Spring 4 for Developing Enterprise Applications:

An End-to-End Approach

Henry H. Liu

PerfMath

ISBN-13: 978-1480284708

ISBN-10: 148028470X

10 9 8 7 6 5 4 3 2 1

05122014

To My Family

Table of Contents

List of Programs and Scripts

Table of Figures

Preface

WHY THIS BOOK

Let us start with the question of why Spring has become so popular. I got my answers from various sources, but a survey as shown in Figure P.1 really puts it into the right perspective (`http://www.springsource.com/node/762`). Although it might be a little bit marketing-driven, it is generally agreed that Spring is simpler and more flexible than Enterprise Java Beans (EJBs) as an enterprise Java application development framework. As is mentioned in Spring's Reference Documentation, Spring offers the following advantages over the *traditional* EJB (mainly EJB 2) technologies:

- It allows a Java method to execute in a database transaction without having to deal with transaction APIs.
- It makes a local Java method:
    - A remote procedure without having to deal with remote APIs
    - A management operation without having to deal with JMX APIs
    - A message handler without having to deal with JMS APIs

My next question is how a developer can learn Spring fast. One can certainly do his own research, read the Spring documentations, and try out various tutorials or samples from many other published Spring texts - presented typically in a piecemeal fashion. However, I feel that it's more effective and efficient to learn Spring from an end-to-end sample enterprise application built with all major Spring technologies, with its source code sufficiently explained and available for anyone to explore and experiment with freely. This is the approach I have decided to adopt to help you get up to speed quickly with Spring so that you can start contributing to the success of your Spring-based project and ultimately to the success of your organization (I wish such an approach were available to me when I started to learn Spring years ago). Now with this end-to-end integrated rather than piecemeal-sample-filled text, more enterprise Java developers can learn Spring in a matter of weeks.

Spring Developer Jobs versus EJB Developer Jobs

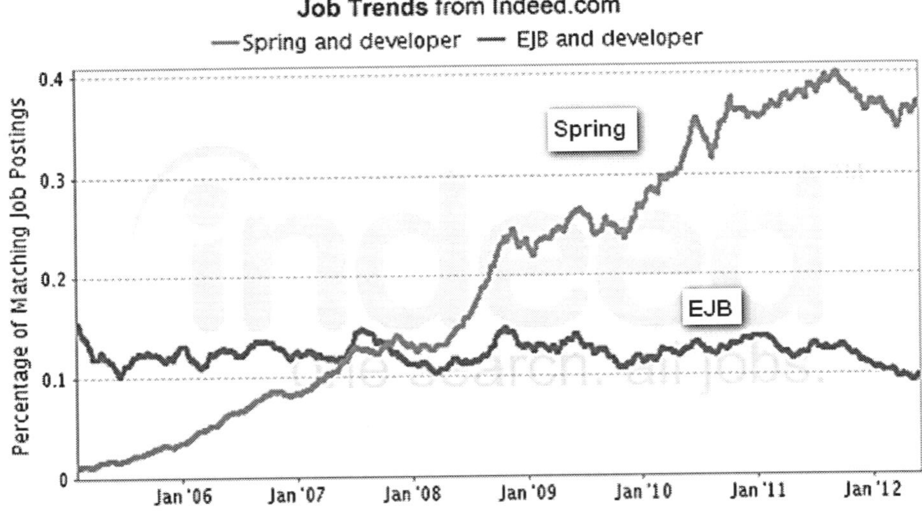

Figure P.1 Comparison between Spring and EJB job trends

Whom This Book Is For

Obviously, this book is for those who are interested in learning Spring. No matter what role you play on your team, a developer, an architect or a manager, this text will help you gain truly applicable Spring skills in a most efficient and relevant manner, mostly because of its unique, end-to-end, integrated approach.

How This Book Is Organized

This book consists of the following three parts:

- **Part I Setting the Stage**: In this part, a gentle introduction to Spring Frameworks is given to help you get an idea on the overall Spring landscape. Then a step-by-step procedure is given about how to set up the sample application named SOBA on Eclipse and a database platform of your choice

(MySQL, PostgreSQL, SQL Server, or Oracle). This serves as a spring board for us to jump into Spring in Part II as is described next.

- **Part II Spring Essential Elements for Building Enterprise Java Applications**: This is the major part of the book. Using the sample application SOBA at each step, we'll explore how those most fundamental Spring Frameworks can be used to build an enterprise application. This part covers a broad range of Spring frameworks, including the core framework, Web MVC framework, RESTful Web Services framework, data access framework, security framework, AOP framework, testing framework, Spring-EJB integration framework, and Spring web flow framework.
- **Appendices**: Appendix A lists a few very useful sources for learning more about Spring. Those sources include some online guides and tutorials as well as the official Spring reference and API documentations. Appendix B describes how to set up the sample application database on MySQL, PostgreSQL, SQL Server, and Oracle, respectively. Appendix C covers how to build another lighter-weight sample application with Maven. The remaining appendices cover various topics associated with building/running SOBA on other platforms as requested by readers of the previous version of the book.

Software And Hardware

I am a firm believer that there is no better way to learn something new than actually do it yourself and gain the first-hand experience. If you decide to take a hands-on approach, then all you need is a PC with all necessary software installed. For your reference, I did all of the development work on the sample application using a latest Intel i7-based 64-bit Windows 7 PC. The dev stack consists of an Eclipse IDE, Apache Maven 3, an Apache Tomcat Web Server, Spring, Hibernate and one of the four database systems of MySQL, PostgreSQL, SQL Server 2012 and Oracle 11g R2. The exact version of each of those software components is given in the main text of this book.

How To Use This Book

There are three ways to use this book:

1 Follow the steps laid out logically in the text and learn progressively from simple to complicated Spring concepts and techniques.
2 Use the sample application as your learning base for trying out more advanced Spring technologies to suit your specific needs.
3 Take a cursory look just for gaining a general understanding about Spring.

Typographic Conventions

Times New Roman indicates normal text blocks.

Italic indicates *emphasis*, *definitions*, *email addresses*, and *URLs* in general.

Calibri font indicates code listings, scripts, and all other types of programming segments.

`Courier` indicates programming elements outside a program or script as well as everything related to executing a program or script such as commands, file names, directoy paths, entries on an HTML form, etc.

How To Reach The Author

All errors in the text are the author's responsibility. You are welcome to email the typos, errors and bugs you found as well as any questions and comments you may have to me at *henry_h_liu@perfmath.com*. Your valuable feedback will be greatly appreciated.

The Book's Web Site

This book has a companion website at http://www.perfmath.com. For downloads and updates, please visit the book's website.

Henry H. Liu, Ph. D.

California

Spring, 2014

Acknowledgements

First, I would really like to thank the self-publishing vendors I have chosen for making this book available to you. This is the most cost-effective and efficient approach for both you as my audience and myself as author. Computer and software technologies evolve so fast that a more timely publishing approach is beneficial for all of us. In addition, my gratitude extends to my wife Sarah and our son William, as I could have not been able to complete this book without their support and patience.

I would also like to thank my audience for valuable feedback and comments, which I have taken whole-heartedly and included every time this book was updated. I especially thank those who kindly sent me the typos, errors and bugs they found in the previous (Spring 3) version of the book, which were very helpful for me to improve the quality of the book in its current version that covers Spring 4. I am reluctant to mention their names here without getting their permission, but I would never forget them for their generosity and professionalism. Authors are not necessarily the smartest, smarter or even smart people – they are just ordinary people who are willing to share and help.

Finally, the cover image is a NASA photo showing a "*Hand in Space*" or the "*Hand of God nebula*," which reminds us of amazing things beyond bits and bytes we struggle with every day while we program.

Part I Setting the Stage

To help you get a smooth warm-up on learning Spring, in this first part, we start with a gentle, high-level overview of a few major Spring Frameworks that are indispensable for building enterprise Java applications. Then, I'll show you how to set up a Spring-based secure online banking application (SOBA) on Eclipse and on one of your preferred databases (MySQL, PostgreSQL, Oracle, or SQL Server). This will help not only get your hands dirty immediately with Spring, but also keep all our Spring learning experiences consistent throughout all the remaining chapters of this book. I hope such an end-to-end, integrated approach with a high-quality, working sample application is more effective and more efficient than for you to go through each individual Spring tutorials piecemeal.

Let's begin with an introduction to Spring Frameworks next.

1 Introduction to Spring Frameworks

1.1 What is an Enterprise Application?

Before introducing Spring frameworks, let's have a good understanding of what an enterprise application is. Not surprisingly, when you ask ten professionals, you might get ten different answers from multiple perspectives. Although you may not completely agree with me, here are some of the typical enterprise applications that all of us may agree that they are *enterprise applications*:

- Billing
- Payroll
- IT Services Management
- Customer Services Management
- Accounting
- Shipping Tracking
- Cost Analysis
- Insurance
- Patient Records
- Banking
- ……

All such enterprise application systems share the following common characteristics:

- The data is persistent that it must be stored in a safe place not only for access in real time but also for future accesses in many years for legal and other reasons.
- The application logic is complex, driven by both business and legal requirements.
- The services must be available to multiple types of clients, including internal employees, system administrators, external customers, and possibly even government regulations.

- Such enterprise systems must satisfy some unique, stringent non-functional requirements such as transactionality, security, performance, scalability, reliability, high availability, and so on, either bound by service level agreements (SLAs) or by laws.
- Such enterprise systems often need to interact with each other either internally in the realm of enterprise application integration (EAI) or mutually among multiple, different business entities in the realm of business-to-business integration (B2B).

A question is how we build such demanding enterprise applications. This has been a topic that the software community has never stopped contemplating. The common wisdom is that such systems need to be divided and conquered in *layers*. Thus, we have come up with a common enterprise application architecture consisting of the backend data layer, application logic layer, frontend UI layer, and so on. For example, when you go to your bank and make a deposit into your account, the clerk enters it on her terminal; then the system behind processes it including calculating your new balance, and in a moment, the clerk hands you a receipt with your new balance on it. Then even in many years, this transaction will be searchable and verifiable. This is just one of the numerous transaction types that flow through countless enterprise application systems in any moment and in anywhere in this world.

The next question is after we figure out that we need to take a layered approach to build such complex software systems, what technologies do we use to accomplish it? Well, more than a decade ago in the frenetic era of e-businesses in earlier 1990's, the Enterprise JavaBeans (EJB) technology was the framework that everyone felt excited about. What did it turn out after all the dusts have settled down? Well, you probably already know the answer. If you are curious about EJB 2, I refer you to a fully functioning EJB 2 sample I developed and posted at this book's website (http://www.perfmath.com/spring_resources.htm) titled "*A Retrospective View on EJB 2*" so that you can get a feel about how convoluted it is. Other than that, all I can say is this book helps you learn how to build enterprise applications with Spring frameworks – a radically different framework than EJB 2.

1.2 WHY AN END-TO-END APPROACH?

We stated that the software community has formed a common wisdom that enterprise applications need to be built in *layers* in order to contain the enormous complexities therein (See Figure 1.1 for an architectural schematic view of a generic enterprise application). What that means is that data flows from the frontend to backend, and maybe back from the backend to the frontend again. For example, everyone uses online banking nowadays. When you log into your banking account online, you would be greeted with your account balance and latest transactions on your screen. When you issue a query on a specific transaction, your online banking application would work behind the scene and get all details related to that transaction to you within seconds. Seeing how a real application such as an online banking application works, I felt that it's better to take an end-to-end approach to presenting how Spring can help build enterprise applications. To be clear, what we mean by "end-to-end" here is that all Spring features are demonstrated in this one single banking context from the frontend to the backend. This is in contrast with other Spring books that in one chapter they use a Vehicle class and in the next chapter they switch to a Contact class, or even worse, they use context-less "foo calls bar and bar calls foo" examples.

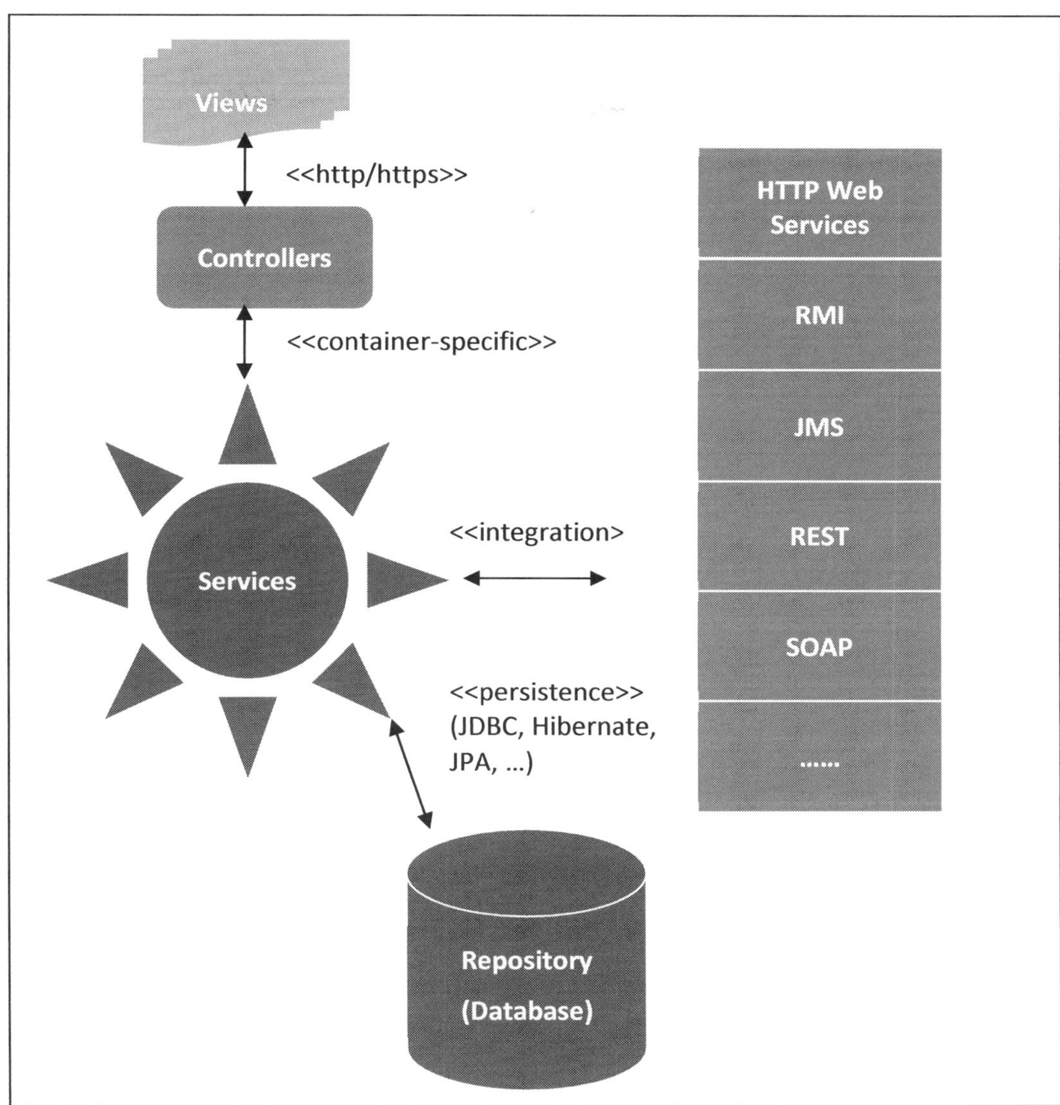

Figure 1.1 An architectural schematic view of a generic enterprise application

In fact, the sample application we use in this book is named SOBA – a Secure Online Banking Application. Besides the end-to-end advantage, this sample provides a better context that everyone is familiar with. In addition, because it's a banking application in nature, it would force us to be rigorous on such implementations as *data persistence*, *security,* and *transactionality* that every enterprise application must deal with seriously.

Spring Frameworks provide a flexible, comprehensive platform for developing Enterprise Java applications. With the Spring frameworks, developers can use so-called *Plain Old Java Objects* (POJOs) as the basic building blocks to construct an enterprise application. Spring frameworks provide infrastructural support for managing and wiring those POJOs so that developers only need to focus on the business logic aspects of POJOs. However, one challenging issue to make POJOs work together is to cope with the dependencies among them. Spring solves this issue with the concepts of *Inversion of Control* (IoC) and *Dependency Injection* (DI), which are discussed next.

1.3 INVERSION OF CONTROL (IOC) AND DEPENDENCY INJECTION (DI)

Enterprise applications are made of components, with either POJOs or EJBs or a mixture of POJOs and EJBs. Those components cannot work standalone – they must work with each other, or they often depend on each other. The specially made software products that manage those components are called *containers*. In Spring, it is called an IoC container. One of the major tasks of an IoC container is to manage dependencies among POJO components.

To explain what an IoC container is about, let's consider a component A that references another two components B and C. When an instance of component A is instantiated, it needs to know how to reference the components B and C it depends on. In this case, component A is called the *dependent* object or the *target* in the context of IoC, whereas components B and C are called *dependencies* or *collaborators*. See Figure 1.2 for the relationships among those components.

Referring to collaborator objects is traditionally made possible with either a *new* operator or a factory class. However, these methods require developers to program manually and become less desirable with more and more complex collaborators. Thus, component-based software technologies such as EJBs emerged, which provide *lookup* services through a component container such as an EJB container. With a container-provided lookup, component A would make a request to its container for referencing components B and C, and the container would look up components B and C from its registries such as JNDI registries and provide component A with the references to components B and C. This approach is termed a *passive* lookup. With an IoC container, component A would not request the references to components B and C. Instead, the lookup process is *inverted* that the references of component A to components B and C would be delivered by the IoC container. So the traditional two-way lookup (one way request and one way delivery) is turned into a one-way service of reference delivery with the concept of an IoC container.

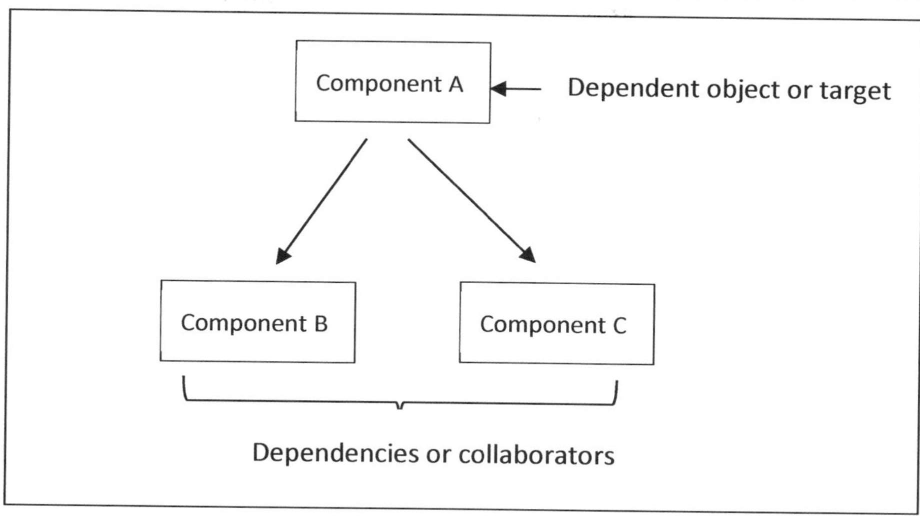

Figure 1.2 Dependent/dependency relationships among objects

So far, an IoC container is only a concept. How an IoC container resolves component dependencies is accomplished with the concept of *dependency injection* (DI). With the above example of components A, B and C, the references of A to B and C are specified (or *injected*) in an external configuration file. It's important to keep in mind that IoC is a generic design principle that many modern containers use to decouple dependencies among components, whereas DI is a concrete design pattern as a mechanism for realizing IoC. However, the terms of IoC and DI are actually interchangeable. We cover more about IoC and DI in Spring's context in Chapter 3.

Like many modern software products, Spring is module-based. Although you may not need to use all Spring modules, and we certainly do not cover all those modules in this text, it's important to know conceptually what modules Spring has to offer, which is the subject of the next section.

1.4 SPRING MODULES

The Spring Framework is a lightweight solution for developing enterprise Java applications. Its prominent features include supporting declarative transaction management, remote access to your business logic residing in the service layer through RMI or Web Services, and a variety of persistence mechanisms for persisting your enterprise data. It offers a MVC framework for Web-enabling your enterprise application. It also provides support for you to integrate AOP transparently into your enterprise software without having to write too much boilerplate code. All these salient features come true due to Spring framework's modularized structure.

The Spring framework is built with as many as about 20 modules, as shown in Figure 1.3. Based on their functionality, these modules are grouped into seven components: the Core Container, Web, Data Access and Integration, AOP (Aspect Oriented Programming), Instrumentation, and Test. What each of these seven components does is explained next.

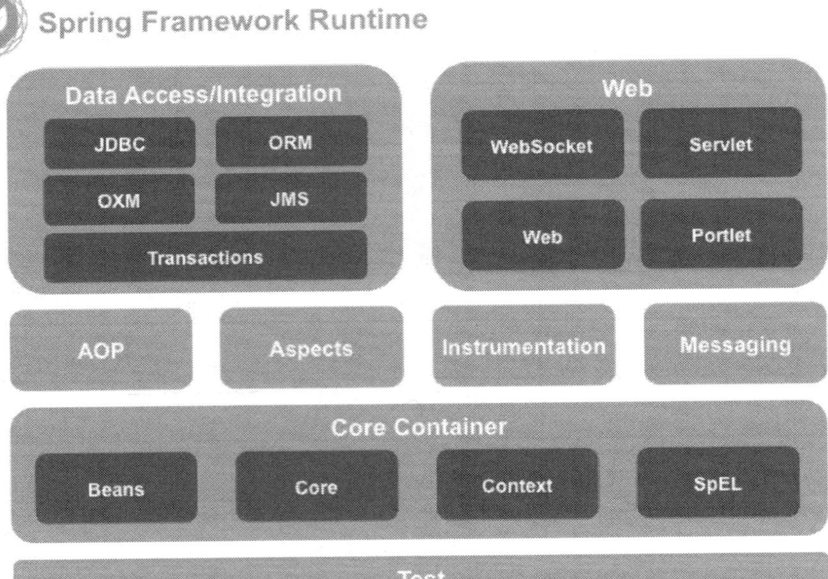

Figure 1.3 Spring modules that constitute the Spring runtime

1.4.1 Core Container

The Spring's core container consists of the following four modules:

- The **Beans and Core** modules: These modules implement the IoC and DI features. These features are implemented with the design pattern of *BeanFactory*, which eliminates the need for programmatic singletons and allows decoupling the configuration and specification of dependencies from the actual application programming logic.
- The **Context** module: This module handles application context creation and resource-loading, etc.
- The **Expression Language** (SpEL) module: This module helps an IoC container retrieve POJOs by name, query and manipulate object graphs at runtime, set and get property values, invoke methods of POJOs, etc.

1.4.2 Data Access and Integration

This component consists of the following modules:

- The **JDBC** (Java Database Connectivity) module: This module encapsulates all complexities in providing data access services required by an enterprise application.

- The **ORM** (Object-Relational Mapping) module: This module enables using popular ORM frameworks such as Hibernate, JPA, JDO and MyBatis, etc., for persisting enterprise data in the form of domain objects.
- The **OXM** (Object/XML Mapping) module: This module provides an abstraction layer for supporting OXM implementations such as JAXB, Castor, XMLBeans, JiBX and XStream.
- The **JMS** (Java Messaging Services) module: This module implements services for producing and consuming messages.
- The **Transaction** module: This module enables programmatic and declarative transaction management for classes implementing special interfaces and for POJOs.

1.4.3 Web

This component consists of the following modules:

- The **Web** module: This module provides initialization of an IoC container using servlet listeners and web application context.
- The **Servlet** module: This module implements Spring's MVC (model-view-controller) framework for building Web applications.
- The **Struts** module: This module supports integrating Struts web tier with Spring web applications.
- The **Portlet** module: This module supports building web portals.

1.4.4 Aspect Oriented Programming (AOP)

This component provides an AOP Alliance-compliant AOP implementation for defining method-interceptors and point-cuts to cleanly decouple code that implements cross-cutting functionality such as logging, transaction management, validation, etc.

1.4.5 Instrumentation

This component provides class instrumentation support as well as class loader implementations.

1.4.6 Test

This component facilitates QA-testing Spring-based applications using JUnit or TestNG. It abstracts the underlying testing framework with the concepts of test context, test context manager, test execution listener, etc. It is heavily oriented toward automating functionality tests using concepts such as mock objects, etc.

Consult the Spring Framework Reference Documentation for more detailed descriptions about the modules mentioned above.

1.5 SPRING JAR FILES

The other way to probe Spring modules and features is by examining the jar files Spring offers. As a developer, no matter what Spring modules you want to use, you need to add the corresponding jar files to your project first. For example, you always need to add some or all jar files from the main framework as shown in Listing 1.1 to your enterprise software project (note that the jars for the modules of *aspects*, *instrument*, *instrument-tomcat*, *jms*, *struts* and *webmvc-portlet* are not listed here). However, these jar files can no longer be downloaded from Spring's website, as Spring 4 encourages users to use Maven to build their Spring-based applications.

Listing 1.1 Major jar files for building Spring-based enterprise applications

spring-**aop**\4.0.1.RELEASE\spring-aop-4.0.1.RELEASE.jar
spring-**beans**\4.0.1.RELEASE\spring-beans-4.0.1.RELEASE.jar
spring-**context**\4.0.1.RELEASE\spring-context-4.0.1.RELEASE.jar
spring-**context-support**\4.0.1.RELEASE\spring-context-support-4.0.1.RELEASE.jar
spring-**core**\4.0.1.RELEASE\spring-core-4.0.1.RELEASE.jar
spring-**expression**\4.0.1.RELEASE\spring-expression-4.0.1.RELEASE.jar
spring-**jdbc**\4.0.1.RELEASE\spring-jdbc-4.0.1.RELEASE.jar
spring-**orm**\4.0.1.RELEASE\spring-orm-4.0.1.RELEASE.jar
spring-**oxm**\4.0.1.RELEASE\spring-oxm-4.0.1.RELEASE.jar
spring-**test**\4.0.1.RELEASE\spring-test-4.0.1.RELEASE.jar
spring-**tx**\4.0.1.RELEASE\spring-tx-4.0.1.RELEASE.jar
spring-**web**\4.0.1.RELEASE\spring-web-4.0.1.RELEASE.jar
spring-**webmvc**\4.0.1.RELEASE\spring-webmvc-4.0.1.RELEASE.jar

Incidentally, for your reference, I'd like to mention that the SOBA sample presented throughout this book was developed several years ago around 2008 using Spring 2.5, and then updated with Spring 3.1 and 3.2 GA in 2013. Now it's updated again with Spring 4.

1.6 SPRING PORTFOLIO

The Spring modules introduced in the preceding section are not all Spring has to offer. In addition to the core Spring Framework, Spring has a rich portfolio including Spring Security, Spring Web Services, Spring Web Flow, Spring Batch, Spring Social, Spring Mobile, Spring LDAP, Spring Rich Client, Spring .NET, Spring Flex, Spring ROO, Spring Integration with Hadoop, and so on. Covering the entire portfolio is obviously beyond the scope of this text. The URL http://spring.io/projects gives more information about the Spring portfolio.

1.7 SUMMARY

I hope that this chapter has given you an idea on what Spring is about. We will get more specific in the remainder of this text. Before getting there, the next chapter helps you set up the SOBA sample application that is built on Spring Core Framework, Spring MVC Web Framework, Spring RESTful Web Services, Spring Security, Spring JDBC and Hibernate support, Spring Validation, Spring

Transaction Management, Spring AOP, on any popular database backend of your choice – MySQL, PostgreSQL, SQL Server or Oracle. This would provide you with a complete experience about how all Spring pieces fit together to make an enterprise application work.

RECOMMENDED READING

It is strongly recommended that you download the *Spring Framework Reference Documentation for 4.x* at this point, as we mention it frequently throughout this book. Part I titled "*Overview of Spring Framework*" of that documentation provides a more detailed overview about these Spring modules we covered briefly in this chapter. You can find all useful resources for Spring in Appendix A of this text.

In addition, if you are interested in the changes introduced in Spring 4, Part II titled "*What's New In Spring 4.x*" of that formal *Spring Framework Reference Documentation* serves this purpose. However, if you are new to Spring, I suggest that you wait until you are through with this book, as it might be challenging to digest those new features in Spring 4 without going through the SOBA sample first that we will focus on next throughout the remainder of this text.

EXERCISES

1.1 Explain the concept of an IoC container and why it's a better choice than that of an EJB.

1.2 Refer to Figure 1.3. Read the *Spring Framework Reference Documentation for 4.x* and learn more about what each module is designed for.

2 Setting up a Spring-Based Sample Enterprise Application

Rather than using disjoint, separate samples to show each feature of the Spring Frameworks, I have decided to use a complete sample enterprise application to show all relevant features in a consistent, end-to-end manner. In this chapter, I'll help you set up this Spring-based sample enterprise application step-by-step. This sample application mimics a secure online banking application, named SOBA for convenience.

Let us begin with a description of what technologies SOBA depends on in addition to Spring next.

2.1 SOBA STACK

A complete SOBA stack includes the following components:

- **A Database System**: I have gone extra miles and tested that SOBA works on MySQL, PostgreSQL, SQL Server, and Oracle. You can choose any one of these database systems based on your preference, but if you don't have a specific preference, I would recommend MySQL. MySQL is one of the most popular open-source RDBMS, and it's very easy to get started with. If you decide to choose another database system beyond these four, then you will need to figure out how to migrate the SOBA database from one of these four database systems covered in this book as well as how to configure SOBA to work with the database system of your choice. I will use MySQL as the reference database system for this book and show you how to switch to a different database system later.
- **A Java Integrated Development Environment (IDE)**: My preference is Eclipse Juno (2012 release). For your reference, Figure 2.1 shows the exact version of Eclipse Juno I used for developing SOBA with Spring 4 for the current edition of this book. Note that there are several download options for a specific Eclipse release, and in my case, I downloaded and installed the *Java EE IDE for Web Developers*.

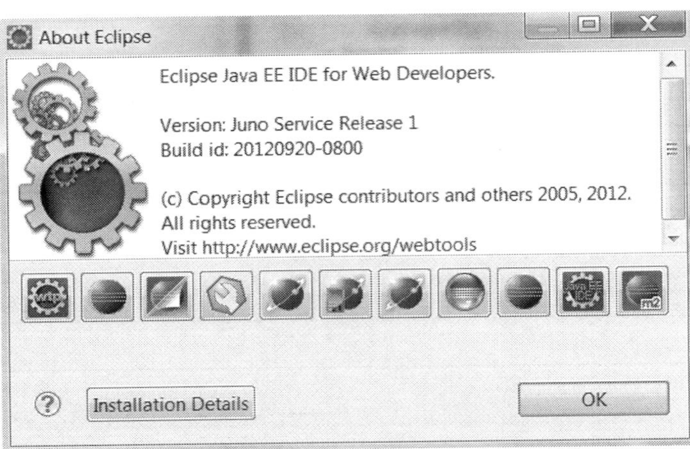

Figure 2.1 Eclipse Java EE IDE (Juno 2012) for Web Developers

- **Apache Maven and Tomcat**: SOBA is an enterprise Web application, and can be configured and deployed to run on Apache Tomcat Web Server. It can be built and deployed with Apache Ant or Maven to run on Tomcat 6 or 7. I built and tested it with Ant 1.8.1/Maven 3 and Tomcat 6.0.26/7.0.27. However, with this edition of the book, I decided to support Maven and Tomcat 7 only, with the choice of Maven driven by Spring's decision to de-support one single place for downloading all Spring jar files. In addition to Tomcat, you can also run SOBA on JEE application servers such as GlassFish, Jboss, and WebLogic. The OS platform for SOBA can be Windows, Linux, or Mac OS X. Consult the appendices at the end of the book if you have such diverse needs.

It will be a lot smoother if you are already familiar with all these technologies mentioned above, and Spring is the only component that you need to learn here. However, I will provide sufficient help so that you can set up a Spring dev environment for SOBA without being blocked due to your less familiarity with any of these technologies mentioned above.

2.2 DIFFERENCES AMONG ORACLE, MYSQL, POSTGRESQL AND SQL SERVER

As an enterprise software developer, it's necessary to get familiar with the backend database that your application depends on, as that's what your app-tier and UI work against. Although it's challenging and even unnecessary to become an expert at every database platform, it's very beneficial to understand at least the differences in data types and features that each of those four database platforms of MySQL, PostgreSQL, SQL Server and Oracle that SOBA supports, which are covered briefly in this section. If you are not interested in this coverage, please feel free to jump to the next section.

2.2.1 Data Types

Each database system has its own specific data types it supports. Data type conversion is the first thing that has to be dealt with when migrating from one database system to another. Some of the major differences in data types involved when creating SOBA database tables on Oracle, MySQL, and SQL Server are summarized in Table 2.1 (we start with Oracle since SOBA was originally developed on Oracle).

Table 2.1 Data Type Conversions among Oracle, MySQL, PostgreSQL and SQL Server

Oracle	**MySQL**	**PostgreSQL**	**SQL Server**
VARCHAR2(n)	VARCHAR(n)	VARCHAR (n)	VARCHAR(n)
NUMBER(p, s)	DECIMAL(p, s)	DECIMAL (p, s)	NUMERIC(p, s)
NUMBER(n)	DECIMAL(n)	DECIMAL (n)	DECIMAL(n)
NUMBER(1)	TINYINT	DECIMAL (1)	BIT
TIMESTAMP	TIMESTAMP*	TIMESTAMP	DATETIME
DATE	DATE	DATE	DATE
CLOB	TEXT	TEXT	TEXT

* Note that with the *TIMESTAMP* date type on MySQL, you need to specify *NULL DEFAULT CURRENT_TIMESTAMP* or *NULL DEFAULT NULL*. Otherwise, it will default to *CURRENT_TIMESTAMP*. This would become an issue when you create a customer account and you don't want the account *CLOSE_DATE* to be set to be the same as *OPEN_DATE* of *CURRENT_TIMESTAMP*.

2.2.2 Features Supported

If your enterprise application needs to support multiple database platforms, decide very carefully on how much you would count on the features provided by a specific flavor of database platform to implement some part of your application logic. My advice is that you determine the least common denominators of the database platform specific features and implement as much application logic as possible at the application layer. This would result in much less changes to coding your application logic and make your application more maintainable over time.

Table 2.2 shows some database features used in SOBA and whether they are supported on those four different database systems of Oracle, MySQL, PostgreSQL and SQL Server. Specifically, the following issues were encountered when migrating SOBA from Oracle to other RDBMS:

- **SEQUENCE**: SQL Server starts supporting 'SEQUENCE' in version 2012. Previously, I had difficulties porting SOBA to SQL Server 2012 that SOBA was stuck with context initialization, but the issue disappeared with SOBA on Spring 4 and SQL Server 2012.
- **TRIGGERS:** SQL Server does not support BEFORE-TRIGGERS (not sure why; patent issue?), which is a huge inconvenience in general (some recommend using "INSTEAD OF" TRIGGERS on SQL Server for "BEFORE" TRIGGERS supported on all other three RDBMS, but it's a totally

different mechanism that "INSTEAD OF" TRIGGERS do not execute the triggering SQL statement.) Because of this, I had to implement the function of '`account_update_balance`' trigger (which is a BEFORE TRIGGER) with an AFTER TRIGGER on SQL Server 2012 to circumvent the issue.

- **SYNONYM**: The other noticeable difference is that SYNONYM is supported on Oracle but not on MySQL and SQL Server except PostgreSQL. However, this can easily be circumvented with VIEW that both MySQL and SQL Server support.

As you might notice, PostgreSQL supports all of these features.

Table 2.2 Feature comparisons among Oracle, MySQL, PostgreSQL and SQL Server

Feature	Oracle	MySQL	PostgreSQL	SQL Server
SEQUENCE	Yes	No	Yes	Yes*
SYNONYM	Yes	No	Yes	Yes*
AFTER TRIGGERS	Yes	Yes	Yes	Yes
BEFORE TRIGGERS	Yes	Yes	Yes	No
ROW LEVEL TRIGGERS	Yes	Yes	Yes	No
INSTEAD OF TRIGGERS	No	No	Yes	Yes

*) Supported on SQL Server 2012.

2.3 SETTING UP MYSQL FOR SOBA

From now on, we focus on MySQL only on 64-bit Windows 7. Please consult the relevant appendices for configuring SOBA on other database and OS platforms.

Note: To proceed, please download the SOBA sample for the current edition of the book, namely Spring 4, at http://www.perfmath.com/download.htm.

For setting up MySQL for SOBA, complete the steps detailed in Appendix B, including installing MySQL 5.5.22, creating the SOBA database, and learning how to get around MySQL with the help of MySQL Workbench, which is a simple GUI for administrating your MySQL server and interacting with your SOBA database on your MySQL. Then, I strongly encourage you to take at least a cursory look at the SOBA schema and all objects introduced in the next two sub-sections so that you would know what domain objects we would deal with. However, if you are in a hurry, you can jump to §2.4 directly next.

2.3.1 SOBA Schema

Next, let us take this opportunity and get familiar with all SOBA objects in terms of tables, views, triggers, functions, etc., as created on MySQL. MySQL Workbench has a helpful feature of Reverse

Engineering for diagramming all objects for a given schema. The model diagram for SOBA reverse engineered on MySQL is shown in Figure 2.2. Note those tables labeled with ACL (Access Control List), which will be discussed later when we discuss implementing SOBA domain object level security with Spring Security. All other tables should be self-explanatory based on their domain context.

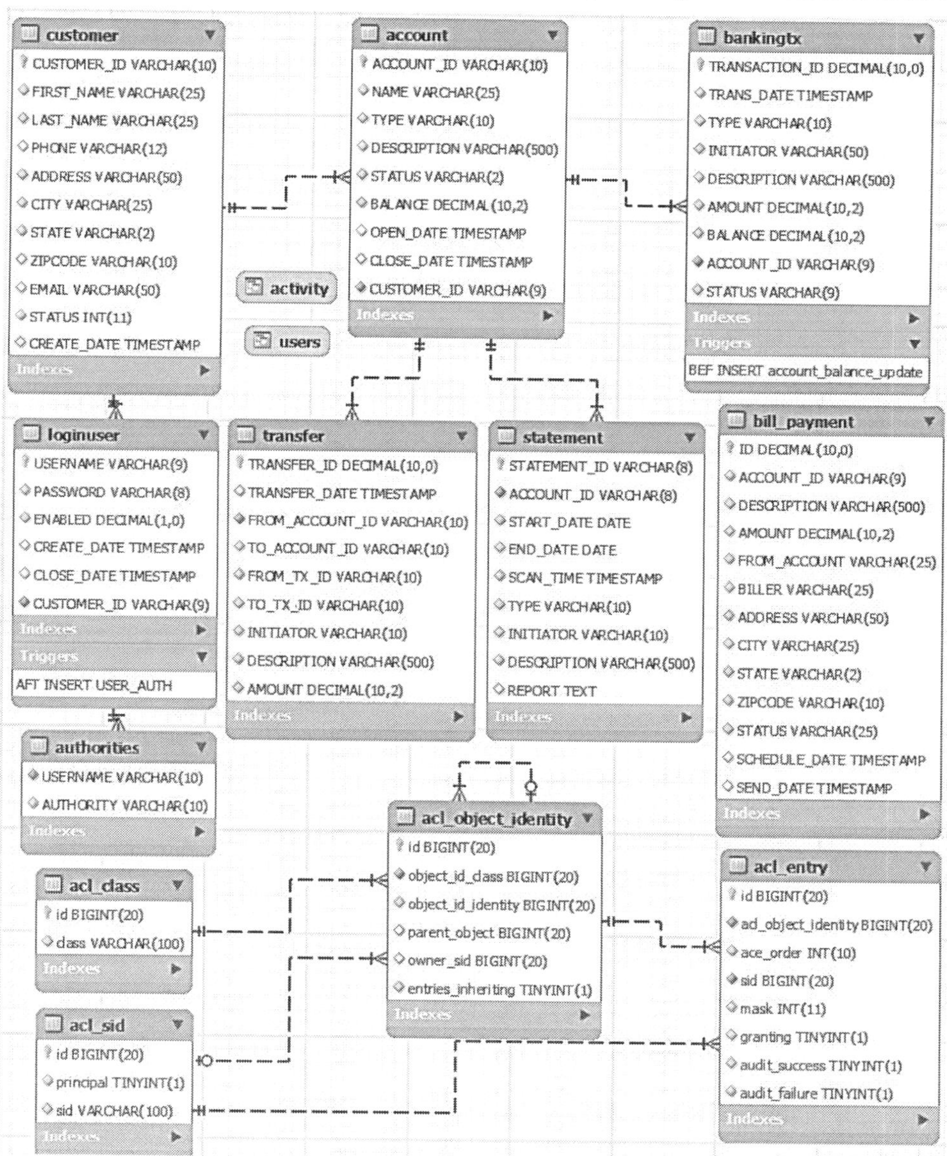

Figure 2.2 SOBA tables, views, and triggers

2.3.2 SQL Statements for Creating SOBA Objects

For those who prefer to see the actual SQL statements used to create those tables, views, and triggers, refer to Listings 2.1 – 2.16 presented next. Some of the specific issues with MySQL are highlighted below:

- MySQL does not support the SEQUENCE feature. This is easily overcome with MySQL's *id auto increment* feature. Note that each of the ACL tables created with its id column like `id bigint unsigned not null auto_increment primary key`. This is actually better than using SEQUENCE in Oracle. SQL Server uses a similar feature called *identity* like `id bigint identity(2000,1) not null primary key`, where `identity(2000, 1)` implies the starting id value of 2000 and incremental value of 1.
- MySQL does not support SYNONYM either. However, this can be circumvented easily with VIEW.
- Fortunately, MySQL supports BEFORE TRIGGER and row-level TRIGGER, which has made it much smoother to migrate SOBA from Oracle to MySQL.

Developing enterprise applications require sufficient knowledge and experience in dealing with domain objects both in Java and in SQL. You should take a look at how each database table is created with this sample application. The access control list tables shown in Listing 2.16 are necessary for securing the domain objects for this sample application, which will be discussed in Chapter 7 later.

Listing 2.1 create_customer.sql

```
create table customer(
 customer_id varchar (10)   not null,
 first_name  varchar (25)   not null,
 last_name   varchar (25)   not null,
 phone       varchar (12)   ,
 address     varchar (50)   not null,
 city        varchar (25)   not null,
 state       varchar (2)    not null,
 zipcode     varchar (10)       ,
 email       varchar (50)   ,
 status      int       not null,
 create_date timestamp null default current_timestamp);
alter table customer add constraint customer_pk_customer_id
primary key (customer_id);
```

Listing 2.2 create_account.sql

```
create table account
(account_id  varchar (10)   not null,
 name        varchar (25)   not null,
 type        varchar (10)   not null,
 description varchar (500) not null,
```

```
 status       varchar (2)    not null,
 balance      decimal (10,2)   not null,
 open_date    timestamp      null default current_timestamp,
 close_date   timestamp      null default null,
 customer_id  varchar (9)    not null);
alter table account
  add constraint account_pk_account_id primary key (account_id);
alter table account
  add constraint account_fk_customer_id foreign key (customer_id)
    references customer (customer_id);
alter table account
  add constraint account_ck_balance check (balance >= 0);
alter table account
  add constraint account_uk_customer_id_type unique (customer_id, type);
```

Listing 2.3 create_banking_tx.sql

```
create table bankingtx
(transaction_id   decimal(10)    not null,
 trans_date       timestamp      not null,
 type             varchar (10)   not null,
 initiator        varchar (50)   not null,
 description      varchar (500)  not null,
 amount           decimal(10,2)  not null,
 balance          decimal(10,2)  not null,
 account_id       varchar (9)    not null,
 status           varchar (9)    not null);
alter table bankingtx
  add constraint tx_pk_transaction_id primary key (transaction_id);
alter table bankingtx
  add constraint tx_fk_account_id foreign key (account_id)
    references account (account_id);
```

Listing 2.4 create_loginuser.sql

```
create table loginuser
(username      varchar (9)    not null,
 password      varchar (8)    not null,
 enabled       decimal (1)    not null,
 create_date   timestamp      null default current_timestamp,
 close_date    timestamp      null default null,
 customer_id   varchar (9)    not null);
alter table loginuser
```

```
 add constraint login_pk_username primary key (username);
alter table loginuser
 add constraint login_fk_customer_id foreign key (customer_id)
    references customer (customer_id);
```

Listing 2.5 create_transfer.sql

```
create table transfer
(transfer_id          decimal(10)   not null,
 transfer_date        timestamp     null default current_timestamp,
 from_account_id      varchar (10)  not null,
 to_account_id        varchar (10)  not null,
 from_tx_id           varchar (10)  not null,
 to_tx_id             varchar (10)  not null,
 initiator            varchar (10)  not null,
 description          varchar (500) not null,
 amount               decimal (10,2)     not null);
alter table transfer
 add constraint tsf_pk_transfer_id primary key (transfer_id);
alter table transfer
 add constraint tsfx_fk_account_id foreign key (from_account_id)
    references account (account_id);
```

Listing 2.6 create_bill_payment.sql

```
create table bill_payment
(id               decimal (10) not null,
 account_id       varchar (9)      not null,
 description      varchar (500) not null,
 amount           decimal (10,2)      not null,
 from_account     varchar (25)   not null,
 biller           varchar (25)   not null,
 address          varchar (50)   not null,
 city             varchar (25)   not null,
 state            varchar (2)    not null,
 zipcode          varchar (10)   not null,
 status           varchar (25)   not null,
 schedule_date    timestamp null default null,
 send_date        timestamp null default  null);
alter table bill_payment add constraint bll_pymnt_pk_id primary key (id);
```

Listing 2.7 create_statement.sql

```
create table statement
(statement_id    varchar (8)     not null,
 account_id      varchar (8)     not null,
 start_date      date       not null,
 end_date        date       not null,
 scan_time       timestamp    not null,
 type            varchar (10)   not null,
 initiator       varchar (10)   not null,
description      varchar (500) not null,
report           text);
alter table statement
  add constraint statement_pk_statement_id
    primary key (statement_id);
alter table statement
  add constraint statement_fk__account_id
    foreign key (account_id)
    references account (account_id);
```

Listing 2.8 create_activity_view.sql

```
create view activity as
 select a.customer_id, a.account_id, a.name, a.type as account_type,
 t.transaction_id, t.trans_date, t.type as tx_type, t.initiator,
 t.description, t.amount, t.balance, t.status
 from account a, bankingtx t
 where a.account_id = t.account_id order by a.account_id;
```

Listing 2.9 create_users_view.sql

```
create view users as select username,password,enabled from loginuser;
```

Listing 2.10 create_authorities.sql

```
create table authorities (
    username       varchar (10)   not null,
    authority      varchar(10)    not null,
    constraint auth_fk_username foreign key (username) references loginuser(username)
);
```

Listing 2.11 create_trigger_user_auth.sql

```
delimiter //
create trigger user_auth
```

```
 after insert on loginuser
 for each row
 begin
    insert into authorities (username, authority) values (new.username, 'role_cust');
 end//
 delimiter ;
```

Listing 2.12 create_trigger_account_balance_update.sql

```
delimiter //
create trigger account_balance_update
  before insert  on bankingtx
  for each row
  begin
  declare account_new_balance decimal (10,2);
     select balance into account_new_balance from account where account.account_id =
new.account_id;
     set account_new_balance = account_new_balance + new.amount;
  update account set balance = account_new_balance where account.account_id = new.account_id;
  set new.balance = account_new_balance;
  end//
  delimiter ;
```

Listing 2.13 create_index_tx_account_id_trans_date_ix.sql

```
create index tx_account_id_tx_date_ix on bankingtx (account_id, trans_date);
```

Listing 2.14 create_func_compute_balance.sql

```
delimiter //
create function compute_balance (acnt_id integer, amount integer)
  returns integer
  begin
    declare curr_balance integer;
    select balance into curr_balance from account
            where account_id = acnt_id;
    return (amount + curr_balance);
  end//
  delimiter ;
```

Listing 2.15 create_func_random_string.sql

```
delimiter //
create function random_string (length  integer)
```

```
returns varchar (500)
begin
  declare rdm_string varchar (500);
  set rdm_string = substring(repeat(md5(rand()), 16) from 1 for length);
  return rdm_string;
end//
delimiter ;
```

Listing 2.16 create_acl.sql

```
create table acl_sid (
   id              bigint unsigned not null auto_increment primary key,
   principal       tinyint(1) not null,
   sid             varchar(100) not null,
   unique index acl_sid_idx_1 (sid, principal)
);

create table acl_class (
   id bigint       unsigned not null auto_increment primary key,
   class           varchar(100) unique not null
) ;

create table acl_object_identity (
   id                     bigint unsigned not null auto_increment primary key,
   object_id_class        bigint unsigned not null,
   object_id_identity     bigint unsigned not null,
   parent_object          bigint unsigned,
   owner_sid              bigint  unsigned,
   entries_inheriting     tinyint(1) not null,
   unique index acl_object_identity_idx_1
      (object_id_class, object_id_identity),
   foreign key (object_id_class) references acl_class (id),
   foreign key (parent_object) references acl_object_identity (id),
   foreign key (owner_sid) references acl_sid (id)
);

create table acl_entry (
   id                      bigint unsigned not null auto_increment primary key,
   acl_object_identity     bigint unsigned not null,
   ace_order               int unsigned not null,
   sid                     bigint unsigned not null,
   mask                    int not null,
   granting                tinyint(1) not null,
```

```
  audit_success          tinyint(1) not null,
  audit_failure                  tinyint(1) not null,
  unique index acl_entry_idx_1 (acl_object_identity, ace_order),
  foreign key (acl_object_identity)
     references acl_object_identity (id),
  foreign key (sid) references acl_sid (id)
);
```

2.4 SETTING UP SOBA ON ECLIPSE

Having created the SOBA database, now it's time to set up and configure SOBA on Eclipse. Let us set up SOBA by following a logic order next.

2.4.1 Installing Eclipse

If you already have *Juno* (2012 release) of Eclipse installed on your system, you are okay. Otherwise, install the latest release of Juno on your system. Note that if you have never used Eclipse, you might need to take a quick self-training on how to get around on an Eclipse Java IDE in general. In addition, between Eclipse and NetBeans, I recommend Eclipse, as according to some statistics, about 70 – 80% developers use Eclipse. I prefer Eclipse as well based on my own personal experience with both.

2.4.2 Importing SOBA

From the SOBA project zip file you downloaded from this book's website at http://www.perfmath.com/, you should see a folder named *soba4*. Copy/paste this folder into your Eclipse workspace, and start up your Eclipse IDE. To import SOBA onto your Eclipse IDE, create a new Java project with exactly the same name of *soba4* and then refresh your project by right-clicking on *soba4* and select *Refresh.* At this point, you should see the entire structure of the SOBA project similar to Figure 2.3 (if you once worked with the previous version of SOBA with Spring 3.x, you might notice that all Ant related items are gone now.)

If, for whatever reasons, red marks appear on any packages from the source folder, then it means that Eclipse needs your help in resolving dependencies. Those dependencies will be resolved automatically after you build SOBA with Maven the first time.

You may notice a source folder named *soba* under *src/main/resources* in Figure 2.3. It was created by right-clicking the soba4 project, choosing Properties/Java Build Path/Source/Link Source, and then entering the name *soba* to link to *C:\mspc\mydev\workspace\soba4\src\main\java* (note that this path is specific to my setup). This is for enabling automatic error checking when you edit a source file in the *soba* folder. (The changes will be reflected in the *src/main/java* folder automatically.)

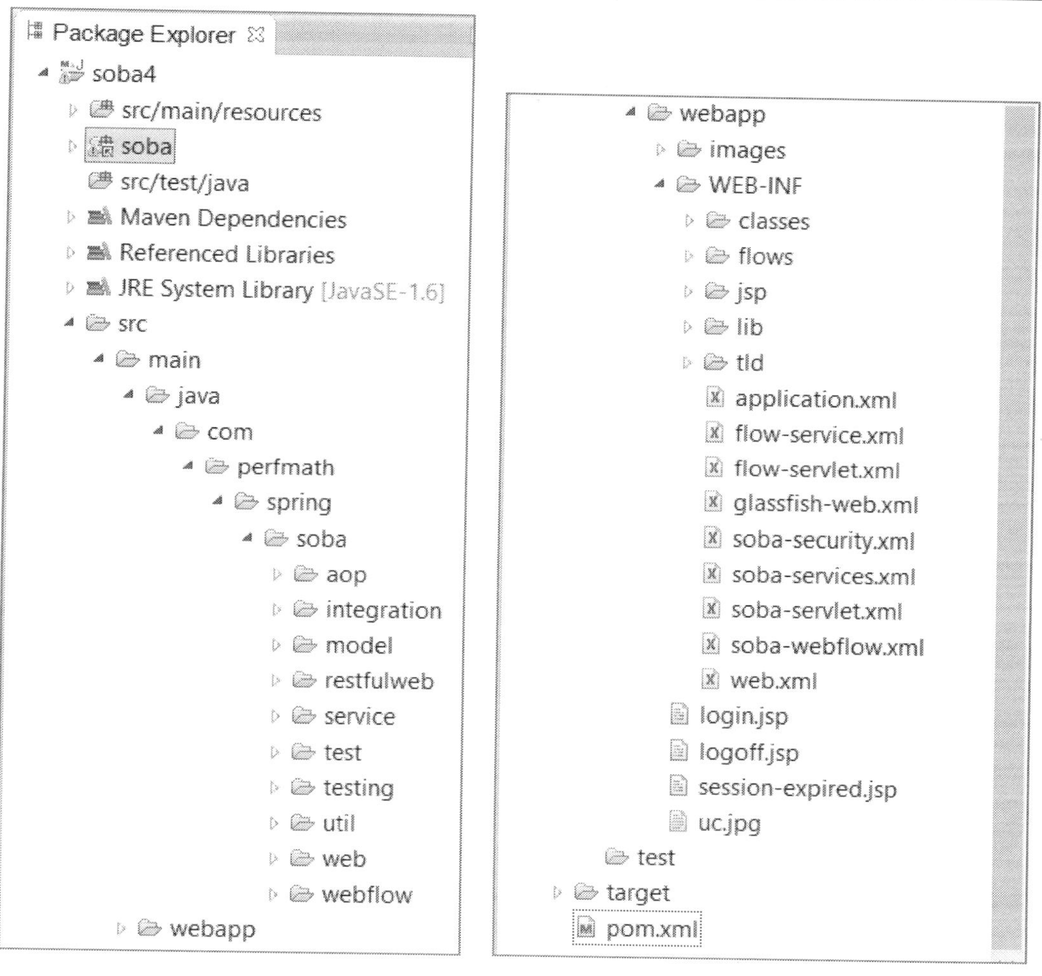

Figure 2.3 The structure of SOBA with Spring 4 on Eclipse (the entire structure was cut into two halves to make it fit on one single page)

Now let us take a look at the SOBA project structure as shown in Figure 2.3. From top to bottom, we see the following three folders:

- ***src/main/java***: This folder contains all Java package and class files. Note the Java packages of `aop`, `integration`, `model`, `restfulweb`, `service`, `test`, `testing`, `util`, `web` and `webflow`. If you expand these packages, you would see all Java class files under them.
- ***src/main/resources***: This folder contains all .properties files and Spring and non-Spring XML configuration files for the project. It also contains a folder named *app-server-lib* for third-party jar files such as JDBC driver jar files.

- ***src/main/webapp***: This folder corresponds to the root folder of SOBA when it is deployed to an application server such as Tomcat. Note the `WEB-INF` folder, which contains a `jsp` folder for all jsp files except the `login.jsp`, `logoff.jsp`, `session-expired.jsp` files and a *uc.jpg* file, which are placed under the `webapp` folder directly. This `WEB-INF` folder will also contain a *classes* folder, which will contain all compiled Java classes together with all resource files in the *src/main/resources* folder after deployment.

Finally, at the bottom of the project structure is the *pom.xml* file for building SOBA with Maven as we discussed above.

I have to mention that this sample project is set up to use MySQL by default. If you are interested in PostgreSQL, Oracle or SQL Server rather than MySQL, you need to replace all MySQL specific files in the *src/main/resources* folder and *src/main/webapp/WEB-INF* folder with the respective configuration files from the downloaded *extras/resourcess* folder and rename them with the *<db>* post-fix removed for each file. However, if possible, please stick to MySQL, as SOBA is configured to run with MySQL out of the box, tested most thoroughly with MySQL, and most readers use MySQL.

2.4.3 Installing Tomcat 7

Although it's possible to configure SOBA to run in an embedded container in Eclipse, it's strongly recommended to configure and run SOBA in a separate, standalone Tomcat server, as this is how a real enterprise application would run, and by doing so, you would learn how to configure and deploy SOBA like in a real production environment. For this purpose, this section gives detailed instructions on how to set up Tomcat for running SOBA in a separate standalone environment using the secured HTTPS protocol.

First, install a JDK 6 or 7 release on your dev machine and set the JAVA_HOME environment variable on your system (I have tested that SOBA works with both Java 6 and 7). Also, add %JAVA_HOME%\bin to your PATH environment variable.

To install Tomcat, first download the proper release from http://tomcat.apache.org/download-70.cgi for Tomcat 7 (I downloaded `apache-tomcat-7.0.27-windows-x64.zip` for my test). Then unzip it to a directory on your system (in my case it's installed at `C:\mspc\myapp\apache-tomcat-7.0.27`). Then follow the procedure below to configure your Tomcat Web Server:

- Execute the following command to create an SSL certificate to enable the HTTPS protocol to be used with your Tomcat Server. Then edit your Tomcat `server.xml` file as described below to enable HTTPS to be used with SOBA:

  %JAVA_HOME%\bin\keytool -genkey -alias tomcat -keyalg RSA

- A few things to pay attention to when you execute the above command:
  - Use "`changeit`" for the keystore password without quotation marks.
  - When asked "What is your first and last name?," enter "localhost/127.0.0.1" or your machine name. If you enter you real first and last names like "henry liu" in my case, then when you try to test a RESTful web API with HTTPS using a URL like https://localhost:8443/soba/..." as will be

illustrated in Chapter 6, an error similar to "hostname didn't match: localhost != henry liu." will occur.

  - At the last step asking for a password for tomcat, choose the default option; otherwise, you might get the "Cannot recover key" error when you try to start up SOBA later. Other than that, all other entries for creating the certificate don't seem to matter much.
  - A question is how one would know if the SSL certificate has been created properly. At this point, all you can do is to check that the *.keystore* file has been created in your *C:\Users\<your_login_id>* folder if you are on Windows 7. Then, when you get to § 2.7.1 later, you can refer to the descriptions there to start up your Tomcat and verify if your Tomcat admin console works after you enter the URL of https://localhost:8443.

- Find your `server.xml` file in the directory of `<tomcat_install>\conf`, un-comment the following XML element, and replace the protocol attribute "HTTP/1.1" with "org.apache.coyote.http11.Http11Protocol" as shown below:

```
<Connector port="8443" protocol="org.apache.coyote.http11.Http11Protocol"
SSLEnabled="true" maxThreads="150" scheme="https" secure="true"
clientAuth="false" sslProtocol="TLS" />
```

The above replacement is required according to *Apache Tomcat 7 SSL Configuration HOW-TO* described at http://tomcat.apache.org/tomcat-7.0-doc/ssl-howto.html. With the above protocol setting, Tomcat 7 would use the *JSSE SSL implementation* as part of the JVM rather than the *APR SSL implementation*, which uses the OpenSSL engine by default. The term APR stands for *Apache Portable Runtime*, which is a highly portable library that provides superior performance, scalability, and better integration with native server technologies. To learn more about APR, please visit http://tomcat.apache.org/tomcat-7.0-doc/apr.html.

- Add the following lines in your `tomcat-users.xml` file in the same *conf* directory:

```
<role rolename="manager-gui" />
<user username="tomcat" password="s3cret" roles="manager-gui"/>
```

Note: Some readers reported having difficulties starting up SOBA on Tomcat. One common cause was that the keystore file was not created properly. To help you verify, here is how I created it (for omitted lines, it means I hit the RETURN key):

```
C:\Users\henry>keytool -genkey -alias tomcat -keyalg RSA
Enter keystore password: changeit
Re-enter new password: changeit
What is your first and last name?
 [Unknown]:  localhost/127.0.0.1
<...omitted...>
Is CN=localhost, OU=Unknown, O=Unknown, L=Unknown, ST=Unknown, C=Unknown correct?
 [no]:  yes
```

You also need to copy the JDBC driver of the database you choose to the *lib* folder of your Tomcat install. The exact jdbc jar file for each database platform is given in Table 2.3. For your convenience, all these jar files can be found in the *extras/lib* directory from the SOBA download.

Table 2.3 JDBC jar Files for MySQL, PostgreSQL, SQL Server and Oracle

Database	**JDBC driver**
MySQL	mysql-connector-java-5.1.18-bin.jar
PostgreSQL	postgresql-9.3-1100.jdbc4.jar
Microsoft SQL Server	sqljdbc4.jar
Oracle	ojdbc6.jar

2.5 BUILDING SOBA WITH MAVEN

In this section, I show you how to build SOBA with Maven 3. I will cover both the basic concepts about Maven and the step-by-step, exact procedure of building SOBA with Maven so that you would have much less research and experimental work to do by yourself . However, you do need to make sure you have set up your Tomcat server and the database server of your choice properly before trying out Maven next.

Next, let me introduce Maven just in case you are new to Maven. If you are familiar with Maven, feel free to jump to §2.5.2.

2.5.1 Introduction to Maven

Maven is an Apache project, which is designed to manage dependent jars required by a generic or an enterprise Java project. It automatically downloads required jars for you so that you don't have to search, download, and add them to your project manually by yourself. However, Maven is more than that – it has become one of the most popular tools for streamlining the process of building and releasing large-scale software projects.

The core concept of Maven is a project object model (POM) file that specifies all the dependencies as well as the entire building process. There is a very helpful document titled *POM Reference* that covers everything about POM, which is available at http://maven.apache.org/pom.html. The most relevant part of a POM file is each of those dependencies specified in the format of, for example:

```
<dependency>
<groupId>javax.servlet</groupId>
<artifactId>servlet-api</artifactId>
<version>2.5</version>
</dependency>
```

With this example dependency, it says that *this application requires version 2.5 of the Java servlet API jar*, and all you have to do is to define it in the right place in your *pom.xml* file. Then, Maven knows how to retrieve it from a remote repository or the local repository on your machine to help resolve that dependency your project requires. So far that's all we need to know about Maven in order to be able to build SOBA with Maven. Let's make it happen step by step next (if you want to spend about 10 minutes and get a deeper understanding on Maven, you can take a look at *Maven Getting Started Guide* available at http://maven.apache.org/guides/getting-started/index.html).

2.5.2 Setting up Maven

Setting up Maven starts with downloading Maven. The version of Maven I used at the time of this writing was 3.0.4, which is available at http://maven.apache.org/download.html . I downloaded and unzipped it to `C:\mspc\myapp\apache-maven-3.0.4` on my dev PC. I also added `C:\mspc\myapp\apache-maven-3.0.4\bin` to my `path` environment variable. You need to do the same and make sure you have set your *JAVA_HOME* environment variable properly. Although the Maven document says you need to add an *M2_HOME* environment variable to point to your Maven installation, I did not set any Maven related environment variable and it works for me on my Windows 7 desktop.

The next step is to enable Maven on Eclipse, as is discussed next.

2.5.3 Enabling Maven on Eclipse

The Maven plug-in for Eclipse is named *m2eclipse* or *m2e*. It is now bundled with the latest (Indigo and newer) versions of Eclipse Java EE IDE for Web Developers. Next, I assume that you already installed Juno on your development system, or download and install it if not.

To enable Maven plug-in on your Eclipse IDE, complete the following steps:

- Open up your Eclipse IDE. Click *Help -> Install New Software*… In the dialog box of *Available Software*, enter http://download.eclipse.org/releases/juno and click *Add*, as shown in Figure 2.4. Under the *Collaboration* category, make sure you select the two m2e entries as well as the proper check boxes in the *Details* pane underneath. Click *Next* and finish the install.
- After Eclipse is restarted, open up the *Available Software* dialog box again. Click the link `already installed`. Verify your m2e install as shown in Figures 2.5 (*Features* tab) and 2.6 (*Plugin Details*).

You are ready to use Maven 3 with Eclipse now.

2.5.4 Building SOBA with Maven

Assuming that you have imported SOBA onto your Eclipse IDE, simply follow the below procedure to build SOBA with Maven:

- Change to the SOBA project directory at an MS-DOS command prompt, for example, *C:\mspc\mydev\workspace\soba4*, in my case.
- Enter `mvn package -DskipTests` and hit *Return*. Since this is your first time to build SOBA with Maven, it may take some time to download all dependent jars to your local Maven repository, which is in *C:\Users\<yourLogin>\.m2* if you are on Windows. The future ones will be much faster. If everything went well, you should see a message of "`BUILD SUCCESS`" at the end of the process.

Now in the *target* directory, you should see a folder named *soba4*. Copy this folder to the *webapps* folder of your Tomcat install, rename it to *soba*, and start up your Tomcat server. You can verify that it works later by following the steps to be described in §2.7. If you are interested in deploying SOBA straight from Maven to Tomcat, refer to the proper appendix for further instructions.

Before moving to the next section, note that you can run "*mvn clean package -DskipTests*" if you want to clean your previous build and have a new build. Next, let's take a cursory look at SOBA's *pom.xml* file available from the project directory on your Eclipse IDE.

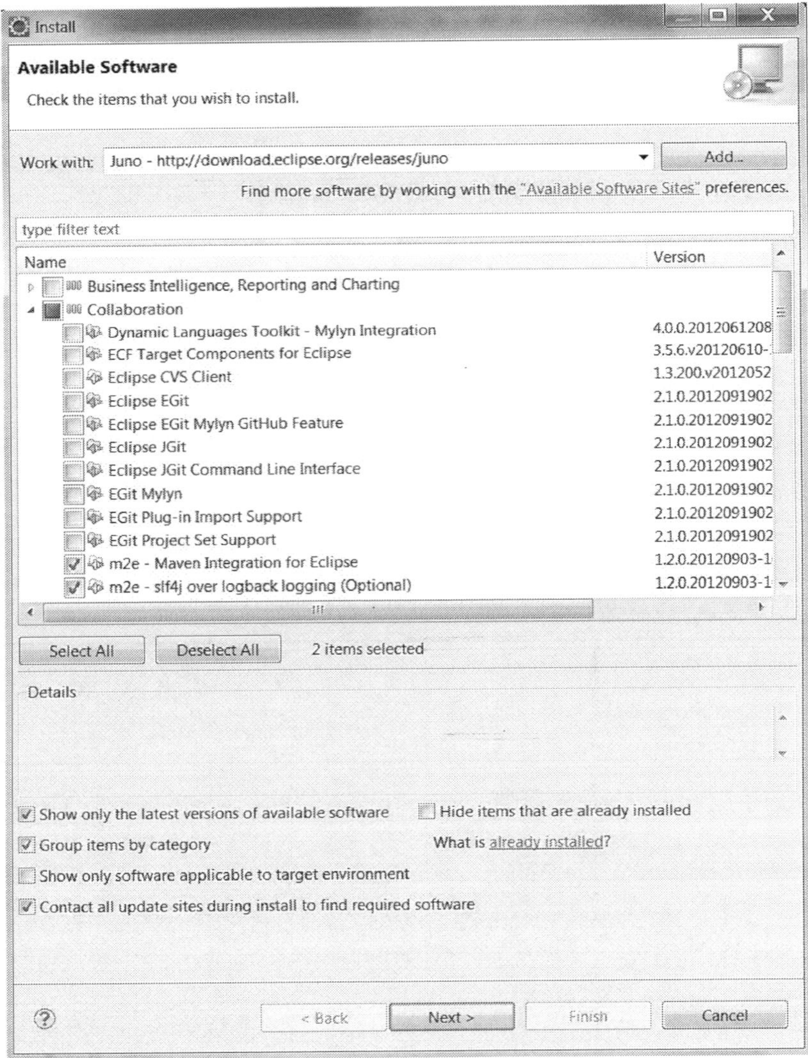

Figure 2.4 Maven plug-in m2e bundled with Eclipse Juno

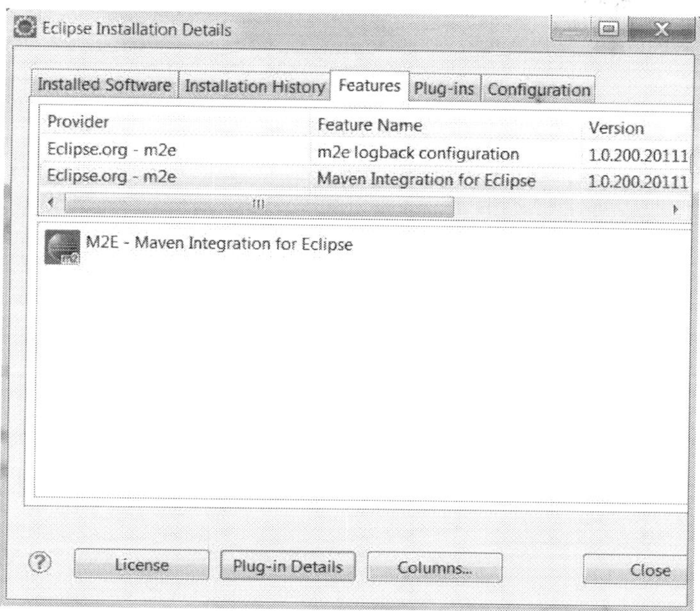

Figure 2.5 Maven plug-in m2e under the Eclipse Juno *Features* tab

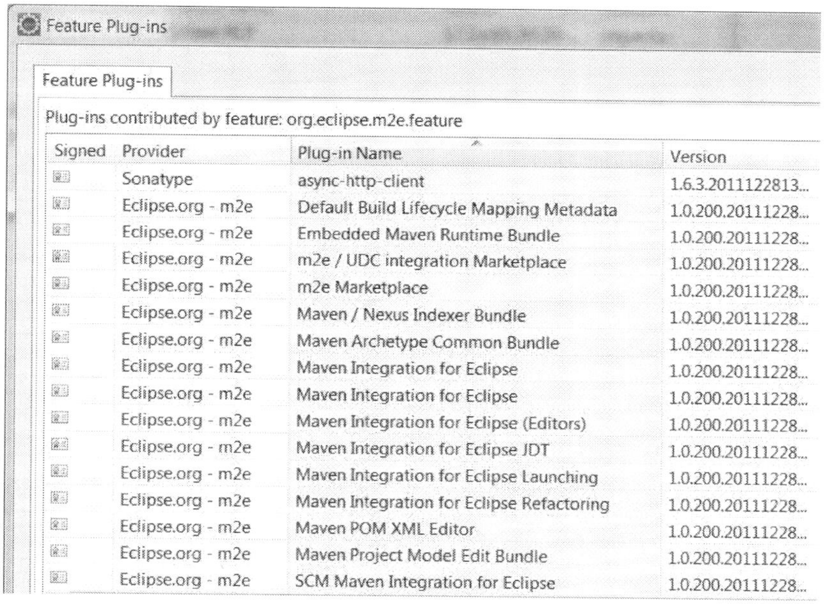

Feature Plug-ins

Feature Plug-ins

Plug-ins contributed by feature: org.eclipse.m2e.feature

Signed	Provider	Plug-in Name	Version
	Sonatype	async-http-client	1.6.3.2011122813...
	Eclipse.org - m2e	Default Build Lifecycle Mapping Metadata	1.0.200.20111228...
	Eclipse.org - m2e	Embedded Maven Runtime Bundle	1.0.200.20111228...
	Eclipse.org - m2e	m2e / UDC integration Marketplace	1.0.200.20111228...
	Eclipse.org - m2e	m2e Marketplace	1.0.200.20111228...
	Eclipse.org - m2e	Maven / Nexus Indexer Bundle	1.0.200.20111228...
	Eclipse.org - m2e	Maven Archetype Common Bundle	1.0.200.20111228...
	Eclipse.org - m2e	Maven Integration for Eclipse	1.0.200.20111228...
	Eclipse.org - m2e	Maven Integration for Eclipse	1.0.200.20111228...
	Eclipse.org - m2e	Maven Integration for Eclipse (Editors)	1.0.200.20111228...
	Eclipse.org - m2e	Maven Integration for Eclipse JDT	1.0.200.20111228...
	Eclipse.org - m2e	Maven Integration for Eclipse Launching	1.0.200.20111228...
	Eclipse.org - m2e	Maven Integration for Eclipse Refactoring	1.0.200.20111228...
	Eclipse.org - m2e	Maven POM XML Editor	1.0.200.20111228...
	Eclipse.org - m2e	Maven Project Model Edit Bundle	1.0.200.20111228...
	Eclipse.org - m2e	SCM Maven Integration for Eclipse	1.0.200.20111228...

Figure 2.6 Maven m2e plug-in details in Eclipse Juno

2.5.5 SOBA's pom.xml Configuration File

At this point, you should open up the *pom.xml* file for SOBA on Spring 4 and examine it if you want. Note the following:

- Remember that a directory of *soba4* was created in the target directory after SOBA was built successfully with Maven? The name of that directory comes from the `artifactId` and `version` entries specified at the beginning of this *pom.xml* file.
- Note the elements of `build`, `plugins`, and `plugin` next. This defines the Maven build process of a project. In our case, it's simple.
- Next, note that this *pom.xml* file mainly consists of `<dependency>` elements, which is because Maven is designed to deal with dependencies, to some extent. If you miss some required dependencies, you will see red cross marks on the items on your project on Eclipse. Such errors must be resolved before the project can be built successfully. To resolve a required dependency, you need the right `groupId`, `artifactId` and `version`, which can be obtained by searching online.

Finally, at the end of this file, note the `properties section`, and note how they are used in defining a dependency in the format of ${...} to help avoid hard-code the version numbers of dependencies.

If you plan to build your own Spring project with Maven, you can use this *pom.xml* as a good start point. The extra dependencies that you do not need are harmless.

2.6 CONFIGURING SOBA TO WORK WITH YOUR DATABASE SYSTEM

In order for SOBA to work properly, you need to make sure that the configuration files specific to the database platform of your choice are in place, which means that you might need to perform some copy/rename/remove operations, with proper entries entered as described below.

Let us go through the database configuration task on a per database platform basis next. For MySQL, locate the configuration files in the *`src/main/resources`* folder in your SOBA project on Eclipse. For PostgreSQL, SQL Server and Oracle, check out the *extras* folder from your SOBA project download.

2.6.1 Configuring SOBA to Work with MySQL 5.5.22

Configure the *jdbc.properties* file and *hibernate.cfg.xml* file as follows:

- In the *jdbc.properties* file as shown below, replace the `url`, `username` and `password` settings with your own (note: do not forget the ':' sign between '`mysql`' and '//')

```
jdbc.driverClassName=com.mysql.jdbc.Driver
jdbc.url=jdbc:mysql://localhost:3306/soba
jdbc.username=sobaadmin
jdbc.password=sobaadmin
```

- In the *hibernate.cfg.xml* file as shown below, make similar changes as you did in the *jdbc.properties* file:

```
<property name="connection.driver_class">com.mysql.jdbc.Driver</property>
<property name="connection.url">jdbc:mysql://localhost:3306/soba</property>
<property name="connection.username">sobaadmin</property>
<property name="connection.password">sobaadmin</property>
<property name="hibernate.dialect">org.hibernate.dialect.MySQLDialect</property>
```

2.6.2 Configuring SOBA to Work with PostgreSQL 9.3

Configure the *jdbc.properties* file and *hibernate.cfg.xml* file as follows:

- In the *jdbc.properties* file as shown below, replace the `url`, `username` and `password` settings with your own:

```
jdbc.driverClassName=org.postgresql.Driver
jdbc.url=jdbc:postgresql://localhost:5432/soba
jdbc.username=sobaadmin
jdbc.password=sobaadmin
```

In the *hibernate.cfg.xml* file, make similar changes as you did in the *jdbc.properties* file.

2.6.3 Configuring SOBA to Work with SQL Server 2012

Configure the *jdbc.properties* file and *hibernate.cfg.xml* file as follows:

- In the *jdbc.properties* file as shown below, replace the `url`, `username` and `password` settings with your own:

```
jdbc.driverClassName=com.microsoft.sqlserver.jdbc.SQLServerDriver
jdbc.url=jdbc:sqlserver://localhost:58600;instanceName=SQLEXPRESS;databaseName=soba
jdbc.username=sobaadmin
jdbc.password=sobaadmin
```

- In the *hibernate.cfg.xml* file, make similar changes as you did in the *jdbc.properties* file.

2.6.4 Configuring SOBA to Work with Oracle 11g R2

Configure the *jdbc.properties* file and *hibernate.cfg.xml* file as follows:

- In the *jdbc.properties* file as shown below, replace the `url`, `username` and `password` settings with your own:

```
jdbc.driverClassName=oracle.jdbc.driver.OracleDriver
jdbc.url=jdbc:oracle:thin:@localhost:1521:Ora11GR2A
jdbc.username=sobaadmin
jdbc.password=sobaadmin
```

- In the *hibernate.cfg.xml* file, make similar changes as you did in the *jdbc.properties* file.

Note: Before you try SOBA with your DB, please use the *JDBCConnectionTest.java* program in the `com.perfmath.spring.soba.test` package to make sure you can connect to your database. This may help save you a lot of time. To perform this task, first build the project with Maven, then change to your SOBA project's *target\soba-4\WEB-INF\classes* directory and execute the following command:

```
java –cp ..\lib\<your jdbc driver name>.jar;. com.perfmath.spring.soba.test.JDBCConnectionTest
```

If successful, you should see the following two output lines:

```
Database connection established
Database connection terminated
```

If any errors, check if you have your JDBC driver jar file in the *lib* directory and if all entries are configured properly. Of course, don't forget that you have your database up and running.

In addition to configuring the *jdbc.properties* and *hibernate.cfg.xml* files properly for each database as stated above, the *soba-security.xml* file and the *soba-services.xml* are database specific as well. You can find these files for each database vendor in the `extras/webapp/WEB-INF` folder from your SOBA download. If you decide not to use MySQL, you need to remove the "_*<db>*" post-fix for each file based on your choice of the database vendor, and overwrite the corresponding files in tomcat's `webapps/soba/WEB-INF/` folder. In the *soba-services.xml* file, a `sobaConfig` bean is specified to designate the database vendor used for SOBA, which should be `mysql`, `postgresql`, `sqlserver` or `oracle` (you can find this bean by opening up the *soba-services.xml* file), depending on the database vendor you chose.

On the other hand, in the *soba-security.xml* file, there is an `aclService` bean that specifies how to get ACL_SID and ACL_CLASS sequence ids from different database vendors. For MySQL and SQL Server, it is configured as follows (you can use the default *soba-security.xml* file for both MySQL and SQL Server as they use the same id queries):

```
<beans:bean id="aclService"
class="org.springframework.security.acls.jdbc.JdbcMutableAclService">
    <beans:constructor-arg ref="dataSource" />
    <beans:constructor-arg ref="lookupStrategy" />
    <beans:constructor-arg ref="aclCache" />
    <beans:property name="sidIdentityQuery"
        value="SELECT max(id) FROM acl_sid" />
    <beans:property name="classIdentityQuery"
        value="SELECT max(id) FROM acl_class" />
</beans:bean>
```

For PostgreSQL, the queries are:

```
select currval(pg_get_serial_sequence('acl_sid', 'id'))
select currval(pg_get_serial_sequence('acl_class', 'id'))
```

This is explained further in Chapter 7, which is dedicated to demonstrating how to secure SOBA with the Spring Security Framework.

Next, build and deploy SOBA in your environment as instructed in §2.5.4. If you are successful with building and deploying SOBA, you are ready to test-drive SOBA next. This is a necessary step before examining how SOBA is implemented with Spring, because you may want to make sure what you will study is a sample that actually works in your environment.

2.7 TESTING SOBA

In this section, we take a step-by-step approach to showing that SOBA works in your environment as expected.

2.7.1 Starting up SOBA

After building and deploying SOBA to your Tomcat server, open up an MS-DOS command prompt, cd to the *bin* directory of your Tomcat install, and run `startup.bat`. In a few seconds, your Tomcat Web server should be up and running. You can access your tomcat admin console at https://localhost:8443 as shown in Figure 2.7. You can try *Server Status* or *Manager App* with the credentials of `tomcat/s3cret` to verify that your Tomcat server works properly.

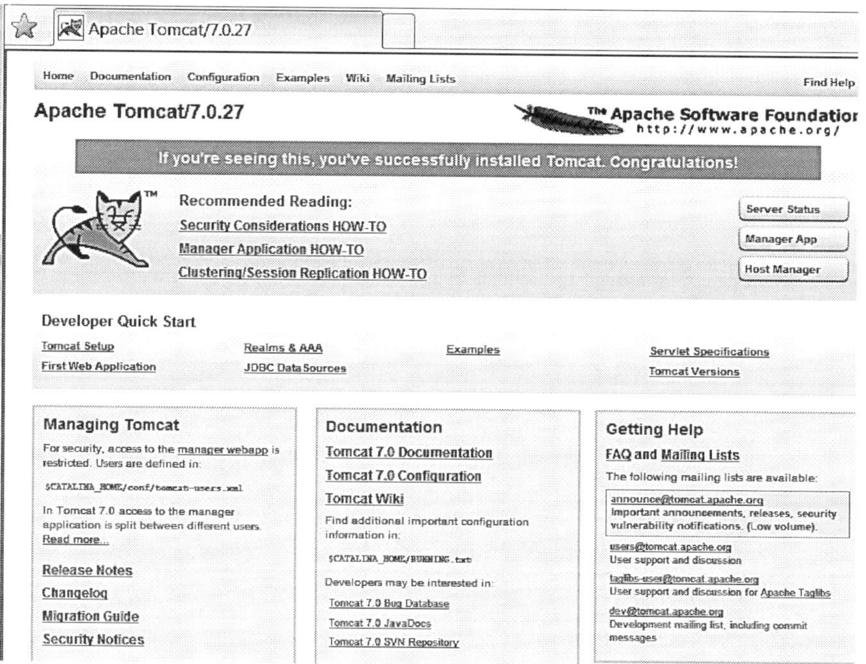

Figure 2.7 Tomcat 7 admin console

If you see errors from your Tomcat startup process, check the newest *localhost* log file in the *logs* directory of your Tomcat install. If not, open up a Web browser and type in https://localhost:8443/soba. If you see an error complaining about this website's security certificate, simply ignore it by clicking *Continuing to this Web site (not recommended)*. Then you should see the SOBA login page as shown in Figure 2.8. If you get this far, it's an indication that your SOBA application has been started successfully. If you encounter any errors, check the *soba.log* file at *<yourTomcatInstall>\logs\soba*.

Next, we test a few functions of SOBA to make sure it works. This is a minimum set of tests that should be conducted whenever new changes are introduced. The tests include creating two new customers with user IDs of `user1001` and `user1002`, posting transactions, and then paying bills between `user1001` and `user1002`. Let us start with creating new customers first.

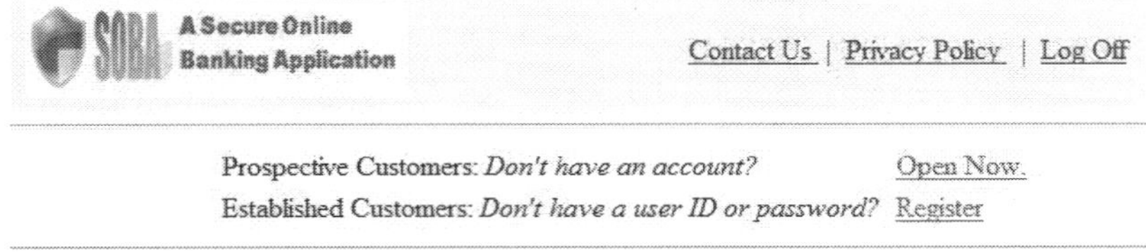

Figure 2.8 SOBA login page

2.7.2 Testing SOBA 1: Creating New Customers

To test creating new customers, follow the below steps:

- Log in to SOBA at https://localhost:8443/soba and click *Open Now* as shown in Figure 2.8 in the previous section. Then you should see the screen as shown in Figure 2.9.
- Note that all fields have been pre-filled. Append "1001" to "user" in the first name field to create a user named "`user1001`." Click *Submit*.

- Now you should get a new screen as shown in Figure 2.10, indicating that the operation is successful. Click the *create* link to create the login ID next.
- Now you should see a screen similar to Figure 2.11. Enter "user1001" and "sobauser" for the loginID and password fields, respectively.
- Now you should see a screen similar to Figure 2.12, indicating that the login ID has been created successfully. Click the *create* link to create an account.
- Now you should see a screen similar to Figure 2.13. All fields have been pre-filled. Click *Submit* and you should see a screen similar to Figure 2.14, indicating that the account has been created successfully.
- Now click *log off* and log in with login ID "user1001" and password "sobauser". You should see a screen similar to Figure 2.15 now.

Now create a new user named user1002 by following the same procedure for creating user1001. In the next section, we test the function of posting transactions by user1001 and user1002 so that they would have some funds in their accounts for testing bill payments.

SOBA :: create a new customer

First Name:	user
Last Name:	soba
Phone:	999-999-9999
Address:	One Way
City:	Any City
State:	CA
Zipcode:	95999
Email:	user@soba.com

Submit

Figure 2.9 SOBA: Creating a new customer

Your customer ID 963465668 has been created successfully.

Use your customer ID to create your login ID for banking online.

Figure 2.10 SOBA: Creating a customer successful

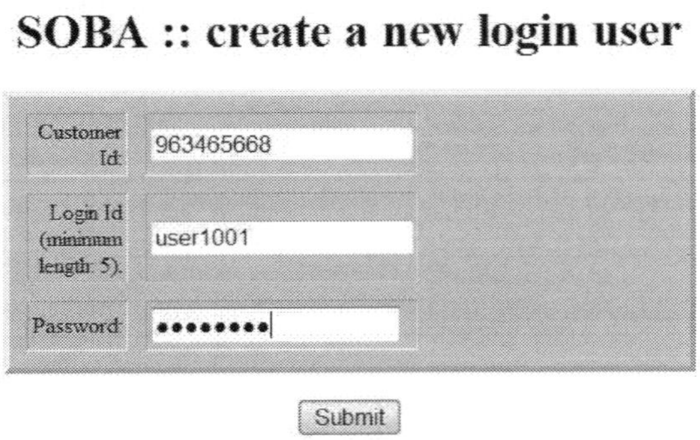

SOBA :: create a new login user
Customer Id:
963465668
Login Id (minimum length: 5).
user1001
Password:
Submit

Figure 2.11 SOBA: Creating a user ID

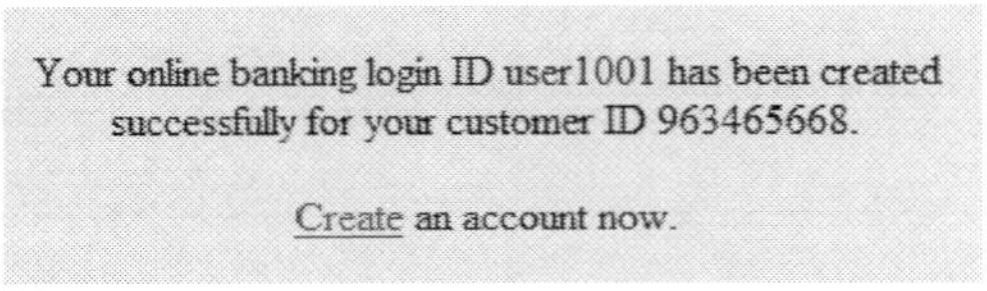

Your online banking login ID user1001 has been created successfully for your customer ID 963465668.
Create an account now.

Figure 2.12 SOBA: Creating login ID successful

CustomerId:
963465668
Name:
my checking
Type:
Checking
Description:
my checking online
Submit

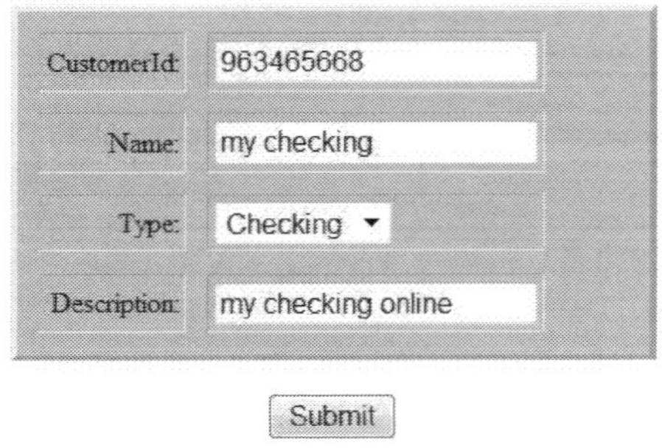

Figure 2.13 SOBA: Creating an account

Your account with your customer ID 963465668 has been created successfully.
Please log off and sign in to access your account(s).

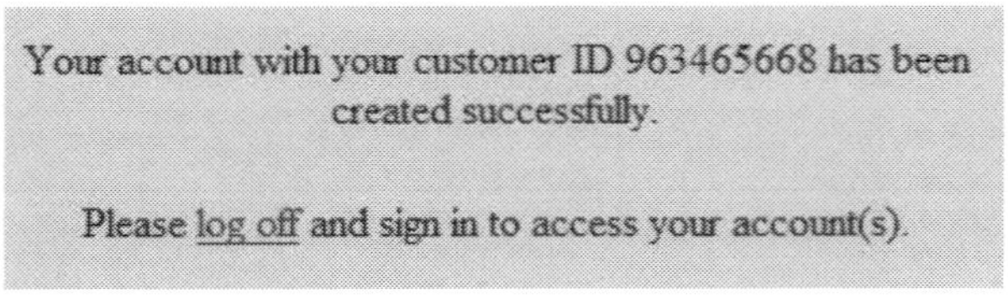

Figure 2.14 SOBA: Creating an account successful

Figure 2.15 Home page of a user logged onto SOBA

2.7.3 Testing SOBA 2: Posting Transactions

To test posting transactions, log onto SOBA as `user1001` and you should see a screen similar to Figure 2.16. Note that since this is a new account, the user does not have any activities yet. Next:

- Click the *Create a Tx* link at the top bar and you should see a screen similar to Figure 2.16. Enter a non-zero amount, say 100, and click *Submit*.
- Now you should see a screen similar to Figure 2.17, showing that posting transaction is successful.
- Click the *View Account Activity* link and you should now see you have $100 in your account, as shown in Figure 2.18. Note that you can now see your account ID on this page now. You will need this account ID when you test bill payment as `user1002`, and vice versa for `user1001`.
- Now click the *Create an ACL Tx* link at the top bar, follow the same procedure and deposit $200. Now you should see you have $300 total in your account, as shown in Figure 2.19.
- Repeat the same steps for `user1002` and we will be ready for testing bill payment next.

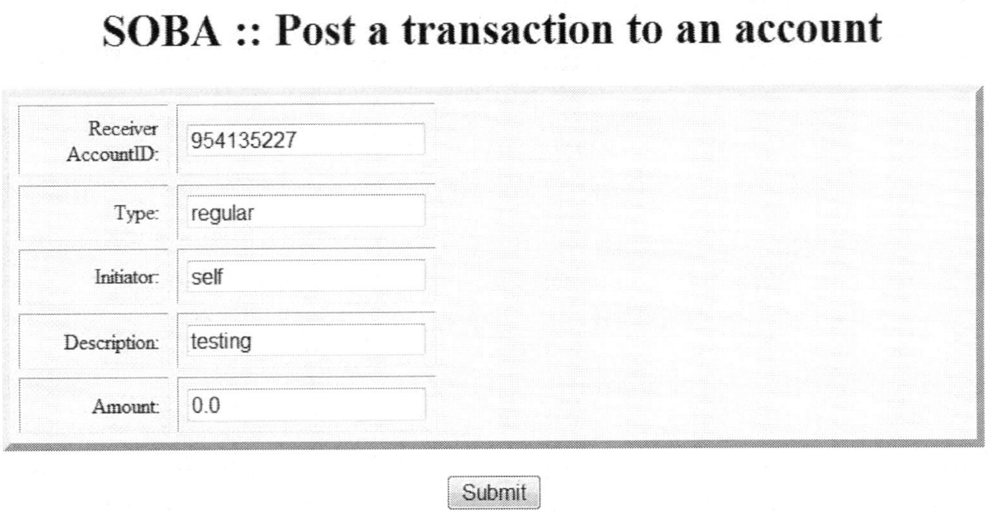

SOBA :: Post a transaction to an account

Receiver AccountID:	954135227
Type:	regular
Initiator:	self
Description:	testing
Amount:	0.0

Submit

Figure 2.16 SOBA: Posting a transaction

The transaction has been created successfully for the customer with ID 963465668.

Create a New Transaction

or

View Account Activity

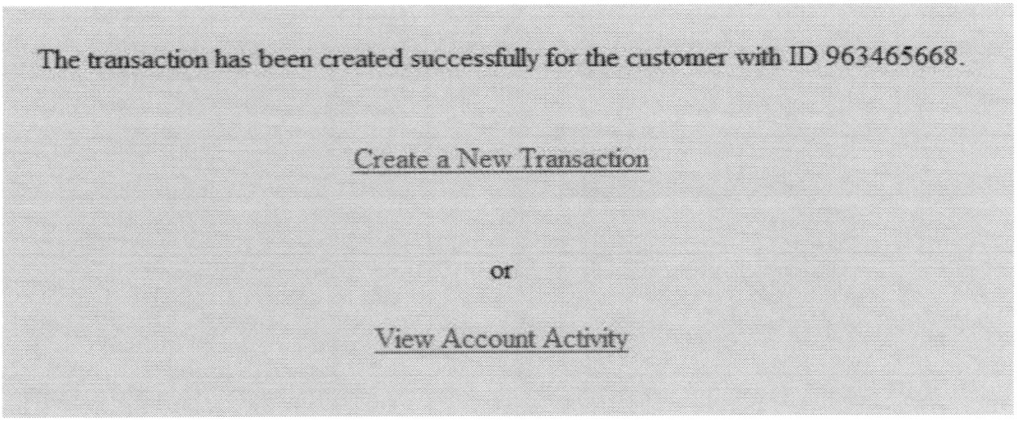

Figure 2.17 SOBA: Posting a transaction successful

Open an Account | Create a Tx | Create an ACL Tx | Bill Payment | Transfers | Dispute Transactions | Messages

Logged in as: anonymousUser

Customer Account Details

Customer ID:	963465668
Account ID:	954135227
Account Name:	my checking
Account Type:	Checking
Account Balance:	100.0

Account Name	Type	Range (date input format: yyyy-mm-dd)
Premium Checking	Checking	Last 30 days From: To: Get History Reset

Date	Type	Description	Debit	Credit	Balance
2012-04-13	regular	testing		100.0	100.0

Figure 2.18 SOBA: Account view with a balance of $100 after a transaction is posted

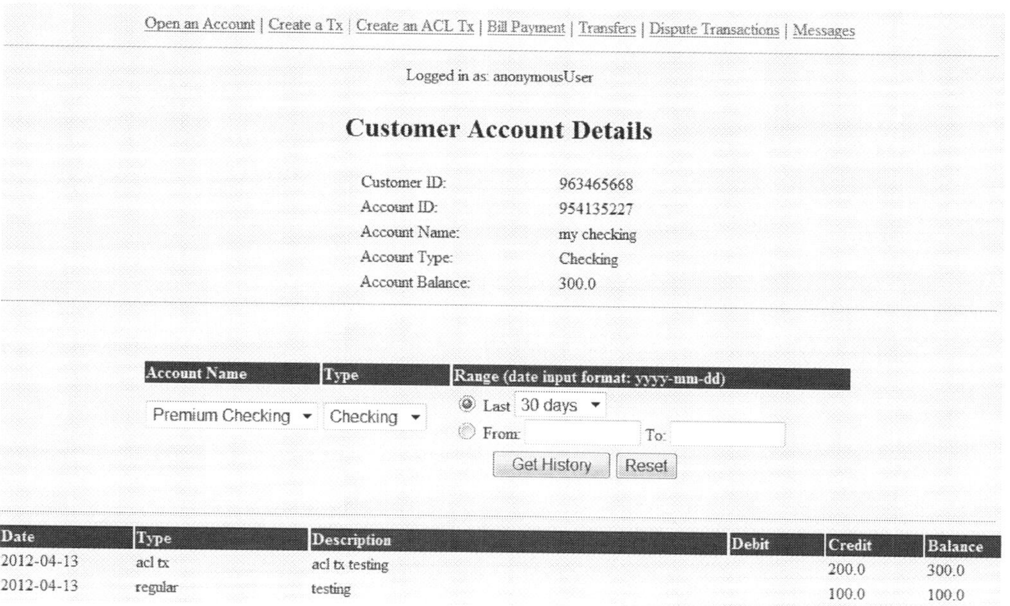

Figure 2.19 SOBA: Account view with a new deposit of $200

2.7.4 Testing SOBA 3: Paying Bills Online

To test paying bills online, log in as `user1002` and follow the procedure below:

- Click the *Bill Payment* link at the top bar. Now you should see a form similar to Figure 2.20. Enter the account ID of `user1001` in the *Receiver AccountID* box, a non-zero amount, e.g., 50, and `user1001` in the *Biller* box. Click *Submit*.
- You should now see bill payment successful in a screen similar to Figure 2.21. Click the *View Account Activity* link and you should see that an amount of $50 has been debited from `user1002's` account, as shown in Figure 2.22.
- Now check `user1001's` account and you should see an amount of $50 has been credited to `user1001's` account, as shown in Figure 2.23. This completes our initial testing on SOBA to make sure everything works so far.

Pay From Account:	677376936
Receiver AccountID:	
Description:	bill pay test
Amount:	0.0
Biller:	
Address:	One Way
City:	Any City
State:	CA
Zipcode:	95999

Submit

Figure 2.20 SOBA: Bill payment form

The bill pay has been created successfully for the customer with ID 36472380.

Create a new Bill Pay

or

View Account Activity

Figure 2.21 SOBA: Bill payment successful

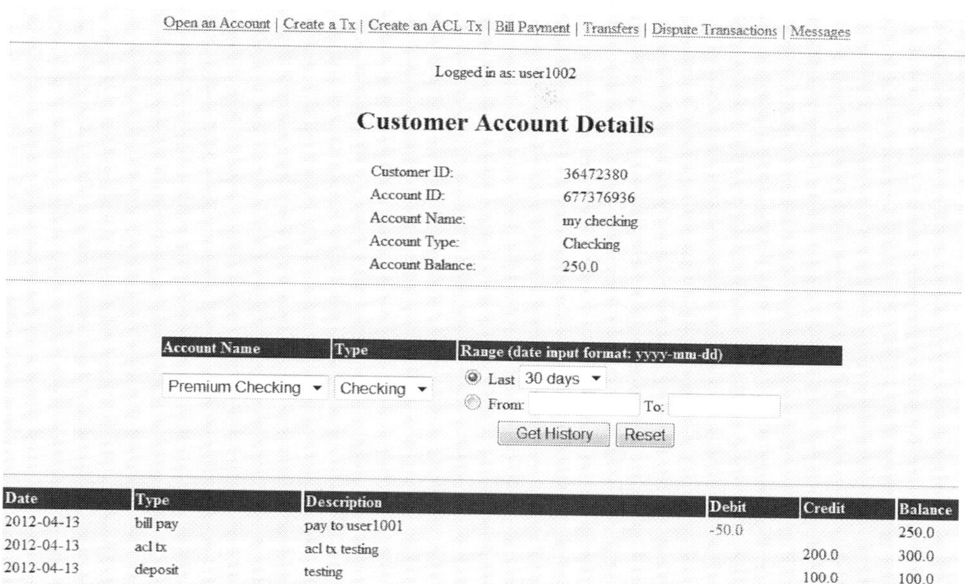

Figure 2.22 SOBA: $50 is debited from user1002's account after a bill pay

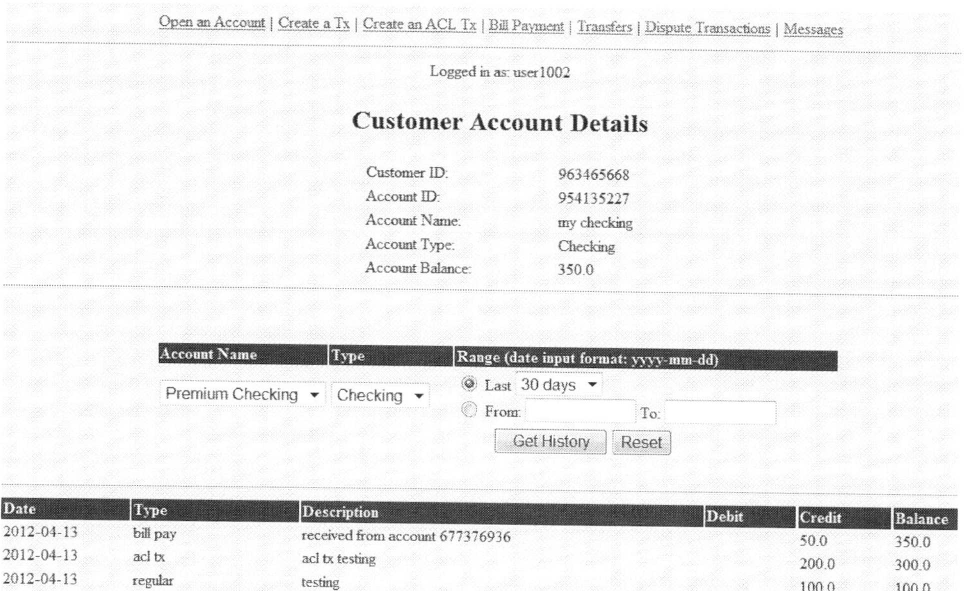

Figure 2.23 SOBA: $50 is credited into user1001's account after a bill pay by user1002

2.8 SUMMARY

In this chapter, we covered how to set up the SOBA sample application with Spring 4 on your system. I hope this exercise itself is a good experience in addition to what you will learn about Spring in the remaining part of this book.

RECOMMENDED READING

As an enterprise application developer, you should be conversant with at least one database platform. If you have not decided which database product you would focus on, MySQL would be a good pick, as many large companies use MySQL to support the services they provide.

To learn more about IoC, refer to Chapter 4 The IoC Container of the Spring Reference Documentation.

EXERCISES

2.1 Take a look at Figure 2.3 and try to get familiar with the general project structure of an enterprise Web application.

2.2 Refer to Listing 1.1. How can you avoid downloading so many jar files manually and separately given the fact there could be many different versions existing? What are the pros and cons between the Ant and Maven based building processes if you are familiar with both?

Part II Spring Essential Elements for Building Enterprise Applications

In this second part, I will help you understand all Spring essential elements for building enterprise applications. Based on the high-level overview of Spring and SOBA sample application you installed and configured in Part I, we will explore the following topics:

- Spring Core Concepts
- Spring Web MVC Framework
- Spring Data Access Framework
- Spring RESTful Web Services Framework
- Spring Security Framework
- Spring AOP Framework
- Spring Testing Framework
- Spring-EJB Integration Framework
- Spring Web Flow Framework

Let's begin with the Spring core concepts next.

3 Spring Core Concepts

In this chapter, we focus on gaining a solid understanding of several Spring core concepts such as an IoC (Inverse of Control) container, Spring beans, dependency injection, and so on. Whenever possible, we will use SOBA to demonstrate these concepts. You can also make changes to SOBA yourself to check your understandings by seeing what happens when you make a change.

3.1 THE IOC CONTAINER

A Spring-based enterprise application consists of beans that developers compose. A bean needs to work with other beans to accomplish a function. The beans that a bean depends on may depend on other beans (refer back to Figure 1.2 for the bean-to-bean dependency relationships). In Spring, a *dependent* bean specifies the beans it depends upon in one of the following three ways:

- Using constructor arguments
- Using arguments to a factory method
- Using properties that are set with setter methods

Then, when a bean is created, the Spring container *injects* the dependencies rather than having the dependent bean look up the references to the instances of the beans it depends upon. This new method is essentially the inversion of the traditional method based on the service lookup pattern, thus the name of *Inversion of Control* (IoC). In summary, with a Spring-based application, dependencies are defined in application beans, but are resolved by a Spring IoC container externally.

A Spring Framework IoC container is built on two Spring Framework packages: the *org.springframework.beans* package and *org.springframework.context* package. Out of the *beans* package, the *BeanFactory* interface provides a generic (and also more advanced) configuration mechanism for managing any type of object, while the *ApplicationContext* interface out of the *context* package, which is a sub-interface of *BeanFactory*, adds more enterprise-oriented functionality such as event publication, message resource handling, AOP integration, and so on. The *ApplicationContext* interface also serves as the basis for supporting even higher-level application-layer specific contexts such as the *WebApplicationContext* interface designed for building enterprise Web applications. Making a mental note that *ApplicationContext* is a sub-interface of *BeanFactory*, whereas *WebApplicationContext* is a sub-interface of *ApplicationContext*, will certainly help you understand the contents covered in this chapter better. See Figure 3.1 for the relationships among the Spring IoC context-related interfaces and some of their implementation classes. The *ClassPathXmlApplicationContext* and *FileSystemXmlApplicationContext* classes are the two implementation classes of the *ApplicationContext* interface, which are discussed in the next section. Incidentally, note the UML conventions here:

- **Generalization:**
  - **Inheritance**: A solid line with a solid arrowhead that points from a sub-interface to a super-interface or from a sub-class to a super-class.
  - **Implementation**: A dotted line with a solid arrowhead that points from a class to the interface that it implements.
- **Dependency:** A dotted line with an open arrowhead that shows one entity depends on another entity; or rather, the *client* depends on the *ApplicationContext* interface in this case.

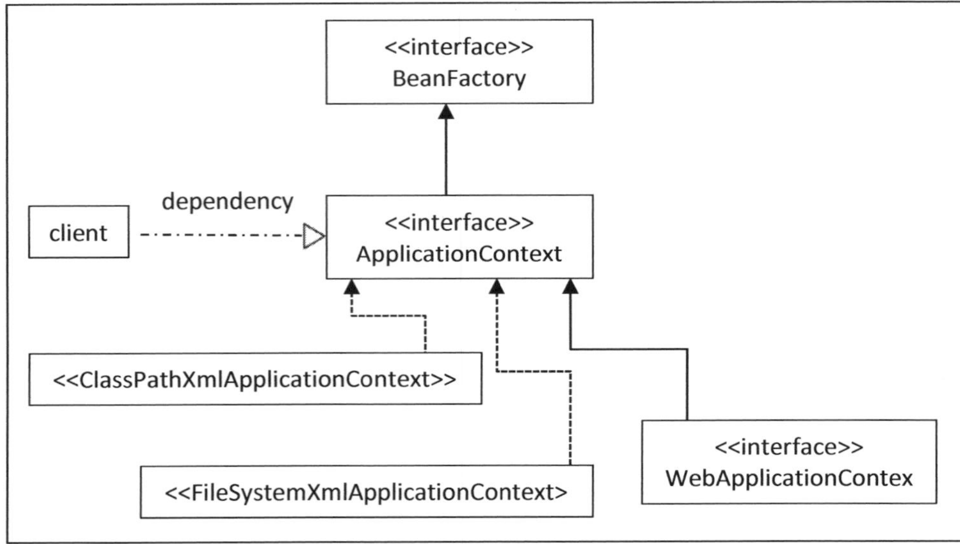

Figure 3.1 Spring IoC interfaces and implementations

Spring is a *context-centric* framework. The Spring IoC container depends heavily on the *ApplicationContext* interface to instantiate, assemble, and manage beans for supporting standalone applications. The *WebApplicationContext* interface works similarly for supporting Web-based applications. In the next section, we discuss how a Spring IoC container loads application context using the *ApplicationContext* interface with XML configuration metadata provided externally. The *WebApplicationContext* interface is discussed in the next chapter.

3.1.1 The POJO and Configuration Metadata

Configuration metadata serves as a media between an application and a Spring IoC container on how to instantiate, configure, and wire beans of the application. Configuration metadata can be supplied in one of the following three mechanisms:

- **XML-based configuration files**: This is the most widely used mechanism.
- **Annotation-based configuration**: This was introduced in Spring 2.5. The *MyNotes* sample presented in Appendix C contains annotation-based configuration examples.
- **Java-based configuration**: This was introduced in Spring 3.0. This feature uses annotations like `@Configuration`, `@Bean`, `@Import` and `@DependsOn`, etc., inside Java code.

Using SOBA as an example, let us say we would like to provide a *SobaConfig* bean so that SOBA clients would know exactly which database vendor is being used with a specific deployment. To accomplish this task, we need to create a POJO as shown in Listing 3.1 first. Note that this is a regular POJO outside the Spring framework, as you can see that it does not require importing any packages from the Spring framework. This POJO depends on an attribute named `databaseVendor` to provide the information on which database vendor SOBA uses. Apparently, the value for this attribute cannot be hard-coded into this POJO, as it would require building a version of SOBA for each database vendor. This is an ideal scenario to demonstrate how this dependency can be *injected externally* into the POJO with Spring's IoC dependency injection mechanism (keep in mind that a dependency doesn't have to be a complex object – it can just be a simple String object as in this case).

Listing 3.1 SobaConfig.java

```
package com.perfmath.spring.soba.service;
public class SobaConfig {
    private static String databaseVendor;
    public static String getDatabaseVendor() {
        return databaseVendor;
    }
    public void setDatabaseVendor(String databaseVendor) {
        SobaConfig.databaseVendor = databaseVendor;
    }
}
```

Next, we compose a *myBeans.xml* file as shown in Listing 3.2 as the *XML configuration metadata* for this bean, which is one of the three configuration metadata mechanisms we mentioned above. It is seen that the `id` attribute identifies the *sobaConfig* bean, while the `class` attribute defines the type of the bean using its fully qualified class name. A value "`mysql`" is assigned to the property named `databaseVendor`. We can configure more beans here as <bean> elements inside the top-level <beans> element, but for this example, we have only this one bean. POJOs described with Spring configuration metadata are now called *Spring beans*. Note this pattern of "*POJOs + Spring configuration metadata => Spring beans*." This simple example shows how Spring makes Spring beans out of regular POJOs with the help of external configuration metadata. It also shows what it means by *dependency injection*.

Listing 3.2 myBeans.xml

```
<?xml version="1.0" encoding="UTF-8"?>
<beans xmlns="http://www.springframework.org/schema/beans"
    xmlns:xsi="http://www.w3.org/2001/XMLSchema-instance"
    xsi:schemaLocation="http://www.springframework.org/schema/beans
       http://www.springframework.org/schema/beans/spring-beans.xsd">
    <bean id="sobaConfig" class="com.perfmath.spring.soba.service.SobaConfig">
    <!--dependency injection here -->
    <property name="databaseVendor" value="mysql" />
    </bean>
    </beans>
```

We will see some examples of annotation-based configuration and Java-based configuration in some chapters later in SOBA's context. Next, we demonstrate how this simple bean can be loaded into the application context to be usable.

3.1.2 Instantiating a Spring IoC Container

Now the Spring framework has to inject the `databaseVendor` dependency into the *sobaConfig* bean before the client can use it to query what database vendor SOBA uses. This can be accomplished by instantiating the Spring IoC container through loading the application context for the *sobaConfig* bean. With the *myBeans.xml* metadata file given above, we can use one of the following implementation classes of the `ApplicationContext` interface to instantiate the Spring IoC container:

- `ClassPathXmlApplicationContext`: This usage requires placing the *myBeans.xml* file in the `CLASSPATH` of SOBA, which is the top directory for class `com.perfmath.spring.soba.service.SobaConfig.class`.
- `FileSystemXmlApplicationContext`: This usage requires placing the *myBeans.xml* file in the root directory of the SOBA project. To execute it on Eclipse, the `myBeans.xml` file needs to be placed in the *src/main/resources* directory.

The actual Java statements are illustrated below:

```
ApplicationContext context = new ClassPathXmlApplicationContext ("myBeans.xml");
ApplicationContext context = new FileSystemXmlApplicationContext ("myBeans.xml");
```

It's worthwhile to notice that the location path provided to an *ApplicationContext* constructor as shown above is a Spring *resource* string that allows the IoC container to load configuration metadata from a variety of external resources such as the Java *CLASSPATH* and local file system as we have demonstrated. This is Spring's resource abstraction feature, which provides a much-needed mechanism for reading *InputStream* from locations defined in a URI syntax. §5.7 in Spring's *reference manual* provides more information on how to use *resource* paths to construct application contexts.

3.1.3 Using the Container

The *ApplicationContext* interface is an advanced factory interface capable of maintaining a registry of all beans and their dependencies. After loading the application context as demonstrated in the preceding section, you can retrieve the bean using the context's `getBean` method. Then you can invoke the methods of the bean retrieved.

Listing 3.3 shows how this works. First, verify that this program works in your environment. To execute this client program on your Eclipse IDE, you can right click on `TestAppContext.java` in the `test` package and then select *Run As → 2 Java Application*. You should see an output message of "`Database vendor for SOBA: mysql`". To switch to `FileSystemXmlApplicationContext`, comment out the line for `ClassPathXMLApplicationContext` and uncomment the line for `FileSystemXmlApplicationContext`, and run it again. The output message should be the same.

Listing 3.3 TestAppContext.java

```
package com.perfmath.spring.soba.test;
import org.springframework.context.ApplicationContext;
import org.springframework.context.support.ClassPathXmlApplicationContext;
import org.springframework.context.support.FileSystemXmlApplicationContext;

import com.perfmath.spring.soba.service.SobaConfig;
public class TestAppContext {

  public static void main (String[] args) {
     ApplicationContext context = new ClassPathXmlApplicationContext ("myBeans.xml");
     //ApplicationContext context = new FileSystemXmlApplicationContext
     // ("myBeans.xml");
     SobaConfig sobaConfig = context.getBean("sobaConfig", SobaConfig.class);
     System.out.println ("Database vendor for SOBA: " +
         sobaConfig.getDatabaseVendor());
     // no need to use the getBean method
     //System.out.println ("Database vendor for SOBA: " +
     //SobaConfig.getDatabaseVendor());
     }
}
```

Figure 3.2 illustrates how the Spring IoC container makes a bean ready for use. Specifically, this is how it works:

- First, you create a *context* object using either `ClassPathXmlApplicationContext` or `FileSystemApplicationContext` based on the *configuration metadata* file provided.
- Then, you use the *context.getBean* () method to get an instance of the bean as defined in the configuration metadata file, which is the *sobaConfig* bean in this case. Note the parameters passed into this method: `sobaConfig` and `SobaConfig.class`, where the first parameter is the bean *instance* and the second parameter is the bean *type*. The Spring IoC container would perform a contextualized dependency lookup (CDL) and pass this bean to the client, or the `TestAppContext.java` class in this case, that depends on this bean.
- You can then call the method of the bean for the information you are interested in.

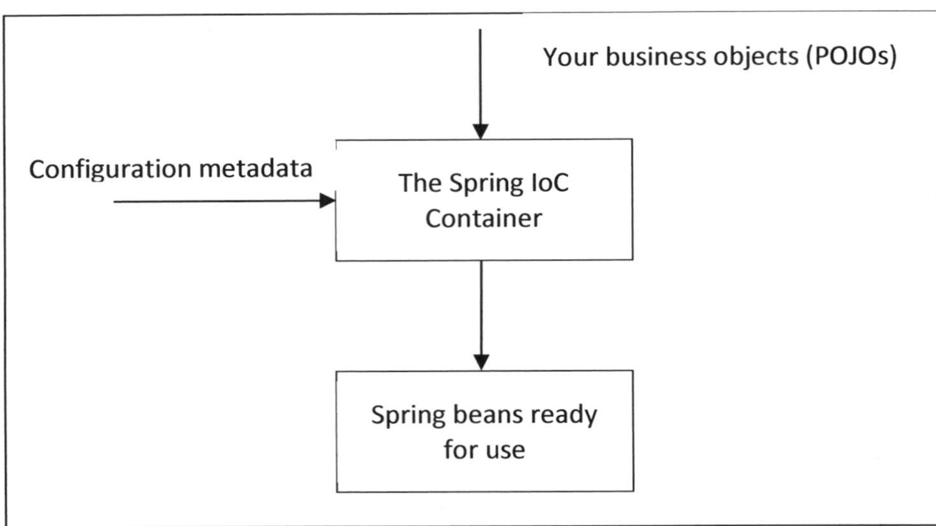

Figure 3.2 The Spring IoC container

Actually, for this example, you do not have to use the context's `getBean` method at all, as implied by the last two statements commented out. In fact, your application code may not have to call the `getBean ()` method at all to access the methods of your beans. This is the case with the `WebApplicationContext` interface (which is a sub-interface of `ApplicationContext` as we described previously) as we will see in the next chapter with the SOBA implementation.

3.1.4 Configuring POJOs As Spring Beans

Do you need to configure every POJO or object for your application as a Spring bean as we have shown in the previous section? Let's take a layered approach to answering this question.

- **Presentation layer objects**: The objects at this layer are typically configured as Spring beans. Such examples include servlets, web controllers, form controllers, JSF and/or Struts Action instances if any, etc. For example, the following beans are configured in the *soba-servlet.xml* file, which maps the transaction/customer/account listing JSP pages to their respective web `controller` objects. We will see plenty of examples as such with SOBA when we get there in the next few chapters.

```
<bean name="/transactionList.htm" class =
        "com.perfmath.spring.soba.web.TxController">
        <property name="txManager" ref="txManager" />
</bean>
<bean name="/customerList.htm" class="com.perfmath.spring.soba.web.CustomerController">
        <property name="customerManager" ref="customerManager" />
</bean>
<bean name="/accountList.htm" class="com.perfmath.spring.soba.web.AccountController">
```

```
        <property name="accountManager" ref="accountManager" />
</bean>
```

- **Service layer objects**: The objects at this layer are typically configured as Spring beans as well. We will see plenty of such examples as `CustomerManager`, `AccountManager`, `BankingTxManager`, and so on, with SOBA when we get there in the next few chapters.

```
<bean id="txManager" class="com.perfmath.spring.soba.service.SimpleTxManager">
        <property name="bankingTxDao" ref="bankingTxDao" />
        <property name="accountManager" ref="accountManager" />
</bean>
<bean id="billPayManager" class="com.perfmath.spring.soba.service.SimpleBillPayManager">
        <property name="billPaymentDao" ref="billPaymentDao" />
        <property name="aclTxManager" ref="aclTxManager" />
  </bean>
```

- **DAO layer objects**: The objects at this layer are typically configured as Spring beans as well. We will see plenty of such examples as `JDBCCustomerDAO`, `JDBCAccountDAO`, `JDBCBankingTxDAO`, and so on, as shown below, with SOBA when we get there in the next few chapters.

```
<bean id="customerDao" class="com.perfmath.spring.soba.model.dao.JdbcCustomerDao">
        <property name="dataSource" ref="dataSource" />
</bean>
<bean id="accountDao" class="com.perfmath.spring.soba.model.dao.JdbcAccountDao">
        <property name="dataSource" ref="dataSource" />
</bean>
<bean id="bankingTxDao" class="com.perfmath.spring.soba.model.dao.JdbcBankingTxDao">
        <property name="dataSource" ref="dataSource" />
</bean>
```

- **Infrastructure layer objects**: These objects provide infrastructural support such as data source objects, transaction management objects, security support objects, the Hibernate `SessionFactories`, `JMS Queues`, and so on. They are typically configured as Spring beans as well. The following bean is the data source bean that SOBA uses. In addition to the usual `id` and `class` attributes, it has the property tags that define the JDBC driver class, `URL`, `username`, `password`, `initialSize` and `maxActive` for the JDBC pool for SOBA. You can find this bean in the *soba-services.xml* file. Note also how this bean is referenced in the DAO beans shown above.

```
<bean id="dataSource" class="org.apache.commons.dbcp.BasicDataSource"
        destroy-method="close">
        <property name="driverClassName" value="${jdbc.driverClassName}" />
        <property name="url" value="${jdbc.url}" />
        <property name="username" value="${jdbc.username}" />
        <property name="password" value="${jdbc.password}" />
        <property name="initialSize" value="5"/>
        <property name="maxActive" value="50"/>
```

```
    </bean>
```

Another infrastructural support bean used in SOBA is the `jaxbMarshaller` bean as shown below, defined in the *soba-servlet.xml* file. The purpose of this bean is for supporting SOBA domain object serialization, and specifically in this case, to support the `BankingTx` domain object. This bean will be discussed further later in §6.3 when we discuss a banking transaction controller implemented with Spring RESTful web services.

```
<bean id="jaxbMarshaller" class="org.springframework.oxm.jaxb.Jaxb2Marshaller">
    <property name="classesToBeBound">
        <list>
            <value>com.perfmath.spring.soba.model.domain.BankingTx</value>
        </list>
    </property>
</bean>
```

One more example is the `messageSource` bean for SOBA as defined below, which defines the file that contains all messages for SOBA to display at proper points.

```
<bean id="messageSource"
    class="org.springframework.context.support.ResourceBundleMessageSource">
    <property name="basename" value="soba_messages" />
</bean>
```

- **Fine-grained domain objects**: These objects are typically not configured as Spring beans. The DAO and services beans create and load these objects.

Having seen one complete example of a Spring bean named *SobaConfig* as illustrated in the previous section, let's explore more about Spring beans next.

3.2 SPRING BEANS

Spring beans are the basic building blocks for composing a Spring-based enterprise application. In this section, we take a closer, more comprehensive look at all aspects of defining a Spring bean, although we may not need to know all of it, since it's always a most basic subset of it that we use in general.

In the previous section, we learnt that a bean can be defined in an external XML configuration metadata file as one of the `<bean>` elements of the `<beans>` top structure. Such a bean is internally represented as a `BeanDefinition` object in a Spring IoC container. The responsibility of the container is to manage the beans defined with the following metadata:

- **A package-qualified class name**: This is typically assigned to the actual implementation class of the bean. We have seen a few such examples in the previous section.
- **Bean behavioral configuration properties**: These properties include *scope*, *lifecycle*, *callbacks*, and so on, which define how the bean should behave in the container. If you refer back to the data source bean introduced in the previous section, you would notice an attribute named "`destroy-method`," which is assigned a value of "`close`." This instructs the container to destroy the bean after the `ApplicationContext` object is closed so that all resources in use can be released.

- **References to other beans**: These references are called *dependencies* as we have repeated in the previous sections. They are also called *collaborators*. The SOBA DAO bean examples shown in the preceding section all reference the `dataSource` bean.
- **Other context specific configuration settings**: For example, if the bean manages a connection pool, the context specific configuration settings may include the connection pool size information such as `min/max` connections in the pool, etc. All the `<property>` tags defined in the `dataSource` bean as described in the previous section belong to this category.

The IoC container constructs a `BeanDefinition` object for each bean defined with the metadata as described above. The metadata eventually translates to a set of attributes for a `BeanDefinition` object, as shown in Table 3.1. The IoC container creates the bean instance based on the attributes listed in Table 3.1. In the next few sections, we elaborate more on these attributes listed here.

Table 3.1 Attributes of the Spring BeanDefinition class

Attribute	Comment
id and/or name	Used to identify beans
class	The implementation class for the bean to be instantiated
scope	Lifecycle definition for the bean to be instantiated
constructor arguments	Constructor parameters for the bean to be instantiated as one of the mechanisms for dependency injection
properties	Properties of the bean to be instantiated as one of the mechanisms for dependency injection
autowiring mode	How beans should be wired together.
lazy-wiring mode	Delaying instantiating a singleton bean if set to true
initialization method	The method to call prior to instantiating the bean
destruction method	The method to call prior to destroying the bean

3.2.1 Identifying and Naming Beans

In your XML-based bean configuration file, you identify your beans with an *id* attribute, as shown in Listing 3.2 in the preceding section. You can also assign a *name* to a bean, when you want to refer to that bean by name through the use of the `ref` element, but most of the time, an `id` attribute is sufficient for identifying a bean. The Spring container distinguishes beans from each other by their `id` attributes; therefore, a bean's id must be unique. The convention for specifying an id for a bean is the same as naming a field or a method for a Java class: You start with a lowercase letter and then capitalize the first letter for each of the subsequent parts such as `sobaConfig`, `accountManager`, and so on.

Also, note that it's not mandatory to specify an *id* for a Spring bean. This is especially the case when you use inner beans and/or auto-wiring collaborators. In such cases, the container assigns a unique id to a bean.

3.2.2 Instantiating Beans

A Spring container instantiates or creates a Spring bean based on the bean definition translated from its configuration metadata. The container looks up the `class` attribute and other attributes of a `BeanDefinition` object and creates the bean accordingly.

Spring provides quite a few mechanisms for instantiating a bean, including:

- **Instantiating a bean with a constructor**: In this case, you only need to specify the `id` and `class` attributes if you are dealing with true JavaBeans with only a default (no-argument) constructor and proper getters and setters. With SOBA, we have a `BillPaymentDAO` bean that falls into this category (you can refer to Listing 5.9 (a) for how this DAO class is defined). Since it is implemented with Hibernate rather than JDBC, unlike other DAO beans, it does not have a dependency on the JDBC `dataSource` object. It is configured in the *soba-services.xml* file with only an `id` attribute and a `class` attribute as follows:

```
<bean id="billPaymentDao"
  class="com.perfmath.spring.soba.model.dao.HibernateBillPaymentDao">
</bean>
```

  This is the simplest case of instantiating a bean with its default empty constructor. However, if the bean has a parameterized constructor, it must be instantiated with a series of `<constructor-arg>` tags with proper `value` and/or `ref` attributes specified in its bean metadata XML descriptor in the form of `<constructor-arg value=<..> />` (for simple types of constructor arguments) or `<constructor-arg ref=<..> />` (for the bean to reference other beans). The container instantiates the bean accordingly with such argument values as defined by the `<constructor-arg ... >` XML tags. Such cases are very common with infrastructural beans which typically are not simple JavaBeans. For example, with SOBA, we have quite a few such beans, one of which is the `permissionEvaluator` bean associated with domain object access control as defined in the *soba-security.xml* file as follows:

```
<beans:bean id="permissionEvaluator"
    class="org.springframework.security.acls.AclPermissionEvaluator">
    <beans:constructor-arg ref="aclService" />
</beans:bean>
```

  In addition to the `id` and `class` attributes, it has a constructor argument as a referential dependency to the `aclService` bean. A more complicated example is the `aclCache` bean defined in the same *soba-security.xml* file as follows (*EhCache* is one of the most widely used caching technologies for building enterprise applications):

```
<beans:bean id="aclCache"
    class="org.springframework.security.acls.domain.EhCacheBasedAclCache">
```

```
    <beans:constructor-arg>
        <beans:bean
            class="org.springframework.cache.ehcache.EhCacheFactoryBean">
            <beans:property name="cacheManager">
                <beans:bean class=
        "org.springframework.cache.ehcache.EhCacheManagerFactoryBean" />
            </beans:property>
            <beans:property name="cacheName" value="aclCache" />
        </beans:bean>
    </beans:constructor-arg>
</beans:bean>
```

This `aclCache` bean is defined with an `id` of `aclCache` and class `EhCacheBasedAclCache`. It has an `EhCacheFactoryBean` as its only parameterized constructor argument, which has two properties defined: `cacheManager` as an instance of `EhCacheManagerFactoryBean` and a cache object named `aclCache` as illustrated above. Note also that the `EhCacheFactoryBean` is an *anonymous* bean without an `id` or `name` defined explicitly.

- **Instantiating a bean with a static factory method**: In this case, you use a static `createInstance ()` method of the factory class containing this method to instantiate the bean and return the reference to the bean. One use for such a bean definition is to call static factories in legacy code. Although we don't deal with legacy code and therefore do not have such an example with SOBA, the following code snippets should suffice to illustrate conceptually how this mechanism works. Note the `factory-method` attribute specified in the `<bean>` element. This is equivalent to creating a `legacyService` bean through a constructor, since the static factory method `createInstance ()` returns a live object.

```
<bean id="legacyService"
class="legacyApp.legacyService"
factory-method ="createInstance"/>
---------------------------------------------
public class LegacyService {
  private static LegacyService legacyServic = new LegacyService ();
  private LegacyService () {}
  public static LegacyService createInstance () {
    return legacyService;
 }
     }
```

- **Instantiating a bean with an instance factory method**: In this case, you specify a `factory-bean` attribute and a (non-static) `factory-method` attribute in your XML metadata bean descriptor to inform the container about how you want your bean instantiated exactly. This is slightly different from specifying a `class` attribute as well as a `factory-method` attribute as in the case of instantiating a bean with a static factory method as discussed above.

These are the bean instantiating mechanisms that Spring offers. However, it makes no sense if we just stop here. A real enterprise application or even our SOBA sample needs more than one object (or `bean` in the Spring parlance) to collaborate with each other to provide services that customers perceive to be coherent and useful. Therefore, we need to charge forward from learning how to define Spring beans standalone to learning how to wire up those beans through the much touted dependency injection (DI) method of Spring, which is the subject of the next section.

3.3 DEPENDENCY INJECTION (DI)

An enterprise application usually consists of many objects that collaborate with each other to provide users with enterprise services. In this regard, dependencies among objects are one of those delicacies that an enterprise application must cope with. Such dependencies are typically reflected in the source code as parameterized constructor arguments, or arguments to a factory method, or properties that need to be set through a self-contained parameterized constructor or an external factory method. With the concept of DI that is implemented in modern containers such as the Spring IoC containers, such dependencies are injected into the object or bean when it is created by the container. The object or bean does not need to know where these dependencies are stored and how to look them up. This is a huge convenience compared with the traditional EJB 2 technologies, a retrospective view of which is provided in a separate PDF file that can be downloaded from this book's website in case you want to know how dependencies are handled differently with EJB 2.

In this section, we focus on elaborating the two major Spring DI style variants: *Setter-based dependency injection* and *constructor-based dependency-injection*. Let's begin with the setter-based dependency injection first in the next section.

3.3.1 Setter-Based Dependency Injection

If you followed the example introduced in Section 3.1 about the *sobaConfig* bean, you already learnt what setter-based dependency injection is about. In that case, we used setter-based DI to inject the "`mysql`" value to the `databaseVendor` string attribute of the *sobaConfig* bean. With setter-based DI, you use one or more setter methods to let the container set the properties or attributes of your bean based on what you specify in the bean XML configuration metadata descriptor. To achieve that, all you need to do is add a `<property name="<attribName>" value="<value>"/>` for a simple-type attribute or `<property name="<attribName>" ref="<otherBean>"/>` for each dependency bean that your bean references.

Setter-based DI is the only way to go for dependency injection if your POJO has no parameterized constructor except regular setter methods. You can open up one of those SOBA XML configuration metadata files and find many such examples. This is a simple, more consistent way to manage dependency injection with Spring.

3.3.2 Constructor-Based Dependency Injection

Constructor-based DI requires a parameterized constructor so that the container can inject dependencies based on what is prescribed in the bean's XML configuration metadata descriptor, such as the elements like <constructor-arg type="int or java.lang.String, etc." value="<yourValue>"/> for simple types or <constructor-arg ref="otherBean"/> for other beans referenced by your bean. In this case, the sequence of the parameter arguments for the constructor is implied. You can also use indices or name attributes to specify how you want to correlate the elements specified in the bean's XML configuration metadata descriptor explicitly without having to follow an implied order. In fact, the last two of the three examples we presented earlier under "*instantiating a bean with a constructor*" are examples of constructor-based DIs. You can review these examples if you need to understand better how constructor-based DI works.

However, the Spring documentation mentions that you need to have your code compiled with the debug flag enabled in order to use this constructor-based DI feature if the arguments were specified by *name*, which makes it much less attractive than the setter-based dependency injection described in the preceding section. With the SOBA sample application, we use the setter-based dependency injection exclusively except those that come from the Spring framework itself or third-party software.

In addition, the Spring documentation mentions that it's a good rule of thumb to use constructor arguments for mandatory dependencies and setters for optional dependencies. It also mentions that one can use a @Required annotation on a setter to make it a required dependency. If such subtleties matter to you, I would recommend using setters with @Required annotation to avoid ambiguities and compiling your code with the debug flag enabled associated with the constructor-based dependency injection.

3.3.3 Dependency Resolution Process

In order to fully understand the inner workings of the Spring DI feature, let's review the dependency resolution process specific to the Spring IoC container in this section. We will use the example shown in Listings 3.1 through 3.3 we presented in the previous sections whenever possible so that we would have something concrete to rely on.

The Spring IoC container resolves bean dependencies by following the steps below:

- **Step 1**: Loading the *ApplicationContext*. As is shown in Listing 3.3, when a standalone Spring-based application starts to run, the first task is to create an *ApplicationContext* object with the configuration metadata that prescribes how each bean should be created. Although we used an external XML file, configuration metadata can also be specified via annotations or Java code.
- **Step 2**: Analyzing how dependencies are specified. The dependencies of a bean can be expressed in the form of attributes with corresponding setter methods, constructor arguments, or arguments to a static factory method of a factory class.
- **Step 3**: The container validates the configuration of each bean, including the validation of whether referenced beans are valid. One issue with referenced beans is that there might exist *circular* references, in which case validation fails. If a bean fails to pass the validation process, the application would not start properly and the root cause must be analyzed and resolved before proceeding further.
- **Step 4**: Converting types for attributes and/or constructor arguments. Each attribute or constructor argument is an actual definition of the value to set or a reference to another bean in the container. By

default, the container can convert a value specified in string format to all simple types such as `int`, `long`, `Boolean`, `String`, and so on.

However, after passing all four steps as described above, a bean may not be created immediately, depending on the scope of the bean, which we will discuss in the next section. By default, Spring pre-instantiates all singleton-scoped beans upfront. Otherwise, the bean is created only when it is needed either by its dependent bean or its client. For large scale enterprise applications, creation of a bean may incur a reaction-chain-like process that a bunch of first-level dependency beans are created, which may invoke the creation of the second level dependency beans that the first-level dependency beans depend on, and so forth. This is because dependency beans must be created prior to being assigned to their dependent bean. This subject is explored further in the next few sub-sections.

3.3.4 Using Depends-On

In a bean's XML configuration metadata descriptor, if you require the dependency beans be forcefully initialized before your bean, you can accomplish this by adding one additional attribute of `depends-on="bean1, bean2,...,"` following the class attribute of your bean. In addition, this feature helps the container decide which beans to destroy first when such a time comes. However, such a hard-coded dependency may not be needed in general. Our SOBA sample application does not use this feature.

3.3.5 Lazy-Initialized Beans

Spring's *ApplicationContext* implementations initialize all singleton beans at startup by default (a singleton bean is a single instance of a class that is initialized and cached at startup, and all subsequent requests return the same bean all the time). This behavior can be altered by adding an attribute of `lazy-init="true"` in the bean's XML configuration metadata descriptor. This might be desirable when you have a very large enterprise application and it takes too long or too much memory to initialize all beans at startup.

3.3.6 Autowiring Collaborators

The Spring IoC container can be enabled to *autowire* your beans with their collaborators if you add an attribute of `autowire` in your bean's XML configuration metadata descriptor. The default autowiring mode is "*no*." To change this default behavior, you can set the autowire attribute to "*byName*," "*byType*," or "*constructor*." These different modes are possible to set as each attribute or constructor argument of a bean is defined with a type-name pair after all. We would not repeat the specifics related to autowiring here, and you should refer to Spring's reference documentation if you are interested in pursuing this subject further.

Although the autowiring feature helps reduce the need to specify properties or constructor arguments when composing your bean's XML configuration metadata descriptor, in the meantime, it increases the chances of introducing extra ambiguities and complexities compared with the explicit wiring approach. It is a good practice to specify the dependencies explicitly, especially with a very large enterprise application that many developers get involved. Spring recommends to use autowiring during the development phase but switch to explicit wiring at the deployment time.

3.3.7 Method Injection

Most of the time, Spring deals with singleton beans. Ideally, a singleton bean should depend only on other singleton beans so that the dependency beans would be always there when the dependent bean needs them. But what if a singleton bean has to depend on one or more non-singleton (prototype) beans? In such a case, the singleton-scoped dependent bean and its prototype-scoped dependency beans have different lifetimes (the concept of *scope* is discussed in the next section). Since the container creates a singleton bean only once, the singleton bean has only one chance to set references to its dependency beans. The container cannot provide the singleton bean with the reference to a dependency bean when the original instance has been destroyed but a new instance is available.

Spring's method injection feature helps circumvent the above situation. However, as you might guess, it is done dynamically by using bytecode generation from the CGLIB library to generate dynamically a subclass that overrides the method. This is a complicated issue, and you should consult Spring's framework reference manual for more information, which actually directs you to a blog entry because of its complexity. Besides, such strategies may incur significant or even unacceptable performance penalty, so avoid using it unless you cannot go by without it.

3.4 BEAN SCOPES

Spring advocates a notion that a bean definition through its configuration metadata is like a *recipe* for creating actual instances of the class specified in that bean definition. This naturally leads to the question of how many bean instances are allowed to create from a single recipe. The `scope` attribute of a Spring bean answers that question.

In general, a Spring bean may have one of the following scopes:

- **Singleton**: This is the default scope that limits to a single object instance per Spring IoC container. Spring maintains a cache for all created singleton beans so that all subsequent requests for an already created singleton bean would be looked up and returned from the cache. Conceptually, a singleton bean is equivalent to a *stateless* bean that maintains no conversational state with a client.
- **Prototype**: In contrast to the singleton bean scope, the prototype scope allows more than one instance of a bean to be created out of a single recipe. Conceptually, a prototype bean is equivalent to a *stateful* bean that maintains a conversational state with a client. However, Spring does not manage the complete lifecycle of a prototype bean. The container instantiates a prototype bean and hands it to the client. After that point, it's up to the client to decide when and how to destroy the prototype bean and release all valuable resources assigned to it. In this regard, the container's role for a prototype bean is similar to the role of the Java `new` operator for regular Java objects.
- **Request**: This scope limits the lifecycle of the bean to a single HTTP request. It's valid only in the context of a Web-aware Spring ApplicationContext. A *login* bean could be an example of a request-scoped bean, which is invoked only when a user logs-in. However, it would cause no harm if such a login bean were scoped singleton so that the container only needs to maintain one single instance of it through its lifecycle.
- **Session**: This scope limits the lifecycle of the bean to a single HTTP Session. It's valid only in the context of a Web-aware Spring ApplicationContext. A `userPreferences` bean could be an example

of a session-scoped bean, since this type of beans do not need to live longer beyond a session that is bound by the login and logout actions of a user.

- **Global**: This scope limits the lifecycle of the bean to a global single HTTP Session, for example, when used in a portlet context. It's valid only in the context of a web-aware Spring ApplicationContext.

The last three scopes of *request*, *session* and *global* are specific to web-scoped beans. If you use the Spring Web MVC framework for your application, or specifically, if you use Spring's `DispatcherServlet` and `DispatcherPortlet`, no special setup is necessary to access such web-scoped beans. However, if you use a Servlet 2.4+ web container for requests processed outside Spring's `DispatcherServlet` and `DispatcherPortlet`, for example, when using other Web MVC frameworks such as JSF or Struts, you need to add `org.springframework.web.context.request.RequestContextListener`, which implements`javax.servlet.ServletRequestListener`, to your *web.xml* file. If you use an older web container such as a Servlet 2.3 web container, you need to add `org.springframework.web.context.request.RequestContextFilter`, which implements`javax.servlet.Filter`, to your *web.xml* file with JSF or Struts. These measures would help bind the HTTP request object to the `Thread` servicing the request when you use non-Spring based Web MVC frameworks like JSF and Struts to handle HTTP requests. Since SOBA is purely based on the Spring Web MVC framework for its frontend, such measures are not necessary for SOBA.

There are other advanced features and specifics related to Spring beans, but they are not very pertinent to the scope of this book and the SOBA sample application. Therefore, we move to the next chapter about the Spring Web MVC Framework, which serves as the indispensable frontend of the SOBA sample application and certainly is one of the central subjects of this book.

3.5 SUMMARY

In this chapter, we covered some of the basic core concepts of the Spring Framework in general. The Spring Framework solves the complexity of building enterprise applications by externalizing dependencies from Java code, and then injecting dependencies with external configuration metadata at the startup of an application. This type of dependency injection style provides developers with the kind of simplicity and flexibility that are not readily available from other frameworks that are heavy-weight in nature.

In the next chapter, after going through how SOBA is built with the Spring Web MVC Framework, you will not only understand those core concepts better, but also gain some real skills for quickly building enterprise applications using Spring Frameworks.

RECOMMENDED READING

Study Chapter 4 of the Spring Reference Documentation to have a more thorough understanding on the concept of a Spring IoC container. Here is a complete list of the sections about the Spring IoC container introduced there (highlighted sections are covered in this chapter).

Chapter 4 of the Spring Reference Documentation:

4.1 Introduction to the Spring IoC container and beans

4.2 Container overview

4.3 Bean overview

4.4 Dependencies

4.5 Bean Scopes

4.6 Customizing the nature of a bean

4.7 Bean definition inheritance

4.8 Container extension points

4.9 Annotation-based container configuration

4.10 Classpath scanning and managed components

4.11 Using JSR 330 Standard Annotations

4.12 Java-based container configuration

4.13 Registering a LoadTimeWeaver

4.14 Additional Capabilities of the ApplicationContext

4.15 The BeanFactory

EXERCISES

3.1 What is the default scope for a Spring bean? What does that mean exactly?

3.2 Where should you place the Spring bean XML configuration file in order to run an associated program using Eclipse's *Run-As* feature?

4 Spring Web MVC Framework

In the preceding chapter, we introduced some of the Spring core concepts, such as a Spring IoC container, Spring beans, Spring dependency injection, and so on. Equipped with the knowledge of those core concepts, we are ready to explore one of the most widely used Spring Frameworks – the Spring Web MVC Framework. Since this is one of the Spring Frameworks that SOBA is built on, this chapter covers it in detail.

Let's start with the architecture of a typical enterprise Web application in the next section.

4.1 Enterprise Web Application Architecture

A typical enterprise Web application consists of multiple tiers, as shown in Figure 4.1. Note that this is only a logical division that you can deploy physically all tiers on one system or several separate systems.

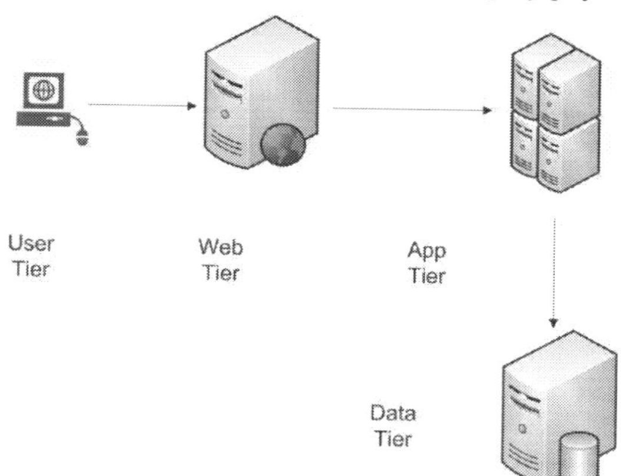

Figure 4.1 Architecture of a typical n-tier enterprise Web application

Next, let us take a brief look at how all those tiers collaborate with each other to fulfill the tasks of an enterprise Web application.

4.1.1 Data Tier

The data tier is also called backend tier, which provides persistence/retrieval services related to your enterprise data. It has to be hosted on a particular database platform, such as MySQL, PostgreSQL, SQL Server, Oracle, or IBM's DB2. DB2 is not covered in this book, though. The common concerns about which database platform to choose are multi-faceted, such as whether your application needs to support multiple database platforms, preferences of your potential customers, strengths of a particular database platform, and the associated development and maintenance costs, etc. My preference is MySQL, because, first, it is a proven platform with successful deployments by many large companies; and secondly, it is one of the most platform-neutral database platforms that it can be deployed on UNIX, Linux, and Windows. In addition, it is quite development-friendly in the sense that all open source development technologies are well supported.

From a functional point of view, the data tier is where your domain objects reside eventually. If you have gone through the SOBA schema covered in §2.3 or you are an experienced enterprise developer, you already understand well what this tier does. We will get more concrete with the data tier later when I walk you through how SOBA is built with JDBC and Hibernate that provide connectivity between the app tier and the data tier.

4.1.2 Application Tier

The application tier implements your business logic. It requires a runtime environment to support executing your business logic, which can be fulfilled with one of the application server products built on Java or other technologies such as the Spring platform combined with a web server such as Tomcat, Oracle's WebLogic, IBM's WebSphere, RedHat's JBoss, and so on.

4.1.3 Web Tier

The basic function of a Web tier is to receive service requests from users, delegate such requests to the application tier, receive and send processed results back to users. In SOBA's context, the application tier and Web tier are inseparable that they run in the same JVM of the Tomcat web server. For large enterprise Web applications, the web tier and application tier can be separated and deployed on two or more separate physical systems or clusters, in which case, some sort of remoting mechanisms such as JAVA RMI (Remote Method Invocation), Web Services, etc., are introduced to enable the communications between the two tiers.

4.1.4 User Tier

The user tier is where a user interacts with an enterprise Web application, mostly through the HTTP/HTTPS protocols. This tier is also called client tier, represented by a variety of client devices, such as PCs, Macs, tablets, mobile devices, etc. At this tier, responses from a frontend Web server are rendered to users through software such as various types of browsers, etc.

In the next section, we introduce a generic Model-View-Controller (MVC) architecture, which serves as the backbone for building enterprise Web applications. We'll see how it maps to the n-tier architecture that we have just described.

4.2 MVC ARCHITECTURE IN GENERAL

In a Model-View-Controller architecture, *model* handles application domain data and business logic, *view* represents what a user would see based on the responses a user receives from the system, whereas *controller* acts more like an orchestrator that coordinates the interactions between a user and the application system. Loosely speaking in the context of the n-tier enterprise architecture, *model* corresponds to the data tier and application tier, *controller* corresponds to the web tier, while *view* corresponds to the user or client tier.

The interactions among the model, view and controller of an MVC architecture are explained in Figure 4.2 further:

1 A user request is sent to the system for viewing, creating, modifying, or deleting data.
2 The dispatcher dispatches the user request to the controller.
3 The controller parses the user requests and calls the model one or multiple times for retrieving data or carrying out the user requested changes to the model.
4 The model queries the database or initiates and commits changes to the database based on a user's request.
5 The controller returns data or outcome of the user request to the user.

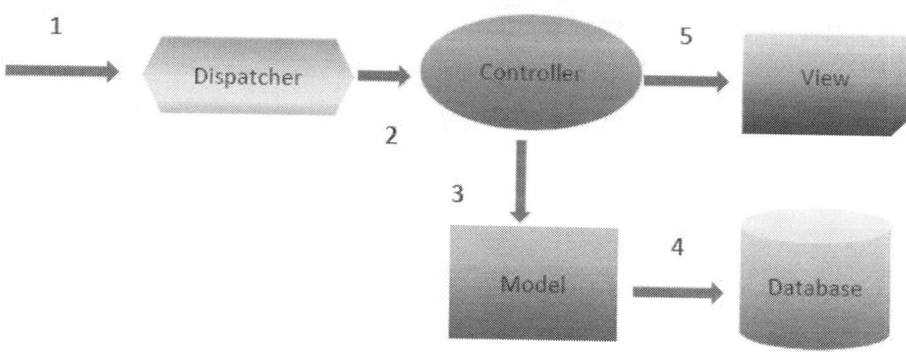

Figure 4.2 A generic MVC architecture

The Spring MVC framework is a concrete implementation of a generic MVC architecture. Next, let's see how such a generic MVC architecture is implemented with the Spring Web MVC Framework.

4.3 SPRING WEB MVC FRAMEWORK

The Spring Web MVC Framework is closely patterned on the generic MVC architecture that we introduced in the previous section. See Figure 4.3 for how Spring MVC Framework works and compare it with the generic MVC architecture shown in Figure 4.2. As is seen, the workflow with the Spring Web MVC Framework gets more specific.

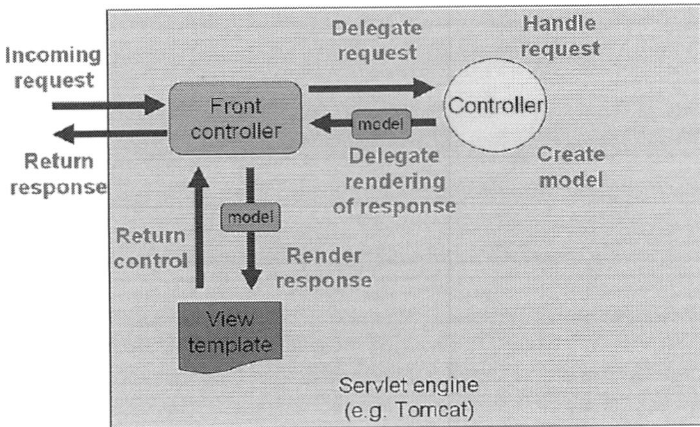

Figure 4.3 Spring Web MVC Framework workflow

Next, let us see how the Spring Web MVC Framework is implemented programmatically.

4.3.1 Spring DispatcherServlet and WebApplicationContext

In Chapter 3, we introduced the `ApplicationContext` interface, which is defined in the `org.springframework.context` package. The `ApplicationContext` interface extends the `BeanFactory` interface, which is defined in the `org.springframework.beans.factory` package. However, in contrast to the `BeanFactory` interface, the `ApplicationContext` interface can be used in a completely declarative manner so that no programming in Java is needed on the developer's side. This is made possible with a support class named `ContextLoader` in conjunction with an XML configuration file that defines all beans. The context loader class automatically instantiates an `ApplicationContext` at the startup time of an application.

Since an `ApplicationContext` is an interface, it must be implemented in order to be usable. The `WebApplicationContext` is one of the implementations of the `ApplicationContext` interface. The `WebApplicationContext` and the `DispatcherServlet` work jointly and play the critical role of *controller* in the Spring MVC Framework, as discussed next.

The `DispatcherServlet` is an expression of the *Front Controller* design pattern. It is defined in the package of `org.springframework.web.servlet`. Its main function is to dispatch user requests to handlers that are managed in a `WebApplicationContext`. Figure 4.4 illustrates the interaction between a `DispatcherServlet` and a `WebApplicationContext` as part of the entire MVC workflow (we'll elaborate on the concepts of controllers, handler mapping, view resolvers, etc., in the Spring's MVC context soon).

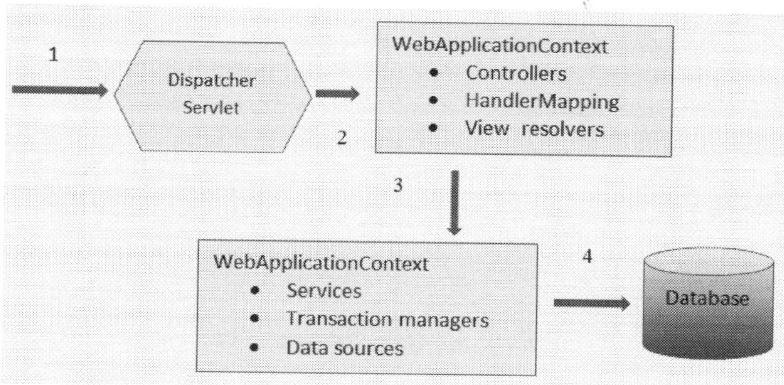

Figure 4.4 Two major elements of the Spring MVC Framework: DispatcherServlet and WebApplicationContext

Since the `DispatcherServlet` inherits from the `HttpServlet` base class, it is an actual servlet, which means that it can be defined in a `web.xml` file like in other non-Spring Web frameworks. To illustrate this, let's examine the `web.xml` file for SOBA next.

4.3.2 Bootstrapping and DispatcherServlet Defined in web.xml File

Since the `DispatcherServlet` inherits from the HttpServlet base class, a Spring-based web application is runnable on a general-purpose Web Server or a servlet engine like Tomcat, which depends on a `web.xml` file to bootstrap the web application. However, what is unique with a Spring MVC-based web application is that it has its own context loader, which provides a flexible mechanism for loading Spring beans defined in various Spring application context configurations.

In this section, we explain how a web application based on the Spring MVC Framework is bootstrapped and how the DispatcherServlet is defined in the `web.xml` file, which is exhibited in Listing 4.1. Now take a closer look at this `web.xml` file, especially those parts that are highlighted, and we will explain them following this listing.

Listing 4.1 web.xml for SOBA

```
<?xml version="1.0" encoding="UTF-8"?>
<web-app version="2.4" xmlns="http://java.sun.com/xml/ns/j2ee"
    xmlns:xsi="http://www.w3.org/2001/XMLSchema-instance"
    xsi:schemaLocation="http://java.sun.com/xml/ns/j2ee
      http://java.sun.com/xml/ns/j2ee/web-app_2_4.xsd">
    <!-- Log4j configuration loading -->
    <listener>
```

```
    <listener-class>org.springframework.web.util.Log4jConfigListener</listener-class>
</listener>
<context-param>
    <param-name>log4jConfigLocation</param-name>
    <param-value>/WEB-INF/classes/log4j.xml</param-value>
</context-param>
<!-- Bootstrapping context loading -->
<listener>
    <listener-class>org.springframework.web.context.ContextLoaderListener</listener-class>
</listener>
<context-param>
    <param-name>contextConfigLocation</param-name>
    <param-value>
     /WEB-INF/soba-servlet.xml
     /WEB-INF/soba-services.xml
      /WEB-INF/soba-security.xml
   </param-value>
</context-param>
<context-param>
    <param-name>webAppRootKey</param-name>
    <param-value>soba.root</param-value>
</context-param>
<!-- session management listener -->
<listener>
    <listener-class>org.springframework.security.web.session.HttpSessionEventPublisher
     </listener-class>
</listener>
<session-config>
    <!-- session times out if no activities for 30 minutes -->
    <session-timeout>30</session-timeout>
</session-config>
<!-- Security entry point -->
<filter>
    <filter-name>springSecurityFilterChain</filter-name>
    <filter-class>org.springframework.web.filter.DelegatingFilterProxy</filter-class>
</filter>
<filter-mapping>
    <filter-name>springSecurityFilterChain</filter-name>
    <url-pattern>/*</url-pattern>
</filter-mapping>
<!-- defining the DispatcherServlet -->
<servlet>
    <servlet-name>soba</servlet-name>
```

```
        <servlet-class>org.springframework.web.servlet.DispatcherServlet</servlet-class>
        <load-on-startup>1</load-on-startup>
    </servlet>
    <servlet-mapping>
        <servlet-name>soba</servlet-name>
        <url-pattern>/</url-pattern>
    </servlet-mapping>
    <servlet-mapping>
        <servlet-name>soba</servlet-name>
        <url-pattern>*.htm</url-pattern>
    </servlet-mapping>
<!-- defining the DefaultServlet -->
    <servlet>
        <servlet-name>DefaultServlet</servlet-name>
        <servlet-class>org.apache.catalina.servlets.DefaultServlet</servlet-class>
    </servlet>
    <servlet-mapping>
        <servlet-name>DefaultServlet</servlet-name>
        <url-pattern>*.jpg</url-pattern>
    </servlet-mapping>
    <servlet-mapping>
        <servlet-name>DefaultServlet</servlet-name>
        <url-pattern>*.html</url-pattern>
    </servlet-mapping>
    <error-page>
        <error-code>404</error-code>
        <location>/WEB-INF/jsp/notfound.jsp</location>
    </error-page>
    <welcome-file-list>
        <welcome-file>
            login.jsp
        </welcome-file>
    </welcome-file-list>
<!-- Spring jsp tag lib -->
    <jsp-config>
        <taglib>
            <taglib-uri>/spring</taglib-uri>
            <taglib-location>/WEB-INF/tld/spring-form.tld</taglib-location>
        </taglib>
    </jsp-config>
</web-app>
```

This `web.xml` file defines a `web-app` as its top structural node indicates. It consists of the following elements:

- **Log4j configuration**: This element defines configuring the log4j logging framework based on the `log4j.xml` file placed in the `/WEB-INF/classes` directory.
- **Bootstrapping context loading**: This element defines a context loader listener for loading contexts specified in the servlet, services, and security XML files. Those files contain all Spring beans in their respective contexts. Note that each of these files is prefixed with `soba-` in its name, which by convention originates from the dispatcher servlet instance name for this application as defined in the servlet element down this file. We will talk more about this later when we discuss the dispatcher servlet entry.
- **Session management listener**: This element defines that each session times out in 30 minutes. You can change this value to suit your needs.
- **Security entry point**: This element defines that the entire app of SOBA is secured with a url-pattern of /*.
- **Defining the DispatcherServlet**: We have discussed this element in the preceding section in detail. First, it defines the `DispatcherServlet` named `soba`. Then it defines a few servlet mappings, such as the root path of "/" and all requests ending with `.htm`. Together with the `welcome-file` of `login.jsp` defined near the end of the `web.xml` file, the URL of https://localhost:8443/soba takes a user to the login page of SOBA as shown in Figure 2.8. We will see later how those requests ending with `*.htm` are mapped to their corresponding Spring MVC controllers defined in the `soab-servlet.xml` file.
- **Defining the DefaultServlet:** This element defines the default servlet, which points to Tomcat's *org.apache.catalina.servlets.DefaultServlet*. Note that this *DefaultServlet* will handle all jpg and HTML files as specified by the two subsequent `<servlet-mapping>` elements.
- **Spring jsp tag lib**: This last element defines the Spring jsp tag lib that can be used in jsp files. We will see such examples later.

The key point to remember is that, upon initialization of a DispatcherServlet, the Spring MVC framework looks for a file named `<servlet-name>-servlet.xml` in the `WEB-INF` directory and creates beans defined there. Then the DispatcherServlet starts to dispatch user requests as users interact with a web application built on the Spring Web MVC Framework. As a Spring developer, it's necessary to fully understand Spring Web MVC programming logic flow from end to end. We will take a full examination at a typical Spring Web MVC programming logic flow using a typical workflow of creating a customer with SOBA as an example, after we explore next how Spring integrates standard view technologies with the Spring Web MVC Framework.

4.3.3 Spring Integration with View Technologies

Standard view technologies such as JSP, JSTL, Tiles (an Apache web template system), and so on, are separate from the Spring Web MVC framework. However, they are fully integrated into the Spring Web MVC Framework to enable a Spring-based enterprise Web application to work seamlessly with them. In this section, we look at how Spring resolves views with those standard view technologies.

As its name implies, Spring resolves views with *View Resolvers*. However, a developer needs to know a lot more about the view technologies than about the Spring View Resolvers, which are easy to configure and just work behind the scene, as is discussed next.

The two most important Spring view interfaces are ViewResolver and View. The ViewResolver interface is a mapping mechanism for resolving a view name to an actual view, while the View interface prepares and hands requests over to a matched view technology. Spring supports XmlViewResolver, ResourceBundleViewResolver, UrlBasedViewResolver, InternalResourceViewResolver, VelocityViewResolver, FreeMakerViewResolver, and ContentNegotiatingViewResolver. Out of these view resolvers, the two most commonly used are the ContentNegotiatingViewResolver and InternalResourceViewResolver, which is a subclass of UrlBasedViewResolver. All these view resolver classes implements the ViewResolver interface.

A view resolving process is defined in the <app-name>-servlet.xml file. To facilitate the discussion, let us look at how view resolving is defined for SOBA in the soba-servlet.xml file, shown in Listing 4.2 (a) below, which applies to both Spring 3.2 and Spring 4. For comparison purposes, how view resolvers are configured with Spring 3.1 is given in Listing 4.2 (b). The main difference is that the mediaTypes property now must be tucked within a ContentNegotiatingManager. Without making this upgrade from 3.1 to 3.2, SOBA would not work with Spring 3.2 and 4.

Spring supports a feature called *chaining* ViewResolvers. What that means is that we can specify multiple view resolvers to work with different view technologies. We chain view resolvers by adding multiple view resolvers to the application context, as is shown exactly in Listing 4.2 (a) with the ContentNegotiatingViewResolver and UrlBasedViewResolver as we mentioned above. A Spring view resolver has an order property, which specifies the precedence among the chained view resolvers. This property has a default value of "0," as is the case with the UrlBasedViewResolver shown in Listing 4.2 (a). The ContentNegotiatingViewResolver has its order property set to "1," which means that it has lower precedence than the UrlBasedViewResolver in the chain. Thus, JSP pages are delegated to the UrlBasedViewResolver, while JSON and XML documents are delegated to the ContentNegotiatingViewResolver based on their types.

Listing 4.2 (a) Spring 3.2 and 4: ViewResolvers defined in soba-servlet.xml for SOBA

```
<bean
        class="org.springframework.web.servlet.view.UrlBasedViewResolver">
        <property name="viewClass"
            value="org.springframework.web.servlet.view.JstlView" />
        <property name="prefix" value="/WEB-INF/jsp/" />
        <property name="suffix" value=".jsp" />
    </bean>
<bean class="org.springframework.web.servlet.view.ContentNegotiatingViewResolver">
        <property name="order" value="1" />
        <property name="contentNegotiationManager">
            <bean class="org.springframework.web.accept.ContentNegotiationManager">
                <constructor-arg>
                    <list>
                        <bean class="org.springframework.web.accept.
                         PathExtensionContentNegotiationStrategy">
```

```
                        <constructor-arg>
                            <map>
                                <entry key="json" value="application/json" />
                                <entry key="xml" value="application/xml" />
                                <entry key="html" value="text/html" />
                            </map>
                        </constructor-arg>
                    </bean>
                    <bean class="org.springframework.web.accept.
                        HeaderContentNegotiationStrategy" />
                </list>
            </constructor-arg>
        </bean>
    </property>
    <property name="defaultViews">
        <list>
            <!-- JSON View -->
            <bean
                class="org.springframework.web.servlet.view.json.
                    MappingJacksonJsonView" />
            <!-- XML View -->
            <bean class="org.springframework.web.servlet.view.xml.MarshallingView">
                <constructor-arg>
                    <bean class="org.springframework.oxm.jaxb.Jaxb2Marshaller">
                        <property name="packagesToScan">
                            <list>
                                <value>com.perfmath.spring.soba.model.domain</value>
                            </list>
                        </property>
                    </bean>
                </constructor-arg>
            </bean>
        </list>
    </property>
</bean>
</beans>
```

Listing 4.2 (b) Spring 3.1: ViewResolvers defined in soba-servlet.xml for SOBA

```
<bean class =    "org.springframework.web.servlet.view.ContentNegotiatingViewResolver">
    <property name="mediaTypes">
        <map>
            <entry key="xml" value="application/xml" />
```

```
            <entry key="json" value="application/json" />
        </map>
    </property>
    <property name="viewResolvers">
        <list>
            <bean id="viewResolver"
                class="org.springframework.web.servlet.view.
                    UrlBasedViewResolver">
                <property name="viewClass"
                    value="org.springframework.web.servlet.view.JstlView" />
                <property name="prefix" value="/WEB-INF/jsp/" />
                <property name="suffix" value=".jsp" />
            </bean>
        </list>
    </property>
    <property name="defaultViews">
        <list>
            <bean class="org.springframework.web.servlet.view.json.
                    MappingJacksonJsonView">
                <property name="prefixJson" value="false" />
            </bean>
        </list>
    </property>
</bean>
```

4.4 PROGRAMMING LOGIC FLOW WITH SPRING WEB MVC FRAMEWORK

First, let us demonstrate what a typical application workflow looks like when using Spring Web MVC to develop an enterprise Web application. The workflow we described for testing SOBA setup in §2.7 is re-usable for our purposes here, as is discussed next.

4.4.1 A Typical Workflow of SOBA Defined in Spring MVC Framework

To make it easier, Figure 4.5 is presented to demonstrate the workflow with the process of *creating a new customer* as described in Chapter 2 with a series of screenshots from Figure 2.9 through Figure 2.15. The steps involved include:

1 **User Gestures**: In this step, a user opens a Web page to initiate an action to interact with the application. In this use scenario, a user opens up the home page of the application.
2 **Requests Sent to the Spring Dispatcher Servlet**: The gesture of a user is formatted into an HTTP request and submitted to the system. The request is then routed to the Spring dispatching servlet.

3 **Requests Dispatched to the Application Controller:** The Spring dispatching servlet automatically sends the requests to the corresponding application controller, based on the handler mappings set up in an external XML configuration file that will be discussed shortly.
4 **User Data Validated by Calling a Validator**: It's very rare that a request would be sent directly to the corresponding service without being validated. This step must be followed rigorously in a real enterprise application, because the application must distinguish between valid and invalid user input data. This is what a validator would be responsible for.
5 **The Corresponding Service Gets Invoked**: After data validation, the corresponding service is invoked to execute the tasks required for fulfilling user's requests. The service at this step typically makes DAO calls to initiate data related operations, as is discussed next.
6 **SQL Execution via a DAO**: The methods of a DAO class mainly consist of a standard set of SQL executions such as `SELECT`, `INSERT`, `UPDATE`, `DELETE`, and so on.
7 **The Data Model Gets Updated**: As the result of the DAO operations as stated in the preceding step, the data model gets updated, which represents the intended operations by the user.
8 **The Result Set is Forwarded to Another Application Controller**: Typically, another application controller is invoked to handle the results returned from the service calls at step 5.
9 **Responses Rendered to a User View**: At this step, the results are reformatted and rendered to a user view to be consumed by the user.
10 **The User Gets the Updated View**: At this step, the user finally sees the responses routed back from the application.

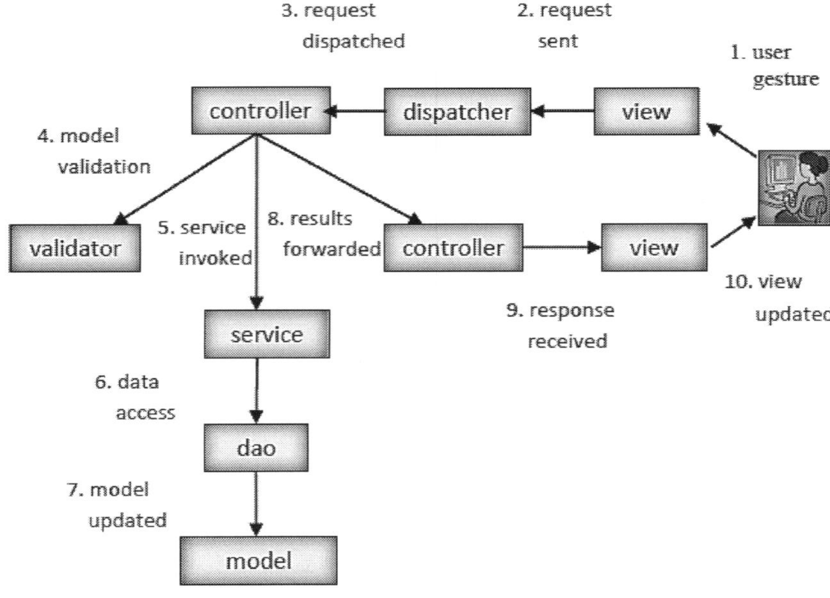

Figure 4.5 SOBA: Workflow for creating a new customer

The programming logic flow for the above workflow using the Spring Web MVC Framework begins with as simple as a `login.jsp` file, as discussed next.

4.4.2 A JSP Login Page Defining a Web Entry Point

To continue our discussion, note the `<welcome-file-list>` XML element in the previous `web.xml` file shown in Listing 4.1. This element specifies the home page of the application. In this case, the home page of SOBA can be invoked with either https://localhost:8443/soba implicitly or https://localhost:8443/soba/login.jsp explicitly. Either way, the `login.jsp` file is called. This file provides an entry point for SOBA.

Listing 4.3 shows the contents of the `login.jsp` file. Note the segment of "`<a href="<c:url value="createCustomerForm.htm"/>"> Open Now`" highlighted in bold face. This is what would work behind the scene when you click the *Open Now* link as shown in Figure 2.8. This link would start the process of creating a new customer. The exact semantics of this segment is defined in the `jsp/jstl/core` tag library, as is indicated by the second line of this `index.jsp` file. We are less concerned with it now, but we would like to know the exact implication of the part of `createCustomerForm.htm`. We know that since it ends with `.htm`, it would be routed by the `DispatcherServlet`, according to what we have learnt from the `web.xml` file previously. But what destination will it be directed to by the `DispatcherServlet`? That is the subject of Handler Mapping and the answer lies in the `soba-servlet.xml` file to be discussed next.

Listing 4.3 login.jsp

```
<%@ include file = "WEB-INF/jsp/include.jsp" %>
<%@ taglib prefix="c" uri="http://java.sun.com/jsp/jstl/core" %>
<html>
<head>
<title>Login</title>
</head>
<%@ include file = "WEB-INF/jsp/banner.jsp" %>
<script language="javascript">
function focusOnUsername () {
    document.loginForm.j_username.focus();
}
</script>
<body onLoad="focusOnUsername ()"> <center>
<table> <tr>
<td> Prospective Customers: <i> Don't have an account? </i></td>
<td> <a href="<c:url value="createCustomerForm.htm"/>"> Open Now </a> </td> <tr>
<td> Established Customers: <i>Don't have a user ID or password? </i></td>
 <td> <a href="<c:url value="createLoginUserForm.htm"/>"> Register </a></td></tr>
</tr></table>
<hr>
```

```
  <br> <br>
<form name="loginForm" method="POST" action="<c:url value="/j_spring_security_check" />">
<div align = "center">
<table align="center" width="300" border="7" CELLPADDING="7" CELLSPACING="10"
BGCOLOR="#C6EFF7">
<th colspan="2" bgcolor="#00184A"><FONT COLOR="#FFFFFF">Existing User Login </FONT></th>
 <tr>
  <td >Username: </td>
  <td><input type="text" name="j_username" /></td>
 </tr>
 <tr>
  <td align="center">Password: </td>
  <td><input type="password" name="j_password" /></td>
 </tr>
 <tr>
  <td> <B><img src="/soba/images/arrow.jpg"/> </B></td><td>
   <select name="signInRole">
   <option value="customer" selected> An Established Customer</option>
   <option value="rep"> A Rep</option>
   <option value="admin"> A System Admin</option>
   </select>
   </td>
   </tr>
 <tr>
  <td colspan="2" align="center">
   <input type="submit" value="Login" />
   <input type="reset" value="Reset" />
  </td>
 </tr>
</table>
</form>
 </div>
</center>
<%@ include file = "WEB-INF/jsp/showLoadTime.jsp" %>
</body>
</html>
```

4.4.3 Handler Mapping

Handler mappings are defined in the `soba-servlet.xml` file, which is shown in Listing 4.4 below. First, we see Spring beans defined in each `<bean>` XML element. Some beans are defined by id, and some beans are defined by name (note that we have to use name rather than id when the string contains symbols such as the "/" character as, for example, "`/customerList.htm`" in Listing 4.4). By default, the

DispatcherServlet uses ControllerClassNameHandlerMapping for its handler mapping task. Thus, a URL pattern like manageTx.htm will be mapped to the corresponding class ManageTxController; similarly, the URL of createCustomerForm.htm will be mapped to CreateCustomerFormController with 'Controller' attached to its name before .htm. This practice is called *Convention over Configuration*. Thus, the six beans from "/customerList.htm" to "/disputeTx.htm" defined in Listing 4.4 are not necessary. However, it's more common to use annotation and auto-detection to handle requests mapping. Note the lines of context:component-scan base-package=<..> in the soba-servlet.xml file. These lines enable all annotated Spring beans to be auto-detected without having to specify the URL mapping in an XML configuration file like soba-servlet.xml.

Now let's take one step back and look at the login.jsp file discussed in the preceding section. Note again the segment highlighted in bold face of "<a href = "<c:url value="createCustomerForm.htm"/>"> Open Now." As we mentioned at the beginning of this section, the URL pattern of createCustomerForm.htm will be mapped by default using ControllerClassNameHandlerMapping to CreateCustomerFormController if it's not specified explicitly in the configuration file. Next, we discuss how to implement this CreateCustomerFormController with Spring annotations, rather than depending on the default ControllerClassNameHandlerMapping.

Listing 4.4 soba-servlet.xml (complete)

```
<?xml version="1.0" encoding="UTF-8"?>
<beans xmlns="http://www.springframework.org/schema/beans"
    xmlns:xsi="http://www.w3.org/2001/XMLSchema-instance"
    xmlns:context="http://www.springframework.org/schema/context"
    xsi:schemaLocation="http://www.springframework.org/schema/beans
   http://www.springframework.org/schema/beans/spring-beans.xsd
   http://www.springframework.org/schema/context
   http://www.springframework.org/schema/context/spring-context.xsd">

    <!-- the application context definition for the soba DispatcherServlet -->
    <context:component-scan base-package="com.perfmath.spring.soba.web" />
    <context:component-scan base-package="com.perfmath.spring.soba.model" />
    <context:component-scan base-package="com.perfmath.spring.soba.service" />
    <context:component-scan base-package="com.perfmath.spring.soba.restfulweb" />
    <context:annotation-config />

    <bean id="myAuthenticationManager"
        class="com.perfmath.spring.soba.util.MyAuthenticationManager">
    </bean>
    <bean id="messageSource"
        class="org.springframework.context.support.ResourceBundleMessageSource">
        <property name="basename" value="messages" />
    </bean>
```

```
<bean name="/customerList.htm"
    class="com.perfmath.spring.soba.web.CustomerController">
    <property name="customerManager" ref="customerManager" />
</bean>
<bean name="/accountList.htm" class="com.perfmath.spring.soba.web.AccountController">
    <property name="accountManager" ref="accountManager" />
</bean>
<bean name="/transactionList.htm" class="com.perfmath.spring.soba.web.TxController">
    <property name="txManager" ref="txManager" />
</bean>
<bean name="/manageTx.htm" class="com.perfmath.spring.soba.web.ManageTxController">
    <property name="aclTxManager" ref="aclTxManager" />
</bean>
<bean name="/reverseTx.htm" class="com.perfmath.spring.soba.web.ReverseTxController">
    <property name="aclTxManager" ref="aclTxManager" />
</bean>
<bean name="/disputeTx.htm" class="com.perfmath.spring.soba.web.DisputeTxController">
    <property name="aclTxManager" ref="aclTxManager" />
</bean>
<!-- spring 3 restful begin -->
<bean id="jaxbMarshaller" class="org.springframework.oxm.jaxb.Jaxb2Marshaller">
    <property name="classesToBeBound">
        <list>
            <value>com.perfmath.spring.soba.model.domain.BankingTx</value>
        </list>
    </property>
</bean>
<bean id="restTxList"
    class="org.springframework.web.servlet.view.xml.MarshallingView">
    <constructor-arg ref="jaxbMarshaller" />
</bean>
<!-- The remaining part is the same as Listing 4.2 (a) and thus onmitted here -->
```

4.4.4 Implementing Spring Controllers with Annotations

Similar to view resolutions, *Controllers* that handle user input can be configured externally, providing developers with options for building flexible, modularized applications. However, since Spring 2.5, handler controllers can be configured based on the `@Controller` and `@RequestMapping` annotations specified in the Java code implementing the handler. Annotation has become more and more popular since Java 5, providing an extra dimension for flexibility. Another benefit of the annotation feature is to allow building applications based on RESTful Web Services painlessly, thanks to the method argument level annotation through the `@PathVariable` annotation and other features. We'll see such examples with SOBA later.

To see how Spring Controller is implemented with the help of Spring's annotation feature, Listing 4.5 shows the actual code of the controller class of `CreateCustomerFormController.java` defined in the package of `com.perfmath.spring.soba.web`. Note that controllers implemented in this style do not have to extend any base classes or implement specific interfaces. In addition, they do not have to depend on Servlet APIs, making them much less constrained and more maintainable over time.

Following Listing 4.5, we focus on understanding how this controller is implemented in an annotated style.

Listing 4.5 CreateCustomerFormController.java

```
package com.perfmath.spring.soba.web;

import org.springframework.beans.factory.annotation.Autowired;
import org.springframework.stereotype.Controller;
import org.springframework.ui.Model;
import org.springframework.validation.BindingResult;
import org.springframework.web.bind.annotation.ModelAttribute;
import org.springframework.web.bind.annotation.RequestMapping;
import org.springframework.web.bind.annotation.RequestMethod;
import org.springframework.web.bind.annotation.RequestParam;
import org.springframework.web.bind.annotation.SessionAttributes;
import org.springframework.web.bind.support.SessionStatus;

import com.perfmath.spring.soba.model.domain.Customer;
import com.perfmath.spring.soba.service.CreateCustomerValidator;
import com.perfmath.spring.soba.service.CustomerManager;

@Controller
@RequestMapping("/createCustomerForm")
@SessionAttributes("customer")
public class CreateCustomerFormController {
    private CreateCustomerValidator validator;
    private CustomerManager customerManager;
    @Autowired
    public CreateCustomerFormController(CustomerManager customerManager,
            CreateCustomerValidator validator) {
        this.customerManager = customerManager;
        this.validator = validator;
    }
    @RequestMapping(method = RequestMethod.GET)
```

```
    public String setupForm(
            @RequestParam(required = false, value = "username") String username,
            Model model) {
        Customer customer = new Customer();
        customer.setFirstName("user");
        customer.setLastName("soba");
        customer.setPhone ("999-999-9999");
        customer.setAddress("One Way");
        customer.setCity("Any City");
        customer.setState("CA");
        customer.setZipcode("95999");
        customer.setEmail("user@soba.com");
        model.addAttribute("customer", customer);
        return "createCustomerForm";
    }
    @RequestMapping(method = RequestMethod.POST)
    public String submitForm(
            @ModelAttribute("customer") Customer customer,
            BindingResult result, SessionStatus status) {
        validator.validate(customer, result);

        if (result.hasErrors()) {
                return "createCustomerForm";
            } else {
                customerManager.createCustomer(customer);
                status.setComplete();
                return "redirect:createCustomerSuccess/customerId/" + customer.getCustomerId();
        }
    }
}
```

By examining the above `CreateCustomerFormController.java` file, we notice the following annotations:

- **@Controller**: This annotation indicates that the annotated class plays the role of a controller. Once again that, in this case, the controller class does not have to extend any controller base class or reference any Servlet APIs. We can also say that the `@Controller` annotation acts as a stereotype for the annotated class, indicating its role. In UML vocabulary, a *stereotype* is an extension mechanism for defining a new kind of model element based on an existing model element. It is expressed by placing its name as a string around a pair of angle brackets or *guillemets* in French, for example, *<<StereoType>>*. So a class with the stereotype *<<Controller>>* is read as "a class of the Controller stereotype." The particular characteristics a Controller class must have are defined when the stereotype is defined. Also, note in Java we use @ instead of *guillemets* to define stereotypes. The annotated beans can be defined explicitly in a configuration file using the URL mapping mechanism. However, they can be more conveniently auto-detected or scanned if it belongs to one of those packages specified in the `<context:component-scan base-package=<..>` XML element. In particular, the controller `CreateCustomerFormController` in the package of `com.perfmath.spring.soba.web` is auto-scanned when the application starts up.

- **@RequestMapping**: This mapping is used to map URLs onto an entire class or a particular handler method. Typically, the class-level annotation maps a specific request path or path pattern onto a form controller, for example, the URL `/createCustomerForm` is mapped to the form controller of `CreateCustomerFormController`. Also, note those `RequestMappings` associated with `HTTP GET` and `POST` methods in Listing 4.5. Such annotations tie HTTP request methods to designated controller class methods unambiguously. For example, with this controller example, a `GET` request is mapped to the `setupForm` method, while a `POST` request is mapped to the `submitForm` method.
- **@SessionAttributes:** This annotation declares session attributes used by a specific handler. It typically lists the names of model attributes that should be maintained in the session, serving as form-backing beans between subsequent requests. In this case, the session attribute defined is `customer`. Note that a `customer` object is created in the `setupForm` method and passed to the validator in the `submitForm` method.
- **@Autowired:** This annotation auto-wires the class with its dependency classes. For example, the class `CreateCustomerFormController` depends on two other classes: `CustomerManager` and `CreateCustomerValidator`. In this case, it's equivalent to the property element of a bean definition explicitly specified in its associated configuration file. Refer to Listing 4.4 and note the `<property>` element for the bean named "`/customerList.htm`." which injects the dependency on `customerManager` into the `CustomerController`.
- **@RequestParam:** This annotation binds the annotated parameter to the corresponding HTTP request parameter if it exists. For example, the `setupForm` method has a method argument named `username` that is annotated with this annotation. Such annotated parameters are required by default, but can be made optional by setting `@RequestParam`'s `required` attribute to `false`.
- **@ModelAttribute:** This annotation provides a mechanism for accessing data stored in the model. As is used with the `submitForm` method of this controller, this annotation binds the specified model attribute of `customer` established in the `setupForm` method to the parameter following it. This is how the controller gets a reference to the data entered in the form.

Note that the `CreateCustomerFormController` form controller has two methods: `setupForm` and `submitForm`. When a URL that contains the destination to this form controller as embedded in the `login.jsp` file is clicked, control is routed to the `DispatcherServlet` that routes control to this form controller based on the URL mapping it knows about. Then the `setupForm` method of this form controller is invoked first. This is where you can pre-populate some of the entries of the form before control is turned over to the form of `createCustomerForm.jsp` as specified in the return statement of the `setupForm` method.

After a user enters all required entries on the form and clicks the *Submit* button, control is returned to the form controller, and the validator is invoked to validate the data entered onto the form. This is another point of time that you can decide how you want to override some of the entries on the form and how you want to validate the data entered on the form (in this sample implementation, validation logic is only for illustrative purposes. Validation should be beefed up significantly in a real application).

Listing 4.6 shows the implementation of the `CreateCustomerFormValidator` class. Note the following:

- This validator class is annotated with @Component, which is a generic stereotype for any Spring-managed component. Other annotations such as @Controller, @Service, and @Repository are specializations of @Component for more specific uses, for example, in the presentation, service, and persistence layers.
- This example demonstrates two validation methods: the ValidationUtils.rejectIfEmptyOrWhitespace (...) and errors.rejectValue (...). With the ValidationUtils.rejectIfEmptyOrWhitespace (Errors errors, String field, String errorCode, String defaultMessage) validation method, the first parameter specifies the Errors instance to register errors on, the second parameter specifies the field, the third parameter specifies the errorCode that is interpretable as a message key, while the last parameter specifies the fallback default message if not defined in an external file. For our SOBA sample, this external file is the *messages.properties* file contained in the *src/main/resources* folder of the SOBA project. The *soba_servlet.xml* file illustrated in Listing 4.4 contains a segment as follows, showing the *basename of messages* as part of the file name *messages.properties*. You can name this file whatever you want as long as you enter the matching *basename* as explained above. The next section further explains how this file is used with jsp files to display messages when needed.

```
<bean id="messageSource"
class="org.springframework.context.support.ResourceBundleMessageSource">
   <property name="basename" value=" messages" />
</bean>
```

- On the other hand, with the errors.rejectValue (String field, String errorCode, String defaultMessage) validation method, the error message is passed back directly via the errors object. Figure 4.6 shows how this validation method and the above ValidationUtils.rejectIfEmptyOrWhitespace (...) validation method work when a non-two-letter state code and an empty lastName are entered on the createCustomerForm. This should be intuitive and we would not explain further.
- In addition to using ValidationUtils, you can implement your own validation classes or methods to be used here. §5.6 introduces more about Spring data validation using the SOBA BillPayment service as an example.

Listing 4.6 CreateCustomerFormValidator.java

```
package com.perfmath.spring.soba.service;

import java.sql.Timestamp;

import org.springframework.validation.Errors;
import org.springframework.validation.ValidationUtils;
import org.springframework.validation.Validator;
import org.springframework.stereotype.Component;

import com.perfmath.spring.soba.model.domain.Customer;
import com.perfmath.spring.soba.util.RandomID;
```

```
@Component
public class CreateCustomerValidator implements Validator {

  public boolean supports(Class clazz) {
    return Customer.class.isAssignableFrom(clazz);
  }

  public void validate(Object target, Errors errors) {
    ValidationUtils.rejectIfEmptyOrWhitespace(errors, "firstName",
        "required.firstName", "firstName is required.");
    ValidationUtils.rejectIfEmpty(errors, "lastName",
        "required.lastName", "lastName is required.");
    ValidationUtils.rejectIfEmpty(errors, "phone",
        "required.phone", "phone is required.");
    ValidationUtils.rejectIfEmptyOrWhitespace(errors, "address",
        "required.address", "address is required.");
    ValidationUtils.rejectIfEmpty(errors, "city",
        "required.city", "city is required.");
    ValidationUtils.rejectIfEmpty(errors, "state",
        "required.state", "state is required.");

    Customer customer = (Customer) target;
      customer.setCustomerId((new RandomID(9)).getId());
      customer.setStatus(0);
      customer.setCreateDate(new Timestamp(System.currentTimeMillis()));

      String state = customer.getState();

    if (state.length() != 2) {
      errors.rejectValue("state", "invalid.stateNameLength",
          "State name must be two letters.");
    }
```

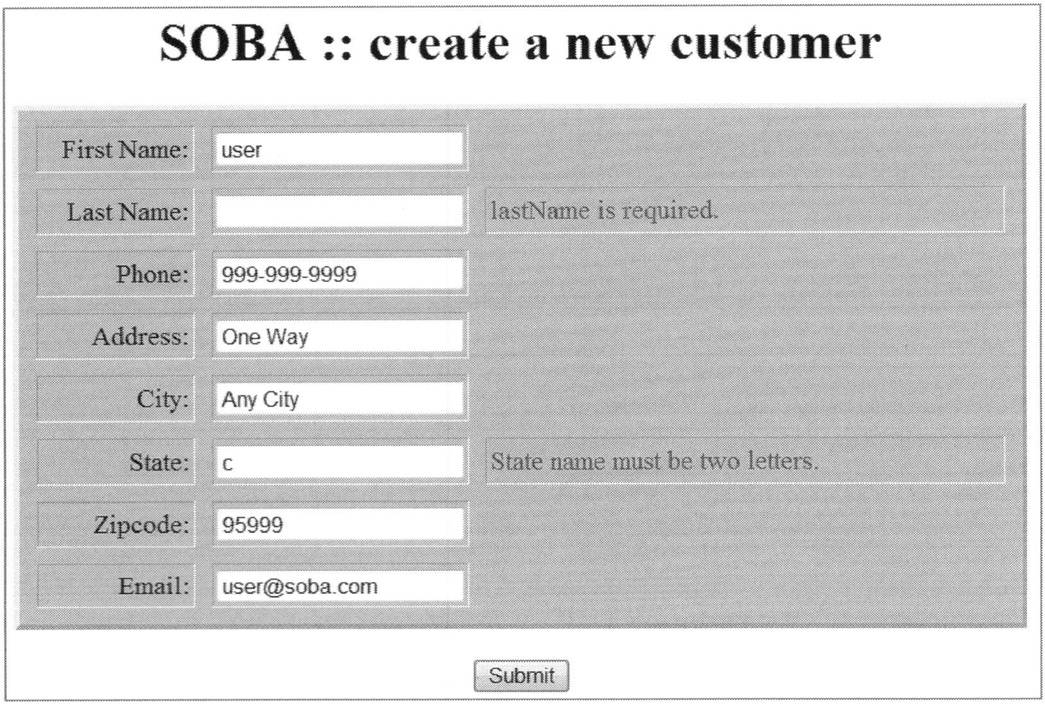

SOBA :: create a new customer

First Name: user
Last Name: lastName is required.
Phone: 999-999-9999
Address: One Way
City: Any City
State: c State name must be two letters.
Zipcode: 95999
Email: user@soba.com
Submit

Figure 4.6 Demonstration of Spring validation methods

If the form data validation is passed, the `createCustomer` service is called, a new customer would be created if everything goes well, and control is turned over to the `createCustomerSuccess.jsp` file that we'll take a look after we look at the `createCustomerForm.jsp` file next. However, before we move to the next section, you might want to take a look at the return statement of the `submitForm` method of the `CreateCustomerFormController` class, which is called out below:

```
return "redirect:createCustomerSuccess/customerId/" + customer.getCustomerId();
```

This is in the form of "…/`customerId/{customerId}`" where the part `{customerId}` represents the actual value of a `customerId`. This is called the *URI Template Pattern* in Spring and we'll talk more about it later.

4.4.5 A Typical View Defined in a Spring MVC Web Form

The `createCustomerForm.jsp` file shown in Listing 4.7 below illustrates a typical view defined in a Spring MVC Web form (we consider a jsp file a Spring MVC Web form if it defines a form that uses the Spring jsp tag library). Consult *Chapter 36 spring-form.tld* of the *Reference Documentation for Spring 4* for valid Spring form entries. Next, let's go over those lines highlighted in bold face.

Listing 4.7 createCustomerForm.jsp

```
<%@ include file="/WEB-INF/jsp/include.jsp" %>
<%@ taglib prefix="form" uri="http://www.springframework.org/tags/form" %>
<html>
<head>
</head>
<%@ include file = "banner.jsp" %>
 <style>
  .error { color: red; }
 </style>  </head>
<body> <center>
<h1><fmt:message key="createcustomer.heading"/></h1>
 <div align = "center">
<form:form method="post" commandName="customer">
 <table align ="center" width="600" bgcolor="#94D6E7" border="3" cellspacing="10" cellpadding="2">
  <tr>
   <td align="right" width="100">First Name:</td>
    <td width="100">
     <form:input path="firstName"/>
    </td>
    <td width="400">
     <form:errors path="firstName" cssClass="error"/>
    </td>
  </tr>
  <tr>
   <td align="right" width="100">Last Name:</td>
    <td width="100">
     <form:input path="lastName"/>
    </td>
    <td width="400">
     <form:errors path="lastName" cssClass="error"/>
    </td>
  </tr>
  <tr>
   <td align="right" width="100">Phone:</td>
    <td width="100">
     <form:input path="phone"/>
    </td>
    <td width="400">
     <form:errors path="phone" cssClass="error"/>
    </td>
  </tr>
```

```
<tr>
 <td align="right" width="100">Address:</td>
  <td width="100">
   <form:input path="address"/>
  </td>
  <td width="400">
   <form:errors path="address" cssClass="error"/>
  </td>
</tr>
<tr>
 <td align="right" width="100">City:</td>
  <td width="100">
   <form:input path="city"/>
  </td>
  <td width="400">
   <form:errors path="city" cssClass="error"/>
  </td>
</tr>
<tr>
 <td align="right" width="100">State:</td>
  <td width="100">
   <form:input path="state"/>
  </td>
  <td width="400">
   <form:errors path="state" cssClass="error"/>
  </td>
</tr>
<tr>
 <td align="right" width="100">Zipcode:</td>
  <td width="100">
   <form:input path="zipcode"/>
  </td>
  <td width="400">
   <form:errors path="zipcode" cssClass="error"/>
  </td>
</tr>
<tr align="center">
 <td align="right" width="100">Email:</td>
  <td width="100">
   <form:input path="email"/>
  </td>
  <td width="400">
   <form:errors path="email" cssClass="error"/>
```

```
      </td>
    </tr>
  </table>
  <br>
<input type="submit" value="Submit">
</form:form>
  </div>
  <%@ include file = "showLoadTime.jsp" %>
</body>
</center>
</html>
```

The first line defines an `include.jsp` file, which contains all common functions shared among all jsp files. The contents of the `include.jsp` file are shown as follows. Note that the first line specifies that page session is not maintained, which is a common jsp performance and scalability practice. The next four lines specify the various jsp tag libraries to be used. The last line defines a JAVA statement that saves the begin time of the jsp file. When used with the line containing `showLoadTime.jsp` at the bottom of the `createCustomerForm.jsp`, the total elapsed time associated with this form can be timed and displayed to the user. Since both the begin and end timing calls are made on the server, the measured elapsed time is the time spent on the server only, namely, it includes neither the page content rendering time nor the network latency between the server and the client.

```
<%@ page session="false"%>
<%@ taglib prefix="c" uri="http://java.sun.com/jsp/jstl/core" %>
<%@ taglib prefix="fmt" uri="http://java.sun.com/jsp/jstl/fmt" %>
<%@ taglib prefix="fn" uri="http://java.sun.com/jsp/jstl/functions" %>
<%@ taglib prefix="security" uri="http://www.springframework.org/security/tags" %>
<%@ page language="java" contentType="text/html;charset=UTF-8" %>
<% long beginPageLoadTime = System.currentTimeMillis();%>
```

Next, note the line containing `fmt:message` in Listing 4.7. This provides an option for specifying text output defined in an external file. For SOBA, this file is named `messages.properties` and stored at the root classpath of `/WEB-INF/classes` after deployment. The contents of this file are shown in Listing 4.8.

Listing 4.8 messages.properties

```
title=SOBA (Safe Online Banking Application)
heading=SOBA :: Safe Online Banking Application
greeting=Greetings, it is now
invalid.stateNamelength=invalid state name length
createcustomer.heading=SOBA :: create a new customer
createloginuser.heading=SOBA :: create a new login user
createaccount.heading=SOBA :: create a new account
createtx.heading=SOBA :: Post a transaction to an account
```

```
required=Entry required.
typeMismatch=Invalid data.
typeMismatch.percentage=That is not a number!!!
invalid.billPayAmount=bill pay amount must be > 0
```

Note the line `<form:form method="post" commandName = "customer">` shown in the above `createCustomerForm.jsp` file. That line defines that the HTTP method to be used to send the form to the `CreateCustomerFormController` would be `POST`, and that the command object to be invoked would be a `customer` object, which is defined in the `Customer.java` file in the `domain` package of SOBA. For the implementation of the Customer class, see Listing 4.9 below.

Listing 4.9 Customer.java

```
package com.perfmath.spring.soba.model.domain;

import java.io.Serializable;
import java.sql.Timestamp;

public class Customer implements Serializable {
    private String customerId;
    private String firstName;
    private String lastName;
    private String phone;
    private String address;
    private String city;
    private String state;
    private String zipcode;
    private String email;
    private int status;
    private Timestamp createDate;

// getters/setters are omitted to save space

    public String toString() {
        StringBuffer buffer = new StringBuffer();
        buffer.append(" customerId: " + customerId + ";");
        buffer.append(" firstName: " + firstName);
        buffer.append(" lastName: " + lastName);
        buffer.append(" phone: " + phone);
        buffer.append(" address: " + address);
        buffer.append(" city: " + city);
        buffer.append(" state: " + state);
        buffer.append(" zipcode: " + zipcode);
        buffer.append(" email: " + email);
```

```
        buffer.append(" status: " + status);
        buffer.append(" createDate: " + createDate);
        return buffer.toString();
    }
}
```

The above createCustomerForm.jsp form contains many lines like, for example, <form:input path = "firstName">. There is a one-to-one corresponding relationship between a path defined on the form and the property of the class to be targeted. This is how a form and a domain class gets associated with each other. Also note that for each line of <form:input ...> there is a corresponding line of <form:errors ...>, which associates the entry with the errors found during validation.

Finally, the line containing "Submit" in createCustomerForm.jsp defines the exit of this jsp file, which returns control to the form's form controller CreateCustomerFormController. After the transaction of creating a new customer is completed successfully, control is returned to the CreateCustomerSuccessController class, which is discussed next.

4.4.6 A Typical Form Success Controller with Spring ModelAndView

Listing 4.10 shows a typical form success controller associated with the transaction of creating a new customer. Note the following specific details in this controller:

- It is annotated with the @Controller annotation.
- It is annotated with @RequestMapping with its value consistent with what is specified in the return statement of the submitForm method of the CreateCustomerFormController class, that is, /createCustomerSuccess/customerId/{customerId}.
- The object returned from this class to DispatcherServlet is a Spring ModelAndView object. ModelAndView is a Spring Web MVC Framework class for holding both model and view in one object. It has six variants based on what arguments to pass in when it is created, but in our case here, it uses the constructor of ModelAndView (String viewName, String modelName, Object modelObject), with viewName = "createCustomerSuccess", modelName="model", and modelObject = myModel of type Map<String, Object>. The view part specifies where control should be routed to, and the model part provides the convenience of accessing the model data in the view.

As stated above, the createCustomerSuccessController returns a ModelAndView object with the return URL of createCustomerSuccess, which is routed to createCustomerSuccess.jsp as shown in Listing 4.11. This jsp file displays a message showing that the transaction is completed successfully. It then waits for the user to initiate the next transaction with an embedded link that is mapped to another controller using the same mapping mechanism discussed previously. Note how the model object is used in createCustomerSuccess.jsp to access the data item customerId.

Listing 4.10 CreateCustomerSuccessController.java

```
package com.perfmath.spring.soba.web;
```

```
import java.util.HashMap;
import java.util.Map;

import org.springframework.stereotype.Controller;
import org.springframework.web.bind.annotation.RequestMapping;
import org.springframework.web.bind.annotation.RequestMethod;
import org.springframework.beans.factory.annotation.Autowired;

import org.springframework.ui.Model;

import org.springframework.web.bind.annotation.ModelAttribute;
import org.springframework.web.bind.annotation.PathVariable;
import org.springframework.web.servlet.ModelAndView;
@Controller
public class CreateCustomerSuccessController {
  @RequestMapping(value="/createCustomerSuccess/customerId/{customerId}",
    method=RequestMethod.GET)
  public ModelAndView createCustomerSuccess(@PathVariable("customerId") String
    customerId) {
    Map<String, Object> myModel = new HashMap<String, Object>();
    myModel.put("customerId", customerId);
    return new ModelAndView("createCustomerSuccess", "model", myModel);
  }
}
```

Listing 4.11 createCustomerSuccess.jsp

```
<%@ include file="/WEB-INF/jsp/include.jsp"%>
<%@ taglib prefix="form" uri="http://www.springframework.org/tags/form"%>
<html>
<head>
<%@ include file="banner.jsp"%>
<title>Create Customer Success</title>
</head>
<body>
    <center>
        Your customer ID
        <c:out value="${model.customerId}" />
        has been created successfully. <br> <br> Use your customer
        ID to <a
            href="<c:url
        value="/createLoginUserForm/customerId/${model.customerId}"/>">
            create</a> your login ID for banking online. <br> <br>
```

```
</center>
</body>
</html>
```

Figure 4.7 summarizes the programming logic flow for creating a customer using the Spring Web MVC framework. The transitional URI's are included at each step. How these transitions should occur is specified in the `web.xml` file and `soba-servlet.xml` file. It might be helpful that you trace this flow one more time by following the detailed descriptions we have provided so far in this section.

Next, we'll dig deeper into how controllers collaborate with POJOs to complete the task of creating a customer in SOBA.

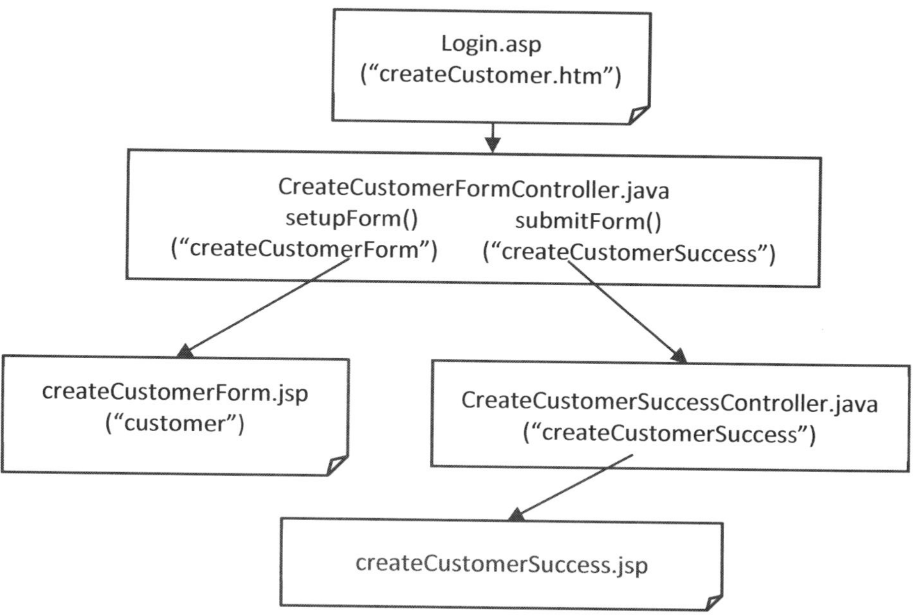

Figure 4.7 Programming logic flow for creating a SOBA customer

4.4.7 POJOs Referenced in the CreateCustomerFormController

Let's take a look at Listing 4.5 for the `CreateCustomerFormController` again. After a customer domain object is successfully constructed, in the `submitForm` method of the `CreateCustomerFormController`, the `createCustomer` method of the `customerManager` class is called to create the customer passed in. Actually, the `customerManager` is only an interface, and its implementation is realized in `SimpleCustomerManager.java`. Listings 4.12 (a) and (b) show how the `CustomerManager` interface is defined in `CustomerManager.java` and how it is implemented in `SimpleCustomerManager.java`, respectively. Note that `customerManager` and `SimpleCustomerManager` are pure POJOs, as by definition of a POJO they don't use any vendor-specific packages. Since these POJOs are ordinary Java objects and what they do are fairly self-explanatory, a more detailed explanation is omitted here. However, I do need to point out that such POJOs need to be defined in an external configuration file, and they are indeed defined in the `soba-services.xml` file. I will remind you of this when we discuss the subject of *Data Access* in the next chapter.

Listing 4.12 (a) CustomerManager.java

```
package com.perfmath.spring.soba.service;
import java.io.Serializable;
import java.util.List;
import com.perfmath.spring.soba.model.domain.Customer;

public interface CustomerManager extends Serializable{
public void createCustomer(Customer customer);
public List<Customer> getCustomers();

}
```

Listing 4.12 (b) SimpleCustomerManager.java

```
package com.perfmath.spring.soba.service;

import java.util.List;
import com.perfmath.spring.soba.model.dao.CustomerDao;
import com.perfmath.spring.soba.model.domain.Customer;

  public class SimpleCustomerManager implements CustomerManager {
  private CustomerDao customerDao;
  public List<Customer> getCustomers() {
    return customerDao.getCustomerList();
  }

  public void createCustomer(Customer customer) {
   customerDao.insert(customer);
  }
  public void setCustomerDao(CustomerDao customerDao) {
    this.customerDao = customerDao;
  }
}
```

You might have noticed that `CustomerManager` depends on `CustomerDao` to persist a customer object into the database. This kind of data access can be implemented either in JDBC or in some object-relational mapping (ORM) frameworks such as Hibernate. This is one of the most important layers in building enterprise applications, and we cover it in detail in the next chapter.

4.5 SUMMARY

In this chapter, we introduced the Spring Web MVC Framework and demonstrated how it is used for building SOBA with a simple workflow of creating a customer. The most important thing is to understand the programming logic flow that needs to be followed when developing an enterprise Web application with the Spring Web MVC Framework. Here is a recap of this programming logic flow we demonstrated in this chapter:

- Spring Web MVC Framework's `DispatcherServlet` inherits from the standard HttpServlet base class. The implication with this is that you can run Spring-based web applications on popular web servers or servlet engines like Tomcat. In this case, your web app is configured with a `web.xml` file, in which you specify a start page such as `login.jsp` among other configurations.
- It's important to understand how URLs are mapped to handlers or controllers with the Spring Web MVC Framework. This is specified in the `<app-name>-servlet.xml` file, e.g., the `soba-servlet.xml` file as you can find in your SOBA project on Eclipse. One important convention to keep in mind is that if you have an `xyzForm.jsp`, then it is implied that it will be mapped to the `xyzFormController` controller. In SOBA, the pair of `createCustomerForm.jsp` and `CreateCustomerFormController.java` is one of such examples.
- Since web applications heavily depend on forms to work, it's crucial to understand how Spring form controllers work. This includes not only how a controller should be properly annotated, but also how its `setupForm` and `submitForm` methods work. We certainly have seen this with the `CreateCustomerFormController.java` class.
- Paired with a form controller, typically a form success controller is used to communicate the final status to the user via a `view`, for example, a jsp page. We demonstrated this with the `CreateCustomerSuccessController.java` class and the `createCustomerSuccess.jsp` file. A very important Spring specific technique here is the Spring `ModelAndView` class, which wraps `view` and `model` in one object so that `view` can consume `model` information within itself.

We certainly have not covered all bits of the Spring Web MVC Framework in this chapter, especially on some more elaborate annotations. Refer to Spring's reference documentation if you need to learn more.

RECOMMENDED READING

Study Chapter 16 of the Spring Reference Documentation 4 to have a more thorough understanding on the Spring MVC framework. Here is a complete list of the sections about the Spring MVC framework introduced there (highlighted subjects are covered in this chapter).

Spring Reference Documentation 4/ Chapter16:

16.1 Introduction to Spring Web MVC framework

16.2 The DispatcherServlet

16.3 Implementing Controllers

16.4 Handler mappings

16.5 Resolving views

16.6 Using flash attributes

16.7 Building URIs

16.8 Building URIs to Controllers and methods

16.9 Using locales

16.10 Using themes

16.11 Spring's multipart (file upload) support

16.12 Handling exceptions

16.13 Convention over configuration support

16.14 ETag support

16.15 Code-based Servlet container initialization

16.16 Configuring Spring MVC

It is particularly worthwhile to try to understand other return types in addition to *ModelAndView* and *String* that we covered in this chapter. Refer to §16.3.3 of the Spring Reference Documentation 4 for a brief description of each return type that Spring 4 supports.

You may also want to review *Chapter 17 View Technologies*, especially the JSP and JSTL sections that we use a lot with SOBA.

EXERCISES

4.1 Is MVC a generic architecture or specific to Spring only?

4.2 What's the purpose of the ApplicationContext interface? Which configuration XML file is for loading application contexts?

4.3 How do you configure your Spring-based application so that it would support Jackson Json view?

4.4 Which configuration file defines Spring handler mappings?

4.5 Which one is more heavily annotated, a Controller or a Validator? Why?

4.6 Identify all annotations in Listing 4.5 and explain how they are used. Especially, what is the purpose of the *Autowired* annotation?

4.7 What's the purpose of Spring context component auto-scan? What are the prerequisites in order to have a Spring component auto-scanned?

4.8 What are the purposes of the *setupForm* and *submitForm* methods with a Spring *Form Controller*? At what points are they initiated?

4.9 How many Controller return types are defined in Spring 4? Which ones are most commonly used?

4.10 This question is about the annotation-based versus XML file based bean configurations. There are pros and cons with each of these approaches. The XML approach wires up beans without touching the source code and thus does not require recompiling of the source code, whereas the annotation-based approach is more contextual and cleaner in contrast to the XML approach. Which approach do you prefer for your project, and what's your justification?

5 Spring Data Access Framework

In order to simplify accessing relational databases from Java, JDBC (Java Database Connectivity) technology was introduced to define a set of standard APIs for all common SQL operations (`SELECT`, `INSERT`, `UPDATE`, `DELETE`, and so on) in a vendor-independent fashion. The Spring JDBC Framework further simplifies this kind of operations by defining an abstract layer on top of the standard JDBC APIs. The core of the Spring JDBC Framework is that it provides template based methods for different types of JDBC operations. In this chapter, I'll give you a brief introduction to Spring JDBC Framework by demonstrating how it is applied to SOBA. I will also show you how Spring Data Access Framework supports Hibernate in addition to JDBC.

5.1 Defining Spring Datasources

Using the Spring JDBC Framework starts with defining a JDBC data source. As an example, SOBA has its JDBC data source defined in the `soba-services.xml` file, which is shown in Listing 5.1. First, note the `datasource` bean with its properties defined with entries like `${jdbc.driverClassName}`, and so on. The values for these entries are read in from the `jdbc.properties` file located at `/Web-INF/classes`. Also note that every manager bean depends on one or more DAO (Data Access Object) beans, and every DAO bean depends on the datasource bean defined based on the external `jdbc.properties` file.

Note also that in Listing 5.1, we specified the *min* and *max* pool sizes for the JDBC connection pool configured. These are arbitrary settings for illustrative purposes. What settings you should have for your application should be determined with your performance and scalability tests based on such non-functional requirements for your customers.

Note: In order to have JDBC connection pool `initialSize` property working, we need the *commons-dbcp-1.4.jar* file in addition to the *commons-dbcp-20030825.184428.jar* file and the *commons-pool-20030825.183949.jar* placed in the *lib* folder of SOBA. Otherwise, SOBA will not be started up properly due to the error of "*Error creating bean with name 'dataSource' defined in ServletContext resource*

[/WEB-INF/soba-services.xml]: Error setting property values; nested exception is org.springframework.beans.NotWritablePropertyException: Invalid property 'initialSize' of bean class [org.apache.commons.dbcp.BasicDataSource]: Bean property 'initialSize' is not writable or has an invalid setter method. Does the parameter type of the setter match the return type of the getter?" There is no need to have the *commons-dbcp-1.4.jar* file in the *lib* folder of SOBA if the `initialSize` property is not specified.

Listing 5.1 soba-services.xml

```
<?xml version="1.0" encoding="UTF-8"?>
<beans xmlns="http://www.springframework.org/schema/beans"
xmlns:xsi="http://www.w3.org/2001/XMLSchema-instance"
xmlns:aop="http://www.springframework.org/schema/aop"
    xmlns:tx="http://www.springframework.org/schema/tx"
    xsi:schemaLocation="http://www.springframework.org/schema/beans
      http://www.springframework.org/schema/beans/spring-beans.xsd
      http://www.springframework.org/schema/aop
      http://www.springframework.org/schema/aop/spring-aop.xsd
      http://www.springframework.org/schema/tx
      http://www.springframework.org/schema/tx/spring-tx.xsd">
    <bean id="sobaConfig" class="com.perfmath.spring.soba.service.SobaConfig">
        <property name="databaseVendor" value="mysql" />
    </bean>
    <bean id="dataSource" class="org.apache.commons.dbcp.BasicDataSource"
        destroy-method="close">
        <property name="driverClassName" value="${jdbc.driverClassName}" />
        <property name="url" value="${jdbc.url}" />
        <property name="username" value="${jdbc.username}" />
        <property name="password" value="${jdbc.password}" />
        <property name="initialSize" value="5" />
        <property name="maxActive" value="20" />
    </bean>

    <bean id="activityManager"
        class="com.perfmath.spring.soba.service.SimpleActivityManager">
        <property name="activityDao" ref="activityDao" />
    </bean>
    <bean id="transferManager"
        class="com.perfmath.spring.soba.service.SimpleTransferManager">
        <property name="transferDao" ref="transferDao" />
        <property name="bankingTxDao" ref="bankingTxDao" />
    </bean>
```

```
<bean id="activityDao" class="com.perfmath.spring.soba.model.dao.JdbcActivityDao">
    <property name="dataSource" ref="dataSource" />
</bean>

<bean id="customerManager"
    class="com.perfmath.spring.soba.service.SimpleCustomerManager">
    <property name="customerDao" ref="customerDao" />
</bean>

<bean id="customerDao" class="com.perfmath.spring.soba.model.dao.JdbcCustomerDao">
    <property name="dataSource" ref="dataSource" />
</bean>

<bean id="transferDao" class="com.perfmath.spring.soba.model.dao.JdbcTransferDao">
    <property name="dataSource" ref="dataSource" />
</bean>

<bean id="accountManager"
    class="com.perfmath.spring.soba.service.SimpleAccountManager">
    <property name="accountDao" ref="accountDao" />
</bean>

<bean id="accountDao" class="com.perfmath.spring.soba.model.dao.JdbcAccountDao">
    <property name="dataSource" ref="dataSource" />
</bean>
<bean id="loginUserManager"
    class="com.perfmath.spring.soba.service.SimpleLoginUserManager">
    <property name="loginUserDao" ref="loginUserDao" />
</bean>

<bean id="loginUserDao" class="com.perfmath.spring.soba.model.dao.JdbcLoginUserDao">
    <property name="dataSource" ref="dataSource" />
</bean>

<bean id="txManager" class="com.perfmath.spring.soba.service.SimpleTxManager">
    <property name="bankingTxDao" ref="bankingTxDao" />
    <property name="accountManager" ref="accountManager" />
    <!-- property name="mutableAclService" ref="aclService"/ -->
</bean>
<bean id="billPayManager"
    class="com.perfmath.spring.soba.service.SimpleBillPayManager">
    <property name="billPaymentDao" ref="billPaymentDao" />
    <property name="aclTxManager" ref="aclTxManager" />
```

```
        <!-- property name="mutableAclService" ref="aclService"/ -->
    </bean>
    <bean id="billPaymentDao"
        class="com.perfmath.spring.soba.model.dao.HibernateBillPaymentDao">
    </bean>
    <bean id="aclTxManager" class="com.perfmath.spring.soba.service.SimpleAclTxManager">
        <property name="aclBankingTxDao" ref="aclBankingTxDao" />
        <property name="loginUserDao" ref="loginUserDao" />
        <property name="accountDao" ref="accountDao" />
        <property name="accountManager" ref="accountManager" />
        <property name="mutableAclService" ref="aclService" />
    </bean>
    <bean id="userDetailsService"
        class="org.springframework.security.core.userdetails.jdbc.JdbcDaoImpl">
        <property name="dataSource" ref="dataSource" />
    </bean>
    <bean id="bankingTxDao" class="com.perfmath.spring.soba.model.dao.JdbcBankingTxDao">
        <property name="dataSource" ref="dataSource" />
    </bean>
    <bean id="aclBankingTxDao"
        class="com.perfmath.spring.soba.model.dao.JdbcAclBankingTxDao">
        <property name="dataSource" ref="dataSource" />
    </bean>

    <bean id="propertyConfigurer"
        class="org.springframework.beans.factory.config.PropertyPlaceholderConfigurer">
        <property name="locations">
            <list>
                <value>classpath:jdbc.properties</value>
            </list>
        </property>
    </bean>
    <tx:annotation-driven />
    <bean id="transactionManager"
        class="org.springframework.jdbc.datasource.DataSourceTransactionManager">
        <property name="dataSource" ref="dataSource" />
    </bean>
</beans>
```

5.2 IMPLEMENTING DAO WITH JDBC

JDBC itself is a broad topic. In order to help you get familiar with it quickly, let's use a real DAO class to illustrate it. My favorite DAO class with SOBA is `BankingTxDao`, and I'll tell you why later.

For a particular domain object, for example, the `BankingTx` domain object, we need a DAO interface and a class that implements the interface. For the `BankingTx` domain object, we have the `BankingTxDao.java` interface and the `JDBCBankingTxDao.java` class. Let's first review the `BankingTx` domain object next.

5.2.1 Defining Domain Objects

The `BankingTx` domain object code in Java is shown in Listing 5.2 (it was originally named `Transaction` instead of `BankingTx`, which was okay with Oracle and MySQL, but I had to rename it because the word `Transaction` is a reserved keyword in SQL Server and SQL Server would not allow me to create a table named *TRANSACTION*). Notice those `@XmlRootElement` and `@XmlElement` annotations? These are *JAXB* annotations, which define the root element and node elements of a standard XML structure (JAXB stands for *Java Architecture for XML Binding*, which is a JAVA standard for defining how to convert Java objects from and to XML). You will see later in §6.3 how this JAXB-based domain object of `BankingTx.java` is marshalled and unmarshalled with Spring's `jaxb2Marshaller` when we discuss a banking transaction controller implemented with Spring RESTful web services.

Listing 5.2 BankingTx.java

```
package com.perfmath.spring.soba.model.domain;

import java.io.Serializable;
import java.sql.Timestamp;
import javax.xml.bind.annotation.XmlRootElement;
import javax.xml.bind.annotation.XmlElement;
import javax.xml.bind.annotation.adapters.XmlJavaTypeAdapter;

import com.perfmath.spring.soba.model.domain.TimestampAdapter;
@XmlRootElement(name="bankingtx")
public class BankingTx implements Serializable {

  private long transactionId;
  private Timestamp transDate;
  private String type;
  private String initiator;
  private String description;
  private double amount;
  private double balance;
  private String accountId;
  private String status;
    @XmlElement(name="transactionId")
    public long getTransactionId() {
        return transactionId;
```

```
}
public long getId() {
    return transactionId;
}
public void setTransactionId(long transactionId) {
    this.transactionId = transactionId;
}
@XmlJavaTypeAdapter(TimestampAdapter.class)
public Timestamp getTransDate() {
    return transDate;
}
public void setTransDate(Timestamp transDate) {
    this.transDate = transDate;
}
@XmlElement(name="type")
public String getType() {
    return type;
}
public void setType(String type) {
    this.type = type;
}
@XmlElement(name="initiator")
public String getInitiator() {
    return initiator;
}
public void setInitiator(String initiator) {
    this.initiator = initiator;
}
@XmlElement(name="description")
public String getDescription() {
    return description;
}
public void setDescription(String description) {
    this.description = description;
}
@XmlElement(name="amount")
public double getAmount() {
    return amount;
}
public void setAmount(double amount) {
    this.amount = amount;
}
@XmlElement(name="balance")
```

```
    public double getBalance() {
        return balance;
    }
    public void setBalance(double balance) {
        this.balance = balance;
    }
    @XmlElement(name="accountId")
    public String getAccountId() {
        return accountId;
    }
    public void setAccountId(String accountId) {
        this.accountId = accountId;
    }
    @XmlElement(name="status")
    public String getStatus() {
        return status;
    }
    public void setStatus(String status) {
        this.status = status;
    }
    public String toString() {
     StringBuffer buffer = new StringBuffer();
     buffer.append("transactionId: " + transactionId + ";");
     buffer.append("accountId: " + accountId + ";");
     buffer.append("amount: " + amount);
     return buffer.toString();
  }
}
```

This is a simple domain object despite those visually noisy XML annotations. Let's move to the `BankingTxDAO` interface next.

5.2.2 Defining a DAO Interface

The DAO interface corresponding to the domain object of `BankingTx` is exhibited in Listing 5.3. This is a very simple Java interface, and it's very self-explanatory. After you take a quick look at it, let's move to the next section which explains in detail how these interfaces are implemented in JDBC, or specifically the Spring JDBC Framework.

Listing 5.3 BankingTxDao.java

```
package com.perfmath.spring.soba.model.dao;

import java.util.List;
```

```
import java.util.Map;
import com.perfmath.spring.soba.model.domain.BankingTx;

public interface BankingTxDao {
    public List<BankingTx> getTransactionList();
    public List<BankingTx> getTransactionList(String accountId);
   public void insert(BankingTx transaction);
   public void update(BankingTx transaction);
   public void delete(String transactionId);
   public BankingTx findByTransactionID(String transactionId);
   public void insertBatch(List<BankingTx> transactions);
   public List<Map<String, Object>> findAll();
   public String getAccountId(String transactionId);
   public int countAll();
}
```

5.3 IMPLEMENTING DAO WITH SPRING JDBC TEMPLATE

This section explains in detail how the `BankingTxDAO` interface defined in the preceding section is implemented with the two major Spring JDBC classes: `JdbcTemplate` and `NamedParameterJdbcTemplate`, against the domain object `BankingTx` defined in Listing 5.2. There are many variations with the Spring JDBC, but I feel that these two classes should be sufficient most of the time. You should refer to *Chapter 13 Data Access with JDBC* of the *Spring Reference Documentation 4* if you want to know every detail about this subject. Here, I'd like to present a succinct example to show how it works.

First, let's show how the `JDBCBankingTxDao.java` class is implemented in Listing 5.4. Note the highlighted parts that we explain next following the code listing.

Listing 5.4 JDBCBankingTxDao.java

```
package com.perfmath.spring.soba.model.dao;

import java.sql.ResultSet;
import java.sql.SQLException;
import java.util.List;
import java.util.Map;

import javax.sql.DataSource;

import org.springframework.jdbc.core.namedparam.BeanPropertySqlParameterSource;
import org.springframework.jdbc.core.namedparam.NamedParameterJdbcDaoSupport;
import org.springframework.jdbc.core.namedparam.NamedParameterJdbcTemplate;
import org.springframework.jdbc.core.namedparam.SqlParameterSource;
```

```
import org.springframework.jdbc.core.namedparam.SqlParameterSourceUtils;
import org.springframework.jdbc.core.simple.ParameterizedRowMapper;
import org.springframework.jdbc.core.JdbcTemplate;

import com.perfmath.spring.soba.model.domain.BankingTx;

public class JdbcBankingTxDao implements BankingTxDao {
    private JdbcTemplate jdbcTemplate;
    private NamedParameterJdbcTemplate namedParameterJdbcTemplate;

    public List<BankingTx> getTransactionList() {
        List<BankingTx> txs = this.jdbcTemplate
                .query("SELECT TRANSACTION_ID, TRANS_DATE, TYPE, "
                        + " INITIATOR, DESCRIPTION, AMOUNT, BALANCE, ACCOUNT_ID, “
                        + “ STATUS FROM BANKINGTX",
                        new TransactionMapper());
        return txs;
    }

    public List<BankingTx> getTransactionList(String accountId) {
        List<BankingTx> txs = this.jdbcTemplate
                .query("SELECT TRANSACTION_ID, TRANS_DATE, TYPE, "
                        + " INITIATOR, DESCRIPTION, AMOUNT, BALANCE, "
                        + " ACCOUNT_ID, STATUS FROM BANKINGTX WHERE
                            ACCOUNT_ID = ?"
                        + " ORDER BY TRANS_DATE DESC", new TransactionMapper(),
                        accountId);
        return txs;
    }

    public void insert(BankingTx transaction) {
        String sql = "INSERT INTO BANKINGTX (TRANSACTION_ID, TRANS_DATE, TYPE,"
            + "INITIATOR, DESCRIPTION, AMOUNT, BALANCE, ACCOUNT_ID, STATUS) “
        + "VALUES (:transactionId, :transDate, :type, :initiator, "
            + ":description, :amount, :balance, :accountId, :status)";
        SqlParameterSource namedParameters = new  BeanPropertySqlParameterSource(
            transaction);

        int count = this.namedParameterJdbcTemplate
                .update(sql, namedParameters);
    }

    public void insertBatch(List<BankingTx> transactions) {
```

```
        String sql = "INSERT INTO BANKINGTX (TRANSACTION_ID, TRANS_DATE, TYPE,"
            + "INITIATOR, DESCRIPTION, AMOUNT, BALANCE, ACCOUNT_ID, STATUS ) "
            + "VALUES (:transactionId, :transDate, :type, :initiator, "
            + ":description, :amount, :balance, :accountId, :status)";


        SqlParameterSource[] parameterSource  =
        SqlParameterSourceUtils.createBatch(transactions.toArray());

        int count[] = this.namedParameterJdbcTemplate
                .batchUpdate(sql, parameterSource);   }

    public BankingTx findByTransactionID(String transID) {

        String sql = "SELECT TRANSACTION_ID, TRANS_DATE, TYPE, "
            + " INITIATOR, DESCRIPTION, AMOUNT, BALANCE, ACCOUNT_ID, STATUS "
            + " FROM BANKINGTX WHERE TRANSACTION_ID = '" + transID + "'";
        BankingTx trans = this.jdbcTemplate.queryForObject(sql,
                new TransactionMapper());

        return trans;
    }

    public void update(BankingTx tx) {
    }

    public void delete(String txId) {
        String sql = "DELETE BANKINGTX WHERE TRANSACTION_ID = ?";

        int count = this.jdbcTemplate.update(sql, txId);
    }

    public List<Map<String, Object>> findAll() {
        String sql = "SELECT * FROM BANKINGTX";

        List<Map<String, Object>> trans = this.jdbcTemplate.queryForList(sql,
                new TransactionMapper());
        return trans;
    }

    public String getAccountId(String transID) {
        String sql = "SELECT ACCOUNT_ID FROM BANKINGTX WHERE TRANSACTION_ID = ?";
        String accountId = this.jdbcTemplate.queryForObject(sql, String.class,
```

```
            transID);
        return accountId;
    }

    public int countAll() {
        String sql = "SELECT COUNT(*) FROM BANKINGTX";

        int count = this.jdbcTemplate.queryForInt(sql);
        return count;
    }

    public void setDataSource(DataSource dataSource) {
        this.jdbcTemplate = new JdbcTemplate(dataSource);
        this.namedParameterJdbcTemplate = new NamedParameterJdbcTemplate(
            dataSource);
    }

    private static class TransactionMapper implements ParameterizedRowMapper<BankingTx> {
        public BankingTx mapRow(ResultSet rs, int rowNum) throws SQLException {
            BankingTx tx = new BankingTx();
            tx.setTransactionId(rs.getLong("TRANSACTION_ID"));
            tx.setTransDate(rs.getTimestamp("TRANS_DATE"));
            tx.setType(rs.getString("TYPE"));
            tx.setInitiator(rs.getString("INITIATOR"));
            tx.setDescription(rs.getString("DESCRIPTION"));
            tx.setAmount(rs.getDouble("AMOUNT"));
            tx.setBalance(rs.getDouble("BALANCE"));
            tx.setAccountId(rs.getString("ACCOUNT_ID"));
            tx.setStatus(rs.getString("STATUS"));
            return tx;
        }
    }
}
```

Here is a generic procedure adopted in implementing the `JDBCBankingTxDao` class shown in the above listing:

- Add two variables of `jdbcTemplate` and `namedParameterJdbcTemplate` as follows:

  ```
  private JdbcTemplate jdbcTemplate;
  private NamedParameterJdbcTemplate namedParameterJdbcTemplate;
  ```

- Add a `setDataSource` method as shown in the above listing. The `datasource` object is configured externally in `soba-services.xml` and you don't have to worry about it here. JDBC DAOs need this `dataSource` to connect to the data store.

- Define a `TransactionMapper` class as shown in the above listing. This mapper converts a row into a domain object. In this case, it converts a row from the `BANKINGTX` table into a `BankingTx` domain object. This conversion is necessary as Java only deals with objects rather than rows directly from the database.

The rule of thumb is that you use the SQL operations from the `JdbcTemplate` class with SQLs that do not use named parameters, but you need to use `NamedParameterJdbcTemplate` class with SQLs that use named parameters. Otherwise, if you use something like `this.jdbcTemplate.update (sql, namedParameters)` (for example, with the `insert` method), it would compile fine, but you would get the following error when it is actually executed, for example, with `createTransaction` calls in SOBA:

```
java.sql.SQLException: Invalid argument value: java.io.NotSerializableException
com.mysql.jdbc.SQLError.createSQLException(SQLError.java:1055)
com.mysql.jdbc.SQLError.createSQLException(SQLError.java:956)
com.mysql.jdbc.SQLError.createSQLException(SQLError.java:926)
com.mysql.jdbc.PreparedStatement.setSerializableObject(PreparedStatement.java:4278)
com.mysql.jdbc.PreparedStatement.setObject(PreparedStatement.java:3922)
org.apache.commons.dbcp.DelegatingPreparedStatement.setObject(DelegatingPreparedStatement.jav
a:255)
org.springframework.jdbc.core.StatementCreatorUtils.setValue(StatementCreatorUtils.java:351)
org.springframework.jdbc.core.StatementCreatorUtils.setParameterValueInternal(StatementCreatorUti
ls.java:216)
org.springframework.jdbc.core.StatementCreatorUtils.setParameterValue(StatementCreatorUtils.java:
144)
org.springframework.jdbc.core.ArgPreparedStatementSetter.doSetValue(ArgPreparedStatementSetter.
java:65)
org.springframework.jdbc.core.ArgPreparedStatementSetter.setValues(ArgPreparedStatementSetter.ja
va:46)
org.springframework.jdbc.core.JdbcTemplate$2.doInPreparedStatement(JdbcTemplate.java:816)
org.springframework.jdbc.core.JdbcTemplate$2.doInPreparedStatement(JdbcTemplate.java:1)
org.springframework.jdbc.core.JdbcTemplate.execute(JdbcTemplate.java:587)
org.springframework.jdbc.core.JdbcTemplate.update(JdbcTemplate.java:812)
org.springframework.jdbc.core.JdbcTemplate.update(JdbcTemplate.java:868)
org.springframework.jdbc.core.JdbcTemplate.update(JdbcTemplate.java:876)
```

Therefore, it's important to know when to use `JdbcTemplate` and when to use `NamedParameterJdbcTemplate`, as explained next with the help of Listing 5.4.

5.3.1 JdbcTemplate.query

This method is for returning a result set of all or partial rows in your database from the table corresponding to your domain object. It is used to implement the two `getTransactionList` methods, one for all transactions, and the other for a specific account. Note that in the second method, a question mark "?" is used in the SQL query to hold the `ACCOUNT_ID` variable. If you have more variables, then you can use more question marks, but you need to make sure the sequence of the values provided after the second argument `new TransactionMapper()` matches. The return type is a Java *List* in this case.

5.3.2 JdbcTemplate.queryForObject

This method is applied to `findByTransactionID` and `getAccountId` for a given `bankingTxID`. In the first case, the returned object is a `BankingTx` object, and in the second case, the returned object is a String representing an account id.

5.3.3 JdbcTemplate.queryForList

This method is applied to the `findAll` method, which returns all banking transactions as a Java List. Note that you need to specify `new TransactionMapper ()` for the second argument of this `queryForList` call, which used to be `BankingTx.class` with the deprecated `getSimpleJdbcTemplate` method.

5.3.4 JdbcTemplate.queryForInt

This method is applied to the `countAll` method, which returns the number of rows of the domain object in the database.

5.3.5 NamedParameterJdbcTemplate.update

This method covers all SQL statements of `INSERT`, `UPDATE and DELETE`. JDBC does not have a method for each of these SQL operations. Instead, the update method applies to all these cases, and the concrete operation is resolved internally.

Note the items preceded with ":" in the SQL statement instead of question marks in the `insert` method. These are called *named parameters*, which is a feature provided with the Spring JDBC Framework. It is used in conjunction with *SqlParameterSource*, which automatically matches the passed-in object with the named parameters. Once again, if you use *this.jdbcTemplate* instead of *namedParameterJdbcTemplate*, you would get the *java.sql.SQLException: Invalid argument value: java.io.NotSerializableException* error as shown previously. However, it's okay for the `delete` method to use *this.jdbc.Template.update*, as it does not use named parameters.

5.3.6 NamedParameterJdbcTemplate.batchUpdate

This method enables batch operations, for example, inserting/deleting/updating multiple rows in one batch to the database. Note that you need to create a `SqlParameterSource` array with `SqlParameterSourceUtils.createBatch` for the second argument of the `batchUpdate` method. Array processing is a common practice to improve the performance and scalability of a database-centric enterprise application.

Next, let's see how these JDBC DAOs are used by service beans to query or persist the model from and to the database.

5.4 SERVICE BEANS

In the beginning of this chapter, you might have noticed that many beans defined in the `soba-services.xml` file have the word 'Manager' in their names. These are service beans that mostly depend on the DAO beans. In this section, we explore one of such examples.

The example we use is the `BankingTxManager` bean. Its interface is defined in `TxManager.java` and its implementation is defined in `SimpleTxManager.java`. This interface and its implementing class are exhibited in Listings 5.5 (a) and (b). The `TxManager` interface is self-explanatory and there is not much to explain. However, a few things worth to notice with the implementation class of `SimpleTxManager.java`:

- First, notice those annotations like `@Transactional` and `@Secured`. The annotation `@Transactional` indicates that all operations within that method should either all succeed or none, while the annotation `@Secured` indicates that only the user who has one of these designated roles is allowed to execute that method.
- From each of the methods, it's easy to see how the `BankingTxDao` is used to carry out various database operations.
- At last, notice the `createTransaction (BankingTx tx)` method. There is a requirement that when a banking transaction is persisted into the `BankingTx` table in the SOBA database, that user's account balance needs to be updated and so does the balance value of that banking transaction. This is a non-issue with Oracle and MySQL, both of which support BEFORE-TRIGGER (refer to Listing 2.12 about this trigger), but since SQL Server does not support BEFORE-TRIGGER, I could not find an easy workaround on SQL Server. Eventually, I have to make it work here by updating the account balance and then setting the new balance for the banking transaction before it is inserted into the database. Because of this interesting twist, I chose the banking transaction domain object as the example for this chapter.

Listing 5.5 (a) TxManager.java

```
package com.perfmath.spring.soba.service;

import java.io.Serializable;
import java.util.List;
import com.perfmath.spring.soba.model.domain.BankingTx;

   public interface TxManager extends Serializable{
   public void createTransaction(BankingTx tx);
   public List<BankingTx> getTransactions();
   public List<BankingTx> getTransactions(String accountId);
   public void updateTransaction(BankingTx tx);
   public BankingTx findByTransactionID(String txId);
```

```
    public void deleteTransaction(String txId);
}
```

Listing 5.5 (b) SimpleTxManager.java

```
package com.perfmath.spring.soba.service;

import java.util.List;
import com.perfmath.spring.soba.model.dao.BankingTxDao;
import com.perfmath.spring.soba.model.domain.BankingTx;
import java.util.ArrayList;
import java.util.LinkedHashMap;
import java.util.List;
import java.util.Map;

  import org.springframework.transaction.annotation.Transactional;
  import org.springframework.security.annotation.Secured;

  public class SimpleTxManager implements TxManager {

    private BankingTxDao bankingTxDao;
    private AccountManager accountManager;

    public List<BankingTx> getTransactions() {
        return bankingTxDao.getTransactionList();
    }
    public List<BankingTx> getTransactions(String accountId) {
        return bankingTxDao.getTransactionList(accountId);
    }
    public void updateTransaction(BankingTx tx) {
        bankingTxDao.update(tx);
    }
    @Transactional
    @Secured("ROLE_REP")
    public void deleteTransaction(String txId) {
        bankingTxDao.delete(txId);
    }

    @Transactional
    @Secured("ROLE_CUST, ROLE_REP")
    public void createTransaction(BankingTx tx) {
        // added due to no BEFORE-TRIGGER in sql server
        if (SobaConfig.getDatabaseVendor().equalsIgnoreCase("SQLServer")) {
```

```
            double balance = accountManager.updateAccountBalance
            (tx.getAmount(), tx.getAccountId());
              tx.setBalance(balance);
          }
          bankingTxDao.insert(tx);

      public BankingTx findByTransactionID(String txId) {
          return bankingTxDao.findByTransactionID(txId);
      }

      public void setBankingTxDao(BankingTxDao bankingTxDao) {
          this.bankingTxDao = bankingTxDao;
      }
      public void setAccountManager(AccountManager accountManager) {
          this.accountManager = accountManager;
      }
}
```

Next, let's take a look at how the Spring Data Access Framework works with Hibernate.

5.5 HIBERNATE DATA ACCESS METHOD

First, there is no barrier with using an ORM framework like Hibernate with Spring, thanks to the architectural pluggability of Spring. Secondly, in general, an ORM framework is favored over plain JDBC for persisting enterprise data. Let's first explore what benefits an ORM framework like Hibernate provides over JDBC.

5.5.1 Benefits of Using Hibernate

As one of the most popular ORM frameworks, Hibernate provides the following benefits:

- Hibernate works by persisting data according to the mapping metadata defined in a mapping file. A mapping file defines mappings between a Java class and a database table by specifying how the attributes of the Java class and the columns of the table map to each other. This provides a natural bridge between the object-oriented programming model and the relational database model.
- Hibernate generates SQL statements at runtime, and therefore its implementation is database vendor neutral. This is especially important if your application has to support multiple database platforms from all major vendors.
- Hibernate goes beyond the basic ORM functionality. It supports additional features like caching, cascading, and lazy loading, which may help enhance the performance and scalability of your application.
- Hibernate defines a powerful query language of its own which is called HQL (Hibernate Query Language). It's very easy to write queries with the HQL.

Next, let's see how metadata mapping works with Hibernate.

5.5.2 Hibernate Mapping (HBM)

Hibernate Mapping (HBM) between a Java object and a database table is straightforward. For example, with the `BillPayment.java` class shown in Listing 5.6, metadata mapping is achieved with a mapping file as shown in Listing 5.7. Note that this mapping file needs to be placed in the class target directory of the java class it is mapped to, or in this case, together with the `BillPayment.class` file rather than the source file.

One needs to pay attention to how the ID field is mapped in Listing 5.7. First, this field is mandatory that both the Java class and the database table must have. Secondly, its type must be *long*. Finally, note how a generator is defined with a property of `class = " ..."`. The values that this property can have include: `assigned`, `increment`, `identity`, `sequence`, `hilo`, `seqhilo`, `uuid`, `native`, `select`, `foreign`, etc. Detailed discussion on what each setting means is beyond the scope of this text, except that the setting of `assigned` chosen in SOBA means that it's assigned by the application.

Listing 5.6 BillPayment.java

```
package com.perfmath.spring.soba.model.domain;
import java.io.Serializable;
import java.sql.Timestamp;
public class BillPayment implements Serializable {
    private Long id = null;
    private String accountId;
    private String description;
    private double amount;
    private String fromAccount;
    private String biller;
    private String address;
    private String city;
    private String state;
    private String zipcode;
    private String status;
    private Timestamp scheduleDate;
    private Timestamp sendDate;
    public BillPayment() {
    }
// All getters and setter methods have been removed to save space
    public String toString() {
        StringBuffer buffer = new StringBuffer();
        buffer.append(" Id: " + id + ";");
        buffer.append(" accountId: " + accountId + ";");
        buffer.append(" description: " + description);
        buffer.append(" amount: " + amount);
        buffer.append(" fromAccount: " + fromAccount);
```

```
        buffer.append(" biller: " + biller);
        buffer.append(" address: " + address);
        buffer.append(" city: " + city);
        buffer.append(" state: " + state);
        buffer.append(" zipcode: " + zipcode);
        buffer.append(" status: " + status);
        buffer.append(" scheduleDate: " + scheduleDate);
        buffer.append(" sendDate: " + sendDate);
        return buffer.toString();
    }
}
```

Listing 5.7 BillPayment.hbm.xml

```
<!DOCTYPE hibernate-mapping
     PUBLIC "-//Hibernate/Hibernate Mapping DTD 3.0//EN"
     "http://hibernate.sourceforge.net/hibernate-mapping-3.0.dtd">
<hibernate-mapping package="com.perfmath.spring.soba.model.domain">
    <class name="BillPayment" table="BILL_PAYMENT">
        <id name="id" type="long" column="ID">
            <generator class="assigned">
                <!-- param name="sequence">BLL_PYMNT_SEQ</param> -->
            </generator>
        </id>
        <property name="fromAccount" type="string">
            <column name="FROM_ACCOUNT" length="9" not-null="true" />
        </property>
        <property name="accountId" type="string">
            <column name="ACCOUNT_ID" length="9" not-null="true" />
        </property>
        <property name="description" type="string">
            <column name="DESCRIPTION" length="500" not-null="true" />
        </property>
        <property name="biller" type="string">
            <column name="BILLER" length="25" not-null="true" />
        </property>
        <property name="address" type="string">
            <column name="ADDRESS" length="50" not-null="true" />
        </property>
        <property name="city" type="string">
            <column name="CITY" length="25" not-null="true" />
        </property>
        <property name="state" type="string">
```

```
            <column name="STATE" length="2" not-null="true" />
        </property>
        <property name="zipcode" type="string">
            <column name="ZIPCODE" length="10" not-null="true" />
        </property>
        <property name="status" type="string" column="STATUS" />
        <property name="amount" type="double" column="AMOUNT" />
        <property name="scheduleDate" type="date" column="SCHEDULE_DATE" />
        <property name="sendDate" type="date" column="SEND_DATE" />
    </class>
</hibernate-mapping>
```

Next, let's take a look at how Hibernate is configured to work with a database system.

5.5.3 Hibernate Connectivity Configuration

Hibernate connectivity with a database platform is defined in a file named `hibernate.cfg.xml` file as shown in Listing 5.8 below. Hibernate looks for this file by default to establish connections with the configured database. Note that although Listing 5.8 is for MySQL, you can find the versions for PostgreSQL, Oracle and SQL Server from the SOBA download as well.

In this Hibernate configuration file, note the last line referring to the metadata mapping file described in the previous section. It tells a Hibernate engine where to find the metadata mapping file, which points to where the mapped object resides at the lowest level. The hibernate configuration file `hibernate.cfg.xml` must be placed in the root classpath directory, which is the `WEB-INF/classes` directory.

Given what we have covered in Chapter 2 and Appendix B, the database connectivity configuration part in Listing 5.8 should be self-explanatory. The last few lines specific to Hibernate are denoted as follows:

- **The property `hibernate.show_sql` = true**: This entry specifies that all SQLs generated by Hibernate at runtime will be output to the console. This is a convenient feature for debugging purposes. However, it should be set to `false` in production due to performance concerns.
- **The property `hibernate.hbm2ddl.auto = update`**: This entry specifies the intention for creating the database schema on deploy if it doesn't exist. It has many other possible settings and which one is most appropriate should be determined with the tests conducted with your application.
- **The property `current_session_context_class = thread`**: This entry specifies the scope of the current session. Valid values include `jta`, `thread`, `managed`, and so on. The setting of `thread` specified here limits the session context to the thread level.

Note that prior to Hibernate 3.6, the DTD file specified in the beginning of Listing 5.8 was `http://hibernate.sourceforge.net/hibernate-mapping-3.0.dtd`, which must be upgraded to the new DTD `http://www.hibernate.org/dtd/hibernate-configuration-3.0.dtd` for Hibernate 3.6. However, do not make this change in Listing 5.7 for `BillPayment.hbm.xml`; otherwise, you would get an error of "The content of element type "property" must match "null"" with each property element.

Listing 5.8 hibernate.cfg.xml

```
<!DOCTYPE hibernate-configuration
    PUBLIC "-//Hibernate/Hibernate Configuration DTD 3.0//EN"
    " http://www.hibernate.org/dtd/hibernate-configuration-3.0.dtd">

<hibernate-configuration>
   <session-factory>
      <property name="connection.driver_class">com.mysql.jdbc.Driver</property>
      <property name="connection.url">jdbc:mysql://localhost:3306/soba</property>
      <property name="connection.username">sobaadmin</property>
      <property name="connection.password">sobaadmin</property>
      <property name="hibernate.dialect">org.hibernate.dialect.MySQLDialect</property>
      <property name="hibernate.show_sql">true</property>
      <property name="hibernate.hbm2ddl.auto">update</property>
      <property name="current_session_context_class">thread</property>
      <mapping resource="com/perfmath/spring/soba/model/domain/BillPayment.hbm.xml"/>
   </session-factory>
</hibernate-configuration>
```

Since this is not a text about Hibernate, please consult more in-depth documentations to learn more about various Hibernate settings. Next, we discuss how a Hibernate DAO class is implemented.

5.5.4 Data Access Methods and Transaction Management for Hibernate

In general, data can be persisted to the backend database with one of the three mechanisms: (1) JDBC, (2) Hibernate, and (3) JPA (Java Persistence Architecture – the persistence framework for EJB 3). Table 5.1 lists the resource, resource factory and exception implementations with each mechanism. It is seen that JDBC uses *Connection* and *DataSource* to persist data, Hibernate uses the concepts of *Session* and *SessionFactory* to persist data, whereas JPA uses *EntityManager* and *EntityManagerFactory* to persist data. The ramifications implied here are that there might be a variety of methods for managing transactions with a Spring-based enterprise application.

Table 5.1 Data Persistence Mechanisms

Mechanism	Resource	ResourceFactory	Exception
JDBC	Connection	DataSource	SQLException
Hibernate	Session	SessionFactory	HibernateException
JPA	EntityManager	EntityManagerFactory	PersistenceException

As shown in Listing 5.1 `soba-services.xml`, a `transactionManager` of `org.springframework.jdbc.dataSource.DataSourceTransactionManager` is defined for the SOBA sample. For Hibernate-based data persistence mechanism, Spring offers transaction managers based on the `org.springframework.orm.hibernate3.HibernateTransactionManager` class for Hibernate 3 or org.springframework.orm.hibernate4.HibernateTransactionManager for Hibernate 4, as is demonstrated with the sample presented in Appendix C (See Listing C.12). Spring also offers a transaction manager based on the org.springframework.orm.jpa.JpaTransactionManager class for managing JPA-based data persistence mechanism, but it is not covered in this book.

The other variable associated with persisting data is how a transaction is managed. While EJB supports *bean-managed transaction (BMT)* and *container-managed transaction (CMT)*, Spring supports *programmatic transaction management (PTM)* and *declarative transaction management (DTM)*. The choice between PTM and DTM is leveraged by a trade-off between flexibility and complexity. DTM is simpler but less flexible than PTM.

Next, let's examine a Hibernate data persisting implementation method based on a POJO domain object with HBM.

POJO Domain Object with HBM

Listings 5.9 (a) and (b) illustrate how a Hibernate DAO is implemented for the BillPayment domain object with PTM. The Java class HibernateBillPaymentDao implements the interface defined in BillPaymentDao.java. Some unique features with this Hibernate DAO method include:

- The Hibernate DAO depends on a Hibernate *SessionFactory* object for all its operations. A *session* needs to be opened and closed within each operation.
- Each operation is managed as a transaction by calling the transactional begin and commit methods directly. This is what we called *PTM,* which allows a programmer to decide when to begin, commit or roll back a transaction precisely. There actually is a conflict with the JDBC-based transaction manager defined with the transactionManager org.springframework.jdbc.dataSource.DataSourceTransactionManager as is shown in Listing 5.1, if we define a Hibernate-based transaction manager for this example, as only one transaction manager can be defined with an application without doing some extra work to accommodate more than one transaction manager. A standalone Spring-Hibernate sample presented in Appendix C shows how to define a transaction manager for Hibernate 4 and use DTM in place of PTM to manage Hibernate data persistence transactions.
- Note the use of the session method saveOrUpdate with the store operation. The rule with this method is that it would perform an INSERT if the row to be inserted does not exist in the database or an UPDATE if the row exists.
- This Hibernate DAO implementation uses a POJO domain object (BillPayment.java defined in Listing 5.6), an *HBM* XML file (BillPayment.hbm.xml defined in Listing 5.7), a Hibernate configuration file (hibernate.cfg.xml defined in Listing 5.8), and *PTM* identifiable in *HibernateBillPaymentDao.java* defined in Listing 5.9 (b).

Next, let's see how an HBM can be eliminated by annotating the domain object class BillPayment.java with JPA.

Listing 5.9 (a) BillPaymentDao.java

```
package com.perfmath.spring.soba.model.dao;
import java.util.List;
```

```
import com.perfmath.spring.soba.model.domain.BillPayment;
    public interface BillPaymentDao {
    public void store(BillPayment billPayment);
    public void delete(String id);
    public BillPayment findById(String id);
    public List<BillPayment> findAll();
}
```

Listing 5.9 (b) HibernateBillPaymentDao.java

```
package com.perfmath.spring.soba.model.dao;
import com.perfmath.spring.soba.model.dao.BillPaymentDao;
import com.perfmath.spring.soba.model.domain.BillPayment;
import org.hibernate.Query;
import org.hibernate.Session;
import org.hibernate.SessionFactory;
import org.hibernate.Transaction;
import org.hibernate.cfg.Configuration;
import java.util.List;
public class HibernateBillPaymentDao implements BillPaymentDao {
    private SessionFactory sessionFactory;
    public HibernateBillPaymentDao() {
        Configuration configuration = new Configuration().configure();
        sessionFactory = configuration.buildSessionFactory();
    }
    public void store(BillPayment billPayment) {
        Session session = sessionFactory.openSession();
        Transaction tx = session.getTransaction();
        try {
            tx.begin();
            session.saveOrUpdate(billPayment);
            tx.commit();
        } catch (RuntimeException e) {
            tx.rollback();
            throw e;
        } finally {
            session.close();
        }
    }
    public void delete(String id) {
        Session session = sessionFactory.openSession();
        Transaction tx = session.getTransaction();
        try {
```

```
                tx.begin();
                BillPayment billPayment = (BillPayment) sessionFactory
                        .getCurrentSession().get(BillPayment.class, id);
                session.delete(billPayment);
                tx.commit();
            } catch (RuntimeException e) {
                tx.rollback();
                throw e;
            } finally {
                session.close();
            }
        }
        public BillPayment findById(String id) {
            Session session = sessionFactory.openSession();
            try {
                return (BillPayment) sessionFactory.getCurrentSession().get(
                        BillPayment.class, id);
            } finally {
                session.close();
            }
        }
        public List<BillPayment> findAll() {
            Session session = sessionFactory.openSession();
            try {
                Query query = sessionFactory.getCurrentSession().createQuery(
                        "from Bill_Payment");
                return query.list();
            } finally {
                session.close();
            }
        }
}
```

JPA Annotated Domain Object without HBM

Listing 5.10 illustrates the Java `BillPayment` class with JPA annotations (note that the `hibernate-jpa-2.0-api-0.1.1.Final.jar` file must be on the SOBA project library path whether ANT or Maven is used to build SOBA). To save space, all setter methods have been omitted. This mechanism eliminates the need for an HBM file as was used in the previous case. In addition, in the `hibernate.cfg.xml` file, one change is required: The `<mapping>` element `resource="com/perfmath/spring/soba/model/domain/BillPayment.hbm.xml"` in Listing 5.8 should be changed to `class="com.perfmath.spring.soba.model.domain.BillPayment"`.

Note that how each attribute is annotated with JPA annotations should be self-explanatory. For example, the `@Entity` annotation signifies the nature of this domain object, that is, it is an entity object, whereas the @Table annotation indicates to which database table this domain object is mapped. In addition, the @Id annotation signifies which PK column the attribute is mapped to; whereas the @Column annotation sets up the attribute-column mapping for each attribute-column pair. Finally, the @Temporal annotation sets the TIMESTAMP data type for the attribute annotated. Chapter 10 *Spring-EJB Integration* further explains how JPA works with a step-by-step procedure showing how to map relationships as well as how to automatically generate JPA entities from database tables directly (Refer to §10.1.2 for more details). We would not repeat such details here as they are not specific to Spring.

Listing 5.10 BillPayment.java (JPA-annotated)

```
package com.perfmath.spring.soba.model.domain;
import java.io.Serializable;
import java.sql.Timestamp;
import java.util.Date;
import javax.persistence.Basic;
import javax.persistence.Column;
import javax.persistence.Entity;
import javax.persistence.Id;
import javax.persistence.Table;
import javax.persistence.Temporal;
import javax.persistence.TemporalType;
@Entity
@Table(name = "BILL_PAYMENT")
public class BillPayment implements Serializable {
    private Long id = null;
    private String accountId;
    private String description;
    private double amount;
    private String fromAccount;
    private String biller;
    private String address;
    private String city;
    private String state;
    private String zipcode;
    private String status;
    private Date scheduleDate;
    private Date sendDate;
    public BillPayment() {
    }
    @Id
    @Column(name = "ID", unique = true, nullable = false, precision = 10, scale = 0)
    public Long getId() {
        return id;
```

```
}
@Column(name = "DESCRIPTION", nullable = false, length = 500)
public String getDescription() {
    return description;
}
@Column(name = "AMOUNT", nullable = false)
public double getAmount() {
    return amount;
}
@Column(name = "ACCOUNT_ID", nullable = false, length = 9)
public String getAccountId() {
    return accountId;
}
@Column(name = "FROM_ACCOUNT", nullable = false, length = 25)
public String getFromAccount() {
    return fromAccount;
}
@Column(name = "BILLER", nullable = false, length = 25)
public String getBiller() {
    return biller;
}
@Column(name = "ADDRESS", nullable = false, length = 50)
public String getAddress() {
    return address;
}
@Column(name = "CITY", nullable = false, length = 25)
public String getCity() {
    return city;
}
@Column(name = "STATE", nullable = false, length = 2)
public String getState() {
    return state;
}
@Column(name = "ZIPCODE", nullable = false, length = 10)
public String getZipcode() {
    return zipcode;
}
@Column(name = "STATUS", nullable = false, length = 25)
public String getStatus() {
    return status;
}
@Temporal(TemporalType.TIMESTAMP)
@Column(name = "SCHEDULE_DATE")
```

```
    public Date getScheduleDate() {
        return scheduleDate;
    }
    @Temporal(TemporalType.TIMESTAMP)
    @Column(name = "SEND_DATE")
    public Date getSendDate() {
        return sendDate;
    }
    public String toString() {
        <omitted>
    }
}
```

Note that whether a DAO is implemented in JDBC or Hibernate, it's used the same way in a service bean, as the service depends on the DAO interface rather than the implementation. Because of this transparency, we could have just stopped here without showing how the service layer of SOBA performs bill payment tasks with `HibernateBillPaymentDao` working behind the scene. However, this actually is a good place for us to get a little deeper on Spring validation framework by picking up where we left off with the bill payment use scenario demonstrated in §2.7. This is the subject of the next section.

5.6 SPRING DATA VALIDATION FRAMEWORK

To get a complete picture about how Spring validation works, let's begin with the programmatic logic flow with the bill pay service implemented in SOBA.

5.6.1 Programmatic Logic Flow with the Bill Pay Service

We start with recapturing the essence of the programmatic logic flow associated with the bill pay service by looking at what classes get involved at each layer. Table 5.2 lists the Java classes associated with this service. It should be clear what each Java class does based on its name and in which layer it is placed.

Table 5.2 Java classes at each layer for the bill pay service

Layer	Java Classes
Domain object	BillPayment.java
DAO	BillPaymentDao.java HibernateBillPayemntDao.java
Service	BillPayManager.java/SimpleBillPayManager.java CreateBillPayValidator.java
Web	CreateBillPayFormController.java CreateBillPaySuccessController.java
View	createBillPayForm.jsp createBillPaySuccess.jsp

Now let us take a look at how the bill pay service flows programmatically based on the Java classes associated with it as listed in Table 5.2. This service is initiated when a user clicks on the Bill Payment tab on the home page as shown in Figure 2.19. That home page was generated with the `activityList.jsp`, which has an embedded link as shown below:

```
<a href = "<c:url value = "createBillPayForm/customerId/${customerId}/
accountId/${accountId}"/>">Bill Payment</a>
```

Note the url value hard-coded in the above HTML element. It is similar to the RequestMapping we introduced in Listing 4.5 `CreateCustomerFormController.java`. Not surprisingly, it is mapped to the `CreateBillPayFormController.java` class, which is shown in Listing 5.11. When control is directed to this class, the `setupForm` method is executed first, which creates a `billPayment` object with some of the attributes pre-populated. Most of the pre-populated attributes here are purely for convenience except the `fromAccount` attribute so that we don't have to type them every time when we test this service. Then, the `setupForm` method returns control to the `createBillPayForm`, namely, the `createBillPayment.jsp`. The form is then presented to the user for entering all required information for a bill payment transaction. Refer back to Figure 2.20 for an actual instance of this form.

Listing 5.11 CreateBillPayFormController.java

```
package com.perfmath.spring.soba.web;

import org.springframework.beans.factory.annotation.Autowired;
import org.springframework.stereotype.Controller;
import org.springframework.ui.Model;
import org.springframework.validation.BindingResult;
import org.springframework.web.bind.annotation.ModelAttribute;
import org.springframework.web.bind.annotation.PathVariable;
import org.springframework.web.bind.annotation.RequestMapping;
import org.springframework.web.bind.annotation.RequestMethod;
import org.springframework.web.bind.annotation.SessionAttributes;
import org.springframework.web.bind.support.SessionStatus;

import com.perfmath.spring.soba.model.domain.BillPayment;
import com.perfmath.spring.soba.service.BillPayManager;
import com.perfmath.spring.soba.service.CreateBillPayValidator;

@Controller
@RequestMapping("/createBillPayForm/customerId/{customerId}/accountId/{accountId}")
@SessionAttributes("billPay")
public class CreateBillPayFormController {
    private CreateBillPayValidator validator;
    private BillPayManager billPayManager;
    @Autowired
    public CreateBillPayFormController(BillPayManager billPayManager,
```

```
            CreateBillPayValidator validator) {
        this.billPayManager = billPayManager;
        this.validator = validator;
    }
    @RequestMapping(method = RequestMethod.GET)
    public String setupForm(
            @PathVariable String accountId,
            Model model) {
        BillPayment billPayment = new BillPayment();
        billPayment.setFromAccount(accountId);
        billPayment.setDescription("bill pay test");
        billPayment.setAddress("One Way");
        billPayment.setCity("Any City");
        billPayment.setState("CA");
        billPayment.setZipcode("95999");
        model.addAttribute("billPayment", billPayment);
        return "createBillPayForm";
    }
    @RequestMapping(method = RequestMethod.POST)
    public String submitForm(
            @PathVariable String customerId,
            @ModelAttribute("billPayment") BillPayment billPayment,
            BindingResult result, SessionStatus status) {
      validator.validate(billPayment, result);

      if (result.hasErrors()) {
            return "createBillPayForm";
        } else {
            billPayManager.storeBillPayment(billPayment);
            status.setComplete();
            return "redirect:/createBillPaySuccess/customerId/" + customerId;
        }
    }
}
```

After a user fills in the bill payment form and hits the *Submit* button, control is redirected back to the class `CreateBillPayFormController.java`, and the `submitForm` is initiated. As is seen from Listing 5.11, the `submitForm` method validates the `billPayment` object using the `validate` method of its `validator`. This is where *validation* gets invoked, as is discussed in the next section. If validation is successful without errors, control is directed to the `CreateBillPaySuccessController`, which presents the responses back to the user via the `createBillPaySuccessForm.jsp` as listed in Table 5.2. If errors occurred during validation, control would be directed back to the bill pay form to display the errors to the user so that the user can correct the errors and resubmit the bill pay again.

Next, we focus on understanding how the Spring Validation Interface works in the specific context of this bill pay service example.

5.6.2 Spring Validation Interface

Refer back to Figure 2.20, which shows an actual instance of a bill pay form. Since the user's own account ID has been pre-populated, we don't have to worry about it at all. Of course, in reality, a user might have an option to decide from which account the fund should be drawn to pay the bill, but that is not very important for our example here. Our concern is how to validate the data entered on this form by the user.

We are particularly concerned about how the bill pay amount is validated. As is shown in Listing 5.12 `CreateBillPayValidator.java`, we use a `Validator` interface in Spring's `validation` package, which is very basic and usable. This `BillPayment` validator has two methods: `supports` (…) and `validate` (…). The `supports` method checks whether the passed-in type supports validation, whereas the `validate` method does the actual validation if this validator supports validation. The `validate` method uses a method of `rejectIfEmptyOrWhitespace (errors, "amount", "required.amount", "amount is required.")` from the Spring `ValidationUtils` class to validate the attribute `amount` of type `double`. This entry is rejected if a user enters an empty or whitespace string or an invalid item in the `amount` field on the `createBillPayForm` form defined in the `createBillPayForm.jsp` file. If a type mismatch occurs, an error message of "`invalid data`" would be displayed near the `amount` field entry, according to the `typeMismatch` entry defined in the `messages.properteis` file located at the root class path of SOBA.

Of course, you can introduce additional validation based on your business context, after form data format is validated. For example, the `validate` method for this example further validates that the bill pay amount must be larger than zero, after a user enters an amount that is syntactically correct. If a less than zero bill pay amount is entered, it would pass the `rejectIfEmptyOrWhitespace` validation, but not the following validation as shown in Listing 5.12, which returns control to the bill pay form with an error message of "`bill pay amount must be > 0`" displayed near the `amount` field:

```
if (billPayment.getAmount() <= 0.0) {
    errors.rejectValue("amount", "invalid.billPayAmount",
    "bill pay amount must be > 0");
}
```

Table 5.3 lists some interesting test cases about how this validation works. Note that the "invalid data" errors like "1.a0" are caught by the Spring form validation APIs before they get to this validator. The "invalid data" message is specified in the `messages.properties` file.

As you can see, this is a very simple, yet very powerful validation framework. You can consult http://static.springsource.org/spring/docs/3.2.x/javadoc-api/org/springframework/validation/ (which applies to Spring 4 as well) to learn more about how this framework works and what other Spring validation APIs are available to meet your specific needs.

Listing 5.12 CreateBillPayValidator.java

```
package com.perfmath.spring.soba.service;
import org.springframework.security.core.context.SecurityContextHolder;
import org.springframework.security.core.userdetails.UserDetails;
import org.springframework.stereotype.Component;
import org.springframework.validation.ValidationUtils;
import org.springframework.validation.Validator;
import org.springframework.validation.Errors;

import org.apache.commons.logging.Log;
import org.apache.commons.logging.LogFactory;
import com.perfmath.spring.soba.model.domain.BillPayment;
import com.perfmath.spring.soba.util.RandomID;

@Component
public class CreateBillPayValidator implements Validator {
    /** Logger for this class and subclasses */
    protected final Log logger = LogFactory.getLog(getClass());
    public boolean supports(Class clazz) {
        return BillPayment.class.isAssignableFrom(clazz);
    }

    public void validate(Object target, Errors errors) {
        BillPayment billPayment = (BillPayment) target;
            ValidationUtils.rejectIfEmptyOrWhitespace(errors, "amount",
                    "required.amount", "amount is required.");
            if (billPayment.getAmount() <= 0.0) {
                errors.rejectValue (“amount”, "invalid.billPayAmount",
"bill pay amount must be > 0");
            }

            billPayment.setId(Long.parseLong(new RandomID(10).getId()));
            billPayment.setScheduleDate(new Timestamp(System.currentTimeMillis()));
            billPayment.setSendDate(new Timestamp(System.currentTimeMillis()));
            billPayment.setStatus("complete");
    }
}
```

Table 5.3 BillPayment form data validation on the *amount* attribute

Input	Comment	Result
1.a0	Letter/number mixed	Error: invalid data
abc	A string	Error: invalid data

1	An integer	Ok ($1.0 was paid)
empty	An empty string	Error: invalid data/amount is required
" "	A two-space string	Error: invalid data/amount is required
1.0 1	A space b/t "0" and "1"	Ok ($1.01 was paid with " " ignored)
1 0.1	A space b/t "1" and "0"	Ok ($10.1 was paid with " " ignored)
10.0.1	Two dots	Error: invalid data
0.0	Zero amount	Error: bill pay amount must be > 0
-10.0	negative amount	Error: bill pay amount must be > 0

5.6.3 JSR-303 Bean Validation

JSR-303 bean validation is a spec about validating domain objects using Java annotations under the package of `javax.validation.constraints`. For example, with the `BillPayment` domain object shown in Listing 5.10, we could have added the following annotations of `@NotNull` and `@Size` to add JSR-303 based validation to limit the length of a required attribute of `description`:

```
...
Import javax.validation.constraints.NotNullNull;
Import javax.validation.constraints.Size;
...
@NotNull
@Size (min=2, max=50)
Private String description;
...
```

Both Spring and Hibernate validators support JSR-303 Bean Validation. However, make a careful decision when choosing which validation mechanism to use with your application. Your application will be less performing and scalable if you have double or even triple validation implemented at all layers for the same validation. Also, keep in mind that it's hard to achieve the same finer granularity with JSR-303 as with Spring validation interface. For example, it might be challenging to use JSR-303 to specify that an entry like "10.0.1" is an invalid input for the `amount` attribute of the bill payment domain object as shown in Table 5.3. Therefore, most of the time, Spring validation interface is a cleaner, more efficient validation mechanism. In a word, try to avoid using JSR-303 bean validation unless you can't do without it.

Before concluding this chapter, we describe how to upgrade the deprecated Spring `SimpleJdbcDAOSupport` used prior to Spring 3.2 next.

5.7 UPGRADING SPRING DEPRECATED SIMPLEJDBCDAOSUPPORT TO 3.2/4 JDBC SUPPORT

If your Spring-based application uses `SimpleJdbcDAOSupport` prior to 3.1, you will get a warning as shown in Figure 5.1 on an Eclipse IDE, indicating that it's deprecated. This is easy to fix, as all you need to do is to remove "`extends SimpleJdbcDaoSupport`" and replace all `getSimpleJdbcTemplate` calls properly. See the upgraded version of this class, Listing 5.4, for more details. Note that the `JdbcBankingTxDAODeprecated.java` class is included in the downloaded *soba4* project as well. Although it is deprecated, it still works.

```
package com.perfmath.spring.soba.model.dao;

import java.sql.ResultSet;
import java.sql.SQLException;
import java.util.ArrayList;
import java.util.List;
import java.util.Map;

import org.springframework.jdbc.core.namedparam.BeanPropertySqlParameterSource;
import org.springframework.jdbc.core.namedparam.SqlParameterSource;
import org.springframework.jdbc.core.simple.ParameterizedRowMapper;
import org.springframework.jdbc.core.simple.SimpleJdbcDaoSupport;

import com.perfmath.spring.soba.model.domain.BankingTx;

public class JdbcBankingTxDaoDeprecated extends SimpleJdbcDaoSupport implements BankingTxDao {
```

Figure 5.1 Deprecated Spring `SimpleJdbcDaoSupport`

5.8 SUMMARY

In this chapter, we explained how the Spring Data Access Framework supports JDBC and Hibernate persistence frameworks. Real SOBA code examples were used to demonstrate the key concepts and technologies associated with JDBC and Hibernate. We also covered the Spring validation interface using the bill pay service. Since SOBA is a fully functioning, integrated sample, you can explore more JDBC and Hibernate features as well as Spring data validations using SOBA as your experimental platform.

The next chapter covers how the RESTful Web Services framework is supported by Spring and applied to SOBA. This is an interesting subject, since RESTful Web Services has become more and more popular for building enterprise applications. Since the JDBC and Hibernate parts are re-usable, they will not be repeated.

RECOMMENDED READING

Study Chapter 13 *Data Access with JDBC* in the *Spring Reference Documentation* to have a more thorough understanding on how Spring supports JDBC. Here is a list of the subjects regarding Spring JDBC support introduced there (highlighted subjects are covered in this chapter):

Spring Reference Documentation / Chapter 13 *Data Access with JDBC*:

13.1 Introduction to Spring Framework JDBC

13.2 Using the JDBC core classes to control basic JDBC processing and error handling

13.3 Controlling database connections

13.4 JDBC batch operations

13.5 Simplifying JDBC operations with the SimpleJdbc classes

13.6 Modeling JDBC operations as Java objects

13.7 Common problems with parameter and data value handling

13.8 Embedded database support

13.9 Initializing a Datasource

You may also want to review *Chapter 14 Object Relational Mapping (ORM) Data Access.* The contents of this chapter are listed below, with those we covered highlighted to help you decide how deep you want to go yourself.

Spring Reference Documentation / Chapter 14 *Object Relational Mapping (ORM) Data Access*:

14.1 Introduction to ORM with Spring

14.2 General ORM Integration Considerations

14.3 Hibernate

14.4 JDO

14.5 JPA

14.6 iBATIS SQL Maps

EXERCISES

5.1 How do you specify the min/max pool sizes for a Spring JDBC connection pool configured as a Spring datasource?

5.2 How do you use Spring's `JdbcTemplate` and `NamedParameterJdbcTemplate` with different types of SQLs?

5.3 What are the benefits of using Hibernate rather than more conventional JDBC?

5.4 Discuss the differences among three different types of data persistence mechanisms (JDBC, Hibernate, and JPA).

5.5 Discuss when you need or don't need an HBM file?

5.6 For the input "1.a0" in Table 5.3, is it caught in the validator or somewhere else?

5.7 How do you validate a Java `BigDecimal` type with Spring's validation framework?

6 Spring RESTful Web Services Framework

RESTful web services refers to a new software architectural style for building software that provides services using the HTTP/HTTPs protocols or any other application layer protocols (note that REST doesn't have to use HTTP). The term REST stands for *REpresentational State Transfer* that originated from Roy Fielding's doctorate dissertation (University of California, Irvine, 2000) titled "*Architectural Styles and the Design of Network-based Software Architectures*." It's claimed that REST has displaced SOAP and WSDL-based web services architectures because of its simplicity and resource-oriented advantages.

Next, a brief introduction to RESTful Web services is given, before we describe how Spring supports RESTful Web Services.

6.1 Introduction to RESTful Web Services

The core concept of REST is *resource*. The most representative format of a resource is a *document*. The content of a document may not matter much from an architectural point of view, although it certainly matters from an application point of view. What makes REST come into the landscape of software design is that a document as a resource is *dynamically* exchanged between a server and a client using the well-understood request/response model. In order for this to happen, a document as a resource must be *addressable* or *identifiable*. How a document is transferred between a client and a server is the main concern of REST. Although REST doesn't have to be exclusively tied to HTTP, it's easier to explain REST with HTTP, as is described next.

6.1.1 Mappings between REST and HTTP

REST calls for four types of operations on resources: CREATE, READ, UPDATE, and DELETE (CRUD), typically from a client to a server. These types of operations happen to be what an HTTP protocol can do well, governed by RFC 2616 which was a Request For Comments (RFC) document on Hypertext Transfer Protocol – HTTP/1.1, authored by Fielding et al (http://tools.ietf.org/pdf/rfc2616.pdf). Table 6.1 maps each of those REST CRUD operations to its corresponding HTTP transfer method. However, REST is beyond just using HTTP or another protocol to achieve those CRUD operations, as is discussed below.

Table 6.1 Mappings between REST and HTTP

REST	HTTP	Comment
CREATE	POST	Create a resource
READ	GET	Retrieve a resource
UPDATE	PUT	Change the state of a resource
DELETE	DELETE	Remove a resource

Note that CRUD operations have been common operations on databases for decades as well. However, the contexts for these operations differ from REST to databases.

6.1.2 RESTful Constraints

The REST style imposes the following constraints at the system level:

- **Client-Server:** This constraint imposes that clients and servers are separated by a uniform interface. Clients are not concerned with, for example, how data is stored on the server, and servers are not concerned with user state so that servers can be simpler and more scalable. Clients and servers can change independently as long as the interface remains intact.
- **Stateless**: This constraint requires that no client context should be stored on the server between requests. However, this is a constraint on the client, not necessarily on the server. Each client request should be self-complete, but the server can be stateful, for example, caching the ID of a client, etc. This makes client/server communications more reliable if network failures occur, and it also helps scalability.
- **Cacheable**: This constraint means that server responses to client requests are cacheable on the client side, which further increases performance and scalability.
- **Transparency**: A client cannot tell or does not need to know whether a response is directly from the end server or an intermediary server. Intermediary servers help improve system performance and scalability by adopting load balancing and providing shared caches.
- **Uniform interface**: The uniform interface simplifies and decouples client/server interactions, which allows each part to evolve independently.
- **Code on demand (optional)**: A server is able to extend/customize temporarily the functionality of a client by transferring logic to it that it can execute.

According to the above constraints, a service is RESTful only if all required constraints are satisfied while leaving code on demand optional. These RESTful constraints are helpful for developing distributed hypermedia systems which can easily collaborate with each other and achieve the desired non-functional requirements such as *performance, scalability, simplicity, reliability, portability, maintainability, modifiability, visibility*, and so on. Retrospectively, these constraints originated from Fielding as he described in his dissertation as follows:

"REST's client–server separation of concerns simplifies component implementation, reduces the complexity of connector semantics, improves the effectiveness of performance tuning, and increases the scalability of pure server components. Layered system constraints allow intermediaries—proxies, gateways, and firewalls—to be introduced at various points in the communication without changing the interfaces between components, thus allowing them to assist in communication translation or improve performance via large-scale, shared caching. REST enables intermediate processing by constraining messages to be self-descriptive: interaction is stateless between requests, standard methods and media types are used to indicate semantics and exchange information, and responses explicitly indicate cacheability."

Next, let's discuss some of the guiding principles for designing RESTful interfaces.

6.1.3 RESTful Interface Design Principles

The uniform interface is the key part of designing any REST interface of a REST service. The following design principles are recommended for maintaining a uniform interface:

- **Separating resource identifications from representations**: With Web-based REST systems, this can be achieved by using URIs (Uniform Resource Identifiers – a string of characters used to identify a resource on the Internet) to identify resources while using payload to contain representations. For example, a server does not send its database connection info, but rather, some HTML, XML or JSON that represents data in its database.
- **Control of resources through representations**: A representation of a resource including any available metadata should be self-complete to allow a client to access the resource on the server, for example, creating or deleting the resource if the client has necessary permission.
- **Self-descriptive messages**: A message should contain sufficient information on how to process the message. One example is to indicate explicitly the type of the message.
- **Hypermedia as the engine of the application state**: The representation returned from the server should provide hypertext links to allow a client to access any related resources.

The above REST interface design principles help the designers of a distributed hypermedia system achieve the goals of: (1) scalability at the system level; (2) simplicity with generic interfaces; (3) flexibility with independent deployment of components or modules; and (4) performance with intermediary components for reducing latency, enforcing security and encapsulating legacy systems.

Next, we explore how Spring supports developing RESTful Web services.

6.2 SPRING'S SUPPORT FOR RESTFUL WEB SERVICES VIA URI TEMPLATE

A RESTful web service uses the HTTP protocol to exchange resources in a manner that is fully compliant to the RESTful constraints as discussed in the previous section. A RESTful web service is also called a RESTful web API. Spring makes developing RESTful web APIs easy by providing a mechanism of URI templates, which is a simple way of identifying a resource.

An example URI template may look like

http://<host:port>/transaction/{id}

In this case, the part in the curly brackets is a variable named *id*. When the variable id is filled with a specific value, the above URI template yields an actual URI. We once touched upon the concept of URI template with an example of /customerId/{customerId} as part of a URI in `CreateCustomerSuccessController` (Listing 4.10). As another example, a URI that represents a transaction in SOBA may look like: https://localhost:8443/soba/transaction/909957218. As is seen, this is conceptually indeed very simple.

To bind a URI with a method, it's required to use `@RequestMapping` in conjunction with `@PathVariable` with one of the following options:

```
// variable name and parameter name same
@RequestMapping (value = "/tx/{txId}", method = RequestMethod.GET)
Public String getTransaction (@PathVariable ("txId") String txId, Model model) {
...
}
// variable name and parameter name different
@RequestMapping (value = "/tx/{txId}", method = RequestMethod.GET)
Public String getTransaction (@PathVariable ("txId") String theTxId, Model model) {
...
}
//multiple variables
@RequestMapping (value = "/account/{accountId}/tx/{txId}", method = RequestMethod.GET)
Public String getTransaction (@PathVariable ("accountId") String accountId, @PathVariable ("txId")
String txId, Model model) {
......
}
```

In the above examples, the method parameters annotated with `@PathVariable` can be of any simple type such as `int`, `long`, `Date`, etc. Spring does type conversion automatically and throws a `TypeMismatchException` if the type mismatches.

Next, let's see some actual REST code on the server side with SOBA.

6.3 SERVER CODE

A RESTful Web API is implemented in SOBA for retrieving a transaction based on a transaction ID (this API is used to implement the *dispute transaction* service). It can be invoked internally with a link in a jsp page as follows:

```
<a href=" /restTx/txId/791111196">791111196</a>
```

In SOBA, this feature is used in `transactionList.jsp`, which is invoked when a customer disputes a transaction. See the second `<td>` element of the following snippet extracted from this jsp file for the embedded link for disputing a transaction:

```
<td> <a href="<c:url value =
"/transactionList.htm?customerId=${model.customerId}&txId=${transaction.transactionId}"/>">
<c:out value="${transaction.transactionId}" />
</a></td>

<td><a href="<c:url value="/restTx/txId/${transaction.transactionId}"/>">
 <c:out value="${transaction.transactionId}" />
</a></td>
```

Note that "/restTx/txId/${transaction.transactionId}" in the second <td> element is a URI template for a RESTful web service while the first <td> element is just a parameterized regular HTTP request. It is part of the *dispute transaction* functionality implemented in SOBA. Refer to Figure 7.5 in the next chapter and you will find two columns: TxId (regular) and TxId (rest), which correspond to the above two parts, respectively (if you are curious about what that c:out means, that's JSTL – JSP Standard Tag Library defined in include.jsp).

When the user clicks the above embedded link in the second <td> element, the RESTful web API getTransactionById implemented in the controller RestTxController is called based on the Spring mapping rule. Listing 6.1 shows how this RESTful web API is implemented in the RestTxController (note the use of Jaxb2Marshaller in the code):

- All URLs starting with /restTx are mapped to the *type (class)* level through @RequestMapping("/restTx") placed prior to the class definition.
- All GET requests with a pattern of /txId/{txId} relative to /restTx are mapped to the method getTransactionById.
- All GET requests with a pattern of /txID/{txId} relative to /restTx are mapped to the method getTransactionByID (note the letter 'D' capitalized). Rather than returning a ModelAndView object as with the getTransactionById method, this method annotated with @ResponseBody returns a BankingTx object. This is necessary for a client that expects a formatted response such as JSON.
- All POST requests are mapped to the method createTransaction.
- All PUT requests are mapped to the method updateTransaction.

Note that in the method createTransaction, Jaxb2Marshaller is used to unmarshall the incoming string source to a transaction object, and then the normal transaction DAO is used to update or insert the banking transaction into the database. Also, note how response body, custom headers, and status are returned to the caller.

A thoughtful reader asked a very good question that since all form controllers we introduced earlier also use the Spring URI template and @RequestMapping in conjunction with @PathVariable like the RestTxController does, does it make all form controllers *RESTful* as well? My answer is "no" according to the RESTful services interface design principles we discussed in §6.1.3:

1. **Separating resource identifications from representations**: The resource identification part is the same, whereas the representation part is different, as form controllers work on Spring forms while the RestTxController uses HTML, XML or JSON documents.

2. **Control of resources through representations**: Form controllers do not provide methods for users to delete objects, whereas the `RestTxController` does.

3. **Self-descriptive messages**: Form controllers have `setupForm` and `submitForm` methods that are internal to the form controllers themselves, while the `RestTxController` doesn't.

4. **Hypermedia as the engine of the application state**: The `RestTxController` provides a link for a user to dispute a transaction (refer to the `XML_VIEW_NAME="disputeTx"` constant above the first @Secured annotation in Listing 6.1), while form controllers do not provide such options for their users.

In summary, using URI template and associated annotations does not determine whether an interface is RESTful. How a resource is identified is only one part of the RESTful services interface design principles. The other parts of *content representation*, *resource control*, *self-descriptiveness of the messages*, and *application state* need to be considered as well.

Listing 6.1 RestTxController.java

```
package com.perfmath.spring.soba.restfulweb;

import java.io.StringReader;
import java.util.HashMap;
import java.util.List;
import java.util.Map;

import javax.xml.transform.Source;
import javax.xml.transform.stream.StreamSource;

import org.springframework.beans.factory.annotation.Autowired;
import org.springframework.http.HttpHeaders;
import org.springframework.http.HttpStatus;
import org.springframework.http.ResponseEntity;
import org.springframework.oxm.jaxb.Jaxb2Marshaller;
import org.springframework.security.annotation.Secured;
import org.springframework.stereotype.Controller;
import org.springframework.transaction.annotation.Transactional;
import org.springframework.web.bind.annotation.PathVariable;
import org.springframework.web.bind.annotation.RequestBody;
import org.springframework.web.bind.annotation.RequestMapping;
import org.springframework.web.bind.annotation.RequestMethod;
import org.springframework.web.bind.annotation.SessionAttributes;
import org.springframework.web.servlet.ModelAndView;
import org.springframework.web.bind.annotation.ResponseBody;

import com.perfmath.spring.soba.model.dao.BankingTxDao;
```

```
import com.perfmath.spring.soba.model.domain.BankingTx;
import com.perfmath.spring.soba.service.AccountManager;
import com.perfmath.spring.soba.service.SobaConfig;
import com.perfmath.spring.soba.service.TxManager;

@Controller
@RequestMapping("/restTx")
@SessionAttributes("restTx")
public class RestTxController implements TxManager {
    private AccountManager accountManager;
    private BankingTxDao bankingTxDao;

    private Jaxb2Marshaller jaxb2Mashaller;

    @Autowired
    public RestTxController(BankingTxDao bankingTxDao,
            Jaxb2Marshaller jaxb2Mashaller) {
        super();
        this.bankingTxDao = bankingTxDao;
        this.jaxb2Mashaller = jaxb2Mashaller;
    }

    public void setJaxb2Mashaller(Jaxb2Marshaller jaxb2Mashaller) {
        this.jaxb2Mashaller = jaxb2Mashaller;
    }

    private static final String XML_VIEW_NAME = "disputeTx";

    @Secured("ROLE_CUST")
    @RequestMapping(value = "/txId/{transactionId}", method = RequestMethod.GET)
    public ModelAndView getTransactionById(@PathVariable String transactionId) {
        String now = (new java.util.Date()).toString();

        Map<String, Object> myModel = new HashMap<String, Object>();
        myModel.put("now", now);

        BankingTx transaction = bankingTxDao.findByTransactionID(transactionId);
        myModel.put("transaction", transaction);
        return new ModelAndView(XML_VIEW_NAME, "model", myModel);
    }
    @Secured("ROLE_CUST")
    @RequestMapping(value = "/txID/{transactionId}", method = RequestMethod.GET)
    public @ResponseBody BankingTx getTransactionByID(@PathVariable String transactionId) {
```

```
        BankingTx transaction = bankingTxDao.findByTransactionID(transactionId);
        return transaction;
    }
    @Secured("ROLE_CUST")
    @RequestMapping(method = RequestMethod.POST)
    public ResponseEntity<String> createTransaction(@RequestBody String body) {
        Source source = new StreamSource(new StringReader(body));
        BankingTx tx = (BankingTx) jaxb2Mashaller.unmarshal(source);
        if (SobaConfig.getDatabaseVendor().equalsIgnoreCase("SQLServer")) {
            double balance = accountManager.updateAccountBalance(tx.getAmount(),
                                    tx.getAccountId());
            tx.setBalance(balance);
        }
        bankingTxDao.insert(tx);
        HttpHeaders responseHeaders = new HttpHeaders ();
        responseHeaders.set ("method", "createTransaction");
        responseHeaders.set ("tx", tx.toString());
        return new ResponseEntity <String> ("Rest createTx succeeded: " + tx.toString(),
                responseHeaders, HttpStatus.CREATED);
    }
    @RequestMapping(method = RequestMethod.PUT, value = "/restTx/txId/{id}")
    public ModelAndView updateTransaction(@RequestBody String body) {
        Source source = new StreamSource(new StringReader(body));
        BankingTx tx = (BankingTx) jaxb2Mashaller.unmarshal(source);
        bankingTxDao.update(tx);
        return new ModelAndView(XML_VIEW_NAME, "object", tx);
    }

    public void setbankingTxDao(BankingTxDao bankingTxDao) {
        this.bankingTxDao = bankingTxDao;
    }

    @Transactional
    @Secured("ROLE_CUST, ROLE_REP")
    public void createTransaction(BankingTx tx) {
        bankingTxDao.insert(tx);
    }

    @Transactional
    @Secured("ROLE_REP")
    public void deleteTransaction(String txId) {
        bankingTxDao.delete(txId);
    }
```

```
    public BankingTx findByTransactionID(String txId) {
        return bankingTxDao.findByTransactionID(txId);
    }

    public List<BankingTx> getTransactions() {
        return bankingTxDao.getTransactionList();
    }

    public List<BankingTx> getTransactions(String customerId) {
        return bankingTxDao.getTransactionList(customerId);
    }

    public void updateTransaction(BankingTx tx) {
        bankingTxDao.update(tx);
    }
}
```

Although this is only one simple example, it's sufficient for demonstrating how Spring supports RESTful web APIs, as all other RESTful web APIs can be developed similarly (note that we have mixed the controller's and manager's responsibilities in this implementation of the `RestTxController` class. In real applications, they should be separated.).

Next, how this RESTful web API can be accessed by an external client is discussed.

6.4 CLIENT CODE

In addition to invoking a REST service via an embedded link in a JSP file as shown in the previous section, Listing 6.2 shows how the same RESTful web API can be accessed in a standalone program external to the server hosting the application (in this case, SOBA). It's indeed as simple as promised. The client program uses Apache HTTP client API. Note the following steps involved with using the `getTransactionById` and `createTransaction` methods of the `RestTxController`:

- **Loading SSL certificate**: Since SOBA is secured with SSL and should be accessed with the secure HTTP protocol (HTTPS), the first step is to set up SSL. Refer to §2.4 about how to create an SSL certificate for Tomcat. Also, note that if you want to test it out on your machine, you need to change the hard-coded path to point to your Tomcat SSL certificate.
- **Setting security provider**: The second step is to set up a security provider to get prepared for authentication.
- **Setting login credentials**: In this step, make sure proper `hostname`, HTTPS `port`, `username` and `password` are entered.
- **Making the REST web API calls**: Note the URI used in creating an HttpGet object. Also note the statement `httpget.addHeader ("Accept", "application/json");`. The acronym *JSON* stands for *JavaScript Object Notation*. It's a format for representing simple data structures and associative

array (map, dictionary, etc.). As an alternative to XML, it is primarily used to transmit data between a web server and a client.

Listing 6.2 RestWebAPITest.java

```
package com.perfmath.spring.soba.test;

import java.io.BufferedReader;
import java.io.File;
import java.io.FileInputStream;
import java.io.InputStreamReader;
import java.security.KeyStore;
import java.security.Security;
import java.sql.Timestamp;

import org.apache.http.Header;
import org.apache.http.HttpEntity;
import org.apache.http.HttpResponse;
import org.apache.http.auth.AuthScope;
import org.apache.http.auth.UsernamePasswordCredentials;
import org.apache.http.client.methods.HttpGet;
import org.apache.http.client.methods.HttpPost;
import org.apache.http.conn.scheme.Scheme;
import org.apache.http.conn.ssl.SSLSocketFactory;
import org.apache.http.impl.client.DefaultHttpClient;
import org.apache.http.entity.StringEntity;

import com.perfmath.spring.soba.util.RandomID;

public class RestWebAPITest {

    public final static void main(String[] args) throws Exception {
        DefaultHttpClient httpclient = new DefaultHttpClient();
        // SSL setup begin
        KeyStore trustStore = KeyStore.getInstance(KeyStore.getDefaultType());
        FileInputStream instream = new FileInputStream(new File(
                "C:\\Users\\henry\\.keystore"));
        try {
            trustStore.load(instream, "changeit".toCharArray());
        } finally {
            instream.close();
        }
```

```
SSLSocketFactory socketFactory = new SSLSocketFactory(trustStore);
Scheme sch = new Scheme("https", socketFactory, 8443);
httpclient.getConnectionManager().getSchemeRegistry().register(sch);
// SSL setup end

// set security provider
String secProviderName = "com.sun.crypto.provider.SunJCE";
java.security.Provider secProvider = (java.security.Provider) Class
        .forName(secProviderName).newInstance();
Security.addProvider(secProvider);

httpclient.getCredentialsProvider().setCredentials(
        new AuthScope("localhost", 8443),
        new UsernamePasswordCredentials("user1001", "sobauser"));

// issue REST web API call
HttpGet httpget = new HttpGet(
        "https://localhost:8443/soba/restTx/txId/27661704");
httpget.addHeader("Accept", "application/json");
System.out.println("Executing request: " + httpget.getRequestLine());

HttpResponse response = httpclient.execute(httpget);
HttpEntity entity = response.getEntity();

System.out.println("----------------------------------------");
System.out.println(response.getStatusLine());

if (entity != null) {
    System.out.println("Response content length: "
            + entity.getContentLength());
    System.out.println("Response content type: "
            + entity.getContentType().getValue());
    BufferedReader reader = new BufferedReader(new InputStreamReader(
            entity.getContent()));
    String line = reader.readLine();
    while (line != null) {
        System.out.println(line);
        line = reader.readLine();
    }
}
if (entity != null) {
    entity.consumeContent();
}
```

```
        createRestTx(httpclient);
        // shut down the connection manager
        httpclient.getConnectionManager().shutdown();
    }

    public static void createRestTx(DefaultHttpClient httpclient)
            throws Exception {
        StringEntity input = new StringEntity(composeATxInXML());
        HttpPost postUrl = new HttpPost("https://localhost:8443/soba/restTx");

        postUrl.addHeader("Content-Type", "application/xml");
        postUrl.setEntity(input);
        HttpResponse response = httpclient.execute(postUrl);
        System.out.println("Response status: " + response.getStatusLine());
        System.out.println("All response headers ----- begin ----------");
        Header[] httpHeaders = response.getAllHeaders();
        for (Header header : httpHeaders) {
            System.out.println ("header: name = " + header.getName() + ",
           value = " + header.getValue());
        }
        System.out.println("All response headers ----- end ----------");
        BufferedReader reader = new BufferedReader(new InputStreamReader(
                (response.getEntity().getContent())));
        String output;
        System.out.println("Response body ----- begin ----------");

        while ((output = reader.readLine()) != null) {
            System.out.println(output);
        }
        System.out.println("Response body ----- end ----------");
    }
    public static String composeATxInXML() {
        String txId = (new RandomID(9)).getId();
        Timestamp ts = new Timestamp(System.currentTimeMillis());
        String newTx = "<bankingtx>" + "<transactionId>" + txId
                + "</transactionId>" + "<transDate>" + ts + "</transDate>"
                + "<type>rest</type>" + "<initiator>rest</initiator>"
                + "<description>rest test</description>"
                + "<amount>1.23</amount>" + "<balance>0</balance>"
                + "<accountId>954135227</accountId>"
                + "<status>pending</status>" + "</bankingtx>";
        return newTx;
    }
```

}

You can run this program by first building SOBA with Maven and then changing to the project's *target\soba-4\WEB-INF\classes* directory and executing the following command (type all on one line):

```
java -cp ..\lib\httpclient-4.1.2.jar;..\lib\httpcore-4.1.2.jar;..\lib\commons-logging-1.1.jar;.
com.perfmath.spring.soba.test.RestWebAPITest
```

After a successful execution, the above program yielded the following output for both `getTransactionByID` and `createTransaction` RESTful Web Services API calls to the `RestTxController` displayed in Listing 6.1. Note the `json` document at the end of this output (if you want to try the above program on your machine, make sure you replace the `txID` 27661704 and the `accountId` 954135227 with your own existing in your database.)

```
----------------------------------------
HTTP/1.1 200 OK
Response content length: -1
Response content type: application/json;charset=UTF-8
{"model":{"transaction":{"id":27661704,"type":"fee","description":"acl tx
testing","status":"complete","accountId":"954135227","amount":-
10.0,"transactionId":27661704,"balance":340.0,"transDate":1334986244000,"initiator":"system"},"now
":"Tue Apr 24 20:20:51 PDT 2012"}}
*** compose a new tx ***
Response status: HTTP/1.1 201 Created
All response headers ----- begin ----------
header: name = Server,    value = Apache-Coyote/1.1
header: name = Pragma,      value = no-cache
header: name = Expires,  value = Thu, 01 Jan 1970 00:00:00 GMT
header: name = Cache-Control,  value = no-cache
header: name = Cache-Control,  value = no-store
header: name = method,      value = createTransaction
header: name = tx,     value = transactionId: 62565488;accountId: 954135227;amount: 1.23
header: name = Content-Type,   value = text/plain;charset=ISO-8859-1
header: name = Content-Length,     value = 82
header: name = Date,      value = Wed, 25 Apr 2012 03:20:51 GMT
All response headers ----- end ----------
Response body ----- begin ----------
Rest createTx succeeded: transactionId: 62565488;accountId: 954135227;amount: 1.23
Response body ----- end ----------
```

You can also use Spring `RestTemplate` in the client in place of the Apache HttpClient API as shown above. Refer to §21.10 in the Spring Framework reference documentation for more information on how to access RESTful services on the client the *Spring-way*.

6.5 SUMMARY

In this chapter, we covered the Spring RESTful Web Services Framework. After a brief introduction to the core concepts and design principles of RESTful web Services in general, we demonstrated how Spring supports RESTful web services within its own framework. The major mechanism of the Spring RESTful Web Services Framework is through *URI Template* in conjunction with the `@RequestMapping` annotation. We illustrated how Spring RESTful Web Services Framework is used to implement some of the SOBA services from both the server and client perspectives.

The next chapter describes the Spring Security Framework, which is an indispensable part of every enterprise Web application.

RECOMMENDED READING

The *Spring Reference Documentation* does not contain a lot about RESTful web Services design except mentioning using its *URI template*, `@RequestMapping` annotation, and the `@PathVariable` annotation for the server side programming and the `RestTemplate` class for the client side programming. It only provides a means for identifying resources and the rest is up to the designers to decide how to design and implement RESTful web services using other technologies. A good text on RESTful web services design is by B. Burke, *RESTful Java with JAX-RS*, O'Reilly, 2010.

EXERCISES

6.1 Explain how those RESTful design principles are followed with the `RestTxController.java` class.

6.2 Explain the pros and cons with the use of Spring's `RestTemplate` class for client side programming associated with consuming RESTful web services.

7 Spring Security Framework

Security is a serious issue that every enterprise application must enforce one way or the other. It's a broad topic that we won't be able to cover in detail here. Instead, I'll help you gain a basic understanding of this subject using the code/configuration examples implemented in SOBA. Let's start with some basic concepts first in the next section.

7.1 Basic Concepts

Some basic concepts related to securing enterprise applications in general include the following:

- **Authentication**: This is the process of verifying the identity of a principal against the credentials provided. It is similar to an airport security check-in process: you show a picture ID and your boarding ticket to prove you are who you are. Then (mostly) you are allowed to pass. Two most commonly encountered types of authentication methods are:
  - *Form-based login authentication:*. In this case, a login form is used to authenticate a user. This is the login authentication type used with SOBA.
  - *HTTP Basic authentication:* In this case, user credentials are embedded in HTTP request headers. It typically is used for authenticating requests made from remoting protocols and web services. The REST client example presented in the previous chapter uses this type of authentication.
- **Authorization**: Note that authentication and authorization are two different concepts. Authorization is the process of determining and granting authorities to an authenticated user or principal for accessing intended resources. Authorities typically are granted in terms of *roles*. You might have noticed some entities like `ROLE_CUST`, `ROLE_REP`, `ROLE_ADMIN`, etc., in some of the code snippets in the previous chapters. These are the roles defined in SOBA for authorizing users. Using the airport example, you are authenticated through the security gate to enter the boarding area does not mean that you can board any plane – you are authorized to board the plane you are checked in for only.
- **A Principal**: A principal is an object to be authenticated, which could be a user, an application, or a device.

- **Access Control**: This is a process to determine *who can access* a resource in question. It's checked by comparing the permission bits of a resource with the roles of the principal attempting to access the resource. This subject is discussed in the ACL (Access Control List) section of this chapter.

Next, let's see how Spring Security Framework works in the domain context of SOBA.

7.2 CONFIGURING SECURITY IN SPRING SECURITY FRAMEWORK

To avoid coding security extensively at low levels, Spring Security Framework enables a developer to configure security in external XML configuration files, supplemented with annotations in Java source code as we have seen in the previous chapters. In this section, we focus on explaining how to configure security in external XML configuration files.

7.2.1 Security Configured in the web.xml File

The entry to invoking Spring security API for a Web application is defined in the `web.xml` file of the application. Refer back to Listing 4.1 for SOBA's `web.xml` file and note the following two XML elements defined there:

```
<filter>
   <filter-name>springSecurityFilterChain</filter-name>
<filter-class>
      org.springframework.web.filter.DelegatingFilterProxy
</filter-class>
</filter>
<filter-mapping>
   <filter-name>springSecurityFilterChain</filter-name>
   <url-pattern>/*</url-pattern>
</filter-mapping>
```

Here, when the login page of SOBA is accessed by a user, the Spring security filter named `springSecurityFilterChain` is invoked, which is a `DelegatingFilterProxy` security bean that delegates security checking to other Spring security beans. The URL pattern of "/*" associated with the filter `springSecurityFilterChain` specifies at the system level that any user who wants to access any page of this web application needs to be authenticated first. Web security authentication is configured using the `<http>` element, as is discussed next.

7.2.2 Security Configured in the soba-security.xml File

This section explains some of the most fundamental Spring security features as applied to SOBA. These features are configured in the `soba-security.xml` file as shown in Listing 7.1 below. The ACL part is omitted as it will be presented and discussed in the next section when we discuss ACL.

The `soba-security.xml` reflects the measures taken to secure SOBA as follows:

- **Secured-annotations**: First, locate the section of `<global-method-security ...>` in Listing 7.1 and note the specification of `secured-annotations = "enabled"`. This means that you can put something like `@Secured ("ROLE_CUST", "ROLE_REP")` prior to a method of a class to make that method secured. We'll see such examples in the next section when we discuss ACLs.
- **HTTPS channel required**: Locate the `<http>` section in Listing 7.1 and note the line of `<intercept-url pattern="/**" requires-channel="https"/>`. This entry specifies that accessing SOBA is enforced with the secure HTTP protocol of HTTPS. The section `<concurrency-control ...>` specifies that at most 10 sessions can be opened by a same user. It can be set to 1 so that when a user is logged in, the second login with the same user credentials will kick off the first user so that the first user would get alerted.
- **Authentication types**: The two authentication types of `basic` and `form-based` are also specified in the `<http>` section through the `<http-basic>` and `<custom-filter>` XML elements, respectively. However, they are configured outside the <http> section separately. We'll describe each of them shortly.
- **Authentication manager**: Locate the `<authentication-manager>` section in Listing 7.1 and note the `jdbc-user-service` configured for user authentication. A table named `USERS` is used for storing user's credentials, as described in Chapter 2 (The table `USERS` is implemented as a `SYNONYM` in ORACLE, and as a `VIEW` in MySQL and SQL Server). Consult Exercise 7.6 on how to enable the use of encrypted password for user authentication.
- **Spring security filter chain**: Locate the line of `<beans:bean id = "springSecurityFilterChain" ...>` section in Listing 7.1 and note that the following three filter chains are defined (keep in mind that the order in which the filters are specified matters):
  - Images require no filters as indicated by `filters="none"` for this URL pattern.
  - URLs with `/rest*/**` are authenticated with the HTTP basic method as indicated by one of the filters specified with the `filters` property - `basicAuthenticationFilter`. This pattern is for external invocation of RESTful web APIs.
  - URLs with all other patterns are authenticated with form-based authentication as indicated by one of the filters specified with the `filters` property - `formLoginFilter` for the URL pattern "/**".

- **Form-based authentication:** Locate the section for form-based authentication in Listing 7.1 and note the properties of the `defaulTargetURL`, `filterProcessesUrl`, `loginFormUrl`, `forceHttps`, and `errorPage`, etc.
- **HTTP basic authentication:** Locate the section for basic type of authentication in Listing 7.1 and note that the realm property is set to `perfmath.com`. You can specify your own realm here.
- **Access decision manager:** The outcome of an authentication action is determined by voting policies. In the access decision manager section, RoleVoter and AuthenticatedVoter are specified. Each of these two voting mechanisms are described as follows:
  - *RoleVote:* This method votes on an access control decision based on a user's *roles*. The access is not granted unless the user has all required roles.
  - *AuthenticatedVoter:* This method votes on an access control decision based on a user's authentication level. It votes to grant the access if the user's authentication level is equal or exceeds the required authentication levels. The authentication levels that Spring supports are:

IS_AUTHENTICATED_FULLY, IS_AUTHENTICATED_REMEMBERED, and IS_AUTHENTICATED_ANONYMOUSLY.

- **Filter security interceptor:** Locate the <beans:bean id = "filterSecurityInterceptor" ..> section in Listing 7.1 and note the intercept-url patterns specified there. Each of these URL patterns has a special intention as is denoted there. For example, the admin page can only be accessed by a user with the ROLE_ADMIN role. In addition, unlike the *login.jsp* file and the *images* folder the RESTful Web APIs cannot be accessed anonymously. For a real application, it might be necessary to divide further.

We have seen how to secure URL access using intercept-url patterns and secure methods using annotated security. Next, let's take a look at how Spring security can be implemented in views.

Listing 7.1 soba-security.xml (ACL part moved to Listing 7.2)

```
<beans:beans xmlns="http://www.springframework.org/schema/security"
    xmlns:beans="http://www.springframework.org/schema/beans"
    xmlns:xsi="http://www.w3.org/2001/XMLSchema-instance"
    xmlns:util="http://www.springframework.org/schema/util"
    xmlns:security="http://www.springframework.org/schema/security"
    xsi:schemaLocation="http://www.springframework.org/schema/beans
        http://www.springframework.org/schema/beans/spring-beans.xsd
        http://www.springframework.org/schema/security
        http://www.springframework.org/schema/security/spring-security.xsd">
<global-method-security pre-post-annotations="enabled"
        secured-annotations="enabled">
        <expression-handler ref="expressionHandler" />
    </global-method-security>
    <http use-expressions="true">
        <intercept-url pattern="/**" requires-channel="https" />
        <http-basic />
        <custom-filter position="FORM_LOGIN_FILTER" ref="formLoginFilter" />
        <session-management>
            <concurrency-control max-sessions="10"
                error-if-maximum-exceeded="true" />
        </session-management>
        <logout logout-success-url="/logoff.jsp" />
    </http>
    <authentication-manager alias="authenticationManager">
        <authentication-provider>
            <jdbc-user-service data-source-ref="dataSource"
                users-by-username-query="SELECT username, password,
                                enabled FROM users WHERE username = ?" />
        </authentication-provider>
    </authentication-manager>
```

```
<beans:bean id="springSecurityFilterChain"
    class="org.springframework.security.web.FilterChainProxy">
    <filter-chain-map path-type="ant">
        <filter-chain pattern="/images/**" filters="none" />
        <filter-chain pattern="/rest*/**"
            filters="
            securityContextPersistenceFilterWithASCFalse,
            basicAuthenticationFilter,
            exceptionTranslationFilter,
            filterSecurityInterceptor" />
        <filter-chain pattern="/**"
            filters="
            securityContextPersistenceFilterWithASCTrue,
            formLoginFilter,
            exceptionTranslationFilter,
            filterSecurityInterceptor" />
    </filter-chain-map>
</beans:bean>
<beans:bean id="securityContextPersistenceFilterWithASCFalse"
class="org.springframework.security.web.context.SecurityContextPersistenceFilter">
</beans:bean>
<beans:bean id="securityContextPersistenceFilterWithASCTrue"
class="org.springframework.security.web.context.SecurityContextPersistenceFilter">
</beans:bean>
<!-- form based authentication -->
<beans:bean id="formLoginFilter" class="org.springframework.security.web.authentication.
        UsernamePasswordAuthenticationFilter">
    <beans:property name="authenticationManager" ref="authenticationManager" />
    <beans:property name="authenticationSuccessHandler">
    <beans:bean class="org.springframework.security.web.authentication.
        SimpleUrlAuthenticationSuccessHandler">
    <beans:property name="defaultTargetUrl"
        value="/loginBroker.htm"></beans:property>
    </beans:bean>
    </beans:property>
    <beans:property name="filterProcessesUrl" value="/j_spring_security_check" />
</beans:bean>
<beans:bean id="formAuthenticationEntryPoint"
class="org.springframework.security.web.authentication.LoginUrlAuthenticationEntryPoint">
    <beans:property name="loginFormUrl" value="/login.jsp" />
    <beans:property name="forceHttps" value="true" />
</beans:bean>
<beans:bean id="formExceptionTranslationFilter"
```

```
        class="org.springframework.security.web.access.ExceptionTranslationFilter">
        <beans:property name="authenticationEntryPoint" ref="formAuthenticationEntryPoint" />
        <beans:property name="accessDeniedHandler" ref="formAccessDeniedHandler" />
    </beans:bean>
    <beans:bean id="formAccessDeniedHandler"
        class="org.springframework.security.web.access.AccessDeniedHandlerImpl">
        <beans:property name="errorPage" value="/login.jsp?error=true" />
    </beans:bean>
    <!-- basic authentication -->
    <beans:bean id="basicAuthenticationFilter"
    class="org.springframework.security.web.authentication.www.BasicAuthenticationFilter">
        <beans:property name="authenticationManager">
            <beans:ref bean="authenticationManager" />
        </beans:property>
        <beans:property name="authenticationEntryPoint">
            <beans:ref bean="basicAuthenticationEntryPoint" />
        </beans:property>
    </beans:bean>
    <beans:bean id="basicAuthenticationEntryPoint"
    class="org.springframework.security.web.authentication.www.BasicAuthenticationEntryPoint">
        <beans:property name="realmName" value="perfmath.com" />
    </beans:bean>

    <beans:bean id="basicExceptionTranslationFilter"
        class="org.springframework.security.web.access.ExceptionTranslationFilter">
        <beans:property name="authenticationEntryPoint" ref="basicAuthenticationEntryPoint" />
        <beans:property name="accessDeniedHandler" ref="basicAccessDeniedHandler" />
    </beans:bean>
    <beans:bean id="basicAccessDeniedHandler"
        class="org.springframework.security.web.access.AccessDeniedHandlerImpl">
    </beans:bean>

    <beans:bean id="accessDecisionManager"
        class="org.springframework.security.access.vote.AffirmativeBased">
        <beans:property name="decisionVoters">
        <beans:list>
        <beans:bean class="org.springframework.security.access.vote.RoleVoter" />
            <beans:bean
              class="org.springframework.security.access.vote.AuthenticatedVoter" />
        </beans:list>
        </beans:property>
    </beans:bean>
```

```
    <beans:bean id="filterSecurityInterceptor"
    class="org.springframework.security.web.access.intercept.FilterSecurityInterceptor">
        <beans:property name="authenticationManager" ref="authenticationManager" />
        <beans:property name="accessDecisionManager" ref="accessDecisionManager" />
        <beans:property name="securityMetadataSource">
            <filter-security-metadata-source>
            <intercept-url pattern="/rest*/**"
                access="ROLE_REST, ROLE_CUST, ROLE_REP)" />
            <intercept-url pattern="/login.jsp"
                access="ROLE_ANONYMOUS,ROLE_CUST, ROLE_REP, ROLE_ADMIN)" />
            <intercept-url pattern="/images/**"
                access="ROLE_ANONYMOUS,ROLE_CUST, ROLE_REP, ROLE_ADMIN)" />
            <intercept-url pattern="/admin.htm*" access="ROLE_ADMIN" />
            <intercept-url pattern="/**"
                access="ROLE_CUST, ROLE_REP, ROLE_ADMIN)" />
            </filter-security-metadata-source>
        </beans:property>
    </beans:bean>
<beans:bean id="expressionHandler"
class="org.springframework.security.access.expression.method.
DefaultMethodSecurityExpressionHandler">
        <beans:property name="permissionEvaluator" ref="permissionEvaluator" />
    </beans:bean>
    <beans:bean id="permissionEvaluator"
        class="org.springframework.security.acls.AclPermissionEvaluator">
        <beans:constructor-arg ref="aclService" />
    </beans:bean>
    <! - - ACL setup. See Section 7.4 -- >
</beans:beans>
```

7.3 IMPLEMENTING SPRING SECURITY IN VIEWS

The resources such as embedded URLs in `jsp` pages can be protected similarly using the Spring Security Framework. The procedure is as follows:

- Enable access to Spring security `jsp` tags. At the beginning of a `jsp` page, add the line `<%@ taglib prefix="security" uri="http://www.springframework.org/security/tags" %>`.
- Then use the `security:authorize` jsp tag to limit access to a URL. For example, the following JSP snippet specifies that only a rep can access the `manageTx` URL:

```
<security:authorize ifAnyGranted="ROLE_REP">
<td> <a href="<c:url value="loginBroker"/>">Rep Console</a>
</td>
<td/>
```

```
<td> <a hre f="<c:url
value="manageTx.htm?customerId=${customerId}&accountId=
${accountId}"/>">Manage Transactions</a> </td>
</security:authorize>
```

The above example is an excerpt from the `activityList.jsp` file of SOBA to limit access to the *Rep Console* to *reps* only. The other option is to use `ifNotGranted` in place of `ifAnyGranted` to handle certain situations more pertinently.

We wrap up this chapter with a discussion on how access control is enforced in Spring and applied to SOBA domain objects next.

7.4 SPRING ACL APPLIED TO SOBA

For complicated enterprise applications, in addition to securing web pages, it's also necessary to control access at the domain object level. For example, a customer should not be allowed to view the transactions of other customers; also, a customer should not be allowed to reverse any of his own transactions – only an authorized bank personnel is allowed to do so. Such requirements demand applying security at the domain object level.

In this section, using the `BANKINGTX` domain object of SOBA, we demonstrate how Spring domain object security can be enforced based on the concept of *Access Control List* (ACL). The same approach applies to other domain objects of SOBA or any other enterprise applications as well. Here, it's necessary to distinguish the context of the term *transaction* between two different situations: one is a banking *business transaction* like *deposit*, *withdraw*, *bill payment*, etc., in SOBA's context, and the other is the usual definition of "*either all or none*" in a non-business or database-specific context. Which one is implied should be clear according to the proper context in question.

Since ACL entries are maintained in separate tables from the domain objects, let's first get familiar with those ACL tables we discussed in Chapter 2.

7.4.1 ACL Tables

Spring ACL requires the following four ACL tables to be created in a relational database (refer to Section 2.3 for how those tables are created in MySQL):

- **ACL_SID:** The ACL_SID table is designed to uniquely identify any principal or authority in the system ("SID" stands for "security identity"). It has only three columns: an ID, a textual representation of the SID, and a flag to indicate whether the textual representation refers to a principal name or a `GrantedAuthority`. Thus, there is a single row for each unique principal or `GrantedAuthority`. When used in the context of receiving permission, a `SID` is generally called a *recipient*.
- **ACL_CLASS**: The ACL_CLASS table is designed to uniquely identify any domain object class in the system. It has only two columns: an ID and a Java class name. Thus, there is a single row for each unique class for which ACL permissions will be created.

- **ACL_OBJECT_IDENTITY**: The ACL_OBJECT_IDENTITY table stores information for each unique domain object instance in the system. It has columns including an ID, a foreign key to the ACL_CLASS table, a unique identifier to indicate which ACL_CLASS instance the information is for, the parent, a foreign key to the ACL_SID table to represent the owner of the domain object instance, and whether ACL entries are allowed to inherit from any parent ACL. There is a single row for every domain object instance for which relevant ACL permissions are created.
- **ACL_ENTRY**: The ACL_ENTRY table stores the individual permissions assigned to each recipient. It has columns including a foreign key to the ACL_OBJECT_IDENTITY, the recipient (i.e., a foreign key to ACL_SID), whether auditing succeeded, and the integer bit mask that represents the actual permission being granted or denied. There is a single row for every recipient that receives permission to work on a domain object.

Next, let's see how to configure Spring ACL.

7.4.2 Configuring Spring ACL

To make it more manageable, one can have all ACL related configuration settings contained in one XML file, and in our case, it would be `soba-acl.xml` file. Then, this `soba-acl.xml` file can be added in the `web.xml` file under `contextConfigLocation`. However, for SOBA, the ACL configuration settings are placed in the `soba-security.xml` file, as is shown in Listing 7.2 below. That is because ACL is really a part of the entire security of an application, and it's more logical to place ACL settings with other security settings in one file.

The core bean here is an ACL service. The Spring Security Framework has two ACL interfaces: `AclService` that defines methods for reading ACLs, and `MutableAclService` that defines methods for creating, updating and deleting ACLs. The corresponding implementations of those two interfaces are `JdbcAclService` and `JdbcMutableAclService`. With SOBA, we use the `MutableAclService`, since we need to perform not only READ but also CREATE, UPDATE and DELETE operations.

Listing 7.2 ACL part of soba-security.xml

```
<beans:beans xmlns="http://www.springframework.org/schema/security"
    xmlns:beans="http://www.springframework.org/schema/beans"
    xmlns:xsi="http://www.w3.org/2001/XMLSchema-instance"
    xmlns:util="http://www.springframework.org/schema/util"
    xmlns:security="http://www.springframework.org/schema/security"
    xsi:schemaLocation="http://www.springframework.org/schema/beans
    http://www.springframework.org/schema/beans/spring-beans.xsd
        http://www.springframework.org/schema/util
            http://www.springframework.org/schema/util/spring-util.xsd
            http://www.springframework.org/schema/security
            http://www.springframework.org/schema/security/spring-security.xsd">
    <global-method-security pre-post-annotations="enabled"
        secured-annotations="enabled">
        <expression-handler ref="expressionHandler" />
```

```
    </global-method-security>
    <! - - Security setup ... See Listing 7.1 -- >
    <!-- ACL start: ACL SERVICE DEFINITIONS -->
    <beans:bean id="aclCache"
        class="org.springframework.security.acls.domain.EhCacheBasedAclCache">
        <beans:constructor-arg>
        <beans:bean class="org.springframework.cache.ehcache.EhCacheFactoryBean">
        <beans:property name="cacheManager">
        <beans:bean  class="org.springframework.cache.ehcache.EhCacheManagerFactoryBean" />
        </beans:property>
        <beans:property name="cacheName" value="aclCache" />
        </beans:bean>
        </beans:constructor-arg>
    </beans:bean>

<beans:bean id="lookupStrategy"
        class="org.springframework.security.acls.jdbc.BasicLookupStrategy">
        <beans:constructor-arg ref="dataSource" />
        <beans:constructor-arg ref="aclCache" />
        <beans:constructor-arg>
        <beans:bean
            class="org.springframework.security.acls.domain.AclAuthorizationStrategyImpl">
            <beans:constructor-arg>
            <beans:list>
            <beans:bean class="org.springframework.security.core.authority.GrantedAuthorityImpl">
            <beans:constructor-arg value="ROLE_ADMIN" />
            </beans:bean>
            <beans:bean class="org.springframework.security.core.authority.GrantedAuthorityImpl">
            <beans:constructor-arg value="ROLE_ADMIN" />
            </beans:bean>
            <beans:bean  class="org.springframework.security.core.authority.GrantedAuthorityImpl">
                <beans:constructor-arg value="ROLE_ADMIN" />
                </beans:bean>
                </beans:list>
                </beans:constructor-arg>
            </beans:bean>
        </beans:constructor-arg>
        <beans:constructor-arg>
        <beans:bean class="org.springframework.security.acls.domain.ConsoleAuditLogger" />
        </beans:constructor-arg>
        </beans:bean>
        <beans:bean id="aclService" class="org.springframework.security.acls.jdbc.
                JdbcMutableAclService">
```

```
        <beans:constructor-arg ref="dataSource" />
        <beans:constructor-arg ref="lookupStrategy" />
        <beans:constructor-arg ref="aclCache" />
        <beans:property name="sidIdentityQuery"
            value=" SELECT max(id) FROM acl_sid " />
        <beans:property name="classIdentityQuery"
            value=" SELECT max(id) FROM acl_class " />
    </beans:bean>
</beans:beans>
```

The aclService as shown above requires three constructor arguments: (1) a dataSource for defining a JDBC source as configured in the soba-services.xml file; (2) a lookupStrategy for performing lookup for an ACL service; and (3) an aclCache for caching ACLs (in this case, a third-party product named Ehcache is used).

Note that the lookupStrategy specified above indicates that only a user who has the ROLE_ADMIN role can modify an ACL. Note also that the aclService specifies a property of sidIdentityQuery and another property of classIdentityQuery. In MySQL and SQL Server, these two id's are implemented with auto-incremental IDs, so the largest ID value would be the current ID value; but in Oracle, they are implemented with SEQUENCE and the actual ID for each query is specified differently, for example, "SELECT ACL_SID_ID_SEQ.CURRVAL FROM DUAL". For PostgreSQL, these two queries are implemented with the pg_get_serial_sequence function as discussed in Chapter 2.

The next step is to implement create/update/delete ACLs in a domain object service, as is discussed next.

7.4.3 Maintaining ACLs for SOBA Domain Objects

In SOBA's context, the ACLs are applied to managing banking transactions of customers. Listing 7.3 shows the SimpleAclTxManager.java class, which has the following methods:

- **createTransaction (BankingTx tx):** After a transaction is posted, the addPermission method is called to insert access control entries (ACEs) for the transaction created (you can verify this by identifying the acl.insertAce (...) statement in the addPermission method, in which the updateAcl method of the mutableAclService also is called to update the ACL). The addPermission method is called three times: once for the principal (the customer in this case) for the READ permission, and twice for the granted authority with the role of ROLE_REP for ADMINISTRATION and DELETE permissions, respectively.
- **disputeTransaction (String txId):** In this case, a zero amount transaction is inserted into the customer's account with the transaction status set to "*disputed.*"
- **reverseTransaction (String txId):** In this reverseTransaction method, the amount of the disputed transaction is credited back to the customer's.

Listing 7.3 SimpleAclTxManager.java

```
package com.perfmath.spring.soba.service;
```

```
import java.sql.Timestamp;
import java.util.List;

import org.springframework.security.access.annotation.Secured;
import org.springframework.security.acls.domain.BasePermission;
import org.springframework.security.acls.domain.GrantedAuthoritySid;
import org.springframework.security.acls.domain.ObjectIdentityImpl;
import org.springframework.security.acls.domain.PrincipalSid;
import org.springframework.security.acls.model.AccessControlEntry;
import org.springframework.security.acls.model.MutableAcl;
import org.springframework.security.acls.model.MutableAclService;
import org.springframework.security.acls.model.NotFoundException;
import org.springframework.security.acls.model.ObjectIdentity;
import org.springframework.security.acls.model.Permission;
import org.springframework.security.acls.model.Sid;
import org.springframework.security.core.context.SecurityContextHolder;
import org.springframework.security.core.userdetails.UserDetails;
import org.springframework.transaction.annotation.Transactional;
import com.perfmath.spring.soba.model.dao.AccountDao;
import com.perfmath.spring.soba.model.dao.AclBankingTxDao;
import com.perfmath.spring.soba.model.dao.LoginUserDao;
import com.perfmath.spring.soba.model.domain.BankingTx;
import com.perfmath.spring.soba.util.RandomID;

public class SimpleAclTxManager implements AclTxManager {
    private AclBankingTxDao aclBankingTxDao;
    private LoginUserDao loginUserDao;
    private AccountDao accountDao;
    private AccountManager accountManager;
    private MutableAclService mutableAclService;
    public LoginUserDao getLoginUserDao() {
        return loginUserDao;
    }

    public void setLoginUserDao(LoginUserDao loginUserDao) {
        this.loginUserDao = loginUserDao;
    }

    public AccountDao getAccountDao() {
        return accountDao;
    }

    public void setAccountDao(AccountDao accountDao) {
```

```
        this.accountDao = accountDao;
    }
    public void setAccountManager(AccountManager accountManager) {
        this.accountManager = accountManager;
    }
    public MutableAclService getMutableAclService() {
        return mutableAclService;
    }

    public void setMutableAclService(MutableAclService mutableAclService) {
        this.mutableAclService = mutableAclService;
    }

    @Secured("AFTER_ACL_READ")
    public BankingTx findByTransactionID(String txId) {
        return aclBankingTxDao.findByTransactionID(txId);
    }

    @Secured("AFTER_ACL_COLLECTION_READ")
    public List<BankingTx> getTransactions() {
        return aclBankingTxDao.getTransactionList();
    }

    public void updateTransaction(BankingTx tx) {
        aclBankingTxDao.update(tx);
    }

    @Transactional
    @Secured({"ROLE_REP", "ACL_TRANSACTION_DELETE", "ACL_TX_DELETE"})

    public void deleteTransaction(String txId) {

    aclBankingTxDao.delete(txId);
        ObjectIdentity oid = new ObjectIdentityImpl(BankingTx.class, txId);
        mutableAclService.deleteAcl(oid, false);
    }

    public List<BankingTx> getTransactions(String accountId) {
        return aclBankingTxDao.getTransactions(accountId);
    }

private String getCustomerUsername (BankingTx tx) {
    String username = "";
```

```
    String authority = SecurityContextHolder.getContext()
    .getAuthentication().getAuthorities().toString();
    if (authority.contains ("ROLE_CUST")) {
        Object principal = SecurityContextHolder.getContext().getAuthentication().getPrincipal();
        if (principal instanceof UserDetails) {
            username = ((UserDetails)principal).getUsername();
        } else {
            username = principal.toString();
        }
    } else {
        String accountId = tx.getAccountId();
        String customerId = accountDao.getCustomerId(accountId);
        username =loginUserDao.getUsernameByCustomerId(customerId);
    }
    return username;
}
    @Transactional
    //@Secured("ROLE_USER")
    public void createTransaction(BankingTx tx) {
        // added due to no BEFORE-TRIGGER in sql server
        if (SobaConfig.getDatabaseVendor().equalsIgnoreCase("SQLServer")) {
            double balance = accountManager.updateAccountBalance(tx.getAmount(),
                tx.getAccountId());
            tx.setBalance(balance);
        }
        aclBankingTxDao.insert(tx);
      addPermission(tx, new PrincipalSid(getCustomerUsername(tx)), BasePermission.READ);
        addPermission(tx, new GrantedAuthoritySid ("ROLE_REP"),
            BasePermission.ADMINISTRATION);
        addPermission(tx, new GrantedAuthoritySid ("ROLE_REP"),
            BasePermission.DELETE);
    }
    @Transactional
    public void disputeTransaction(String txId) {
        BankingTx tx = aclBankingTxDao.findByTransactionID(txId);
        System.out.println ("dispute Tx " + txId);
        tx.setAmount(0.0);
        tx.setDescription ("Customer disputed (txTd = " + txId + "): " +
            tx.getDescription());
        tx.setStatus ("disputed");
        tx.setTransactionId (Integer.parseInt((new RandomID(9)).getId()));
        tx.setTransDate(new Timestamp(System.currentTimeMillis()));
        aclBankingTxDao.insert(tx);
```

```
        addPermission(tx, new PrincipalSid(getCustomerUsername(tx)),
            BasePermission.READ);
        addPermission(tx, new GrantedAuthoritySid ("ROLE_REP"),
            BasePermission.ADMINISTRATION);
        addPermission(tx, new GrantedAuthoritySid ("ROLE_REP"),
            BasePermission.DELETE);
    }

    @Transactional
    public void reverseTransaction(String txId) {
        BankingTx tx = aclBankingTxDao.findByTransactionID(txId);
        System.out.println ("Reverse Tx " + txId);
        tx.setAmount(-tx.getAmount());
        tx.setDescription ("Reversed: " + tx.getDescription());
        tx.setTransactionId (Integer.parseInt((new RandomID(9)).getId()));
        tx.setTransDate(new Timestamp(System.currentTimeMillis()));
        aclBankingTxDao.insert(tx);
        addPermission(tx, new PrincipalSid(getCustomerUsername(tx)), BasePermission.READ);
        addPermission(tx, new GrantedAuthoritySid ("ROLE_REP"),
            BasePermission.ADMINISTRATION);
        addPermission(tx, new GrantedAuthoritySid ("ROLE_REP"), BasePermission.DELETE);
    }

    public void setaclBankingTxDao(AclBankingTxDao aclBankingTxDao) {
        this.aclBankingTxDao = aclBankingTxDao;
    }

  public void addPermission(BankingTx tx, Sid recipient, Permission permission) {
    MutableAcl acl;
    ObjectIdentity oid = new ObjectIdentityImpl(BankingTx.class, tx.getId());

    try {
      acl = (MutableAcl) mutableAclService.readAclById(oid);
    } catch (NotFoundException nfe) {
      System.out.println ("oid=" + oid.toString());
      acl = mutableAclService.createAcl(oid);
    }

    acl.insertAce(acl.getEntries().size(), permission, recipient, true);
    mutableAclService.updateAcl(acl);
  }

  public void deletePermission(BankingTx tx, Sid recipient, Permission permission) {
```

```
        ObjectIdentity oid = new ObjectIdentityImpl(BankingTx.class, tx.getTransactionId());
        MutableAcl acl = (MutableAcl) mutableAclService.readAclById(oid);
        // Remove all permissions associated with this particular recipient (string equality to KISS)
        List<AccessControlEntry> entries = acl.getEntries();

        for (int i = 0; i < entries.size(); i++) {
          if (entries.get(i).getSid().equals(recipient) &&
               entries.get(i).getPermission().equals(permission)) {
            acl.deleteAce(i);
          }
        }
        mutableAclService.updateAcl(acl);
    }
}
```

You might have noticed the annotation `@Transactional` placed in front of each ACL related methods introduced in the above code. This is specific to the Spring Security Framework that the `JdbcMutableAclService` requires all the methods containing ACL insert/update/delete operations run in a JDBC transactional context. To enable the `@Transactional` annotation, it's necessary to add the following elements in the service XML configuration file (in this case, the `soba-services.xml` file), together with the JDBC data source `transactionManager` and the `aclTxManager` bean added as well:

```
<...>
<tx:annotation-driven />
  <bean id="transactionManager"
  class="org.springframework.jdbc.datasource.DataSourceTransactionManager">
          <property name="dataSource" ref="dataSource" />
  </bean>
<bean id="aclTxManager" class="com.perfmath.spring.soba.service.SimpleAclTxManager">
      <property name="aclBankingTxDao" ref="aclBankingTxDao" />
      <property name="loginUserDao" ref="loginUserDao" />
      <property name="accountDao" ref="accountDao" />
      <property name="accountManager" ref="accountManager" />
      <property name="mutableAclService" ref="aclService" />
  </bean>
<...>
```

7.4.4 Applying ACLs to Business Operations

When a domain object is ACL-enabled, which means that it will have ACL information created as well when the domain object is inserted into the database, you can use that ACL information to grant or hide the access privilege based on the permissions set to the domain object. For example, if you want to hide the `Reverse` link of a transaction that does not have the ADMINISTRATION permission, you can make it happen by using the `<security:accesscontrollist>` tag as is shown in Listing 7.4 below in the manageTx.jsp file. This tag's function is to filter the access based on a domain object's ACL bits, which would correspond to the permissions of READ, WRITE, CREATE, DELETE and ADMINISTRATION.

Listing 7.4 manageTx.jsp

```
<%@ include file="include.jsp"%>
<%@ taglib prefix="c" uri="http://java.sun.com/jsp/jstl/core"%>
<%@ taglib prefix="security"
uri="http://www.springframework.org/security/tags"%>
<html>
<head>
<title>Tx List</title>
</head>
<%@ include file="banner.jsp"%>
<body>
<center>
<h2>You are logged in as <i> <security:authentication
    property="name" /> </i> with the following authorities:</h2>

<security:authentication property="authorities" var="authorities" />
<ul>
    <c:forEach items="${authorities}" var="authority">
        <li>${authority.authority}</li>
    </c:forEach>
</ul>
<hr> <br>  <br> <hr>
<security:authorize ifAnyGranted="ROLE_REP">
 Back to <a href="<c:url value="loginBroker"/>"> Rep Console</a>
</security:authorize>
<hr/>
<security:authorize ifAnyGranted="ROLE_REP, ROLE_CUST">
<table>
<tr>
<c:forEach var="column" items="Date, Type, Description, Debit, Credit, Balance,
Tx ID, ction">
    <th align="left" bgcolor="#00184A"><FONT COLOR="#FFFFFF">${column}
</FONT></th>
</c:forEach>
</tr>
<c:forEach items="${txs}" var="tx">
<tr>
<!-- formatDate doesn't work  if yyyy-mm-dd. must be MM-->
<td width=100><fmt:formatDate value="${tx.transDate}"
```

```
pattern="yyyy-MM-dd" /></td>
<td width=80>${tx.type}</td>
<td width=300>${tx.description}</td>
    <c:choose>
    <c:when test="${tx.amount > 0.0}">
    <td width=100></td>
    <td width=100>${tx.amount}</td>
    </c:when>
    <c:otherwise>

    <td width=100><FONT  COLOR="#FF0000">${tx.amount} </FONT></td>
    <td width=100></td>
    </c:otherwise>
    </c:choose>
    <td width=100>${tx.balance}</td>
    <td>${tx.transactionId}</td>
<security:accesscontrollist domainObject="${tx}"
hasPermission="ADMINISTRATION">
<c:if test="${tx.amount != 0}">
<td><a   href="reverseTx.htm?txId=${tx.transactionId}&accountId=${tx.accountId}">
Reverse </a></td>
</c:if>
</security:accesscontrollist>
</tr>
</c:forEach>
</table>
</security:authorize> <br>
<br>
<%@ include file="showLoadTime.jsp"%></center>
</body>
</html>
```

There are two more uses with ACL-enabled domain objects:

- Using the object's ACL to make access control decisions on the methods that operate on the object. In this case, it's necessary to configure an `AclEntryVoter` to help decide whether a method is allowed to be invoked.
- Making access control decisions based on the permissions of the domain objects returned from the methods that are subject to the ACL constraints. In this case, it's necessary to configure an `AclAfterInvocationProvider` if the method returns one domain object; or if the method returns a collection of domain objects, configure an `AclAfterInvocationCollectionFilteringProvider`. Accordingly, a decision can be made on whether allowing the domain object or the collection of domain objects to be returned to the user.

These two cases of applying ACL at the method level are significantly more complicated than the above jsp example, though. They are not used in SOBA.

7.4.5 Testing ACLs with SOBA

In this section, let's construct a complete test case to see Spring ACL in action with SOBA. The test scenario is that a bank representative logs into SOBA and post a charge of $10 to a customer's checking account. Then the customer (`user1001` in this example) disputes the charge, and the bank rep then honors the dispute by reversing the transaction. Follow the step-by-step procedure below for this test scenario (if you have not created `sobarep`, use the `create_test_users.sql` script from the SOBA download to create this user):

1. Log into SOBA as `sobarep` with the password `sobarep` as shown in Figure 7.1.

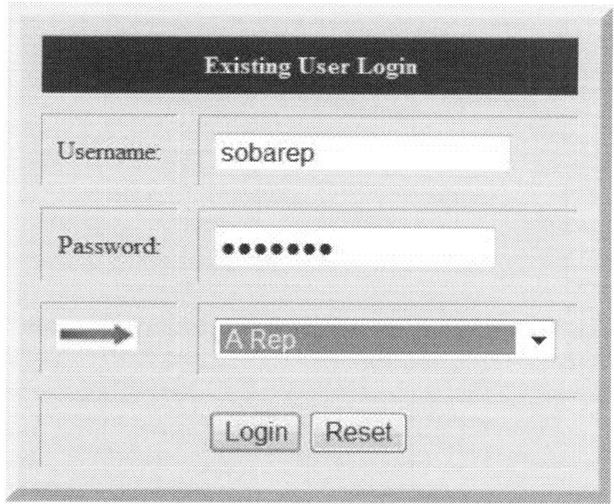

Figure 7.1 SOBA: Login as sobarep

2. Enter `user1001's` customer ID (in my case, it's `963465668`) and click *Submit*. The *rep* should see a view similar to Figure 7.2.

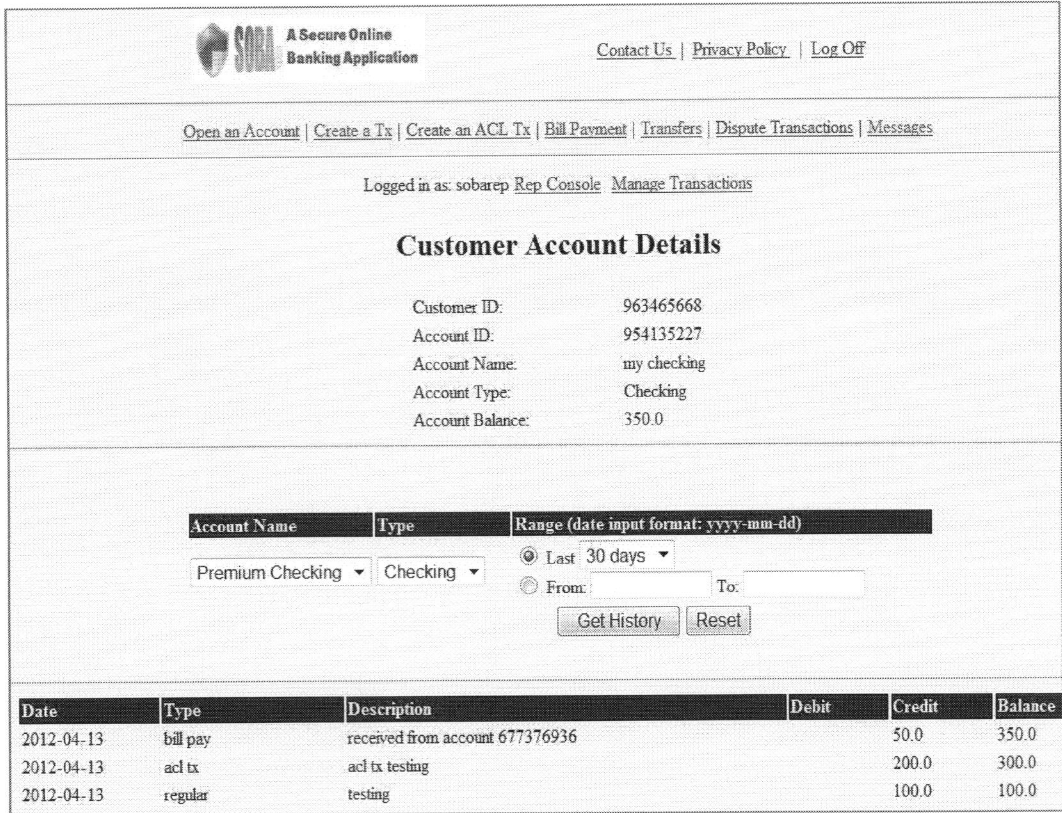

Figure 7.2 SOBA: `user1001`'s banking activities

3. Click the *Create an ACL Tx* link, fill an ACL tx as shown in Figure 7.3, and click *Submit*. At this point, you can query the `bankingtx` table and put down the `TRANSACTION_ID` for this transaction (in my case, it's `27661704`). Then query the `acl_object_identity` table and you would notice that an entry corresponding to this transaction had been inserted into this table. Use the value of the `id` column of this entry (in my case, it's `37`) to check the granted permissions in the `acl_entry` table for each `sid` that can be looked up from querying the `acl_sid` table. In my case, three rows were found with the masks of 1, 8 and 16, with the mask bit "1" assigned to `user1001` with a `sid` of "5" and masks of "8" and "16" assigned to `ROLE_REP` with a `sid` of "2" (Refer to Table 7.1 for the Spring ACL mask-permission mappings). Recall that we did not want customers to have DELETE and ADMINISTRATION permissions for their transactions for obvious reasons. Now, click the *View Account Activity* link to get to the account activity page.

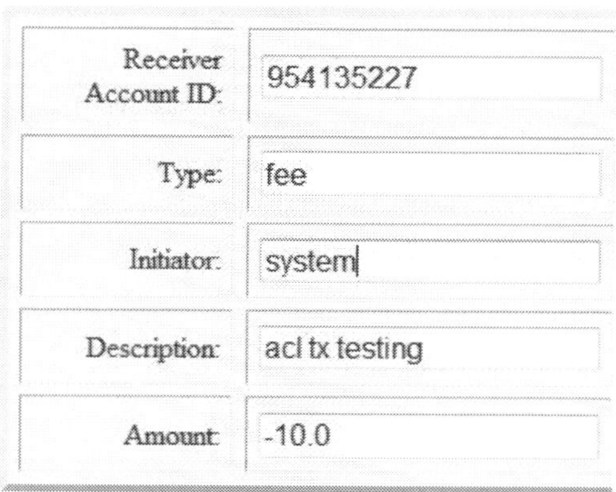

Figure 7.3 SOBA: Posting a $10 charge to user1001's checking account

Table 7.1 Spring ACL mask-permission mappings

Mask	Permission
1	READ
2	WRITE
4	CREATE
8	DELETE
16	ADMINISTRATION

4. Now open up another Web browser and log into SOBA as `user1001`. You should see a view similar to Figure 7.4.

5. Dispute the $10 fee transaction by following the below sequence of actions:

   a. Click the *Dispute Transactions* tab and you should see a list of transactions as shown in Figure 7.5. Then dispute the $10 fee transaction by clicking its ID (`27661704`) under the second column of `TxId (rest)`. If successful, you should see the *Dispute* view page similar to Figure 7.6. At this point, you can verify that only ACL transactions are disputable.

   b. Click the *Dispute* button to dispute the transaction. You should now see a page similar to Figure 7.7. Note that this dispute action by the customer does not change the account balance.

6. Now switch to `sobarep`'s browser. Reverse the $10 fee transaction by following the below sequence of actions:

   a. Click the *Manage Transactions* tab and you should see a list of transactions for user1001 as shown in Figure 7.8. Note the Reverse action following the disputed transaction.

b. Click the *Reverse* link and you should see that the $10 fee has been credited back to `user1001`'s account as shown in Figure 7.9.

7. Switch to `user1001`'s activity view and you should see the $10 fee credited back as shown in Figure 7.10.

This wraps up our ACL testing with SOBA project, and I hope you have enjoyed it.

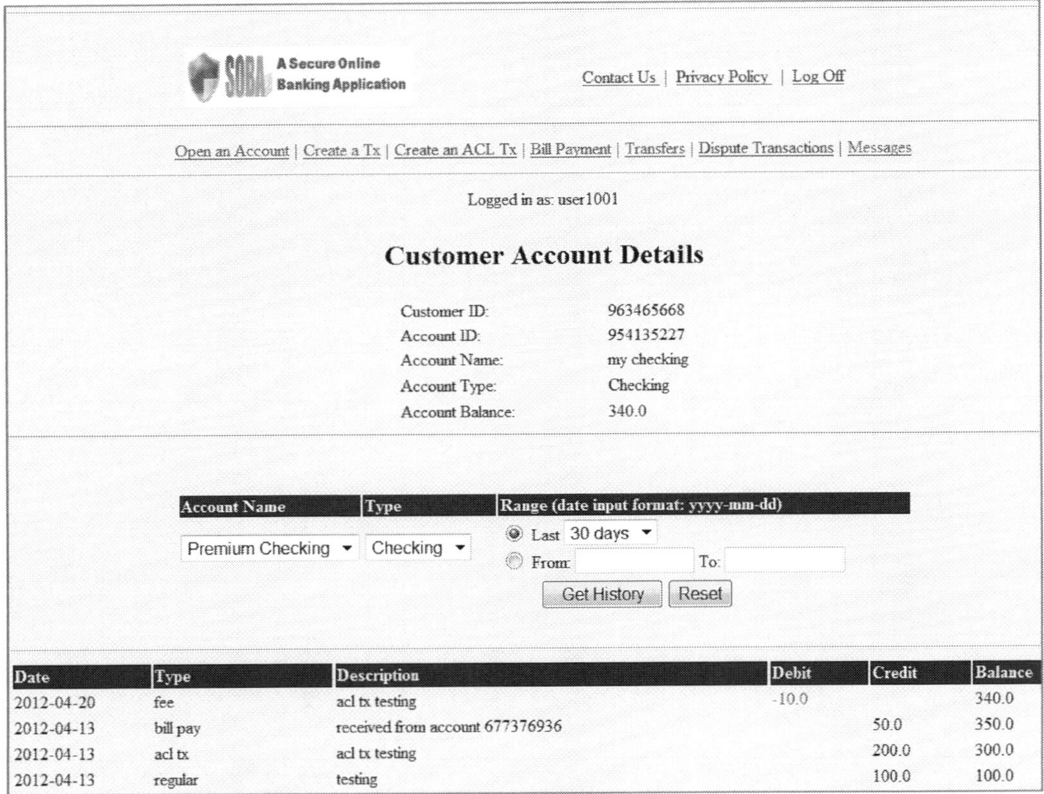

Date	Type	Description	Debit	Credit	Balance
2012-04-20	fee	acl tx testing	-10.0		340.0
2012-04-13	bill pay	received from account 677376936		50.0	350.0
2012-04-13	acl tx	acl tx testing		200.0	300.0
2012-04-13	regular	testing		100.0	100.0

Figure 7.4 SOBA: `user1001`'s account activity page after a $10 fee was charged

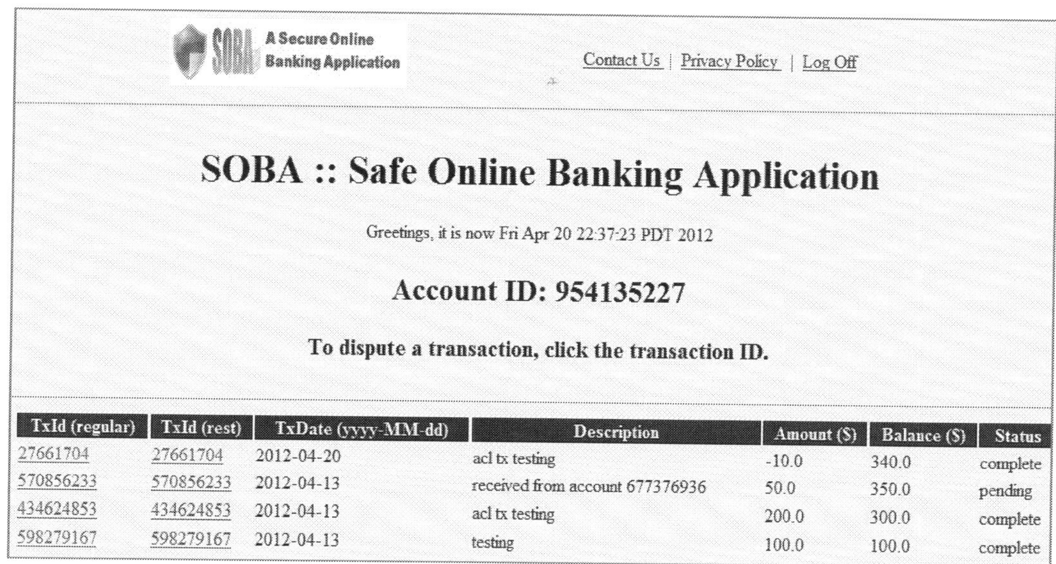

Figure 7.5 SOBA: *Dispute Transaction* page

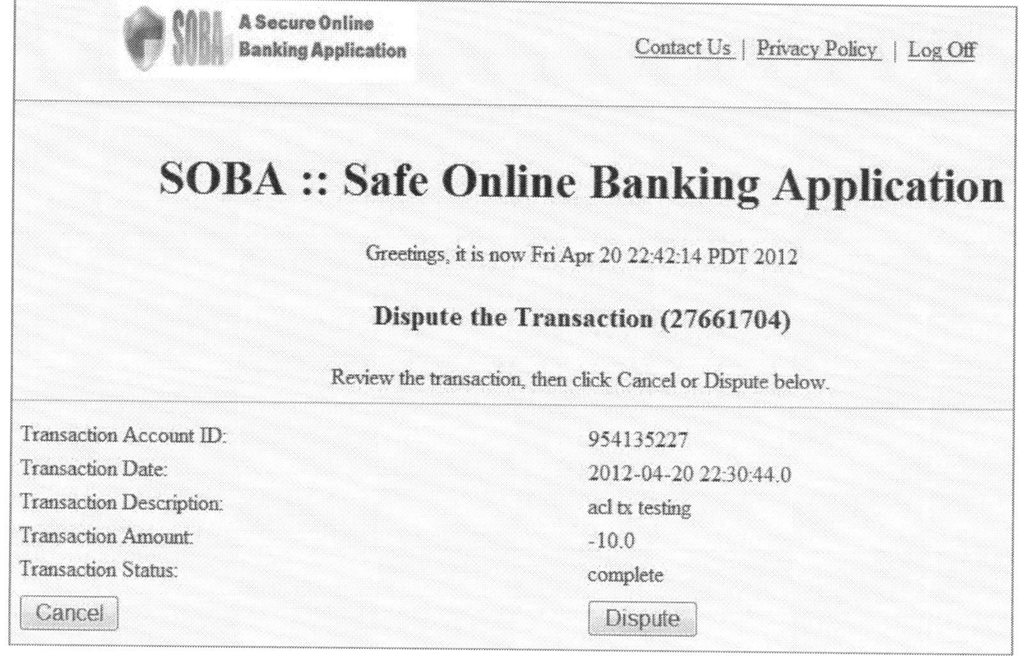

Figure 7.6 SOBA: *Dispute* or *Cancel* transaction page

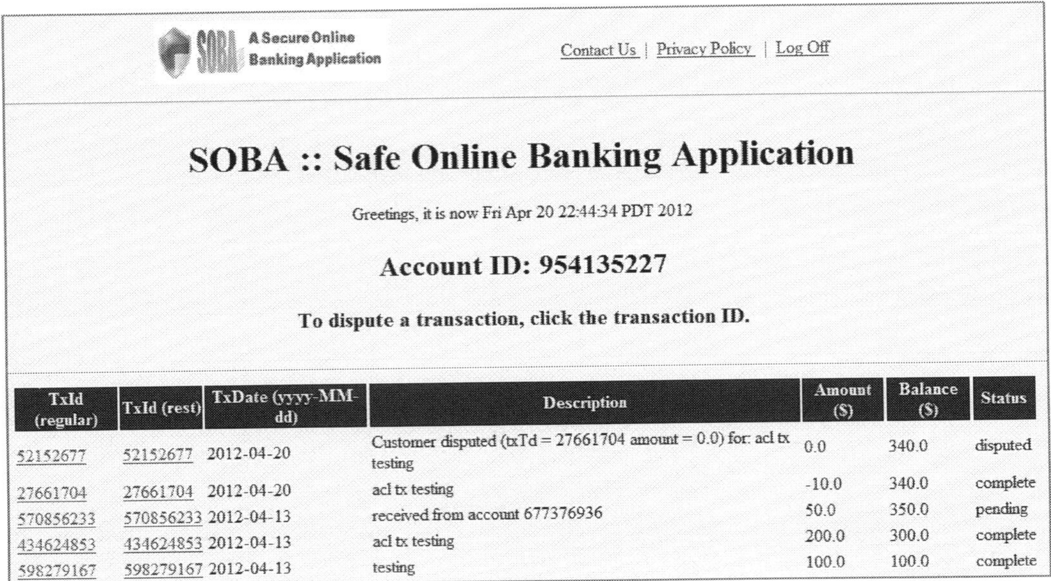

TxId (regular)	TxId (rest)	TxDate (yyyy-MM-dd)	Description	Amount ($)	Balance ($)	Status
52152677	52152677	2012-04-20	Customer disputed (txTd = 27661704 amount = 0.0) for: acl tx testing	0.0	340.0	disputed
27661704	27661704	2012-04-20	acl tx testing	-10.0	340.0	complete
570856233	570856233	2012-04-13	received from account 677376936	50.0	350.0	pending
434624853	434624853	2012-04-13	acl tx testing	200.0	300.0	complete
598279167	598279167	2012-04-13	testing	100.0	100.0	complete

Figure 7.7 SOBA: user1001's activity page after disputing the $10 fee transaction

Date	Type	Description	Debit	Credit	Balance	Tx ID	Action
2012-04-20	fee	Customer disputed (txTd = 27661704 amount = 0.0) for: acl tx testing	0.0		340.0	52152677	
2012-04-20	fee	acl tx testing	-10.0		340.0	27661704	Reverse
2012-04-13	bill pay	received from account 677376936		50.0	350.0	570856233	
2012-04-13	acl tx	acl tx testing		200.0	300.0	434624853	
2012-04-13	regular	testing		100.0	100.0	598279167	

Figure 7.8 SOBA: *Reverse Transaction* page

Date	Type	Description	Debit	Credit	Balance	Tx ID	Action
2012-04-20	fee	Reversed: amount = 10.0 for acl tx testing		10.0	350.0	390679540	Reverse
2012-04-20	fee	Customer disputed (txTd = 27661704 amount = 0.0) for: acl tx testing	0.0		340.0	52152677	
2012-04-20	fee	acl tx testing	-10.0		340.0	27661704	Reverse
2012-04-13	bill pay	received from account 677376936		50.0	350.0	570856233	
2012-04-13	acl tx	acl tx testing		200.0	300.0	434624853	
2012-04-13	regular	testing		100.0	100.0	598279167	

Figure 7.9 SOBA: The $10 fee credited back to `user1001`'s account

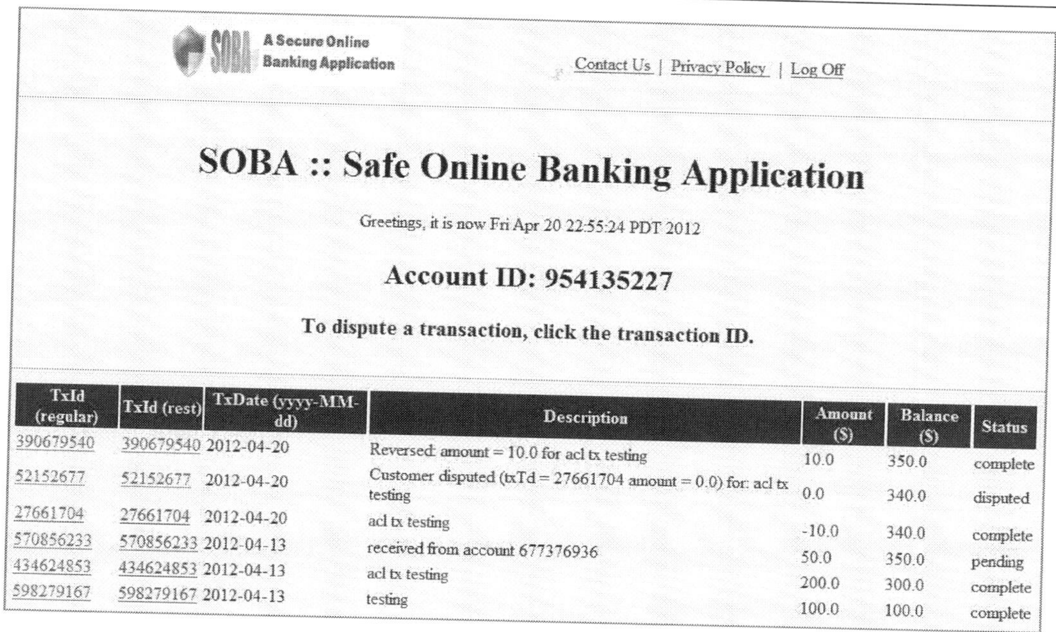

TxId (regular)	TxId (rest)	TxDate (yyyy-MM-dd)	Description	Amount ($)	Balance ($)	Status
390679540	390679540	2012-04-20	Reversed: amount = 10.0 for acl tx testing	10.0	350.0	complete
52152677	52152677	2012-04-20	Customer disputed (txTd = 27661704 amount = 0.0) for: acl tx testing	0.0	340.0	disputed
27661704	27661704	2012-04-20	acl tx testing	-10.0	340.0	complete
570856233	570856233	2012-04-13	received from account 677376936	50.0	350.0	pending
434624853	434624853	2012-04-13	acl tx testing	200.0	300.0	complete
598279167	598279167	2012-04-13	testing	100.0	100.0	complete

Figure 7.10 SOBA: The $10 fee credited back to user1001's account as is seen on the customer's own browser

7.5 SUMMARY

In this chapter, we introduced some basic security concepts both in general and in Spring's contexts for securing enterprise Web applications from multiple perspectives. Using SOBA, we have illustrated how to configure Spring security with various entries in the `web.xml` and `soba-security.xml` files. We have also covered ACL for securing domain objects, which is rarely covered anywhere else in such an end-to-end, integrated, consistent approach as we did here.

Although this is not a complete coverage about the Spring Security Framework, it provides you with sufficient information for you to take off and explore more on your own, especially experimenting on your own with SOBA as a platform for you to try various things freely. Spring has a separate document about Spring Security Framework, which should be used as the first-hand source for any subjects related to the Spring Security Framework.

I hope you have achieved your Spring learning objectives with the help of this book. The next chapter introduces Spring's AOP framework, which is a very interesting subject but not easy to learn and master. I decided to defer introducing the AOP Spring framework until up to this point, as it's a lot easier to digest it after you have gone through all the basic Spring elements introduced so far. Also, you may or may not need to learn it, depending on the scale of your project. It may not be worth it if your project scale is small to medium. However, I encourage you to finish it, as I have tried to make it as easy and practical as possible. Please keep going if you are interested. Otherwise, thank you and good luck with your Spring endeavors on your way to help make your organization and yourself more successful!

RECOMMENDED READING

The best reference for the Spring Security Framework is Spring's own security framework reference documentation, which is a separate documentation from the Spring's main reference documentation. It is available at Spring's website.

EXERCISES

7.1 Explain the basic concepts of authentication, authorization, principal, and access control in general security contexts.

7.2 What's the difference between form-based authentication and HTTP basic authentication?

7.3 Identify the part of the `soba-security.xml` file that is database-specific.

7.4 How is security implemented in *views*?

7.5 Explain the concept of ACL and when it is needed.

7.6 This exercise shows how you can explore more Spring features by using SOBA as a learning platform rather than depending on the book to provide you with everything you need for your project. The exercise is about how to enable the use of encrypted password for user authentication. For your reference, here is a tested procedure about how to implement this feature using one of the methods as documented in the Spring security reference documentation (note that for your convenience, all code snippets are available from the files mentioned in the download project zip file):

1 Increase the size of the `password` column of the `loginuser` table with the following MySQL commands:

- cmd> mysql soba –h 127.0.0.1 –u root –p
- mysql> alter table loginuser modify password VARCHAR (80);
- mysql> commit;
- mysql> exit

2 Add an `encoder` bean and a `<password-encoder>` XML element as shown below in `soba-security.xml` (this part is commented out in this file):

```
<beans:bean id="encoder"
        class="org.springframework.security.crypto.password.StandardPasswordEncoder">
</beans:bean>
   <authentication-manager alias="authenticationManager">
      <authentication-provider>
         <password-encoder ref="encoder">
         </password-encoder>
         <jdbc-user-service data-source-ref="dataSource"
```

```
        users-by-username-query="SELECT username, password, enabled FROM users
  WHERE username = ?" />
   </authentication-provider>
 </authentication-manager>
```

3 Explore the password encoding feature provided by the Spring Security Framework as follows (a convenient class to try it out is the `CreateLoginUserValidator.java` class):

```
import org.springframework.security.crypto.password.*;
...
StandardPasswordEncoder encoder = new StandardPasswordEncoder ();
   String encyptedPassword = encoder.encode (user.getPassword ());
   user.setPassword(encyptedPassword);
```

4 If you use Maven-based build of the SOBA project, you also need to add the following dependency in the project's `pom.xml` file (if you use Ant-based approach to building SOBA, it's necessary to add `spring-security-crypto-3.1.0.RELEASE.jar` to SOBA, which is already included in the downloaded SOBA project zip file):

```
<dependency>
<groupId>org.springframework.security</groupId>
<artifactId>spring-security-crypto</artifactId>
<version>${spring-security.version}</version>
</dependency>
```

5 Test it by following the procedure presented in Section 2.7.2 (you can verify the encrypted password by querying the `loginuser` table).

For more details about the above implementation, refer to the *Spring Security Reference Documentation Section 7.3 Password Encoding.*

8 Spring AOP Framework

In building enterprise applications, the tasks like logging, performance profiling, validation, error checking and handling, transaction management, and so on, are called *crosscutting concerns*, meaning that they are intermingled with the main business logic code dealt with a separate paradigm of *object oriented programming* (OOP). How to deal with such crosscutting concerns effectively and efficiently is an important task for building an enterprise application. *Aspect oriented programming* (AOP) is generally considered a standard practice for addressing such crosscutting concerns.

Spring has its own AOP framework, which is limited to the beans declared in its IoC container only. In addition, it supports integration with the AspectJ AOP framework (http://www.eclipse.org/aspectj). As an aspect oriented extension to the Java programming language, AspectJ is a very popular AOP framework for modularizing crosscutting concerns.

Throughout this chapter, we use a performance profiling framework (*perfBasic*) I described in my other text *Software Performance and Scalability: A Quantitative Approach* (Wiley, 2009) as a concrete crosscutting concern to demonstrate how to apply Spring AOP framework to solving real crosscutting concerns. You can apply the same AOP techniques illustrated in this chapter by substituting the perfBasic profiling concern with your crosscutting contexts.

Let's begin with the admin console for SOBA next, which enables configuring log4j logging and *perfBasic* profiling for SOBA. Using SOBA admin console as a stepping stone, we illustrate how logging can be implemented with multiple approaches, from the most primitive one to the state-of-the-art one.

8.1 SOBA Admin Console – A Rendezvous for Crosscutting Concerns

Two crosscutting requirements need to be addressed for SOBA:

- Logging levels should be configurable dynamically.
- Performance profiling based on the *perfBasic* profiling framework should be configurable dynamically.

Figure 8.1 shows the SOBA admin console, which is what one would see after logging in with the user *appadmin/appadmin*. This admin user have been created when the SOBA schema was created initially by executing the `create_all.sql` script, which includes the `create_test_users.sql` script for creating the *appadmin* user.

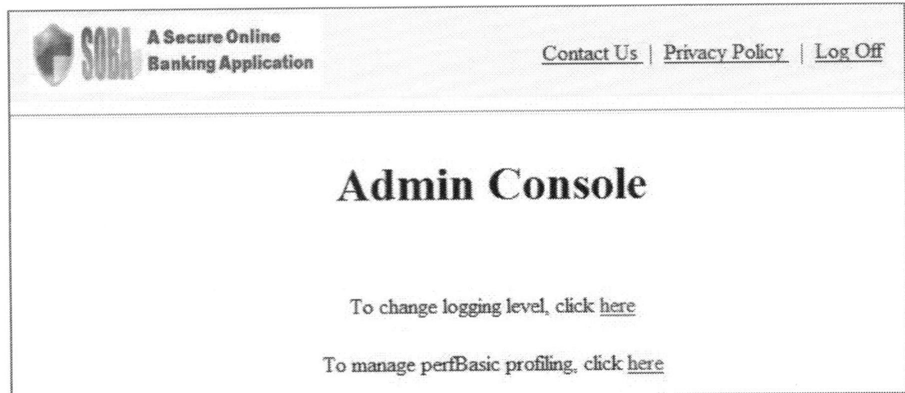

Figure 8.1 SOBA admin console

8.1.1 SOBA Logging Controller and Performance Profiling Controller

A SOBA admin can change the logging level and manage perfBasic profiling, both at runtime on the admin console. Figure 8.2 shows the SOBA admin console with all Log4j loggers for SOBA, while Figure 8.3 shows SOBA perfBasic profiling admin console, which enables an admin to toggle profiling between on and off.

The logic behind the SOBA admin console works as follows:

- When you log in as *appadmin/appadmin*, after passing authentication, control is transferred to the `LoginBroker` controller, which redirects to `adminConsole.jsp` based on the role of "ADMIN" assigned to the *appadmin* user. Listing 8.1 shows the contents of the `adminConsole.jsp`, with the two embedded URLs of `log4jConsole` and `perfBasicConsole` highlighted. The `LoginBroker` controller is discussed when we discuss log4j in the next section.
- On the admin console page shown in Figure 8.1, control is transferred to the `log4jConsole` controller or `perfBasicConsole` controller, depending on which URL is clicked (See Figure 8.1 for those two URLs available). Listing 8.2 shows the `Log4jConcolseController.java` class, while Listing 8.3 shows the `PerfBasicConsoleController.java` class. As is seen, it addition to those familiar annotations such as @`Controller`, @`RequestMapping`, and @`SessionAttributes` that we covered previously, both controllers extend the `AbstractController` class from Spring's `org.springframework.web.servlet.mvc` package and override its `handleRequestInternal` method. The major difference between the two is that the `Log4jConcolseController` returns to `log4jConsole.jsp` while `PerfBasicConsoleController` returns to `perfBasicConsole.jsp`. The other difference is that the `Log4jConcolseController` has a `setLogLevel` method to reset the

logging level for a given logger, while the `PerfBasicConsoleController` has a `resetProfiling` method to toggle the profiling status between on and off.

Parent	Logger	Level
root	com.perfmath.spring.soba	INFO
com.perfmath.spring.soba	com.perfmath.spring.soba.service.CreateAclTxValidator	INFO
com.perfmath.spring.soba	com.perfmath.spring.soba.service.CreateBillPayValidator	INFO
com.perfmath.spring.soba	com.perfmath.spring.soba.service.CreateTxValidator	INFO
com.perfmath.spring.soba	com.perfmath.spring.soba.service.TransferValidator	INFO
com.perfmath.spring.soba	com.perfmath.spring.soba.web.ActivityListController	INFO
com.perfmath.spring.soba	com.perfmath.spring.soba.web.AdminConsoleController	INFO
com.perfmath.spring.soba	com.perfmath.spring.soba.web.DisputeTxController	INFO
com.perfmath.spring.soba	com.perfmath.spring.soba.web.Log4jConsoleController	INFO
com.perfmath.spring.soba	com.perfmath.spring.soba.web.LoginBroker	INFO
com.perfmath.spring.soba	com.perfmath.spring.soba.web.LogoffController	INFO
com.perfmath.spring.soba	com.perfmath.spring.soba.web.ManageTxController	INFO
com.perfmath.spring.soba	com.perfmath.spring.soba.web.PerfBasicConsoleController	INFO
com.perfmath.spring.soba	com.perfmath.spring.soba.web.RepConsoleController	INFO
com.perfmath.spring.soba	com.perfmath.spring.soba.web.ReverseTxController	INFO

Figure 8.2 Log4j loggers for SOBA

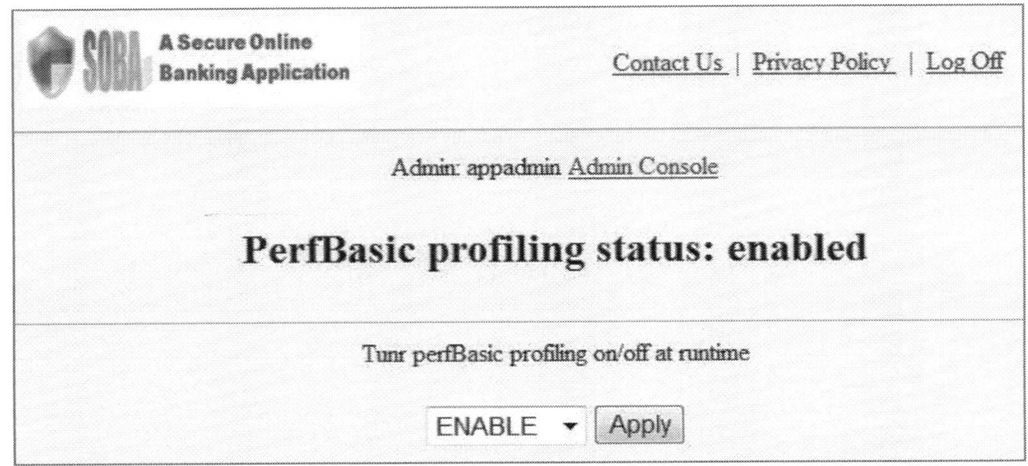

Figure 8.3 PerfBasic admin console

Listing 8.1 adminConsole.jsp

```
<%@ include file="include.jsp" %>
<%@ taglib prefix="form" uri="http://www.springframework.org/tags/form" %>
<html>
<head>
<title>Admin Console</title>
</head>
<%@ include file = "banner.jsp" %>
<body>
<center>
<h1> Admin Console</h1>
<br> <br>
   To change logging level, click <a href="<c:url value="log4jConsole"/>">here</a>
<p>
   To manage perfBasic profiling, click <a href="<c:url
                  value="perfBasicConsole"/>">here</a>
  <br> <br>
  </center>
</body>
</html>
```

Listing 8.2 Log4jConsoleController.java

```
package com.perfmath.spring.soba.web;
```

```
import javax.servlet.http.HttpServletRequest;
import javax.servlet.http.HttpServletResponse;

import java.util.ArrayList;
import java.util.HashMap;
import java.util.SortedMap;
import java.util.TreeMap;
import java.util.Iterator;

import java.util.Map;
import org.apache.log4j.LogManager;
import org.apache.log4j.Logger;
import org.apache.log4j.Level;
import org.springframework.stereotype.Controller;
import org.springframework.web.bind.annotation.RequestMapping;
import org.springframework.web.bind.annotation.RequestMethod;
import org.springframework.web.bind.annotation.SessionAttributes;
import org.springframework.web.servlet.ModelAndView;
import org.springframework.web.servlet.mvc.AbstractController;
import java.util.Enumeration;
import java.util.List;

import com.perfmath.spring.soba.util.MyLogger;

@Controller
@RequestMapping("/log4jConsole")
@SessionAttributes("log4j")
public class Log4jConsoleController extends AbstractController {

    @RequestMapping(value="/log4jConsole", method = RequestMethod.GET)
    protected ModelAndView handleRequestInternal(HttpServletRequest request,
            HttpServletResponse response) throws Exception {
        String loggerSelected = request.getParameter("loggerSelected");
        if (loggerSelected != null && loggerSelected.length() > 0) {
            String levelSelected = request.getParameter("levelSelected");
            setLogLevel(loggerSelected, levelSelected);
        }

        ModelAndView mav = new ModelAndView ();
        mav.setViewName("log4jConsole");
        String name = "";
        String effectiveLevel = "";
        String parent = "";
```

```
        Map<String, Object> model = new HashMap<String, Object> ();
        Enumeration loggers = LogManager.getCurrentLoggers();

        SortedMap sm = new TreeMap();

        while (loggers.hasMoreElements()) {
            Logger logger = (Logger) loggers.nextElement();
            name = logger.getName().toString();
            effectiveLevel = logger.getEffectiveLevel().toString();
            parent = logger.getParent().getName().toString();
            if (name.startsWith("com.perfmath")) {
                sm.put (name, new MyLogger (name, effectiveLevel,parent));
            }
        }

        List<MyLogger> myLoggers = new ArrayList<MyLogger>();
        Iterator it = sm.keySet().iterator();
        while (it.hasNext() ) {
            Object key = it.next();
            myLoggers.add ((MyLogger) sm.get(key));
        }
        model.put ("myLoggers", myLoggers);
        mav.addObject ("model", model);
        return new ModelAndView("log4jConsole", model);
    }
    public void setLogLevel(String loggerSelected, String levelSelected) {
        Logger rootLogger = Logger.getRootLogger();
        Logger logger = rootLogger.getLoggerRepository().getLogger(loggerSelected);
        logger.setLevel((Level)Level.toLevel(levelSelected));
    }
}
```

Listing 8.3 PerfBasicConsoleController.java

```
package com.perfmath.spring.soba.web;

import javax.servlet.http.HttpServletRequest;
import javax.servlet.http.HttpServletResponse;
import java.util.HashMap;
import java.util.Map;
import org.springframework.beans.factory.annotation.Autowired;
import org.springframework.stereotype.Controller;
import org.springframework.web.bind.annotation.RequestMapping;
```

```
import org.springframework.web.bind.annotation.RequestMethod;
import org.springframework.web.bind.annotation.SessionAttributes;
import org.springframework.web.servlet.ModelAndView;
import org.springframework.web.servlet.mvc.AbstractController;

import com.perfmath.spring.soba.util.PerfBasicUtil;

@Controller
@RequestMapping("/perfBasicConsole")
@SessionAttributes("perfBasic")
public class PerfBasicConsoleController extends AbstractController {
    @RequestMapping(value="/perfBasicConsole", method = RequestMethod.GET)
    protected ModelAndView handleRequestInternal(HttpServletRequest request,
            HttpServletResponse response) throws Exception {
        String profilingStatus = request.getParameter("profilingStatus");
        if (profilingStatus != null ) {
            resetProfiling(profilingStatus);
        }

        ModelAndView mav = new ModelAndView ();
        mav.setViewName("perfBasicConsole");

        Map<String, Object> model = new HashMap<String, Object> ();

        model.put ("profilingStatus", PerfBasicUtil.getProfilingStatus());
        mav.addObject ("model", model);
        return new ModelAndView("perfBasicConsole", model);
    }
    public void resetProfiling(String profilingStatus) {
        if (!PerfBasicUtil.getProfilingStatus().equals(profilingStatus)) {
            PerfBasicUtil.setProfilingStatus(profilingStatus);
            if (PerfBasicUtil.getProfilingStatus().equals("disabled")){
                PerfBasicUtil.flushApfWriter();
            }
        }
    }
}
```

8.1.2 Log4jConsole and PerfBasic Profiling Views

Listings 8.4 and 8.5 show `log4jConsole.jsp` and `perfBasicConsole.jsp`, respectively. You might want to take a quick look at these two jsp files to understand what Spring features they use and how they interact with their corresponding Spring controllers exactly. Next, we describe how log4j and perfBasic profiling work with SOBA for logging and performance profiling.

Listing 8.4 log4jConsole.jsp

```
<%@ include file="include.jsp"%>
<%@ taglib prefix="c" uri="http://java.sun.com/jsp/jstl/core"%>
<%@ taglib prefix="security"
    uri="http://www.springframework.org/security/tags"%>
<html bgcolor='blue'>
<head>
<script language="javascript" src="init.js"></script>
<title>Log4J Console</title>
</head>
<%@ include file="banner.jsp"%>
<body bgcolor="F7FFCE" >
    <center>
        <security:authorize ifAnyGranted="ROLE_ADMIN">
            <table>
                <tr><td>Admin: <security:authentication property="name" /></td>
                <td><a href="<c:url value="loginBroker"/>">Admin Console</a></td>
                </tr>
            </table>
        </security:authorize>
        <h2>Log4j Loggers</h2>
        <hr>
        <!-- reset log level for a given class -->
        Reset Log4j Logging Level at Runtime <br>
        <form name="setLogLevel" method="POST"
            action="<c:url value="/log4jConsole" />">
            <table border="2" CELLPADDING="2" CELLSPACING="2"
                    BGCOLOR="#C6EFF7">
                <c:forEach var="column" items="Logger, New Level, Change">
                    <th align="left" bgcolor="#00184A"><FONT
                    COLOR="#FFFFFF">${column}
                    </FONT></th>
                </c:forEach>
                <tr>
                    <td><select name="loggerSelected">
                            <c:forEach items="${myLoggers}" varStatus="status"
                                var="myLogger">
                                <option
                            value="${myLogger.name}">${myLogger.name}</option>
```

```
                    </c:forEach>
                </select></td>
                <td><select name="levelSelected">
                    <option value="debug">DEBUG</option>
                    <option value="info">INFO</option>
                    <option value="warn">WARN</option>
                    <option value="error" selected>ERROR</option>
                    <option value="fatal">FATAL</option>
                    <option value="off">OFF</option>
                </select></td>
                <td colspan="2" align="center">
                <input type="submit" value="Apply" /></td>
            </tr>
        </table>
    </form>
    <!-- display loggers -->
    <hr>
    <br> <a href="<c:url value="/log4jConsole.htm"/>"> Refresh </a> <br>
    <table border="2" CELLPADDING="2" CELLSPACING="2"
BGCOLOR="#C6EFF7">
        <c:forEach var="column" items="Parent, Logger, Level ">
            <th align="left" bgcolor="#00184A"><FONT
                COLOR="#FFFFFF">${column}
            </FONT></th>
        </c:forEach>
        <c:forEach items="${myLoggers}" varStatus="status" var="myLogger">
            <tr>
                <td>${myLogger.parent}</td>
                <td>${myLogger.name}</td>
                <td>${myLogger.effectiveLevel}</td>
            </tr>
        </c:forEach>
    </table>
  </center>
</body>
```

Listing 8.5 perfBasicConsole.jsp

```
<%@page import="com.perfmath.spring.soba.util.PerfBasicUtil"%>
<%@ include file="include.jsp"%>
<%@ taglib prefix="c" uri="http://java.sun.com/jsp/jstl/core"%>
<%@ taglib prefix="security"
  uri="http://www.springframework.org/security/tags"%>
```

```
<html bgcolor='blue'>
<head>
<title>PerfBasic Console</title>
</head>
<%@ include file="banner.jsp"%>
<body bgcolor="F7FFCE">
    <center>
        <security:authorize ifAnyGranted="ROLE_ADMIN">
            <table>
                <tr>
                    <td>Admin: <security:authentication property="name" />
                    </td>
                    <td><a href="<c:url value="loginBroker"/>">Admin
                        Console</a></td>
                </tr>
            </table>
        </security:authorize>
        <h2>PerfBasic profiling status: ${profilingStatus}</h2>
        <hr> Turn perfBasic profiling on/off at runtime <br>
        <form name="resetProfiling" method="POST"
            action="<c:url value="/perfBasicConsole" />">
            <select name="profilingStatus">
                <option value="enabled">ENABLE</option>
                <option value="disabled">DISABLE</option>
            </select> <input type="submit" value="Apply" />
            </td>
        </form>
    </center>
</body>
</html>
```

8.1.3 Logging with Log4j for SOBA

First, let us understand how log4j works.

Log4j is a specific implementation that implements the generic logging interface defined by a common framework such as the *Apache Commons Logging* or *SLF4J* (Simple Logging Façade for Java). Other similar Java logging implementations include *Java Logging API* (`java.util.logging`) that comes with Oracle JREs and *logback*, which is intended as a successor to log4j, and so on.

To use Log4j with a Java application, a `log4j.xml` file needs to be configured and placed in the right directory. With SOBA, this file is initially placed in the *src/main/resources* directory, which will be copied to the *WEB-INF/classes* directory at deployment time. Listing 8.6 shows the log4j configuration file for SOBA. As is seen, log4j has three main elements:

- **Appender**: An *appender* defines where the log should go – *Console* or *File*. In Listing 8.6, we see three appenders: one *Console* appender as set with the class `org.apapche.log4j.ConsoleAppender` and two *File* appenders (File and PERF) as set with the class `org.apapche.log4j.RollingFileAppender`. With each file appender, file name and path are explicitly specified. The log4j log file is named `soba.log` whereas the performance profiling log file is named `soba_perf_log4j.log`, both of which are placed in Tomcat's *logs/soba* folder.
- **Layout**: A layout specifies the logging format, which heavily depends on the symbol of "%" sign followed by a letter. Common patterns include:
    - %d for date/time
    - %t for thread name
    - %m for user-defined message
    - %r for milliseconds since program start
    - %C for class name
    - %c{n} for the category of the event – last *n* sub-categories only
    - %M for method name
    - %m for application supplied message associated with the logging event
    - %n for carriage return, etc.
    - %-np for the priority of the logging event – right pad with spaces if the category name is less than *n* characters long
- **Logger**: A *logger* associates a package with a log level. A logger can also have an *appender-ref* attribute specified specifically so that the log can be directed to a separate file. See the logger for *com.perfmath.spring.soba* defined below with PERF specified as the value for the *appender-ref* attribute. Note also the root logger defined in Listing 8.6, from which all other loggers inherit.

After setting up a `log4j.xml` file, the next step is to use it in your Java application to perform logging tasks. Let's use the `LoginBroker.java` class shown in Listing 8.7 to demonstrate how log4j can be used. This `LoginBroker` controller simply directs the user to the corresponding view based on his/her role. This controller is similar to the `Log4jConsoleController` and the `PerfBasicConsoleController` we discussed previously, and therefore, we would not explain further about how it is implemented.

To demonstrate how to use log4j with both *Apache Commons Logging* and SLF4J (note that you only need to pick one for your project, e.g., SLF4J), as is seen in Listing 8.7, we import the packages of `org.apache.commons.logging.Log`, `org.apache.commons.logging.LogFactory` from Apache Commons Logging and `org.slf4j.Logger` from SLF4J. Then, we define a `log` object of type `Log` from the `LogFactory` interface of the Apache Commons Logging framework as well as a `logger` object of type `Logger` from the SLF4J framework with the following two statements, respectively:

```
private Log log = LogFactory.getLog (this.getClass());
    private Logger logger = org.slf4j.LoggerFactory.getLogger(this.getClass());
```

Then, we use `log.info (String message)` or `logger.info (String message)` to log a message anywhere in an executable location of the class. These two statements are equivalent and you can pick only one of them with your project. In addition, since is there are six logging levels of `TRACE`, `DEBUG`, `INFO`, `WARN`, `ERROR`, and `FATAL`, you can replace `info` in `log.info` or `logger.info` with one of the other logging levels of `trace`, `debug`, `warn`, `error`, and `fatal`. Keep in mind that when you use log.info (...) or logger.info (...) in your program, the message is logged only if the current logging level is equal to or higher than "INFO," or in other words, all statements of log.trace (...) and log.debug (...) will be ignored. This is the mechanism that log4j uses to control how verbose you want to go with your logging in your application.

Now note the use of log.info (...) statement at the beginning and end of the getModelAndView method. The SLF4J logger.info (…) statement is included here only for demonstration purposes. To see how log4j works, perform a login onto SOBA with appadmin/appadmin and check the *soba.log* file in Tomcat's *logs/soba* folder, which should contain lines similar to the following as I obtained on my system at the time of this writing (note the use of the line continuation mark "➥"):

```
2013-02-15 17:34:25,843 http-bio-8443-exec-5 INFO  web.LoginBroker +
2013-02-15 17:34:25,843 http-bio-8443-exec-5 INFO  web.LoginBroker Testing logging from SLF4J ➥...
it works
2013-02-15 17:34:25,843 http-bio-8443-exec-5 INFO  web.LoginBroker –
```

The above log format is determined by the "%d{ISO8601}%t%-5p%c{2}%m%n" ConversionPattern as specified in Listing 8.6 for the soba.log file, namely, *date*, *thread name*, *logging level*, *<class_name>.<method_name>*, and *message*. The first and third lines were from the log.info (...) statements (*Apache Commons Logging*) at the beginning and the end of the getModelAndView method, while the second line was from logger.info (...) (*SLF4J*).

Now check the *soba_perf_log4j.log* file in Tomcat's *logs/soba* folder, and you should find lines similar to the following as I obtained on my system at the time of this writing:

```
2013-02-15 17:34:25,843|API|http-bio-8443-exec-5
➥|18070+com.perfmath.spring.soba.web.LoginBroker.getModelAndView
2013-02-15 17:34:25,843|API|http-bio-8443-exec-5|18070Testing logging from SLF4J ... it
➥workscom.perfmath.spring.soba.web.LoginBroker.getModelAndView
2013-02-15 17:34:25,843|API|http-bio-8443-exec-5|18070-
➥com.perfmath.spring.soba.web.LoginBroker.getModelAndView
```

The above log format is determined by the "%d{ISO8601}|API|%t|%r%m%C.%M%n" ConversionPattern as specified in Listing 8.6 for the soba_perf_log4j.log file, namely, *date*, API, *thread name*, *milliseconds since program startup*, mark '+' or '-' or message, *<class_name>.<method_name>*, and *message*. The mark '+' or '-' indicate whether the logging event occurred at the beginning or at end of the method. The timing difference between the two gives the elapsed time of the method executed. Next, we discuss performance-profiling logging with perfBasic for SOBA in the next section.

Listing 8.6 log4j.xml configuration file

```
<?xml version="1.0" encoding="UTF-8" ?>
<!DOCTYPE log4j:configuration SYSTEM "log4j.dtd">
<log4j:configuration>
 <appender name="CONSOLE" class="org.apache.log4j.ConsoleAppender">
  <layout class="org.apache.log4j.PatternLayout">
   <param name="ConversionPattern"
```

```
        value="%d [%t] %-5p %c - %m%n"/>
    </layout>
  </appender>
  <appender name="FILE" class="org.apache.log4j.RollingFileAppender">
    <param name="File" value="../logs/soba/soba.log"/>
    <param name="Append" value="true"/>
    <layout class="org.apache.log4j.PatternLayout">
      <param name="ConversionPattern" value="%d{ISO8601} %t %-5p %c{2} – %m%n"/>
    </layout>
  </appender>
  <appender name="PERF" class="org.apache.log4j.RollingFileAppender">
    <param name="File" value="../logs/soba/soba_perf_log4j.log"/>
    <param name="Append" value="true"/>
    <layout class="org.apache.log4j.PatternLayout">
      <param name="ConversionPattern"
          value="%d{ISO8601}|API|%t|%r|%m%C.%M%n"/>
    </layout>
    <filter class="org.apache.log4j.varia.LevelRangeFilter" >
     <param name="LevelMin" value="INFO"/>
     </filter>
  </appender>
  <logger name="org.apache">
   <level value="INFO"/>
  </logger>
  <logger name="org.springframework.web">
   <level value="INFO"/>
     </logger>
      <logger name="org.springframework.security">
   <level value="INFO"/>
     </logger>
 <logger name="com.perfmath.spring.soba">
   <level value="INFO"/>
    <appender-ref ref="PERF"/>
 </logger>
 <root>
 <priority value="INFO" />
 <appender-ref ref="FILE"/>
 </root>
</log4j:configuration>
```

Listing 8.7 LoginBroker.java

```
package com.perfmath.spring.soba.web;
```

```
import javax.servlet.http.HttpServletRequest;
import javax.servlet.http.HttpServletResponse;
import org.apache.commons.logging.Log;
import org.apache.commons.logging.LogFactory;
import org.slf4j.Logger;
import org.springframework.security.core.context.SecurityContextHolder;
import org.springframework.stereotype.Controller;

import org.springframework.web.bind.annotation.RequestMapping;
import org.springframework.web.bind.annotation.SessionAttributes;
import org.springframework.web.servlet.ModelAndView;
import org.springframework.web.servlet.mvc.AbstractController;

@Controller
@RequestMapping("/loginBroker")
@SessionAttributes("login")
public class LoginBroker extends AbstractController {
private Log log = LogFactory.getLog (this.getClass());
private Logger logger = org.slf4j.LoggerFactory.getLogger(this.getClass());
    protected ModelAndView handleRequestInternal(HttpServletRequest request,
            HttpServletResponse response) throws Exception {

        ModelAndView mav = new ModelAndView ();
        mav= getModelAndView(request);
        return mav;
    }

    public ModelAndView getModelAndView(HttpServletRequest request) {
        log.info ("+");
logger.info("Testing logging from SLF4J ... it works");
        String authority = SecurityContextHolder.getContext()
                .getAuthentication().getAuthorities().toString();
        String viewString = "";
        if (authority.contains("ADMIN")) {
            viewString = "adminConsole";
        } else if (authority.contains("REP")) {
            viewString = "repConsole";
        } else if (authority.contains("CUST") ) {
            viewString = "redirect:activityList";
        }
        log.info ("-");
        return new ModelAndView (viewString);
```

```
    }
}
```

8.1.4 Performance Profiling with perfBasic for SOBA

Recall that we have a PERF appender configured in Listing 8.6 `log4j.xml` as follows:

```
<appender name="PERF" class="org.apache.log4j.RollingFileAppender">
  <param name="File" value="../logs/soba/soba_perf_log4j.log"/>
  <param name="Append" value="true"/>
  <layout class="org.apache.log4j.PatternLayout">
    <param name="ConversionPattern" value="%d{ISO8601}|API|%t|%r|%m%C.%M%n"/>
  </layout>
  <filter class="org.apache.log4j.varia.LevelRangeFilter" >
    <param name="LevelMin" value="INFO"/>
  </filter>
</appender>
```

Note that this appender specifies a logging format of **%d** for date, **%t** for thread name, **%r** for milliseconds since program startup, **%m** for user-defined message, and **%C.%M** for *className.methodName*. This format conforms to the perfBasic profiling logging format I once proposed in my other text *Software Performance and Scalability: A Quantitative Approach* (Wiley, 2009). However, there is a problem here: although all log data is written to a separate file, it cannot be independently turned on or off at runtime. Therefore, I needed to have decouple it from log4j. That is why I have a `PerfBasicUtil.java` class and the associated `perfBasicConsoleController.java` and `perfBasicConsole.jsp` for using my perfBasic profiling framework with SOBA.

Listing 8.8 shows the `PerfBasicUtil.java` class, which illustrates how it helps implement the perfBasic profiling framework. Note the following:

- **The attribute apfWriter**: This attribute makes it possible to separate perfBasic logging from the regular log4j logging by creating a separate writer from the file designated by the value of the attribute `apfFileName`. Be default, this file is named `perfLogData.apf` and is placed in Tomcat's `logs/soba` folder as well.
- The attribute **profilingStatus**: This is the variable that controls how profiling can be turned on and off dynamically at runtime. The actual work is done with the `resetProfiling (...)` method as shown below with the code snippet extracted from the class `PerfBasicConsoleController.java` illustrated in Listing 8.3. It specifies that if current `profilingStatus` and requested `profilingStatus` are not equal to each other, then reset it; also, the `ApfWriter` needs to be flushed to flush all performance log data after profiling is turned off.

```
public void resetProfiling(String profilingStatus) {
  if (!PerfBasicUtil.getProfilingStatus().equals(profilingStatus)) {
      PerfBasicUtil.setProfilingStatus(profilingStatus);
      if (PerfBasicUtil.getProfilingStatus().equals("disabled")){
          PerfBasicUtil.flushApfWriter();
```

```
            }
        }
    }
```

- The **log** method: This is the method that writes performance log data. Note how the class name and method name are extracted from the stack trace of the executing thread. In addition, we are not concerned with the server, client and user, so we just put "`unknownServer`," "`unknownClient`" and "`unknownUser`" there. We are more interested in how to enable logging than what performance metrics are logged here. In general, the other performance metrics such as thread, time-stamps, and fully-qualified class name with the method invoked are sufficient for performance profiling purposes.

Listing 8.8 PerfBasicUtil.java

```
package com.perfmath.spring.soba.util;

import java.io.FileWriter;
import java.io.IOException;
import java.io.PrintWriter;
import java.net.*;

public class PerfBasicUtil {

    private String apfFileName;
    private static String profilingStatus;
    private static  PrintWriter apfWriter;

// getters/setters and less relevant methods omitted here to save space

    public void createApfWriter() {

        try {
            if (apfWriter == null) {
                apfWriter = new PrintWriter(new FileWriter(apfFileName, true));
            }
        } catch (IOException io) {
            System.out.println("Failed to create " + apfFileName + " "
                    + io.getMessage());
            System.exit(-1);
        }
        System.out.println("apfWriter created: ");
    }

    public void closeApfWriter() {
```

```
        if (apfWriter != null) {
            apfWriter.flush();
            apfWriter.close();
        }
    }

    public void flushApfWriter() {
        if (apfWriter != null) {
            apfWriter.flush();
        }
    }

public static void log() {
        StackTraceElement[] stacktrace = Thread.currentThread().getStackTrace();
        if (getProfilingStatus().equals("enabled")) {
            String data = "/API" + "," + Thread.currentThread().getName()
                    + "," + System.currentTimeMillis() + "," + "unknownServer"
                    + "," + Thread.currentThread().getThreadGroup().getName()
                    + "," + "unknownClient" + "," + "unknownUser" + ","
                    + stacktrace[2].toString();
            if (apfWriter != null) {
                apfWriter.println(data);
            } else {
                System.out.println (data);
            }
        }
    }
}
```

Now functional logging through *log4j* and performance logging through *perfBasic* are separated and can be controlled independently from each other – both dynamically. PerfBasic logging is not limited by logging levels any more. However, there is a common problem, which is where the concept of *crosscutting concern* comes in, that is, you have to insert those logging statements into every method to be logged manually. This is not efficient, for example, if you have 20k classes and on average five methods per class need to have those logging statements inserted, it would sum up to 200k statements (log4j and perfBasic together). For perfBasic, it's not a huge deal, because we only need to add at the beginning and end of a method and the logging statement is the same, namely, *PerfBasicUtil.log()*; which can be done by using a simple program (in fact I did provide such a program when I first introduced perfBasic several years ago). Still, it would be more desirable if we could have other alternatives, which is what we would strive throughout the remainder of this chapter. Our first attempt would be with the method of dynamic proxy, as discussed in the next section.

8.2 SOLVING CROSSCUTTING CONCERNS WITH DYNAMIC PROXY

Proxy is a design pattern that belongs to the *structural pattern* category. With the proxy pattern, the caller calls the proxy and the proxy acts on behalf of the original object. Therefore, a proxy is basically a wrapper of an object. Figure 8.4 shows the concept of a proxy and a *proxied object*. A proxied object is also known as a *target object* or *advised object* as is explained later in context of AOP.

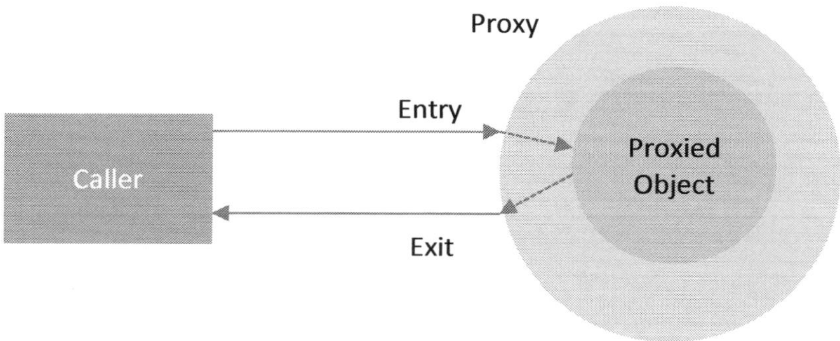

Figure 8.4 The concept of a proxy.

There are two types of proxies: static proxies and dynamic proxies. A static proxy works on a one-to-one basis that a proxy is needed for each interface and it is resolved at compile time. Obviously, this is worse than manually inserting those logging statements one by one in each method that requires logging.

A dynamic proxy is different that it is created at runtime dynamically and it works with any object. There are two types of dynamic proxies: those provided by the JDKs and CGLIB proxies (http://cglib.sourceforge.net – a powerful, high performance and quality Code Generation Library for extending Java classes and implementing interfaces at runtime). The difference between the two is that the JDK proxy requires at least one interface is implemented and only the methods declared in the interface are processed through the proxy, whereas the CGLIB proxy does not have this restriction since it uses sub-classing as opposed to the interface approach of the JDK proxies. Therefore, if you look at the `LoginBroker.java` class shown in Listing 8.7, it's clear that a JDK-based dynamic proxy would not work and only a CGLIB dynamic proxy would work. It appears that all classes in the `services` and `dao` packages do follow the interface-implementation pattern, and therefore a JDK-based dynamic proxy should work, but that's not the case either, because those objects are *injected* by Spring under the hood and we do not create them externally. These constraints become clear after we demonstrate how to apply JDK-based dynamic proxies to classes outside the Spring framework next.

In fact, the JDK and CGLIB proxies are used under the cover in the implementation of AspectJ, which will be discussed later. Let us now demonstrate how to apply JDK-based dynamic proxies to non-Spring-based classes. In order to demonstrate this, we have a few classes created in the `com.perfmath.spring.soba.aop.proxy` package. The first class is the `PerfBasicLoggingHandler.java` in this package. This class is shown in Listing 8.9. It is seen that:

- It does not import any Spring or Apache packages and it's purely standard Java without vendor specific packages.
- It implements the `InvocationHandler` from the `java.lang.reflect` package.

- It uses a `createProxy` method to create a proxy for a target object.
- It has an `invoke` method that would invoke the method of the target object. You can put your logging statements before and after the `method.invoke` (..) statement, but for perfBasic logging, we only need to insert a statement after the statement, because we only want to know how long it took for that `method.invoke` (..) method to be executed as an approximate time for the elapsed time of that method. With the `PerfBasicUtil.java` class, we could no longer use the *stacktrace* to extract the class and method of the profiled object, because the *stacktrace* has become more complicated due to the introduction of proxies. Therefore, we extract such information based on what's available in the *handler's invoke* method, that is, `target.toString ()` as shown in Listing 8.10.

Listing 8.9 PerfBasicLoggingHandler.java

```
package com.perfmath.spring.soba.aop.proxy;

import java.lang.reflect.InvocationHandler;
import java.lang.reflect.Method;
import java.lang.reflect.Proxy;

public class PerfBasicLoggingHandler implements InvocationHandler {
   private Object target;

   public static Object createProxy(Object target) {
      return Proxy.newProxyInstance(
            target.getClass().getClassLoader(),
            target.getClass().getInterfaces(),
            new PerfBasicLoggingHandler(target));
   }

   public PerfBasicLoggingHandler(Object target) {
      this.target = target;
   }

   public Object invoke(Object proxy, Method method, Object[] args)
        throws Throwable {
     long startTime = System.currentTimeMillis();
      Object result = method.invoke(target, args);
      PerfBasicUtil.log(target.toString() + "@" + method.getName() +
            ":" + (System.currentTimeMillis() - startTime));
      return result;
   }
}
```

Listing 8.10 A new method of PerfBasicUtil.log (String message) to be used with JDK-based dynamic proxy

```
// for proxy-based calls
public static void log(String message) {
        int index1 = message.indexOf("@");
        int index2 = message.lastIndexOf("@");
        if (index1 > 0) {
            message = message.substring (0, index1) + "." + message.substring
(index2 + 1);
        }
        if (getProfilingStatus().equals("enabled")) {
            String data = "API" + "," + Thread.currentThread().getName()
                    + "," + System.currentTimeMillis() + "," + "unknownServer"
                    + "," + Thread.currentThread().getThreadGroup().getName()
                    + "," + "unknownClient" + "," + "unknownUser" + ","
                    + message;
            if (apfWriter != null) {
                apfWriter.println(data);
            } else {
                System.out.println (data);
            }
        }
    }
```

Now let's say we want to profile a `MySQLJDBCConnection` object that checks and measures how long it takes to create a new JDBC connection. According to what we explained about what a JDK-based dynamic proxy can and can't do, we have to make it work as follows:

- Creating an interface, which is defined in `IJDBCConnection.java` as shown in Listing 8.11. This simple interface attempts to make a connection based on the connector information provided and returns a `java.sql.Connection` object.
- Creating an implementation of the `IJDBCConnection` interface, which is the `MySQLJDBCConnection.java` class as shown in Listing 8.12. This simple Java class implements the `checkConnection` method as described above.
- Creating a `JDBCConnectionTest.java` class, which does the actual work of testing the JDBC connection with a given implementation, which is the `MySQLJDBCConnection.java` class in this case, as is shown in Listing 8.13. This is how this `JDBCConnectionTest.java` class works :
    - First, a `mySQLJDBCConnection` object is instantiated as usual.
    - Then, the object is passed to the `PerfBasicLoggingHandler's createProxy` method to create a `jdbcConnection` object, which is the target object to be worked on.

Note: During upgrading SOBA from Spring 3.1 to 3.2 GA, a red mark appeared on the `JDBCConnectionTest.java` class in the `com.perfmath.spring.soba.aop.proxy` package, complaining that "*The type IJDBCConnection cannot be resolved.*" The issue was eventually resolved by unchecking *Project → Build Automatically* and then clicking *Clean….* In case you encounter similar issues and nothing else seems to be helpful, you might want to try to clean and re-build your project as well.

This example shows all the logistics necessary for using JDK-based dynamic proxies to solve a crosscutting concern. Listing 8.14 shows the output of a test run, indicating that the proxy-based call to create a JDBC connection against a MySQL server on an Intel i7-3770 system took 170 milliseconds.

This dynamic proxy worked fine when executed standalone on Eclipse and produced the expected output as shown in Listing 8.14. However, when it was built with Maven and deployed with the rest of SOBA on Tomcat 7, SOBA could not be started up, due to the following error:

```
Jul 22, 2012 7:47:00 PM org.apache.catalina.core.StandardContext startInternal
SEVERE: Error listenerStart
Jul 22, 2012 7:47:00 PM org.apache.catalina.core.StandardContext startInternal
SEVERE: Context [/soba] startup failed due to previous errors
Jul 22, 2012 7:47:00 PM org.apache.catalina.loader.WebappClassLoader
    clearReferencesJdbc
SEVERE: The web application [/soba] registered the JDBC driver [com.mysql.jdbc.Driver] but failed to
unregister it when the web application was stopped. To prevent a memory leak, the JDBC Driver has
been forcibly unregistered.
Jul 22, 2012 7:47:00 PM org.apache.catalina.loader.WebappClassLoader clearReferencesThreads
SEVERE: The web application [/soba] appears to have started a thread named [MySQL Statement
Cancellation Timer] but has failed to stop it. This is very likely to create a memory leak.
```

The above error is reported here just to show that AOP programming is a lot more challenging than regular Java programming. It has very stringent rules to follow and associated error messages are less indicative. After hours of debugging, I finally resolved it by making the following changes:

- Changed the arguments for `checkConnection` shown in Listing 8.11 into:

```
checkConnection (String connectionDescriptor)
```

- Changed the `checkConnection` implementation in Listing 8.12 into:

```
public class MySQLJDBCConnection implements IJDBCConnection {
    public Connection checkConnection(String connectionDescriptor) {
        Connection conn = null;
        long startTime = System.nanoTime ();
        String[] part = new String[4];
        StringTokenizer st = new StringTokenizer(connectionDescriptor, "+");
        int i = 0;
        while (st.hasMoreElements()) {
            part[i] = st.nextElement().toString();
            i++;
```

```
        }
    try {
            Class.forName(part[0]).newInstance();
            conn = DriverManager.getConnection(part[1], part[2], part[3]);
    }
    catch (Exception e) {
        System.out.print ("Cannot connect to database server: " + e.getMessage());
        }
    return conn;
  }
```

- Changed the `checkConnection` call in Listing 8.13 into:

```
String connectionDescriptor = "com.mysql.jdbc.Driver+"
                + "jdbc:mysql://localhost:3306/soba32+" + "soba32admin+"
                + "soba32admin";
    conn = jdbcConnection.checkConnection(connectionDescriptor);
```

This trick helped resolve the above error magically (I figured that somehow *it* knew that a MySQL connection was being made with given *driver*, *url*, *username*, and *password*, so I won't let it know that by introducing a `StringTokenizer` to reconstruct all pieces of information from one String object of `connectionDescriptor`).

Listing 8.11 IJDBCConnection interface

```
package com.perfmath.spring.soba.aop.proxy;
import java.sql.Connection;
public interface IJDBCConnection {
public Connection checkConnection (String username,
String password, String url, String driver);
}
```

Listing 8.12 MySQLJDBCConnection.java class that implements the IJDBCConnection interface

```
package com.perfmath.spring.soba.aop.proxy;

import java.sql.Connection;
import java.sql.DriverManager;

public class MySQLJDBCConnection implements IJDBCConnection {
    public Connection checkConnection(String username, String password, String url,
            String driver) {
        Connection conn = null;
    try {
        Class.forName (driver).newInstance ();
```

```
        conn = DriverManager.getConnection (url, username, password);
      }
      catch (Exception e) {
        System.out.print ("Cannot connect to database server: " + e.getMessage());
        }
      return conn;
    }
}
```

Listing 8.13 JDBCConnectionTest.java

```
package com.perfmath.spring.soba.aop.proxy;
import java.sql.*;

import com.perfmath.spring.soba.util.PerfBasicUtil;

public class JDBCConnectionTest
{
  public static void main (String[] args)
  {
    Connection conn = null;
    try {
      IJDBCConnection mySQLJDBCConnection = new MySQLJDBCConnection ();
      IJDBCConnection jdbcConnection =
          (IJDBCConnection) PerfBasicLoggingHandler.createProxy
         (mySQLJDBCConnection);
      conn = jdbcConnection.checkConnection("sobaadmin", "sobaadmin",
            "jdbc:mysql://localhost:3306/soba", "com.mysql.jdbc.Driver");
      if (conn != null) {
      System.out.println ("   --> calling by proxy completed with " +
          " database connection established");
      }
    } catch (Exception e) {
      System.err.println ("Cannot connect to database server: " + e.getMessage());
    } finally {
      if (conn != null) {
        try
        {
          conn.close ();
          System.out.println ("   --> Database connection terminated");
        }
        catch (Exception e) { /* ignore close errors */ }
      }
```

```
      }
      PerfBasicUtil.setProfilingStatus("disabled");
   }
}
```

Listing 8.14 The output of a JDBCConnection test run

```
API,main,1361065936494,unknownServer,main,unknownClient,unknownUser,
➥com.perfmath.spring.soba.aop.proxy.MySQLJDBCConnection.checkConnection:170
  --> calling by proxy completed with  database connection established
  --> Database connection terminated
```

Dynamic proxy does not require inserting crosscutting statements in every class or method of an application. However, as you can see from Listing 8.13, it requires manually creating an object through the `createProxy` method of a crosscutting handler. What if an application consists of 20k or 100k classes? And what if an application has already been developed and in use for quite some time and it's not so easy to modify it? And as you can see that it's even hard to use with SOBA because all objects are *injected*. A better, preferred solution is to use Spring AOP-AspectJ support, as is discussed in the next section.

8.3 SOLVING CROSSCUTTING CONCERNS WITH SPRING AOP-ASPECTJ SUPPORT

Before getting deep with Spring AOP and its support for AspectJ, let's first review some of the basic AOP concepts next.

8.3.1 Basic AOP Concepts

The following concepts are essential for understanding AOP in general:

- **Joinpoint**: A joinpoint is basically an *execution point* in a program. It defines *where* an event occurs, for example, before or after a method execution event, or after an exception is thrown, etc., or where you could insert crosscutting statements if it was done in an intrusive way.
- **Pointcut**: A pointcut is a *predicate* for matching desired joinpoints. A pointcut defines on which package/class/method to apply an action or *advice* in AOP's term as explained next. It is essentially a matchmaker between an AOP advice and one or more joinpoints. Spring uses the AspectJ *pointcut expression* by default.
- **Advice**: An advice advises what action to take at well-defined joinpoints matched by one or more pointcuts. Spring supports the following five types of advice:
  - *Before advice*: Advice to be executed *before* a method execution.
  - *Around advice*: Advice to be executed *around* (or prior to and following) a join point such as a method invocation.
  - *After returning advice* : Advice to be executed after a join point completes normally without throwing an exception.

- *After throwing advice*: Advice to be executed after a method exits due to an exception thrown.
- *After (finally) advice*: Advice to be executed regardless of whether an exception is thrown or not.

- **Aspect**: An aspect is a modularization of a crosscutting concern that applies to more than one class. An *aspect* is essentially a class that can be applied to altering the behavior of the base code by applying *advice* (additional crosscutting behavior) at various *join points* (places to apply advised operations) specified in a quantification or query called a *pointcut* (a matching condition for helping determine whether the *advice* should be invoked). Spring offers two approaches to implementing an aspect class: using the @AspectJ annotation style or using a schema-based approach that is independent of AspectJ. The @AspectJ style is preferred in general, because it gives more flexibilities to tap into the vast possibilities of solving crosscutting concerns than Spring's own schema-based approach. Later in this section, we present an example of using the @AspectJ style to implement an aspect class. Nevertheless, keep in mind the limitations with Spring's own AOP that:
  - It is limited to the classes that implement an interface.
  - It is limited to method execution joinpoints only.
  - It is limited to Spring beans only.
- **Target object**: A target object is the object to receive advice from one or more aspects. Because the Spring AOP is implemented using runtime proxies, a target object is also called a *proxied* object or *advised* object, to be more pertinently.
- **Introduction**: An introduction provides opportunities for adding additional attributes and methods on behalf of a type or introducing new interfaces to advised objects. In the AspectJ community, an introduction is known as an inter-type declaration.
- **Weaving**: This is a mechanism for linking or weaving aspects with other application types or objects to create an advised object. Although weaving can be done at compile time, load time, or runtime, Spring AOP *weaves* at runtime.

Instead of giving each permutation a light touch, let us go through a concrete, easier to understand example next to help explain the AOP concepts and the most likely approach you would use if you really need to use AOP a lot with your product, that is, how Spring supports AspectJ framework within its own AOP framework. You should refer to the Spring reference documentation and AspectJ texts to learn more if AOP is really a big deal to your project.

8.3.2 Spring and AspectJ Mixed AOP

My suggested approach to learning anything new is to focus on one good example, understand the concepts and the underlying mechanism really well, and then expand. The example presented next follows this guideline.

To illustrate how a Spring and AspectJ mixed AOP scenario might work, we focus on the *around advice*. This scenario consists of the following four classes:

1 A `JDBCConnection` class: This `JDBCConnection.java` class is contained in the package of `com.perfmath.spring.soba.aop.aspectj` and shown in Listing 8.15. It has two methods: a method named `getConnection` with a given connection descriptor and a method named `returnConnection` with a given open connection to close it.

2 A ManageJDBCConnection class: This ManageJDBCConnection.java class is shown in Listing 8.16. It depends on the preceding JDBCConnection class to manage JDBC connections. It has three methods: openConnection, closeConnection, and setJdbcConnection. The first two methods are for normal operations with JDBC connections, while the last method auto-wires it to the dependent class of JDBCConnection.

3 A PerfBasicLoggingAspect class: This PerfBasicLoggingAspect.java class is shown in Listing 8.17. This is the *aspect* to be applied to an advised object. It defines two *pointcuts* and one *around advice* as follows:

- The first pointcut annotation specifies all methods with their method names starting with getConnection (String) from all classes in the com.perfmath.spring package with an argument of connDescriptor of *String* type, which matches the getConnectionExecution () method of the JDBCConnection class. In this pointcut expression, the first wildcard ("*") matches methods with any modifier (public, private, and protected), while the second wildcard ("*") matches method names starting with the prefix of getConnection and have an argument of String type; the two dots ".." in "com.perfmath.spring..getConnection*(String)" specify all classes with their fully qualified names starting with "com.perfmath.spring"; and the part "args(connDescriptor)" specifies the methods with an argument named connDescriptor.
- The second pointcut annotation specifies *all* method executions of the Spring beans whose names are prefixed with 'jdbcConnection'.
- The around annotation specifies that the logAround (...) method should be applied when both pointcuts match, namely, all beans with their names prefixed with jdbcConnection and their methods satisfying the condition specified by the first pointcut.

Listing 8.18 shows the Spring bean configuration file springaopaspectj.xml for this example. In addition to the relevant schemas declared, there are only two tags: One is to specify @AspectJ autoproxy with <aop:aspectj-autoproxy> and the other is <context:component-scan>. The first tag enables Spring to create proxies for advised objects automatically (remember that it's always the proxies that work behind the scene), whereas the second tag instructs Spring to scan beans from the base package of com.perfmath.spring.soba.aop, which is where the advised objects reside. By default, the JDK-based dynamic proxies are created. If you rewrite the first tag like <aop:aspectj-autoproxy proxy-target-class ="true"/>, the CGLIB dynamic proxies will be created instead (refer to Chapter 9 of the *Spring 4 Reference Documentation* for more details).

Listing 8.19 shows the AOPDriver.java program that is used to drive the test. It first creates an application context from the springaopaspectj.xml Spring bean configuration file. It then gets the Spring bean named manageJDBCConnection from the context created in the preceding step. This is made possible with the @Component annotation in Listing 8.16 ManageJDBCConnection.java and the tag <context:component-scan> in Listing 8.18 springaopaspectj.xml. It then calls the openConnection and closeConnection methods to drive the test.

Listing 8.20 shows the output with the JDK-based dynamic proxies, while Listing 8.21 shows the output with the CGLIB-based dynamic proxies obtained by changing "false" to "true" in <aop:aspectj-autoproxy proxy-target-class ="false"/> in the springaopaspectj.xml file. Let's trace back how it worked:

- The ManageJDBCConnection bean depends on the jdbcConnection bean. These beans were created when the AOPDriver started to run. When the statement "Connection conn = jdbcConnection.openConnection(connectionDescriptor);" was invoked, the openConnection () method of the jdbcConnection bean was invoked, which triggered the logAround () advice as both pointcuts matched. Then, three events occurred in sequence in the logAround () method:
  - The first "perfBasic logging: startTime=..." was output as shown in Listings 8.20 and 8.21.
  - Next, when the statement "joinPoint.proceed()" was executed, the openConnection () method of the jdbcConnection bean was executed, which output the next three lines preceded with "-->" as shown in Listings 8.20 and 8.21.
  - After returning from the openConnection () method of the jdbcConnection bean, the next "perfBasic logging: endTime=..." was output as shown in Listings 8.20 and 8.21.
- When the next statement of jdbcConnection.closeConnection () was executed in the AOPDriver, those two pointcuts were not met, and therefore the logAround advice was not applied. That's why we had only one line of "--> Database connection terminated" in Listings 8.20 and 8.21.

I'd like to mention that both outputs were obtained on an Intel i7-3770 based system. It is seen that there is not much difference in performance between these two different types of dynamic proxies (121 milliseconds versus 120 milliseconds – in this case the openConnection is an long operation. It may make a larger difference for sub-millisecond operations). However, they were significantly faster than the non-AOP based approach, which took 170 milliseconds as shown in Listing 8.14. It seems that the non-AOP based approach was slower than the AOP based approach. This probably is because that with the non-aspect-based example, the proxy was created in the test driver program manually, while with the aspect-based examples, the proxies were created already when they were initialized for each test case since they were configured rather than manually created as was the case with the non-aspect-based example. These test results seem to hint that people should not try to create proxies in their programs manually. Instead, they should use Spring-configured proxies as much as possible both for performance and flexibility reasons.

If you want to learn more about Spring AOP and AspectJ, refer to the *Recommended Reading* section at the end of this chapter.

This wraps up our AOP chapter.

Listing 8.15 JDBCConnection.java

```
package com.perfmath.spring.soba.aop.aspectj;

import java.sql.Connection;
import java.sql.DriverManager;
import java.util.StringTokenizer;

import org.springframework.stereotype.Component;
```

```
@Component("jdbcConnection")
public class JDBCConnection {

    public Connection getConnection(String connectionDescriptor) {
        long startTime = System.nanoTime ();
        String[] part = new String[4];
        StringTokenizer st = new StringTokenizer(connectionDescriptor, "+");
        int i = 0;
        while (st.hasMoreElements()) {
            part[i] = st.nextElement().toString();
            i++;
        }
        System.out.println("    --> Parsing took  " +
                (System.nanoTime () - startTime)/1000 +
                " microseconds inside JDBCConnection");
        Connection conn = null;
        try {
            Class.forName(part[0]).newInstance();
            conn = DriverManager.getConnection(part[1], part[2], part[3]);
            System.out.println("    --> Connect to database server " + part[1]
                    + " successful");
        } catch (Exception e) {
            System.out.println("Cannot connect to database server: "
                    + e.getMessage());
        }
        System.out.println("    --> getConnection took  " +
            (System.nanoTime () - startTime)/1000000 +
             " ms inside JDBCConnection");
        return conn;
    }

    public void returnConnection(Connection conn) {
        if (conn != null) {
            try {
                conn.close();
                System.out.println("  --> Database connection terminated");
            } catch (Exception e) {
            }
        }
    }
}
```

Listing 8.16 ManageJDBCConnection.java

```
package com.perfmath.spring.soba.aop.aspectj;

import java.sql.Connection;

import org.springframework.beans.factory.annotation.Autowired;
import org.springframework.stereotype.Component;

@Component("manageJDBCConnection")
public class ManageJDBCConnection {
    private JDBCConnection jdbcConnection;

    public Connection openConnection(String connectionDescriptor) {
        Connection conn = jdbcConnection.getConnection(connectionDescriptor);
        return conn;
    }

    public void closeConnection(Connection conn) {
        jdbcConnection.returnConnection(conn);
    }

    @Autowired
    public void setJdbcConnection(JDBCConnection jdbcConnection) {
        this.jdbcConnection = jdbcConnection;
    }
}
```

Listing 8.17 PerfBasicLoggingAspect.java

```
package com.perfmath.spring.soba.aop;

import java.util.Arrays;

import org.aspectj.lang.ProceedingJoinPoint;
import org.aspectj.lang.annotation.Around;
import org.aspectj.lang.annotation.Aspect;
import org.aspectj.lang.annotation.Pointcut;
import org.springframework.stereotype.Component;

@Component
@Aspect
public class PerfBasicLoggingAspect {
```

```
    @Pointcut("execution(* com.perfmath.spring..getConnection*(String))
&& args(connDescriptor)")
    public void getConnectionExecution(String connDescriptor) {
    }

    @Pointcut("bean(jdbcConnection*)")
    public void inJDBCConnection() {
    }

    @Around("getConnectionExecution(connDescriptor) && inJDBCConnection ()")
    public Object logAround(ProceedingJoinPoint joinPoint, String connDescriptor)
            throws Throwable {
        long startTime = System.currentTimeMillis();
        String signature = joinPoint.getTarget().getClass().getName() + "."
                + joinPoint.getSignature().getName();
        try {
            System.out.println("perfBasic logging: startTime=" + startTime
                    + " for " + signature);
            Object result = joinPoint.proceed();
            long endTime = System.currentTimeMillis();
            String logData = "perfBasic logging: endTime=" + endTime + " for "
                    + signature + ":elapsed time=" + (endTime - startTime)
                    + " ms";
            System.out.println(logData);
            return result;
        } catch (IllegalArgumentException e) {
            System.out.println("Illegal argument "
                    + Arrays.toString(joinPoint.getArgs()) + " in "
                    + joinPoint.getSignature().getName() + "()");
            throw e;
        }
    }
}
```

Listing 8.18 springaopaspectj.xml

```
<?xml version="1.0" encoding="UTF-8"?>
<beans xmlns="http://www.springframework.org/schema/beans"
    xmlns:xsi="http://www.w3.org/2001/XMLSchema-instance"
    xmlns:aop="http://www.springframework.org/schema/aop"
    xmlns:context="http://www.springframework.org/schema/context"
    xsi:schemaLocation="http://www.springframework.org/schema/aop
    http://www.springframework.org/schema/aop/spring-aop.xsd
```

```
        http://www.springframework.org/schema/beans
    http://www.springframework.org/schema/beans/spring-beans.xsd
        http://www.springframework.org/schema/context
    http://www.springframework.org/schema/context/spring-context.xsd">

    <!-- "false" for JDK-generated proxies (default) -->
    <aop:aspectj-autoproxy proxy-target-class="false" />

    <!-- "true" for CGLIB generated proxies -->
    <!-- aop:aspectj-autoproxy proxy-target-class="true" / -->

    <context:component-scan base-package="com.perfmath.spring.soba.aop.aspectj" />

</beans>
```

Listing 8.19 AOPDriver.java

```
package com.perfmath.spring.soba.aop.aspectj;

import org.springframework.context.ApplicationContext;
import org.springframework.context.support.ClassPathXmlApplicationContext;
import java.sql.Connection;

import com.perfmath.spring.soba.aop.ManageJDBCConnection;

public class AOPDriver {
    public static void main(String[] args) {
        {
            ApplicationContext context = new ClassPathXmlApplicationContext(
                    "springaopaspectj.xml");
            ManageJDBCConnection jdbcConnection =
                (ManageJDBCConnection) context
                    .getBean("manageJDBCConnection");
            String connectionDescriptor = "com.mysql.jdbc.Driver+"
                    + "jdbc:mysql://localhost:3306/soba+" + "sobaadmin+"
                    + "sobaadmin";
            Connection conn = jdbcConnection.openConnection(connectionDescriptor);
            jdbcConnection.closeConnection(conn);
        }
    }
}
```

Listing 8.20 Output from an AOP Test Run with JDK-based dynamic proxies

```
perfBasic logging: startTime=1361065254813 for
↪com.perfmath.spring.soba.aop.aspectj.JDBCConnection.getConnection
  --> Parsing took 31 microseconds inside JDBCConnection
  --> Connect to database server jdbc:mysql://localhost:3306/soba successful
  --> getConnection took 121 ms inside JDBCConnection
perfBasic logging: endTime=1361065254943 for
↪com.perfmath.spring.soba.aop.aspectj.JDBCConnection.getConnection:elapsed time=130 ms
 --> Database connection terminated
```

Listing 8.21 Output from an AOP test run with CGLIB-based dynamic proxies

```
perfBasic logging: startTime=1361065546673 for
↪com.perfmath.spring.soba.aop.aspectj.JDBCConnection.getConnection
  --> Parsing took 64 microseconds inside JDBCConnection
  --> Connect to database server jdbc:mysql://localhost:3306/soba successful
  --> getConnection took 120 ms inside JDBCConnection
perfBasic logging: endTime=1361065546803 for
↪com.perfmath.spring.soba.aop.aspectj.JDBCConnection.getConnection:elapsed time=130 ms
 --> Database connection terminated
```

8.4 SUMMARY

In this chapter, we introduced the concept of crosscutting concerns such as logging, validation, security, transaction management, exception handling, etc., that have to be dealt with in developing enterprise applications. Examples of SOBA functional logging and performance logging based on the perfBasic profiling framework I proposed several years ago were used to help corroborate those crosscutting concerns.

Then, we focused on two approaches to solving crosscutting concerns: The proxy-based approach and the AOP-based approach. From an application development point of view, the AOP-based approach is more flexible and practical, and out of many AOP-based implementations, Spring-AspectJ mixed implementation is arguably the best implementation strategy for Spring-based enterprise Java applications. We presented a concrete example to help explain the AOP concepts such as a joinpoint, pointcut, advice, aspect, and so on. The example also illustrated the procedure to develop and apply an aspect for solving a crosscutting concern.

Apparently, Spring AOP is a broad subject that is hard to explain all in one chapter of a book. If you really need to use AOP with your product, you need to study further, as explained in the Recommend Reading section next.

RECOMMENDED READING

The Spring Reference Documentation covers the following AOP topics in Chapters 8 and 9 (the topics we covered are highlighted):

- Chapter 8 Aspect Oriented Programming with Spring:
    - **8.1 Introduction**
    - **8.2 @AspectJ support**
    - 8.3 Schema-based AOP support
    - **8.4 Choosing which AOP style to use**
    - 8.5 Mixing aspect types
    - **8.6 Proxying mechanisms**
    - 8.7 Programmatic creation of @AspectJ Proxies
    - 8.8 Using AspectJ with Spring applications
    - 8.9 Further resources
- Chapter 9 Spring AOP APIs

If you are interested in exploring more Spring AOP features, you can continue to try them out with SOBA. In fact, there is a self-review exercise next that I hope you can try it. AOP is a very powerful concept for solving large scale crosscutting concerns, but programming it is not easy at all. If you have never worked on it, you will know it after you try the AOP programing exercise 8.3 as described next.

EXERCISES

8.1 What are the major differences conceptually between JDK-based dynamic proxies and CGLIB-based proxies?

8.2 What are the major limitations with pure Spring AOP implementations?

8.3 Modify the *aspect* listed in section 8.3 so that it would work for all methods of all classes to be proxied.

9 Spring Testing

Testing is an indispensable part of developing high quality, reliable enterprise software. Testing can typically be divided into two broad categories: functional and non-functional tests. Functional tests help verify whether the product under test executes correctly with a pre-determined set of use cases, whereas non-functional tests help verify whether the product under test can meet the performance, reliability, scalability and/or any other requirements that are operational-driven.

In this chapter, we are more concerned with functional tests. The first level of functional testing is *unit testing*, which verifies that the methods of a class work as expected with one or more given states as represented by the attributes of the class. The next level of functional testing is *integration testing*, which verifies that a class or component works as expected when other components get involved. The third level of functional testing is *system testing*, which verifies that the product still work as expected when it is deployed to an internal test environment and driven with realistic use cases that mimic how real users would use it. The scope becomes broader and broader as we go higher from one level to the next. For example, with the SOBA sample included in this book, I have to verify that it does not only work in a base environment of MySQL/Tomcat/Windows, but also works with other commonly used databases, application servers and operating systems such as Oracle, SQL Server, Jboss, GlassFish, WebLogic, Linux and Mac OS X. However, if you are working with a real enterprise software product, you should convince your company to minimize the variety of DB/AppServer/OS that your product has to support. That will help your company save time and money in the end.

In this chapter, we start with how to use JUnit and TestNG to perform functional tests in general. Then we cover how Spring Testing supports testing Spring components with features such as TestContext, automatically injecting test fixtures, transactional support, and so on. If you are already familiar with JUnit and TestNG, feel free to jump to Spring Testing directly.

9.1 Unit Testing with JUnit and TestNG

JUnit is a testing framework that has been in use widely for testing Java applications. At the time of this writing, the latest formal release is 4.11. Spring 2.5 and prior releases supported JUnit 3.8, which was referred to as JUnit 3.8 legacy support, while Spring 3.x started supporting JUnit 4. JUnit 3.x depends on the following two features:

- The testing class must extend the JUnit framework class `TestCase`.
- Each test case must be a public method and the method name must be prefixed with `test`.

In contrast, JUnit 4 takes advantages of the Java annotation feature introduced in Java 1.5. It provides a framework `@Test` annotation so that any public methods can be run as a test case. Next, we use an example to illustrate how JUnit 4 works in general.

9.1.1 Unit Testing with JUnit 4

Let us use our SOBA sample as the context for demonstrating how JUnit 4 works. Let's say we have a requirement that dividend should be paid with an banking account on a monthly basis. This requirement can be implemented with a `DividentCalculator.java` interface and a `SimpleDividentCalculator.java` class that implements the interface. Listings 9.1 and 9.2 illustrates the Java source code for this interface and class.

Note: In order to build the project successfully, it's necessary to add the `junit-4.9.jar` file to the `SOBA-lib` if you use Ant. If you use Maven, add the following dependency to the `pom.xml` file (I tried 4.10, which didn't work):

```
<dependency>
    <groupId>junit</groupId>
    <artifactId>junit</artifactId>
    <version>4.9</version>
</dependency>
```

As we see from the interface and the implementation class shown in Listings 9.1 and 9.2, the method `calculate (double balance, int numOfDays)` returns the amount of dividend to be credited to the customer's account, which can be initiated on a monthly basis.

Listing 9.1 DividentCalculator.java

```
package com.perfmath.spring.soba.testing;

public interface DividentCalculator {

   public void setDailyRate(double dailyRate);
   public double calculate(double balance, int numOfDays);
}
```

Listing 9.2 SimpleDividentCalculator.java

```
package com.perfmath.spring.soba.testing;
```

```
public class SimpleDividentCalculator implements DividentCalculator {

  private double dailyRate;

  public void setDailyRate(double dailyRate) {
    this.dailyRate = dailyRate;
  }

  public double calculate(double balance, int numOfDays) {
    if (numOfDays <0) {
      throw new IllegalArgumentException("number of days must be positive");
    } else if (balance < 0) {
      return 0;
    } else {
      return balance * numOfDays * dailyRate;
    }
  }
}
```

Listing 9.3 shows how to test the `SimpleDividentCalculator.java` class as shown in Listing 9.2. Unlike JUnit 3.x, this JUnit test class does not extend the JUnit framework `TestCase` base class. Besides, it does not have to prefix each public method with `test`. Instead, it uses the `@Test` annotation to indicate that the annotated method is a test case. In addition, you can use the `assertEquals` to ensure that the dividend would be $15.0 with a daily rate of 0.1%, an average balance of $500 over a 30-day period. This method has the signature of

```
Public static void assertEquals (double expected, double actual, double delta)
```

which asserts that the `expected` and `actual` doubles will be considered `equal` within a positive `delta` as specified. Finally, you can use the `expected` attribute of the `@Test` annotation to specify the exception to be thrown when an invalid parameter is input.

Listing 9.3 SimpleDividentCalculatorJUnitTest.java

```
package com.perfmath.spring.soba.testing.junit;

import static org.junit.Assert.*;

import org.junit.Before;
import org.junit.Test;

import com.perfmath.spring.soba.testing.DividentCalculator;
import com.perfmath.spring.soba.testing.SimpleDividentCalculator;

public class SimpleDividentCalculatorJUnitTest {
```

```
    private DividentCalculator dividentCalculator;

    @Before
    public void init() {
        dividentCalculator = new SimpleDividentCalculator();
        dividentCalculator.setDailyRate(0.001);
    }

    @Test
    public void calculate() {
        double divident = dividentCalculator.calculate(500.0, 30);
        assertEquals(divident, 15.0, 0);
    }

    @Test(expected = IllegalArgumentException.class)
    public void illegalCalculate() {
        dividentCalculator.calculate(100.0, -10);
    }
}
```

To run the above JUnit test class `SimpleDividentCalculatorJUnitTest`, first, make sure you build the project with either Maven or Ant without encounter any errors. Then, you can right-click on the class name of `SimpleDividentCalculatorJUnitTest.java` in the *src/main/java/testing/junit* package, and select *Run As … 2 JUnit Test*, as shown in Figure 9.1. If you built the project with Maven, you should see an output as shown in Figure 9.2, indicating zero errors and failures. However, if you built the project with Ant, you might get the notorious exception of `ClassDefNotFound`, complaining that the `SimpleDividentCalculatorJUnitTest` class cannot be found. Next, we describe how to resolve this error.

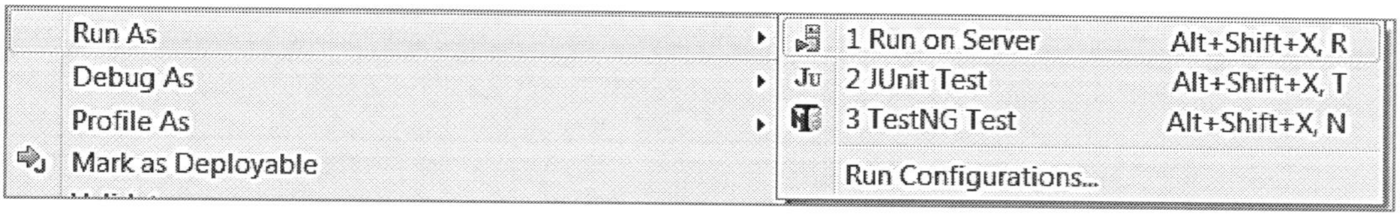

Figure 9.1 Running JUnit test on Eclipse IDE

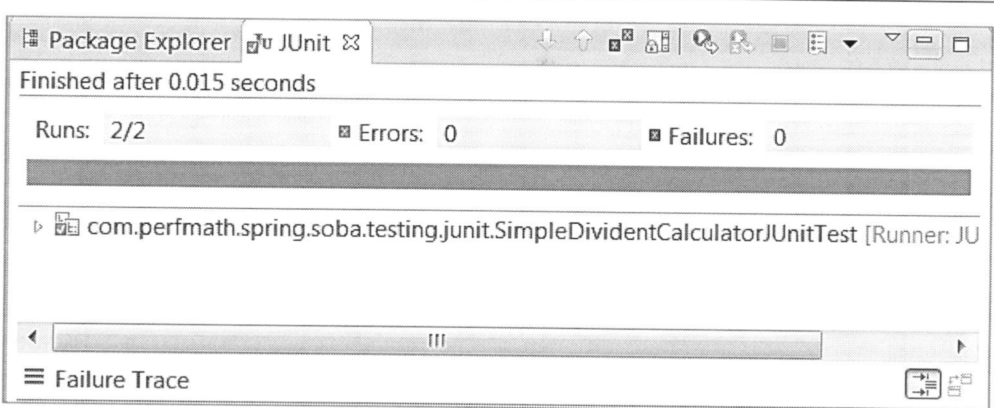

Figure 9.2 Output from running the JUnit test

The error of `ClassDefNotFound` typically is a CLASSPATH issue. When Maven is enabled on Eclipse, the *target/classes* folder is automatically added to the project's classpath. However, this is not the case when the project is built with Ant. In this case, you have to add the *build/classes* folder according to the instructions given in the *SOBA_project_ReadMeFirst.PDF* file included in the project download zip file.

Next, we discuss how to use TestNG to perform unit testing.

9.1.2 Unit Testing with TestNG

TestNG is marketed as the *Next Generation Java Testing Framework* (http://testng.org). As it is stated at its website, it is inspired from JUnit and NUnit and introduces the following new features:

- Annotations
- Run your tests in arbitrarily big thread pools (all methods in their own thread and one thread per test case, etc.)
- Test your code is multithread safe
- Supper for data-driven testing with `@DataProvider`
- Support for parameters
- Powerful execution model with no more need to extend `TestCase`
- Supported by a variety of tools and plug-ins such as Eclipse, Maven, IDEA, etc.
- Dependent methods for application server testing

TestNG is designed to cover all categories of testing such as unit testing, functional testing, end-to-end testing, integration testing, and so on. However, a detailed coverage of TestNG is beyond the scope of this text. We can only present a few examples to help you get a glimpse of how it works.

Listing 9.4 shows how to use TestNG to test the `SimpleDividentCalculator` class as an alternative to JUnit. First, it applies the `@BeforeMethod` annotation to the `init ()` method to create a new `DividentCalculator` instance and sets the `dailyRate` to 0.1%. Then, note the two methods of `createLegalDividentParameters()` and `createIllegalDividentParameters()`, annotated with

@DataProvider named with "legal" and "illegal", respectively. Note how the Object[] and Object[][] are used with the @DataProvider annotation. Finally, note how these two DataProviders are used with the calculate and illegalCalculate methods, both of which are annotated with the @Test annotation.

You can build and execute this test class using the Eclipse *Run As …* feature as shown in Figure 9.1. Listing 9.5 shows the output obtained in my environment.

Note: In order to build the project successfully, it's necessary to add the testng6.8.jar file to the SOBA-lib if you use Ant. If you use Maven, add the following dependency to the pom.xml file:

```
<dependency>
    <groupId>org.testng</groupId>
    <artifactId>testng</artifactId>
    <version>6.8</version>
</dependency>
```

Listing 9.4 SimpleDividentCalculatorTestNGTest.java

```
package com.perfmath.spring.soba.testing.testng;

import static org.testng.Assert.*;

import org.testng.annotations.BeforeMethod;
import org.testng.annotations.DataProvider;
import org.testng.annotations.Test;

import com.perfmath.spring.soba.testing.DividentCalculator;
import com.perfmath.spring.soba.testing.SimpleDividentCalculator;

public class SimpleDividentCalculatorTestNGTest {

  private DividentCalculator dividentCalculator;

  @BeforeMethod
  public void init() {
   dividentCalculator = new SimpleDividentCalculator();
   dividentCalculator.setDailyRate(0.001);
  }

  @DataProvider(name = "legal")
  public Object[][] createLegalDividentParameters() {
     return new Object[][] { new Object[] { 500, 30, 15.0 } };
```

```
    }

    @DataProvider(name = "illegal")
    public Object[][] createIllegalDividentParameters() {
        return new Object[][] {new Object[] { 500, -30 }, new Object[] { -500, -30 }};
    }

    @Test(dataProvider = "legal")
    public void calculate(double balance, int numOfDays, double result) {
        double divident= dividentCalculator.calculate(balance, numOfDays);
        assertEquals(divident, result);
    }

    @Test(dataProvider = "illegal", expectedExceptions = IllegalArgumentException.class)
    public void illegalCalculate(double balance, int numOfDays) {
       dividentCalculator.calculate(balance, numOfDays);
    }
}
```

Listing 9.5 TestNG output from running SimpleDividentCalculatorTestNGTest

```
[TestNG] Running:
  C:\Users\henry\AppData\Local\Temp\testng-eclipse--972939339\testng-customsuite.xml

PASSED: calculate(500, 30, 15.0)
PASSED: illegalCalculate(500, -30)
PASSED: illegalCalculate(-500, -30)

===============================================
    Default test
    Tests run: 3, Failures: 0, Skips: 0
===============================================
```

9.2 INTEGRATION TESTING WITH TESTNG

The scope of a unit test is limited to a single programming unit, which is typically a class with its methods in object-oriented languages. As we described earlier, the next level of testing is integration testing, the scope of which becomes wider that it has to deal with the inter-dependencies among multiple units or objects. In this section, let us explore how to conduct integration testing with TestNG. We start with testing DAO units with InMemoryDaos.

9.2.1 Integration Testing DAOs with InMemoryDaos

In principle, a DAO unit or class should be tested against a real database. However, during the early stage of a product development process, it's very common to test DAOs with InMemoryDaos. In this section, we present an example of integration-testing DAOs with InMemoryDaos.

The example we use in this section is the `Account` domain object and the `AccountDao` interface from the SOBA project. Listings 9.6 and 9.7 show the `Account` domain object and the `AccountDao` interface, while Listing 9.8 shows the `InMemoryAccountDao` class that implements the `AccountDao` interface. You can take a quick look at these listings, but our main subject here is how to test the InMemoryDAO with TestNG. In addition, we focus on the `insert`, `update`, `delete` and `findByAccountID` methods only, as highlighted in Listing 9.8. Note that this InMemoryDao is implemented with a synchronized `HashMap`.

Listing 9.6 Account.java

```
package com.perfmath.spring.soba.model.domain;

import java.io.Serializable;
import java.sql.Timestamp;

public class Account implements Serializable {

   private String accountId;
   private String name;
   private String type;
   private String description;
   private String status;
   private double balance;
   private Timestamp openDate;
   private Timestamp closeDate;
   private String customerId;

   // getters and setters are omitted to save space
   public boolean equals(Object obj) {
      if (!(obj instanceof Account)) {
         return false;
      }
      Account account = (Account) obj;
      return account.accountId.equals(accountId) && account.balance == balance;
   }
}
```

Listing 9.7 AccountDao.java

```
package com.perfmath.spring.soba.model.dao;
```

```
import java.util.List;
import java.util.Map;

import com.perfmath.spring.soba.model.domain.Account;

public interface AccountDao {
   public List<Account> getAccountList();
   public void insert(Account account);
   public void update(Account account);
   public double updateAccountBalance (double amount, String accountID);
   public void delete(Account account);
   public Account findByAccountID(String accountID);
   public void insertBatch(List<Account> accounts);
   public List<Map<String, Object>> findAll();
   public String getCustomerId(String accountID);
   public int countAll();
   public String getAccountIdByCustomerId (String customerId, String accountType);
}
```

Listing 9.8 InMemoryAccountDao.java

```
package com.perfmath.spring.soba.testing;

import java.util.ArrayList;
import java.util.Collections;
import java.util.HashMap;
import java.util.Iterator;
import java.util.List;
import java.util.Map;

import java.util.Set;

import com.perfmath.spring.soba.model.domain.Account;
import com.perfmath.spring.soba.model.dao.AccountDao;

public class InMemoryAccountDao implements AccountDao {

   private Map<String, Account> accounts;

   public InMemoryAccountDao() {
      accounts = Collections.synchronizedMap(new HashMap<String, Account>());
   }
```

```
public boolean accountExists(String accountNo) {
   return accounts.containsKey(accountNo);
}

public void insert(Account account) {
   if (accountExists(account.getAccountId())) {
      throw new DuplicateAccountException();
   }
   accounts.put(account.getAccountId(), account);
}

public void update(Account account) {
   if (!accountExists(account.getAccountId())) {
      throw new AccountNotFoundException();
   }
   accounts.put(account.getAccountId(), account);
}

public void delete(Account account) {
   if (!accountExists(account.getAccountId())) {
      throw new AccountNotFoundException();
   }
   accounts.remove(account.getAccountId());
}

public Account findByAccountID(String accountId) {
   Account account = accounts.get(accountId);
   if (account == null) {
      throw new AccountNotFoundException();
   }
   return account;
}

 public List<Account> getAccountList() {
      List<Account> list = (List<Account>) accounts.values();
      return list;
 }
public double updateAccountBalance (double amount, String accountID) {
 Account account = findByAccountID(accountId);
 double balance = amount + account.getBalance();
 account.setBalance(balance);
 update (account);
 return balance;
```

```
  }
  public void insertBatch(List<Account> accounts) {
    ;
  }
  public List<Map<String, Object>> findAll() {
    List<Map<String, Object>> list = new ArrayList ();
    Map <String, Object> objectMap = new HashMap <String, Object>();
    Set set = (Set) accounts.entrySet();
    Iterator it = set.iterator ();
    while (it.hasNext()) {
         Map.Entry<String, Account> map = (Map.Entry)it.next();
         objectMap.put (map.getKey().toString(), (Object) map.getValue());
         list.add(objectMap);
    }
    return list;
  }
  public String getCustomerId(String accountID) {
    return "";
  }
  public int countAll() {
    return 0;
  }
  public String getAccountIdByCustomerId (String customerId, String accountType) {
    return "";
  }
}
```

Listing 9.9 shows the `InMemoryAccountDaoTest.java` class implemented with TestNG. If you have gone through the TestNG unit testing example with the `SimpleDividentCalculator.java` class presented earlier, the annotations used in this `InMemoryAccountDaoTest.java` class should look familiar to you. You can build this project with either Ant or Maven and run the test as you did with the previous TestNG example. For your reference, Listing 9.10 shows the console output from running this test in my Eclipse environment. You can also view the results of running class `InMemoryAccountDaoTest` by clicking on the tab next to the Console tab as shown in Figure 9.3.

Listing 9.9 InMemoryAccountDaoTest.java

```
package com.perfmath.spring.soba.testing.testng;

import static org.testng.Assert.*;

import org.testng.annotations.BeforeMethod;
import org.testng.annotations.Test;
```

```
import com.perfmath.spring.soba.model.domain.Account;
import com.perfmath.spring.soba.testing.InMemoryAccountDao;
import com.perfmath.spring.soba.testing.AccountNotFoundException;
import com.perfmath.spring.soba.testing.DuplicateAccountException;

public class InMemoryAccountDaoTest {

   private static final String EXISTING_ACCOUNT_ID = "88888888";
   private static final String NEW_ACCOUNT_ID = "99999999";

   private Account existingAccount;
   private Account newAccount;
   private InMemoryAccountDao accountDao;

   @BeforeMethod
   public void init() {
      existingAccount = new Account();
      existingAccount.setAccountId(EXISTING_ACCOUNT_ID);
      existingAccount.setBalance(800.0);

      newAccount = new Account();
      newAccount.setAccountId(NEW_ACCOUNT_ID);
      newAccount.setBalance(900.0);

      accountDao = new InMemoryAccountDao();
      accountDao.insert(existingAccount);
   }

   @Test
   public void createNewAccount() {
      accountDao.insert(newAccount);
      assertEquals(accountDao.findByAccountID(NEW_ACCOUNT_ID), newAccount);
   }

   @Test
   public void accountExists() {
      assertTrue(accountDao.accountExists(EXISTING_ACCOUNT_ID));
      assertFalse(accountDao.accountExists(NEW_ACCOUNT_ID));
   }

   @Test(expectedExceptions = DuplicateAccountException.class)
   public void createDuplicateAccount() {
      accountDao.insert(existingAccount);
```

```
  }

  @Test
  public void updateExistingAccount() {
    existingAccount.setBalance(20);
    accountDao.update(existingAccount);
    assertEquals(accountDao.findByAccountID(EXISTING_ACCOUNT_ID), existingAccount);
  }
  @Test
  public void updateAccountBalance() {
   accountDao.updateAccountBalance(UPDATE_AMOUNT, EXISTING_ACCOUNT_ID);
    assertEquals(accountDao.findByAccountID(EXISTING_ACCOUNT_ID).getBalance(),
           (EXISTING_ACCOUNT_INITIAL_BALANCE + UPDATE_AMOUNT), 0);
  }

  @Test(expectedExceptions = AccountNotFoundException.class)
  public void updateNonExistingAccount() {
    accountDao.update(newAccount);
  }

  @Test
  public void removeExistingAccount() {
    accountDao.delete(existingAccount);
    assertFalse(accountDao.accountExists(EXISTING_ACCOUNT_ID));
  }

  @Test(expectedExceptions = AccountNotFoundException.class)
  public void removeNonExistingAccount() {
    accountDao.delete(newAccount);
  }

  @Test
  public void findExistingAccount() {
    Account account = accountDao.findByAccountID(EXISTING_ACCOUNT_ID);
    assertEquals(account, existingAccount);
  }

  @Test(expectedExceptions = AccountNotFoundException.class)
  public void findNonExistingAccount() {
    accountDao.findByAccountID(NEW_ACCOUNT_ID);
  }
}
```

Listing 9.10 Console output from running the InMemoryAccountDao TestNG testing

```
[TestNG] Running:
  C:\Users\henry\AppData\Local\Temp\testng-eclipse-1229054272\testng-customsuite.xml

PASSED: accountExists
PASSED: createDuplicateAccount
PASSED: createNewAccount
PASSED: findExistingAccount
PASSED: findNonExistingAccount
PASSED: removeExistingAccount
PASSED: removeNonExistingAccount
PASSED: updateAccountBalance
PASSED: updateExistingAccount
PASSED: updateNonExistingAccount

===============================================
    Default test
    Tests run: 10, Failures: 0, Skips: 0
===============================================
```

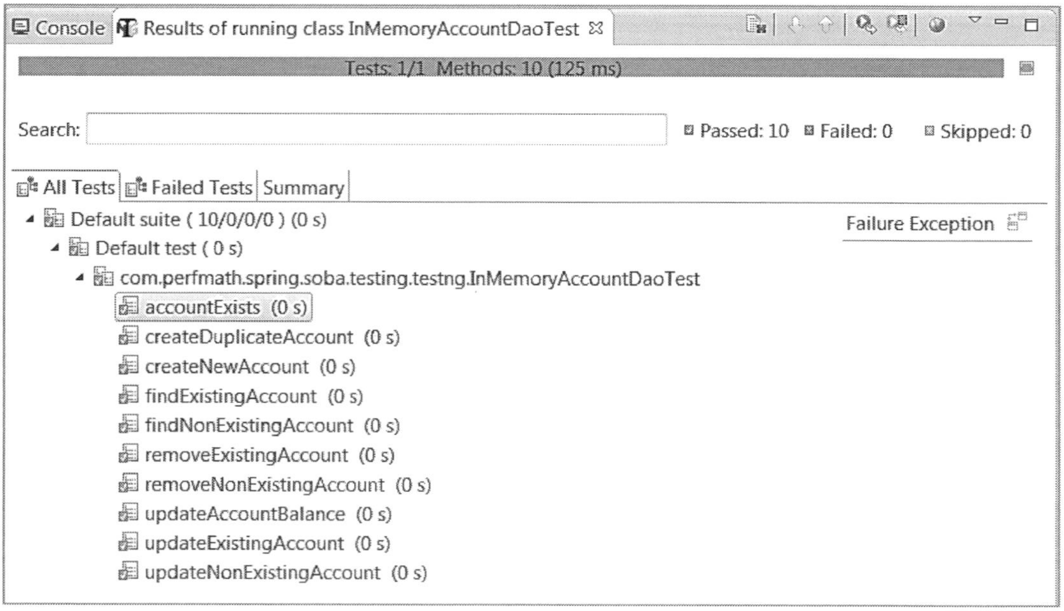

Console | Results of running class InMemoryAccountDaoTest
Tests: 1/1 Methods: 10 (125 ms)
Search: Passed: 10 Failed: 0 Skipped: 0
All Tests | Failed Tests | Summary
Failure Exception
Default suite (10/0/0/0) (0 s)
Default test (0 s)
com.perfmath.spring.soba.testing.testng.InMemoryAccountDaoTest
accountExists (0 s)
createDuplicateAccount (0 s)
createNewAccount (0 s)
findExistingAccount (0 s)
findNonExistingAccount (0 s)
removeExistingAccount (0 s)
removeNonExistingAccount (0 s)
updateAccountBalance (0 s)
updateExistingAccount (0 s)
updateNonExistingAccount (0 s)

Figure 9.3 Tab for the Results of running class InMmemoryAccountDaoTest

9.2.2 Integration Testing Service Layer Classes with TestNG

Since the service layer of an enterprise application typically depends on the DAO layer, the scope of testing a service layer classes belongs in the category of integration testing. In this section, we use the example of AccountManager in the package of com.perfmath.spring.soba.service of the SOBA project to demonstrate how to conduct integration testing with TestNG. We continue using the InMemoryAccountDao class used in the previous section for this example. In the next section, we replace this class with a mock DAO object to demonstrate how to use mock objects to assist integration testing.

For this example, we continue using Account.java as the domain object class, AccountDao.java as the DAO class, and InMemoryAccountDao.java as the DAO implementation class. In addition, we introduce the AccountManager.java interface and the SimpleAccountManager.java class as the service layer class to be tested. Listings 9.11 and 9.12 show how this interface and the implementation class are coded.

Note from Listing 9.12 that the SimpleAccountManager class depends on the AccountDao class. Therefore, testing the SimpleAccountManager class cannot be conducted without getting the class AccountDao involved. Listing 9.13 shows the SimpleAccountManagerIntegrationTest.java class, implemented with TestNG. In addition to the TestNG specific annotations such as @BeforeMethod, @Test, and @AfterMethod, note the account instance created in the init() method and how an InMemoryAccountDao object is hooked up with the accountManager object, which characterizes this testing being integration testing.

Note in Listing 9.13 that, for demonstrating how to conduct integration testing with TestNG, only two test cases are included: createAccount and updateAccountBalance. The createAccount test case creates the account set up in the init method, and then asserts that the ACCOUNT_ID and BALANCE of the account created match the account id and the initial balance as set in the init method. The two asserts are accomplished with the help of the findByAccountID method.

In addition, keep in mind that the init method only creates an account instance, which is not persisted into the InMemoryAccountDao object. Therefore, in the updateAccountBalance test case, the account instance created in the init method must be persisted into the HashMap of the InMemoryAccountDao object; otherwise, an AccountNotFound exception will be thrown when the test case is executed. We cannot simply assume that the createAccount test case would always be executed first so that the account instance would be available in the updateAccountBalance test case without creating it again as shown in the updateAccountBalance method.

You can build the project with either Ant or Maven and run the test as you did with the previous TestNG example. For your reference, Listing 9.13 shows the console output from running this test in my Eclipse environment, indicating that the test was executed successfully.

Listing 9.11 AccountManager.java

```
package com.perfmath.spring.soba.service;

import java.io.Serializable;
import java.util.List;
```

```
import com.perfmath.spring.soba.model.domain.Account;

public interface AccountManager extends Serializable{

   public void createAccount(Account account);
   public List<Account> getAccounts();
   public String getAccountIdByCustomerId (String customerId, String accountType);
   public double updateAccountBalance (double amount, String accountID);
   public void deleteAccount(String accountID);
}
```

Listing 9.12 SimpleAccountManager.java

```
package com.perfmath.spring.soba.service;
import java.util.List;
import com.perfmath.spring.soba.model.dao.AccountDao;
import com.perfmath.spring.soba.model.domain.Account;

public class SimpleAccountManager implements AccountManager {

   private AccountDao accountDao;

   public List<Account> getAccounts() {
      return accountDao.getAccountList();
   }

   public void createAccount(Account account) {
     accountDao.insert(account);
   }
   public void updateAccount(Account account) {
     accountDao.update(account);
   }
   public void setAccountDao(AccountDao accountDao) {
      this.accountDao = accountDao;
   }

   public String getAccountIdByCustomerId (String customerId, String accountType) {
         return accountDao.getAccountIdByCustomerId(customerId, accountType);
   }

   public double updateAccountBalance (double amount, String accountID) {
     Account account = accountDao.findByAccountID(accountID);
     double balance = amount + account.getBalance();
```

```
    account.setBalance(balance);
    accountDao.update(account);
    return balance;
  }
  public void deleteAccount(String accountID) {
    Account account = accountDao.findByAccountID(accountID);
    accountDao.delete(account);
  }
}
```

Listing 9.13 SimpleAccountManagerIntegrationTest.java

```
package com.perfmath.spring.soba.testing.testng;

import static org.testng.Assert.*;
import org.testng.annotations.AfterMethod;
import org.testng.annotations.BeforeMethod;
import org.testng.annotations.Test;
import com.perfmath.spring.soba.model.domain.Account;
import com.perfmath.spring.soba.model.dao.AccountDao;
import com.perfmath.spring.soba.service.SimpleAccountManager;
import com.perfmath.spring.soba.testing.InMemoryAccountDao;

public class SimpleAccountManagerIntegrationTest {

private static final String TEST_ACCOUNT_ID = "88889999";
  private static final double INITIAL_BALANCE = 200.0;
  private static final double UPDATE_AMOUNT = 50.0;
  private AccountDao accountDao;
  private SimpleAccountManager accountManager;
  private Account account;

  @BeforeMethod
  public void init() {
    account = new Account ();
    account.setAccountId (TEST_ACCOUNT_ID);
    account.setBalance (200.0);

    accountManager = new SimpleAccountManager ();
    accountDao = new InMemoryAccountDao();
    accountManager.setAccountDao (accountDao);
  }
```

```
  @Test
  public void createAccount () {
    accountManager.createAccount(account);
    assertEquals((accountDao.findByAccountID(TEST_ACCOUNT_ID)).getAccountId(),
       TEST_ACCOUNT_ID);
    assertEquals((accountDao.findByAccountID(TEST_ACCOUNT_ID)).getBalance(),
       INITIAL_BALANCE, 0);
  }

  @Test
  public void updateAccountBalance () {
   accountManager.createAccount(account);
   accountManager.updateAccountBalance(UPDATE_AMOUNT, TEST_ACCOUNT_ID);
   assertEquals((accountDao.findByAccountID(TEST_ACCOUNT_ID)).getBalance(),
        (UPDATE_AMOUNT + INITIAL_BALANCE), 0);
  }

  @AfterMethod
  public void cleanup () {
   accountManager.deleteAccount (TEST_ACCOUNT_ID);
  }
}
```

Listing 9.14 Console output of running SimpleAccountManagerIntegrationTest

```
[TestNG] Running:
 C:\Users\henry\AppData\Local\Temp\testng-eclipse--289187755\testng-customsuite.xml

PASSED: createAccount
PASSED: updateAccountBalance

===============================================
  Default test
  Tests run: 2, Failures: 0, Skips: 0
===============================================
```

9.2.3 Integration Testing with Mock Objects

As we pointed earlier, using mock objects is a helpful approach to conducting integration testing that has to resolve dependencies for the class under test. To demonstrate how to use mock objects to facilitate integration testing, we re-use the `SimpleAccountManager` example presented in the preceding section, with one change that instead of using an `InMemoryAccountDao` object, we use mock objects.

For this example, we use EasyMock (http://www.easymock.org), which is a Java testing framework for creating mock objects on the fly using Java's proxy mechanism. To demonstrate how mock objects generated with EasyMock can help conduct integration testing on the `SimpleAccountManager` class that was tested with an `InMemoryAccountDao` object in the preceding section, Listing 9.15 shows the integration testing implemented with TestNG and EasyMock. Let's summarize how EasyMock is used for this integration testing:

- **Creating the mock object**: This is accomplished in the `init` method with the statement of `mock = createMock(AccountDao.class)`. This is a mock object that mocks an `AccountDao` object.
- **Hooking up the mock object with the class under test**: This is accomplished in the `init` method with the statement of `accountManager.setAccountDao (mock)`. As is seen, the mocking `AccountDao` object named `mock` is assigned to the class under test as its `AccountDao` object. This mock object will play the role of a DAO object like a more real DAO object such as the `InMemoryAccountDao` object we used in the preceding section or a real JDBC or Hibernate DAO object that actually persists domain objects into a real database.
- **A mock object in replay**: Let's use the `createAccount` test case to demonstrate how this works. First, the statement of `mock.insert(account)` is executed. Since `mock` is an `accountDao` mocking object, this statement can be considered *inserting* an `account` object into a "mocking" store just as if this mock object were a real DAO object. Once a mock object is created, it will be put into the *record* state, meaning that any operations performed upon it will be recorded for future referencing and verification. The next statement of `replay (mock)` will put the `mock` object in the *replay* state, meaning that the mock object is active so that you can perform operations like `accountManager.createAccount(account)` (note that without this mock object, the account instance would have no place to persist). Finally, the `verify (mock)` statement verifies that the `accountManager.createAccount(account)` statement has achieved the same result as the `mock.insert(account)` statement recorded earlier.
- **Returning a domain object from the mock object**: Note this interesting feature with the `expect (mock.findByAccountID(TEST_ACCOUNT_ID)).andReturn (account)` statement in the `updateAccountBalance` test case. This `expect` statement finds the `account` object stored in the mock object and returns it to the executing thread. This `account` object can then be used as if it were retrieved from an `InMemoryAccountDao` object or a real relational store. The rest of the `updateAccountBalance` test case is similar to what we explained with the `createAccount` test case, so we would not repeat it again.

You can build the project with either Ant or Maven and run the test as you did with the previous TestNG example. For your reference, Listing 9.16 shows the console output from running this test in my Eclipse environment, indicating that the test was executed successfully.

In the next section, we explore Spring testing support for testing various Spring components. You will see that the concept of a mock object is equally applicable to testing Spring components. Of course, Spring has introduced its own more advanced concepts such as `MockHttpSession`, `MockHttpServletRequest`, `MockHttpServletResponse`, `TestContext`, and so on.

Note: In order to build the project successfully, it's necessary to add the `easymock-3.1.jar` file to the `SOBA-lib` if you use Ant. If you use Maven, add the following dependency to the `pom.xml` file:

```
<dependency>
    <groupId>org.easymock</groupId>
    <artifactId>easymock</artifactId>
    <version>3.1</version>
</dependency>
```

Listing 9.15 SimpleAccountManagerMockTest.java

```
package com.perfmath.spring.soba.testing.testng;

import static org.easymock.EasyMock.*;
import org.testng.annotations.BeforeMethod;
import org.testng.annotations.Test;
import static org.testng.Assert.*;

import com.perfmath.spring.soba.model.domain.Account;
import com.perfmath.spring.soba.model.dao.AccountDao;
import com.perfmath.spring.soba.service.SimpleAccountManager;

public class SimpleAccountManagerMockTest {

  private static final String TEST_ACCOUNT_ID = "88889999";
  private static final double AMOUNT = 50.0d;
  private AccountDao mock;
  private SimpleAccountManager accountManager;
  private Account account;

  @BeforeMethod
  public void init() {
    account = new Account ();
    account.setAccountId (TEST_ACCOUNT_ID);
    account.setBalance (200.0);

    mock = createMock(AccountDao.class);
    accountManager = new SimpleAccountManager ();
    accountManager.setAccountDao (mock);
  }

  @Test
  public void createAccount () {
   mock.insert(account);
   replay (mock);
```

```
        accountManager.createAccount(account);
        verify (mock);
    }

    @Test
    public void updateAccountBalance() {
        expect (mock.findByAccountID(TEST_ACCOUNT_ID)).andReturn (account);
        account.setBalance(AMOUNT + account.getBalance());
        mock.update(account);
        replay(mock);

        accountManager.updateAccountBalance(AMOUNT, TEST_ACCOUNT_ID);
        verify(mock);
    }
}
```

Listing 9.16 Console output from running SimpleAccountManagerMockTest

```
[TestNG] Running:
  C:\Users\henry\AppData\Local\Temp\testng-eclipse-1570924868\testng-customsuite.xml

PASSED: createAccount
PASSED: updateAccountBalance

===============================================
    Default test
    Tests run: 2, Failures: 0, Skips: 0
===============================================
```

9.3 SPRING TESTING SUPPORT

As one of the most popular enterprise Java development framework, Spring takes testing seriously and supports testing various Spring components on top of the generic Java testing frameworks such as TestNG and JUnit. In this section, we explore Spring testing support using the SOBA project as an example. Let's start with testing Spring MVC controllers next.

9.3.1 Testing Spring MVC Controllers

Note: In order to build the project with all test cases presented in this section successfully, it's necessary to add the `spring-mock-2.0.8.jar` file and `spring-test-3.2.0.RELEASE.jar` file to the `SOBA-lib` if you use Ant. If you use Maven, add the following dependencies to the `pom.xml` file (note that I used spring-mock-version 2.0.8 and spring-test version 3.2.0- RELEASE at the time of this writing):

```
<dependency>
    <groupId>org.springframework</groupId>
    <artifactId>spring-mock</artifactId>
    <version>${spring-mock.version}</version>
</dependency>
<dependency>
    <groupId>org.springframework</groupId>
    <artifactId>spring-test</artifactId>
    <version>${org.springframework.version}</version>
</dependency>
```

To demonstrate how to test Spring MVC controllers, we use the `AccountController` class in the SOBA project. As you have learnt from the previous chapters of this text, a Spring MVC controller can be either annotation-based or configuration-based. We present an example for each case. Let's start with testing an annotation-based Spring MVC controller next.

#1 Testing Annotation-based Spring MVC Controllers

Listing 9.17 shows the annotated `AccountController` class to be tested. Note that we name it `AccountControllerAnnotated` to distinguish it from the configuration-based version to be discussed next. For your Spring MVC controllers, you should pick either annotation-based or configuration-based without having *Annotated* or *Configured* to be part of the name of your controller).

First, note the annotations of @`Controller`, @`Autowired`, @`RequestMapping`, and @`RequestParam` that we covered in the earlier chapters. These annotations should look familiar to you and we would not repeat explaining them here. Next, note that this controller depends on an `accountManager` object, which is used to update the account balance by calling its `updateAccountBalance` method. This method can be multiple purposes, for example, customer initiated transactions such as *deposit* and *withdraw*, or transactions such as *debit* and *credit* conducted by the bank or third parties, depending on whether the amount parameter value is positive or negative (refer to Listing 9.12 for more details about this method). Finally, note the `accountId` and `balance` model attributes and the `success` *viewName* returned at the exit of this method call.

Listing 9.17 AccountControllerAnnotated.java

```
package com.perfmath.spring.soba.web;

import org.springframework.beans.factory.annotation.Autowired;
import org.springframework.stereotype.Controller;
import org.springframework.ui.ModelMap;
import org.springframework.web.bind.annotation.RequestMapping;
import org.springframework.web.bind.annotation.RequestParam;
```

```
import com.perfmath.spring.soba.service.AccountManager;

@Controller
public class AccountControllerAnnotated {

   private AccountManager accountManager;
   @Autowired
   public AccountControllerAnnotated(AccountManager accountManager) {
      this.accountManager = accountManager;
   }
   @RequestMapping("/updateAccountBalance.htm")
     public String updateAccountBalance (
         @RequestParam("accountId") String accountId,
         @RequestParam("amount") double amount,
         ModelMap model) {
      double balance = accountManager.updateAccountBalance(amount, accountId);
      model.addAttribute("accountId", accountId);
      model.addAttribute("balance", balance);
      return "success";
   }
}
```

Listing 9.18 shows the `AccountControllerAnnotatedTest.java` class. Given what we have covered so far about TestNG and EasyMock, it should be easy to comprehend this test class. However, I have to mention that a common exception of "`missing behavior definition for the preceding method call`" as shown in Listing 9.19 would occur if the first two statements in the `updateAccountBalance` method were implemented as follows:

```
mock.updateAccountBalance (TEST_AMOUNT, TEST_ACCOUNT_ID);
expect (mock.getBalance(TEST_ACCOUNT_ID)).andReturn(NEW_BALANCE);
replay (mock);
```

That is because the `mock.updatAccountBalance` call has a `double` return type instead of `void`. It would work properly if the mock call prior to the `expect` statement had a `void` return type. Other than that, this class is straightforward, and you can just build and run it as you did with all previous TestNG-based examples. For your reference, Listing 9.20 shows the console output obtained from running this class in my Eclipse environment.

Listing 9.18 AccountControllerAnnotatedTest.java

```
package com.perfmath.spring.soba.testing.spring;
import static org.junit.Assert.*;
import static org.easymock.EasyMock.*;
import org.testng.annotations.BeforeMethod;
```

```
import org.testng.annotations.Test;
import org.springframework.ui.ModelMap;
import com.perfmath.spring.soba.service.AccountManager;
import com.perfmath.spring.soba.web.AccountControllerAnnotated;

public class AccountControllerAnnotatedTest {

  private static final String TEST_ACCOUNT_ID = "88889999";
  private static final double TEST_AMOUNT = 100;
  private static final double NEW_BALANCE = 200;
  private AccountManager mock;
  private AccountControllerAnnotated accountController;

  @BeforeMethod
  public void init() {
   mock = createMock (AccountManager.class);
    accountController = new AccountControllerAnnotated(mock);
  }

  @Test
  public void updateAccountBalance() {
    expect (mock.updateAccountBalance(TEST_AMOUNT,
      TEST_ACCOUNT_ID)).andReturn(NEW_BALANCE);
    replay(mock);

    ModelMap model = new ModelMap();
    String viewName =
      accountController.updateAccountBalance (TEST_ACCOUNT_ID, TEST_AMOUNT, model);
    verify(mock);

    assertEquals(viewName, "success");
    assertEquals(model.get("accountId"), TEST_ACCOUNT_ID);
    assertEquals(model.get("balance"), NEW_BALANCE);
  }
}
```

Listing 9.19 The exception caused by the improper use of mock objects

```
[TestNG] Running:
 C:\Users\henry\AppData\Local\Temp\testng-eclipse--701496993\testng-customsuite.xml

FAILED: updateAccountBalance
java.lang.IllegalStateException: missing behavior definition for the preceding method call:
```

```
AccountManager.updateAccountBalance(100.0, "88889999")
Usage is: expect(a.foo()).andXXX()
    at org.easymock.internal.MockInvocationHandler.invoke(MockInvocationHandler.java:42)
    at org.easymock.internal.ObjectMethodsFilter.invoke(ObjectMethodsFilter.java:85)
    at $Proxy6.getBalance(Unknown Source)
    at com.perfmath.spring.soba.testing.spring.AccountControllerAnnotatedTest.
        updateAccountBalance(AccountControllerAnnotatedTest.java:30)
    at sun.reflect.NativeMethodAccessorImpl.invoke0(Native Method)
    at sun.reflect.NativeMethodAccessorImpl.invoke(NativeMethodAccessorImpl.java:39)
    at sun.reflect.DelegatingMethodAccessorImpl.
        invoke(DelegatingMethodAccessorImpl.java:25)
    at java.lang.reflect.Method.invoke(Method.java:597)
    at org.testng.internal.MethodInvocationHelper.
        invokeMethod(MethodInvocationHelper.java:80)
    at org.testng.internal.Invoker.invokeMethod(Invoker.java:714)
    at org.testng.internal.Invoker.invokeTestMethod(Invoker.java:901)
    at org.testng.internal.Invoker.invokeTestMethods(Invoker.java:1231)
    at org.testng.internal.TestMethodWorker.invokeTestMethods(TestMethodWorker.java:128)
    at org.testng.internal.TestMethodWorker.run(TestMethodWorker.java:111)
    at org.testng.TestRunner.privateRun(TestRunner.java:767)
    at org.testng.TestRunner.run(TestRunner.java:617)
    at org.testng.SuiteRunner.runTest(SuiteRunner.java:334)
    at org.testng.SuiteRunner.runSequentially(SuiteRunner.java:329)
    at org.testng.SuiteRunner.privateRun(SuiteRunner.java:291)
    at org.testng.SuiteRunner.run(SuiteRunner.java:240)
    at org.testng.SuiteRunnerWorker.runSuite(SuiteRunnerWorker.java:52)
    at org.testng.SuiteRunnerWorker.run(SuiteRunnerWorker.java:86)
    at org.testng.TestNG.runSuitesSequentially(TestNG.java:1203)
    at org.testng.TestNG.runSuitesLocally(TestNG.java:1128)
    at org.testng.TestNG.run(TestNG.java:1036)
    at org.testng.remote.RemoteTestNG.run(RemoteTestNG.java:111)
    at org.testng.remote.RemoteTestNG.initAndRun(RemoteTestNG.java:204)
    at org.testng.remote.RemoteTestNG.main(RemoteTestNG.java:175)

===============================================
  Default test
  Tests run: 1, Failures: 1, Skips: 0
===============================================
```

Listing 9.20 Console output of running AccountControllerAnnotatedTest.java class

```
[TestNG] Running:
  C:\Users\henry\AppData\Local\Temp\testng-eclipse-480456488\testng-customsuite.xml
```

```
PASSED: updateAccountBalance

===============================================
    Default test
    Tests run: 1, Failures: 0, Skips: 0
===============================================
```

#2 Testing Configuration-based Spring MVC Controllers

Listing 9.21 shows the configuration-based `AccountController` to be tested. It has the same dependency on an `accountManager` object and is *HttpServlet*-based with the `accountId` and `amount` parameters extracted using the `ServletRequestUtils` class. It then calls the `accountManager's` `updateAccountBalance` with the `amount` and `accoundId` parameters extracted from the `HttpServletRequest` argument of the `handleRequestInternal` method. Finally, it returns a `ModelAndView` object with the *viewName*, *accountId* and *balance* attributes as specified.

Listing 9.21 AccountControllerConfigured.java

```
package com.perfmath.spring.soba.web;

import javax.servlet.http.HttpServletRequest;
import javax.servlet.http.HttpServletResponse;

import org.springframework.web.bind.ServletRequestUtils;
import org.springframework.web.servlet.ModelAndView;
import org.springframework.web.servlet.mvc.AbstractController;

import com.perfmath.spring.soba.service.AccountManager;

public class AccountControllerConfigured extends AbstractController{

   private AccountManager accountManager;

   public AccountControllerConfigured(AccountManager accountManager) {
      this.accountManager = accountManager;
   }

     public ModelAndView handleRequestInternal (HttpServletRequest request,
            HttpServletResponse response) throws Exception {
      String accountId =
            ServletRequestUtils.getRequiredStringParameter (request, "accountId");
      double amount =
            ServletRequestUtils.getRequiredDoubleParameter (request, "amount");
```

```
    double balance = accountManager.updateAccountBalance (amount, accountId);
    return new ModelAndView ("success", "accountId", accountId).addObject("balance",
      balance);
  }
}
```

Listing 9.22 shows the `AccountControllerConfiguredTest.java` class. Note that this test class uses Spring's `MockHttpServletRequest` and `MockHttpServletResponse` to facilitate testing this configuration-based `accountController`. The mock object is used similarly in terms of *expect*, *replay* and *verify*. However, instead of using `assertEquals` as is the case with the preceding class, it uses Spring-specific `assertViewName` and `assertModelAttributeValue` for asserting the `ModelAndView` object. Figure 9.4 shows the TestNG console output of running this test class, indicating that the test was executed successfully.

Listing 9.22 AccountControllerConfiguredTest.java

```
package com.perfmath.spring.soba.testing.spring;

import static org.springframework.test.web.ModelAndViewAssert.*;
import static org.easymock.EasyMock.*;
import org.testng.annotations.BeforeMethod;
import org.testng.annotations.Test;
import org.springframework.mock.web.MockHttpServletRequest;
import org.springframework.mock.web.MockHttpServletResponse;
import org.springframework.web.servlet.ModelAndView;
import com.perfmath.spring.soba.service.AccountManager;
import com.perfmath.spring.soba.web.AccountControllerConfigured;

public class AccountControllerConfiguredTest {

  private static final String TEST_ACCOUNT_ID = "88889999";
  private static final double TEST_AMOUNT = 100.0;
  private static final double NEW_BALANCE = 200.0;

  private AccountManager mock;
  private AccountControllerConfigured accountController;

  @BeforeMethod
  public void init() {
    mock = createMock (AccountManager.class);
     accountController = new AccountControllerConfigured(mock);
  }

  @Test
```

```
  public void updateAccountBalance() throws Exception {
    MockHttpServletRequest request = new MockHttpServletRequest ();
    request.setMethod ("POST");
    request.addParameter ("accountId", TEST_ACCOUNT_ID);
    request.addParameter ("amount", String.valueOf(TEST_AMOUNT));
    MockHttpServletResponse response = new MockHttpServletResponse ();

     expect (mock.updateAccountBalance(TEST_AMOUNT,
        TEST_ACCOUNT_ID)).andReturn(NEW_BALANCE);
     replay(mock);

    ModelAndView modelAndView =
         accountController.handleRequest (request, response);
    verify (mock);

    assertViewName (modelAndView, "success");
    assertModelAttributeValue (modelAndView, "accountId", TEST_ACCOUNT_ID);
    assertModelAttributeValue (modelAndView, "balance", NEW_BALANCE);
  }
}
```

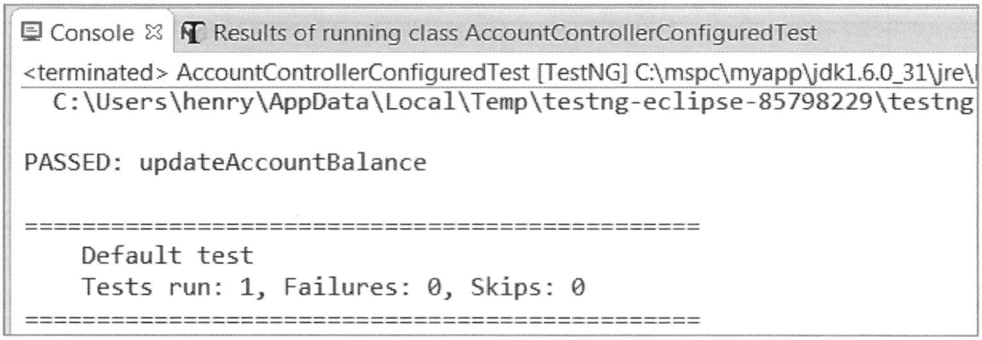

```
Console ☒   Results of running class AccountControllerConfiguredTest
<terminated> AccountControllerConfiguredTest [TestNG] C:\mspc\myapp\jdk1.6.0_31\jre\
  C:\Users\henry\AppData\Local\Temp\testng-eclipse-85798229\testng

PASSED: updateAccountBalance

===============================================
    Default test
    Tests run: 1, Failures: 0, Skips: 0
===============================================
```

Figure 9.4 Console output of running class AccountControllerConfiguredTest

9.3.2 Spring's TestContext Support for Integration Testing

Recall that in §9.2.2, we tested a service layer class named `SimpleAccountManager.java` as shown in Listing 9.13. We used the Java `new` operator to create the dependency object `accountDao` in the TestNG's `init` method as follows:

```
accountDao = new InMemoryAccountDao();
```

By doing that, we have completed by-passed the application context configuration file. It's okay to test a pure POJO that way, but for most Spring beans, it's preferable to test them against their application contexts. Spring provides TestContext support to manage application context for this kind of integration testing. Specifically, the Spring TestContext framework provides the following two test execution listeners related to context management:

- **DependencyInjectionTestExecutionListener**: This listener helps inject dependencies into the tests.
- **DirtiesContextTestExecutionListener**: This listener handles the @DirtiesContext annotation, which may trigger the re-loading of the application context when necessary.

The good news is that these listeners are registered by default if we don't specify our own explicitly so that we don't have to worry about them. However, the test classes we create must implement the following interface or extend the following base class:

- The ApplicationContextAware for both TestNG and JUnit4.
- The AbstractTestNGSpringContextTests base class for TestNG or the AbstractJUnit4SpringContextTests base class for JUnit4.

Next, let's explore this Spring TestContext feature with the same SimpleAccountManager.java class we mentioned at the beginning of this section. Since the TestNG and JUnit test classes share the same application context configuration file, Listing 9.23 shows the beans-app-context.xml file to be used for the examples presented in this section. We start with the TestNG-based example for demonstrating Spring TestContext feature following Listing 9.23.

Listing 9.23 beans-app-context.xml file

```
<beans xmlns="http://www.springframework.org/schema/beans"
  xmlns:xsi="http://www.w3.org/2001/XMLSchema-instance"
  xsi:schemaLocation="http://www.springframework.org/schema/beans
    http://www.springframework.org/schema/beans/spring-beans.xsd">

  <bean id="accountDao"
    class="com.perfmath.spring.soba.testing.InMemoryAccountDao">
  </bean>

  <bean id="accountManager"
    class="com.perfmath.spring.soba.service.SimpleAccountManager">
    <property name="accountDao" ref="accountDao" />
  </bean>
</beans>
```

#1 TestNG-based example for demonstrating the Spring TestContext feature

Listing 9.24 shows the AccountManagerTestNGContextAbstractTest.java class, which demonstrates how the AbstractTestNGSpringContextTests class is extended with this test class. First, note the @ContextConfiguration (locations = "/beans-app-context.xml") annotation applied to this class. This annotation instructs the Spring testing framework about where to find the application context configuration file, which is specified with the locations property as is shown. The locations are classpath locations relative to the test class by default. Keep in mind that the application context will be cached and reused for each test case if the test case under test is not annotated with the `@DirtiesContext` annotation to reload the application context. The `createAccount` and `updateAccountBalance` test cases are similar to what we discussed before, so we would not explain them here again. For the console output of running this class with TestNG on Eclipse, see Listing 9.25.

Listing 9.24 AccountManagerTestNGContextAbstractTest.java

```
package com.perfmath.spring.soba.testing.testng;

import static org.junit.Assert.assertEquals;
import org.springframework.test.context.ContextConfiguration;
import org.springframework.test.context.testng.AbstractTestNGSpringContextTests;
import org.testng.annotations.BeforeMethod;
import org.testng.annotations.Test;
import com.perfmath.spring.soba.model.domain.Account;
import com.perfmath.spring.soba.service.AccountManager;

@ContextConfiguration(locations = "/beans-test-app-context.xml")
public class AccountManagerTestNGContextAbstractTest extends
    AbstractTestNGSpringContextTests {

  private static final String TEST_ACCOUNT_ID = "88889999";
  private static final double INITIAL_BALANCE = 500.0;
  private static final double TEST_AMOUNT = 300.0;
  private AccountManager accountManager;

  @BeforeMethod
  public void init() {
    accountManager = (AccountManager) applicationContext.getBean("accountManager");
  }

  @Test
  public void createAccount () {
    Account account = new Account ();
    account.setAccountId(TEST_ACCOUNT_ID);
    account.setBalance(INITIAL_BALANCE);
    accountManager.createAccount(account);
    assertEquals(accountManager.getBalance(TEST_ACCOUNT_ID), INITIAL_BALANCE, 0);
  }

  @Test
  public void updateAccountBalance () {
    accountManager.updateAccountBalance (TEST_AMOUNT, TEST_ACCOUNT_ID);
```

```
        assertEquals(accountManager.getBalance(TEST_ACCOUNT_ID),
            (INITIAL_BALANCE + TEST_AMOUNT), 0);
    }
}
```

Listing 9.25 Console output of running the AccountManagerTestNGAbstractTest class

```
[TestNG] Running:
  C:\Users\henry\AppData\Local\Temp\testng-eclipse--1205327052\testng-customsuite.xml

PASSED: createAccount
PASSED: updateAccountBalance

===============================================
    Default test
    Tests run: 2, Failures: 0, Skips: 0
===============================================
```

#2 JUnit4-based example for demonstrating the Spring TestContext feature

We have an `AccountManagerTJUnit4ContextAbstractTest.java` class in SOBA's `testing/junit` package, but it's almost identical with the TestNG-based example we have just presented above except that it extends the `Abstract`**`JUni4`**`SpringContextTests` interface rather than the `Abstract`**`TestNG`**`SpringContextTests` base class. Therefore, we present a JUnit 4 example that implements the `ApplicationContextAware` interface next.

Listing 9.26 demonstrates how the `ApplicationContextAware` interface is implemented with this test class. First, in addition to the `@ContextConfiguration (locations = "/beans-app-context.xml")` annotation as we saw in the previous example, note the `@RunWith` annotation, which instructs the Spring testing framework explicitly to use this test runner of `SpringJUnit4ClassRunner` to run this test. Next, note the `applicationContext` attribute and its setter method. These features are unique with the test classes that implement the `ApplicationContextAware` interface. Similarly, the `locations` for the application context configuration file are classpath locations relative to the test class by default. The `createAccount` and `updateAccountBalance` test cases are similar to what we discussed before, so we would not explain them here again. For the console output of running this class with JUnit4 on Eclipse, see Figure 9.5.

Listing 9.26 AccountManagerJUnit4ContextAwareTest.java

```
package com.perfmath.spring.soba.testing.junit;

import static org.junit.Assert.assertEquals;
import org.junit.Before;
import org.junit.Test;
import org.junit.runner.RunWith;
```

```
import org.springframework.context.ApplicationContext;
import org.springframework.context.ApplicationContextAware;
import org.springframework.test.context.ContextConfiguration;
import org.springframework.test.context.junit4.SpringJUnit4ClassRunner;
import com.perfmath.spring.soba.service.AccountManager;
import com.perfmath.spring.soba.model.domain.Account;

@RunWith (SpringJUnit4ClassRunner.class)
@ContextConfiguration(locations = "/beans-test-app-context.xml")
public class AccountManagerJUnit4ContextAwareTest implements
      ApplicationContextAware {

   private static final String TEST_ACCOUNT_ID = "88889999";
   private static final double INITIAL_BALANCE = 500.0;
   private static final double TEST_AMOUNT = 300.0;
   private ApplicationContext applicationContext;
   private AccountManager accountManager;

   public void setApplicationContext (ApplicationContext applicationContext ) {
     this.applicationContext = applicationContext;
   }

   @Before
   public void init() {
      accountManager = (AccountManager) applicationContext.getBean("accountManager");
   }

   @Test
   public void createAccount () {
      Account account = new Account ();
      account.setAccountId(TEST_ACCOUNT_ID);
      account.setBalance(INITIAL_BALANCE);
      accountManager.createAccount(account);
      assertEquals(accountManager.getBalance(TEST_ACCOUNT_ID), INITIAL_BALANCE, 0);
   }

   @Test
   public void updateAccountBalance () {
      accountManager.updateAccountBalance (TEST_AMOUNT, TEST_ACCOUNT_ID);
      assertEquals(accountManager.getBalance(TEST_ACCOUNT_ID),
            (INITIAL_BALANCE + TEST_AMOUNT), 0);
   }
}
```

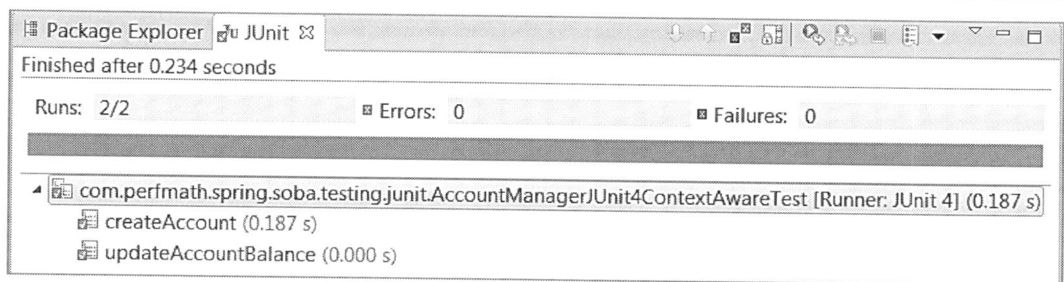

Figure 9.5 Console output of running AccountManagerJUnit4ContextAwareTest class

9.3.3 Automatically Injecting Spring Test Fixtures into Integration Tests

Note in the test cases presented in the preceding section, such as Listing 9.26 `AccountManagerJUnit4ContextAwareTest.java`, that the `accountManager` dependency bean needs to be injected into the test class explicitly in its `init` method with the following statement:

```
@Before
  public void init() {
    accountManager = (AccountManager) applicationContext.getBean("accountManager");
  }
```

Such dependency beans are called *test fixtures* and in fact can be injected into the test classes automatically. The fixture can be injected by type with the `@Autowired` annotation or by name with the `@Resource` annotation. Listing 9.27 shows how this feature works exactly with the `AccountManagerTestNGContextFixtureAbstractTest.java` class, which is retrofitted from Listing 9.24 `AccountManagerTestNGContextAbstractTest.java` presented in §9.3.2. Note that the `@Autowired` annotation, applied to the `accountManager` dependency bean, has eliminated the need to create the `accountManager` bean in the `init` method of the test class. Refer to Listing 9.28 for the console output of running this class. Note that this feature applies to JUnit as well, but we would not repeat it here.

Listing 9.27 AccountManagerTestNGContextFixtureAbstractTest.java

```
package com.perfmath.spring.soba.testing.testng;

import static org.junit.Assert.assertEquals;
import org.springframework.beans.factory.annotation.Autowired;
import org.springframework.test.context.ContextConfiguration;
import org.springframework.test.context.testng.AbstractTestNGSpringContextTests;
import org.testng.annotations.BeforeMethod;
import org.testng.annotations.Test;
import com.perfmath.spring.soba.model.domain.Account;
import com.perfmath.spring.soba.service.AccountManager;
```

```
@ContextConfiguration(locations = "/beans-test-app-context.xml")
public class AccountManagerTestNGContextFixtureAbstractTest extends
AbstractTestNGSpringContextTests {

    private static final String TEST_ACCOUNT_ID = "88889999";
    private static final double INITIAL_BALANCE = 500.0;
    private static final double TEST_AMOUNT = 300.0;
    @Autowired
    private AccountManager accountManager;

    @BeforeMethod
    public void init() {
    }

    @Test
    public void createAccount () {
        Account account = new Account ();
        account.setAccountId(TEST_ACCOUNT_ID);
        account.setBalance(INITIAL_BALANCE);
        accountManager.createAccount(account);
        assertEquals(accountManager.getBalance(TEST_ACCOUNT_ID), INITIAL_BALANCE, 0);
    }

    @Test
    public void updateAccountBalance () {
        accountManager.updateAccountBalance (TEST_AMOUNT, TEST_ACCOUNT_ID);
        assertEquals(accountManager.getBalance(TEST_ACCOUNT_ID),
                (INITIAL_BALANCE + TEST_AMOUNT), 0);
    }
}
```

Listing 9.28 The console output of running AccountManagerTestNGContextFixtureAbstractTest class

```
[TestNG] Running:
  C:\Users\henry\AppData\Local\Temp\testng-eclipse-583467160\testng-customsuite.xml

PASSED: createAccount
PASSED: updateAccountBalance

===============================================
    Default test
```

```
Tests run: 2, Failures: 0, Skips: 0
===============================================
```

9.3.4 Spring's Transactional Support for Integration Testing

So far, we have been using either mock objects or an in-memory database to facilitate integration testing. It might be more meaningful to use real databases to test Spring-based enterprise applications at the integration testing level to close the gap between artificiality and reality. In this section, we explore Spring's transactional support for integration testing with real data persistence, while in the next section, we explore Spring's support for conducting integration testing using real databases to facilitate assertions.

Spring 3.x provides two abstract base classes to support transactionality for conducting JUni4-based and TestNG-based integration testing. For JUnit4, the abstract base class is named `AbstractTransactionalJUnit4SpringContextTests`, while for TestNG, the counterpart abstract base class is named `AbstractTransactionalTestNGSpringContextTests`. These classes are registered with a test context manager by default if it's not specified explicitly. In addition, a Spring `TransactionalTestExecutionListener` makes it possible to use @`Transactional` annotation to mark a class or method to be transactional. By default, those two abstract base classes for the JUnit4 and TestNG frameworks enable a test class with @Transactional at the class level, meaning that all the test cases will be transactional. However, keep in mind that when we say a test class or method is transactional in Spring's test context, what that really means is that all persistence related operations will be rolled back at the end of a test so that the state of the database remains the same before and after the test. This helps save us time restoring database to its state before testing if we need to make multiple tests repeatable.

To proceed, we need to create an application context configuration file and have a JDBC Dao class in place. Listing 9.29 shows the application context configuration file for the examples presented in this section, while Listing 9.30 shows the `JdbcAccountDao.java` class we will use for the examples in this section and in the next section. This application context configuration file and the `JdbcAccountDao.java` class should look familiar to you, so we would not spend time here explaining how they work. However, note that we have to specify a `transactionManager` in the `beans-test-tx.xml` file to support the transactionality under test.

Listing 9.29 beans-test-tx.xml

```
<beans xmlns="http://www.springframework.org/schema/beans"
  xmlns:xsi="http://www.w3.org/2001/XMLSchema-instance"
  xsi:schemaLocation="http://www.springframework.org/schema/beans
    http://www.springframework.org/schema/beans/spring-beans.xsd">

  <bean id="dataSource"
    class="org.springframework.jdbc.datasource.DriverManagerDataSource">
    <property name="driverClassName"
      value="com.mysql.jdbc.Driver" />
```

```
        <property name="url"
          value="jdbc:mysql://localhost:3306/soba32" />
        <property name="username" value="soba32admin" />
        <property name="password" value="soba32admin" />
    </bean>

    <bean id="transactionManager"
        class="org.springframework.jdbc.datasource.DataSourceTransactionManager">
        <property name="dataSource" ref="dataSource" />
    </bean>

    <bean id="accountDao"
        class="com.perfmath.spring.soba.model.dao.JdbcAccountDao">
        <property name="dataSource" ref="dataSource" />
    </bean>

    <bean id="accountManager"
        class="com.perfmath.spring.soba.service.SimpleAccountManager">
        <property name="accountDao" ref="accountDao" />
    </bean>
</beans>
```

Listing 9.30 JdbcAccountDao.java

```
package com.perfmath.spring.soba.model.dao;

import java.sql.ResultSet;
import java.sql.SQLException;
import java.util.List;
import java.util.Map;
import javax.sql.DataSource;
import org.springframework.jdbc.core.namedparam.BeanPropertySqlParameterSource;
import org.springframework.jdbc.core.namedparam.NamedParameterJdbcTemplate;
import org.springframework.jdbc.core.namedparam.SqlParameterSource;
import org.springframework.jdbc.core.namedparam.SqlParameterSourceUtils;
import org.springframework.jdbc.core.simple.ParameterizedRowMapper;
import org.springframework.jdbc.core.JdbcTemplate;
import com.perfmath.spring.soba.model.domain.Account;

public class JdbcAccountDao  implements AccountDao {
    private JdbcTemplate jdbcTemplate;
    private NamedParameterJdbcTemplate namedParameterJdbcTemplate;
    public List<Account> getAccountList() {
```

```
    List<Account> accounts = this.jdbcTemplate.query("SELECT ACCOUNT_ID, NAME, TYPE,
        DESCRIPTION, STATUS, "
                + " BALANCE, OPEN_DATE, CLOSE_DATE, CUSTOMER_ID FROM ACCOUNT",
                new AccountMapper());
    return accounts;
}

public String getAccountIdByCustomerId(String customerId, String accountType) {
    String sql = "SELECT ACCOUNT_ID FROM ACCOUNT WHERE CUSTOMER_ID = ?
        AND TYPE = ?";

    String accountId = this.jdbcTemplate.queryForObject(sql,
            String.class, customerId, accountType);
    return accountId;
}

public void insert(Account account) {
    String sql = "INSERT INTO ACCOUNT (ACCOUNT_ID, NAME, TYPE, DESCRIPTION, STATUS, "
            + " BALANCE, OPEN_DATE, CLOSE_DATE, CUSTOMER_ID) "
            + "VALUES (:accountId, :name, :type,:description, "
            + ":status, :balance, :openDate, :closeDate, :customerId)";

    SqlParameterSource parameterSource = new BeanPropertySqlParameterSource(
            account);

    int count = this.namedParameterJdbcTemplate.update(sql, parameterSource);
}

public void insertBatch(List<Account> accounts) {
    String sql = "INSERT INTO ACCOUNT (ACCOUNT_ID, NAME, TYPE, DESCRIPTION, STATUS, "
            + " BALANCE, OPEN_DATE, CLOSE_DATE, CUSTOMER_ID) "
            + "VALUES (:accountId, :name, :type,:description, "
            + ":status, :balance, :openDate, :closeDate, :customerId)";
    SqlParameterSource[]  batch = SqlParameterSourceUtils.createBatch(accounts.toArray());
    namedParameterJdbcTemplate.batchUpdate (sql, batch);
}

public Account findByAccountID(String accountID) {
    String sql = "SELECT ACCOUNT_ID, NAME, TYPE, DESCRIPTION, STATUS, BALANCE, " +
            "  OPEN_DATE, CLOSE_DATE, CUSTOMER_ID FROM ACCOUNT WHERE
                ACCOUNT_ID = ?";
    Account account = this.jdbcTemplate.queryForObject(sql, new AccountMapper(),
            accountID);
```

```
        return account;
    }

    public void update(Account account) {
        String sql = "UPDATE ACCOUNT SET NAME = ?, SET TYPE = ?," +
                " SET DESCRIPTION = ?, SET STATUS = ?, SET BALANCE = ?," +
                " SET OPEN_DATE = ?, SET CLOSE_DATE = ?, SET CUSTOMER_ID = ? " +
                " WHERE ACCOUNT_ID = ?";
        this.jdbcTemplate.update(sql, account.getName(), account.getType(),
                account.getDescription(), account.getStatus(), account.getBalance(),
                account.getOpenDate(), account.getCloseDate(), account.getCustomerId(),
                account.getAccountId());
    }
    public double updateAccountBalance (double amount, String accountID) {
        String sql0 = "SELECT BALANCE FROM ACCOUNT WHERE ACCOUNT_ID = ?";

        Double Balance = this.jdbcTemplate.queryForObject(sql0,
                Double.class, accountID);
        double currBalance = Balance.doubleValue();

        String sql1 = "UPDATE ACCOUNT SET BALANCE = ? WHERE ACCOUNT_ID = ?";
        int count = this.jdbcTemplate.update(sql1, (amount + currBalance), accountID);
        return (amount + currBalance);
    }

    public void delete(Account account) {
        String sql = "DELETE FROM ACCOUNT WHERE ACCOUNT_ID = ?";
        this.jdbcTemplate.update(sql, account.getAccountId());
    }

    public List<Map<String, Object>> findAll() {
        String sql = "SELECT * FROM ACCOUNT";

        List<Map<String, Object>> accounts = this.jdbcTemplate.queryForList(sql, new
            AccountMapper());
        return accounts;
    }

    public String getCustomerId(String accountID) {
        String sql = "SELECT CUSTOMER_ID FROM ACCOUNT WHERE ACCOUNT_ID = ?";

        String customerId = this.jdbcTemplate.queryForObject(sql,
                String.class, accountID);
```

```
        return customerId;
    }
    public double getBalance (String accountID) {
        String sql = "SELECT BALANCE FROM ACCOUNT WHERE ACCOUNT_ID = ?";

        double balance = this.jdbcTemplate.queryForObject(sql, Double.class, accountID);
        return balance;
    }
    public int countAll() {
        String sql = "SELECT COUNT(*) FROM ACCOUNT";

        int count = this.jdbcTemplate.queryForInt(sql);
        return count;
    }
    public void setDataSource(DataSource dataSource) {
        this.jdbcTemplate = new JdbcTemplate(dataSource);
        this.namedParameterJdbcTemplate = new NamedParameterJdbcTemplate (dataSource);
    }
    private static class AccountMapper implements
            ParameterizedRowMapper<Account> {
        public Account mapRow(ResultSet rs, int rowNum) throws SQLException {
            Account account = new Account();
            account.setAccountId(rs.getString("ACCOUNT_ID"));
            account.setName(rs.getString("NAME"));
            account.setType(rs.getString("TYPE"));
            account.setDescription(rs.getString("DESCRIPTION"));
            account.setStatus(rs.getString("STATUS"));
            account.setBalance(rs.getInt("BALANCE"));
            account.setOpenDate(rs.getTimestamp("OPEN_DATE"));
            account.setCloseDate(rs.getTimestamp("CLOSE_DATE"));
            account.setCustomerId(rs.getString("CUSTOMER_ID"));
            return account;
        }
    }
}
```

#1 Transactional integration testing with JUnit4

Our first example in this section is the `AccountManagerJUnit4ContextTxTest.java` as shown in Listing 9.31. First, note the @`RunWith` annotation, which specifies that the `SpringJUnit4ClassRunner` class should be used as the test runner. Next, note the @`Transactional` annotation as we explained at the beginning of this section. Another annotation of @`NotTransactional` used to be available for marking the test cases that are expected to be non-transactional, but has been deprecated as of Spring 3.0. Finally, note that this test class does not need to extend an abstract base class. I have run this test class in my environment successfully as indicated in Figure 9.6. I have also double checked my MySQL database and verified that no traces left in the database by this test run.

Listing 9.31 AccountManagerJUnit4ContextTxTest.java

```
package com.perfmath.spring.soba.testing.junit;

import static org.junit.Assert.assertEquals;
import java.sql.Timestamp;
import org.junit.Before;
import org.junit.Test;
import org.junit.runner.RunWith;
import org.springframework.beans.factory.annotation.Autowired;
import org.springframework.test.context.ContextConfiguration;
import org.springframework.test.context.junit4.SpringJUnit4ClassRunner;
import org.springframework.transaction.annotation.Transactional;
import com.perfmath.spring.soba.model.domain.Account;
import com.perfmath.spring.soba.service.AccountManager;

@RunWith (SpringJUnit4ClassRunner.class)
@ContextConfiguration(locations = "/beans-test-tx.xml")
@Transactional
public class AccountManagerJUnit4ContextTxTest {

  private static final String TEST_ACCOUNT_ID = "88889999";
  private static final double INITIAL_BALANCE = 500.0;
  private static final double TEST_AMOUNT = 300.0;
  @Autowired
  private AccountManager accountManager;

  @Before
  public void init() {
  }

  @Test
  public void createAccount () {
    Account account = new Account ();
    account.setAccountId(TEST_ACCOUNT_ID);
    account.setCustomerId("585855478");
    account.setName("Testing");
    account.setType("Testing");
    account.setDescription("Spring integration testing");
    account.setBalance(INITIAL_BALANCE);
```

```
        account.setStatus("0");
        account.setOpenDate(new Timestamp(System.currentTimeMillis()));
        accountManager.createAccount(account);
        assertEquals(accountManager.getBalance(TEST_ACCOUNT_ID), INITIAL_BALANCE, 0);
    }
    @Test
    public void updateAccountBalance () {
      createAccount ();
        double balance = accountManager.updateAccountBalance (TEST_AMOUNT,
            TEST_ACCOUNT_ID);
        assertEquals(accountManager.getBalance(TEST_ACCOUNT_ID),
            (INITIAL_BALANCE + TEST_AMOUNT), 0);
    }
}
```

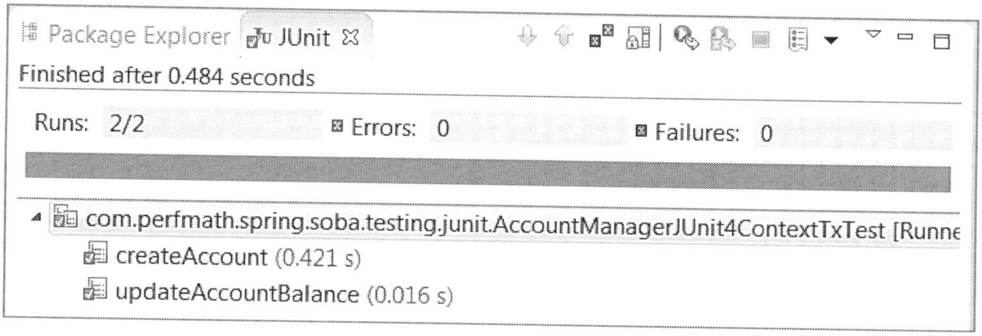

Figure 9.6 Successful execution of a transactional test case with JUnit 4

Note that the `@RunWith` and `@Transactional` annotations can be avoided if the test class as shown in 9.31 extends the `AbstractTransactionalJUnit4SpringContextTests` base class. You can find the `AccountManagerJUnit4ContextAbstractTxTest.java` class in the same package as the `AccountManagerJUnit4ContextTxTest.java` class and try it out yourself if you are interested in it. This is a trivial change and we would not repeat it here.

#2 Transactional integration testing with TestNG

Our second example is the `AccountManagerTestNGAbstractContextTxTest.java` as shown in Listing 9.32. Since it extends the `AbstractTransactionalTestNGSpringContextTests` base class, this test class does not need the `@RunWith` annotation and the `@Transactional` annotation. I have run this test class in my environment and got successful results for the two test cases as indicated in Listing 9.33. I have also double checked my MySQL database and verified that no traces left in the database by this test run.

Listing 9.32 AccountManagerTestNGAbstractContextTxTest.java

```
package com.perfmath.spring.soba.testing.testng;

import java.sql.Timestamp;
import org.springframework.beans.factory.annotation.Autowired;
import org.springframework.test.context.ContextConfiguration;
import org.springframework.test.context.testng.AbstractTransactionalTestNGSpringContextTests;
import static org.junit.Assert.assertEquals;
import org.testng.annotations.BeforeMethod;
import org.testng.annotations.Test;
import com.perfmath.spring.soba.model.domain.Account;
import com.perfmath.spring.soba.service.AccountManager;

@ContextConfiguration(locations = "/beans-test-tx.xml")
public class AccountManagerTestNGContextAbstractTxTest extends
    AbstractTransactionalTestNGSpringContextTests {

  private static final String TEST_ACCOUNT_ID = "88889999";
  private static final double INITIAL_BALANCE = 500.0;
  private static final double TEST_AMOUNT = 300.0;
  @Autowired
  private AccountManager accountManager;

  @BeforeMethod
  public void init() {
  }

  @Test
  public void createAccount () {
    Account account = new Account ();
    account.setAccountId(TEST_ACCOUNT_ID);
    account.setCustomerId("585855478");
    account.setName("Testing");
    account.setType("Testing");
    account.setDescription("Spring integration testing");
    account.setBalance(INITIAL_BALANCE);
    account.setStatus("0");
    account.setOpenDate(new Timestamp(System.currentTimeMillis()));
    accountManager.createAccount(account);
    assertEquals(accountManager.getBalance(TEST_ACCOUNT_ID), INITIAL_BALANCE, 0);
  }

  @Test
  public void updateAccountBalance () {
```

```
    createAccount ();
     accountManager.updateAccountBalance (TEST_AMOUNT, TEST_ACCOUNT_ID);
     assertEquals(accountManager.getBalance(TEST_ACCOUNT_ID),
           (INITIAL_BALANCE + TEST_AMOUNT), 0);
  }
}
```

Listing 9.33 Console output of running AccountManagerTestNGContextAbstractTxTest

```
[TestNG] Running:
  C:\Users\henry\AppData\Local\Temp\testng-eclipse--1910367704\testng-
customsuite.xml

PASSED: createAccount
PASSED: updateAccountBalance

===============================================
    Default test
    Tests run: 2, Failures: 0, Skips: 0
===============================================
```

9.3.5 Spring Integration Testing against Real Databases

In the previous section, we discussed how to make a test case and its methods *transactional* by having the test case extend either `AbstractTransactionalJUnit4SpringContextTests` base class for JUnit4 or the `AbstractTransactionalTestNGSpringContextTests` base class for TestNG. However, note from both Listing 9.31 and 9.32 that `assertEquals` are done by calling the proper method of the dependent object. In fact, one can issue SQLs directly to prepare data or retrieve results from the database for verification purposes if such needs arise. Listing 9.34 shows an example of extending the `AbstractTransactionalTestNGSpringContextTests` base class for TestNG (Junit4 case would be similar). Note those Spring `jdbcTemplate` API calls in the `init` method for creating the account and add an initial balance to it. Then, the Spring `jdbcTemplate.queryForObject` calls are made in the `deposit` and `withdraw` methods to verify the balance in the account.

This test class as shown in Listing 9.34 was executed successfully in my environment with the console output as shown in Listing 9.35. There is a similar JUnit4-based test case named `AccountManagerJUnit4ContextDBTest.java` in the `testing.junit` package, and you can try it out if you are interested.

Listing 9.34 AccountMangerTestNGContextDBTest.java

```
package com.perfmath.spring.soba.testing.testng;

import static org.testng.Assert.assertEquals;
```

```
import java.sql.Timestamp;
import org.springframework.beans.factory.annotation.Autowired;
import org.springframework.test.context.ContextConfiguration;
import org.springframework.test.context.testng.AbstractTransactionalTestNGSpringContextTests;
import org.testng.annotations.BeforeMethod;
import org.testng.annotations.Test;

import com.perfmath.spring.soba.service.AccountManager;

@ContextConfiguration(locations = "/beans-test-tx.xml")
public class AccountManagerTestNGContextDBTest extends
    AbstractTransactionalTestNGSpringContextTests {

  private static final String TEST_ACCOUNT_ID = "88889999";
  private static final double INITIAL_BALANCE = 500.0;
  private static final double TEST_AMOUNT = 300.0;

  @Autowired
  private AccountManager accountManager;

  @BeforeMethod
  public void init() {
    jdbcTemplate.update ( "INSERT INTO ACCOUNT (ACCOUNT_ID, NAME, TYPE,
      DESCRIPTION, STATUS, "
          + " BALANCE, OPEN_DATE, CLOSE_DATE, CUSTOMER_ID) "
          + "VALUES (?, ?, ?,?, ?, ?, ?, ?, ?)", TEST_ACCOUNT_ID,
          "Testing", "Testing", "Spring integration testing",  "0", INITIAL_BALANCE,
          new Timestamp(System.currentTimeMillis()), null, "585855478");
    jdbcTemplate.update ("UPDATE ACCOUNT SET BALANCE = ? WHERE ACCOUNT_ID = ?",
          (INITIAL_BALANCE + TEST_AMOUNT), TEST_ACCOUNT_ID);
  }

  @Test
  public void deposit() {
    accountManager.updateAccountBalance (TEST_AMOUNT, TEST_ACCOUNT_ID);
    double balance = jdbcTemplate.queryForObject (
        "SELECT BALANCE FROM ACCOUNT WHERE ACCOUNT_ID = ?",
        Double.class, TEST_ACCOUNT_ID);
    assertEquals(balance, (INITIAL_BALANCE + 2*TEST_AMOUNT), 0);
  }

  @Test
  public void withdraw() {
```

```
        accountManager.updateAccountBalance (-TEST_AMOUNT, TEST_ACCOUNT_ID);
        double balance = jdbcTemplate.queryForObject (
            "SELECT BALANCE FROM ACCOUNT WHERE ACCOUNT_ID = ?",
            Double.class, TEST_ACCOUNT_ID);
        assertEquals(balance, INITIAL_BALANCE, 0);
    }
}
```

Listing 9.35 Console output of running AccountManagerTestNGContextDBTest

```
[TestNG] Running:
  C:\Users\henry\AppData\Local\Temp\testng-eclipse--598883244\testng-customsuite.xml

PASSED: deposit
PASSED: withdraw

===============================================
    Default test
    Tests run: 2, Failures: 0, Skips: 0
===============================================
```

9.4 SPRING JUNIT TESTING ANNOTATIONS

Spring supports annotations such as `@Timed`, `@Repeat (n)`, `@IfProfileValue`, and so on. However, according to Spring Reference Documentation 3.2, these annotations are supported on JUnit only; or in other words, they are not supported on TestNG. In this section, we present a simple example to demonstrate how some of these annotations work.

Listing 9.36 shows an example, which uses: (1) the `@Timed` annotation to limit that the `deposit` method should complete its execution within 900 milliseconds, and (2) the `@Repeat` (5) annotation to specify that the `withDraw` method should repeat five times. Because how these annotations work is so obvious, I'd like to show the result of running this test class in my environment in Figure 9.7, which verifies that the deposit method completed within 359 milliseconds. This wraps up our coverage on Spring testing support.

Listing 9.36 AccountManagerJUnit4ContextCommonTest .java

```
package com.perfmath.spring.soba.testing.junit;
import static org.junit.Assert.assertEquals;
import java.sql.Timestamp;
import org.junit.Before;
import org.junit.Test;
import org.springframework.beans.factory.annotation.Autowired;
import org.springframework.test.annotation.Repeat;
```

```
import org.springframework.test.annotation.Timed;
import org.springframework.test.context.ContextConfiguration;
import org.springframework.test.context.junit4.AbstractTransactionalJUnit4SpringContextTests;
import com.perfmath.spring.soba.service.AccountManager;

@ContextConfiguration(locations = "/beans-test-tx.xml")
public class AccountManagerJUnit4ContextCommonTest extends
    AbstractTransactionalJUnit4SpringContextTests {

  private static final String TEST_ACCOUNT_ID = "88889999";
  private static final double INITIAL_BALANCE = 1500.0;
  private static final double TEST_AMOUNT = 300.0;

  @Autowired
  private AccountManager accountManager;

  @Before
  public void init () {
    jdbcTemplate.update( "INSERT INTO ACCOUNT (ACCOUNT_ID, NAME, TYPE,
            DESCRIPTION, STATUS, "
            + " BALANCE, OPEN_DATE, CLOSE_DATE, CUSTOMER_ID) "
            + "VALUES (?, ?, ?,?, ?, ?, ?, ?, ?)", TEST_ACCOUNT_ID,
            "Testing", "Testing", "Spring integration testing",  "0", INITIAL_BALANCE,
            new Timestamp(System.currentTimeMillis()), null, "585855478");
      jdbcTemplate.update("UPDATE ACCOUNT SET BALANCE = ? WHERE ACCOUNT_ID = ?",
            (INITIAL_BALANCE + TEST_AMOUNT), TEST_ACCOUNT_ID);
  }

  @Test
  @Timed(millis = 900)
  public void deposit() {
    accountManager.updateAccountBalance (TEST_AMOUNT, TEST_ACCOUNT_ID);
    double balance = jdbcTemplate.queryForObject(
        "SELECT BALANCE FROM ACCOUNT WHERE ACCOUNT_ID = ?",
        Double.class, TEST_ACCOUNT_ID);
    assertEquals(balance, (INITIAL_BALANCE + 2*TEST_AMOUNT), 0);
  }

  @Test
  @Repeat(3)
  public void withDraw() {
    accountManager.updateAccountBalance (-TEST_AMOUNT, TEST_ACCOUNT_ID);
    double balance = jdbcTemplate.queryForObject(
```

```
            "SELECT BALANCE FROM ACCOUNT WHERE ACCOUNT_ID = ?",
            Double.class, TEST_ACCOUNT_ID);
        assertEquals(balance, INITIAL_BALANCE, 0);
    }
}
```

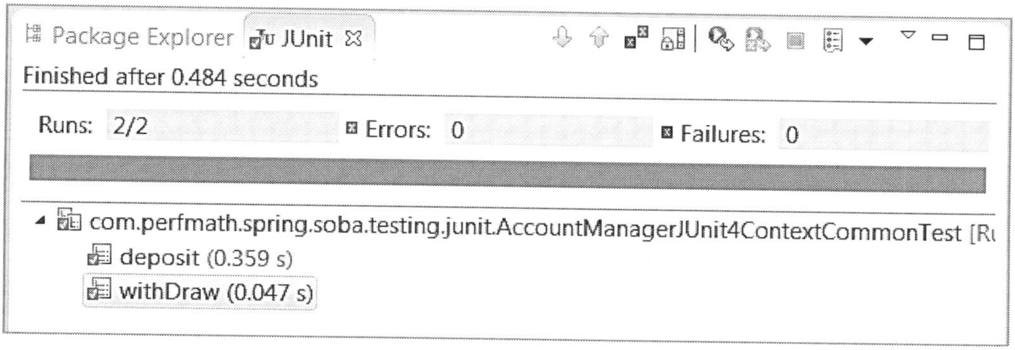

Package Explorer JUnit
Finished after 0.484 seconds
Runs: 2/2 Errors: 0 Failures: 0
com.perfmath.spring.soba.testing.junit.AccountManagerJUnit4ContextCommonTest [Ru
deposit (0.359 s)
withDraw (0.047 s)

Figure 9.7 Test result of running AccountManagerJUnit4ContextCommonTest

9.5 SUMMARY

This chapter covered Spring testing support for testing Spring MVC controllers, service and DAO layer Spring beans. We presented test cases in association with both JUnit4 and TestNG Java testing frameworks, as Spring testing framework really is not a standalone testing framework. We demonstrated three most important Spring testing framework features: TestContext, automatically injecting Spring test fixtures, and transaction-related annotations. These features should meet most of your testing needs for your Spring-based project. Another equally important subject is test automation, which is much needed for every large-scale enterprise application. However, a detailed coverage of such a broad topic is beyond the context and scope of this book.

9.6 RECOMMENDED READING

Chapter 10 of the Spring Framework Reference Documentation is dedicated to Spring testing. It includes the following sections that you can reference if you need more information on certain specific features:

- **10.1 Introduction to Spring Testing**
- **10.2 Unit Testing**
- **10.3 Integration Testing**
- 10.4 Further Resources

9.7 EXERCISES

9.1 If you have experience with both JUnit and TestNG, what are the pros and cons of each test framework from your perception, and which one is in use with your project (and what was the main reason for choosing one over the other)?

9.2 What are the advantages and disadvantages of using some artifacts such as mock objects and in-memory databases in place of real backend layers?

9.3 What is test context and how is it managed in Spring's testing framework? How does it facilitate testing Spring beans?

9.4 What issue does the Spring test fixture injection attempt to resolve? How do you inject test fixtures automatically into Spring-specific test classes?

9.5 Which abstract base classes do the test classes need to extend to enable transactionality to work with the JUnit4 and TestNG testing frameworks?

10 Spring-EJB Integration

Although Spring is considered an EJB replacement, sometimes, the choice of "replacement" may not be available and one has to integrate Spring with existing EJB systems. For example, your legacy EJB enterprise application has been working just fine and it would be too costly to re-write it in Spring; however, you might want to re-use some functionality of your existing legacy EJB application without having to re-code it in Spring. In such situations, Spring offers solutions for integrating your Spring-based enterprise application with your existing legacy EJB-based enterprise application.

In this chapter, we demonstrate how Spring-EJB integration works using a concrete, Jboss-based EJB 3 sample. We will create an EJB 3 sample first. This sample will serve as the base for our Spring-EJB integration coverage. It provides an opportunity for us to evidence how those complexities imposed on earlier EJB technologies as discussed in my article "*A Retrospective View on EJB 2,*" posted on this book's website, have been taken out from EJB 2 to EJB 3. Then, we demonstrate how you can integrate your Spring 3.x enterprise application with your EJB 3.x legacies. The sample is not only fully verifiable in your environment but also adaptable for your project if you have such needs to meet.

10.1 Creating an EJB 3 Sample

In order to demonstrate Spring support for accessing EJB 3 components, we need to create an EJB 3 sample. In this section, we create such an EJB 3 sample using Eclipse and JPA, which will run on Jboss. To make it as realistic as possible, we create a relevant database on MySQL for this purpose in the next section.

10.1.1 Creating the MySQL Database

The procedure for creating a MySQL database for our EJB 3 sample consists of the following two steps:

1 Creating an *ejb3db* database with the user credentials of "*ejb3admin/ejb3admin*" by executing the following command (note that you need to enter *root's* password for this step):

```
cmd>mysql –h 127.0.0.1 –u root –p <create_ejb3db.sql
```

2 Creating the two tables of CUSTOMER and BANKINGTX by executing the following command (note that you need to enter *ejb3admin*'s password for this step, which is the same as '*ejb3admin*'):

```
cmd>mysql ejb3db –h 127.0.0.1 -u ejb3admin –p < create_ejb3_tables.sql
```

Refer to Listings 10.1 and 10.2 for the contents of the two SQL scripts executed above. Note that we have created two tables: CUSTOMER and BANKINGTX, with the BANKINGTX table containing a foreign key (FK) of `customer_id` referencing the primary key of `id` from the CUSTOMER table. This constraint will be reflected in the entities we create as is discussed next.

Listing 10.1 create_ejb3db.sql

```
create database ejb3db;
grant usage on *.* to ejb3admin@localhost identified by 'ejb3admin';
grant all privileges on ejb3db.* to ejb3admin@localhost;
show databases;
```

Listing 10.2 create_ejb3tables.sql

```
create table customer (
id              bigint unsigned not null auto_increment primary key,
name            varchar (30) not null,
password        varchar(30) not null,
email           varchar (30) not null,
locked          tinyint(1) not null
);

create table bankingtx (
id              bigint unsigned not null auto_increment primary key,
description     varchar(45) default null,
amount          decimal(10,2) default null,
type            varchar(30) not null,
customer_id     bigint unsigned not null,
foreign key     (customer_id) references customer (id)
);
alter table bankingtx add constraint fk_bankingtx foreign key (customer_id) references customer (id) on
delete cascade on update cascade;
```

10.1.2 Creating Entities with an EJB 3 project

As we know, EJB 3 replaced Entity EJBs with *entities* as specified by the Java Persistence API. In this section, we demonstrate how to create EJB 3 entities using the JPA-enabled Eclipse IDE (Juno version) for our EJB 3 sample, which includes the following two tasks:

- Creating an EJB 3 sample project
- Creating JPA entities

Task #1: Creating an EJB 3 sample project

To create our EJB 3 sample, we start with creating a new EJB project by clicking *File → New → Other → EJB Project* on the Eclipse IDE, as is shown in Figure 10.1.

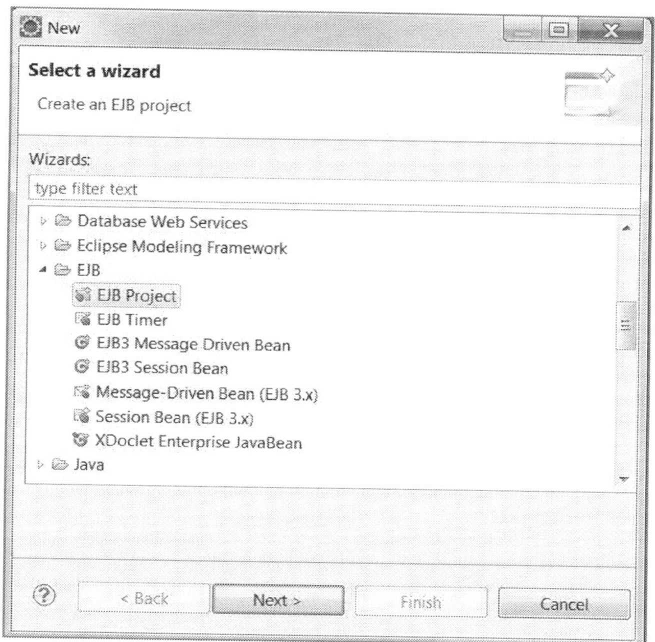

Figure 10.1 Creating an EJB project on Eclipse

After clicking *Next*, you should see a dialog similar to Figure 10.2. Now configure this EJB project as follows:

- **Project name**: Enter a project name like "*Customer_EJB3*."
- **Target runtime**: Select a Target Runtime like "Jboss 6.x Runtime" from the drop-down list, since we will run this EJB 3 sample on Jboss, and we need the Jboss JPA runtime to proceed. If this runtime does not show up on your IDE, it means that you need to install it. To install the required Jboss 6.x Runtime for this specific EJB 3 sample, click on the *New Runtime...* button to bring up the dialog similar to Figure 10.3. If you don't see the Jboss Community category, click the "*Download additional server adapters*" link above the "*type filter text*" box and get it installed. Then you should see those Jboss community server runtimes as shown in Figure 10.3.
- **EJB module version**: Select 3.0.
- **Configuration**: Make sure <custom> is selected. Also, click *Modify...* and make sure you have selected all project facets including *EJB Module 3.0, Java 1.6* (note that the default 1.7 is not recommended at this time), *JPA 2.0* and *Jboss 6.x Runtime* as shown in Figure 10.4.

Note: You might think why we didn't create a faceted project in the first place by going through the clicks of File → New → Other → General → Faceted Project, and then add EJB modules and classes to it. This approach turned out to be more problematic than creating the EJB project first and then adding the facets as shown above.

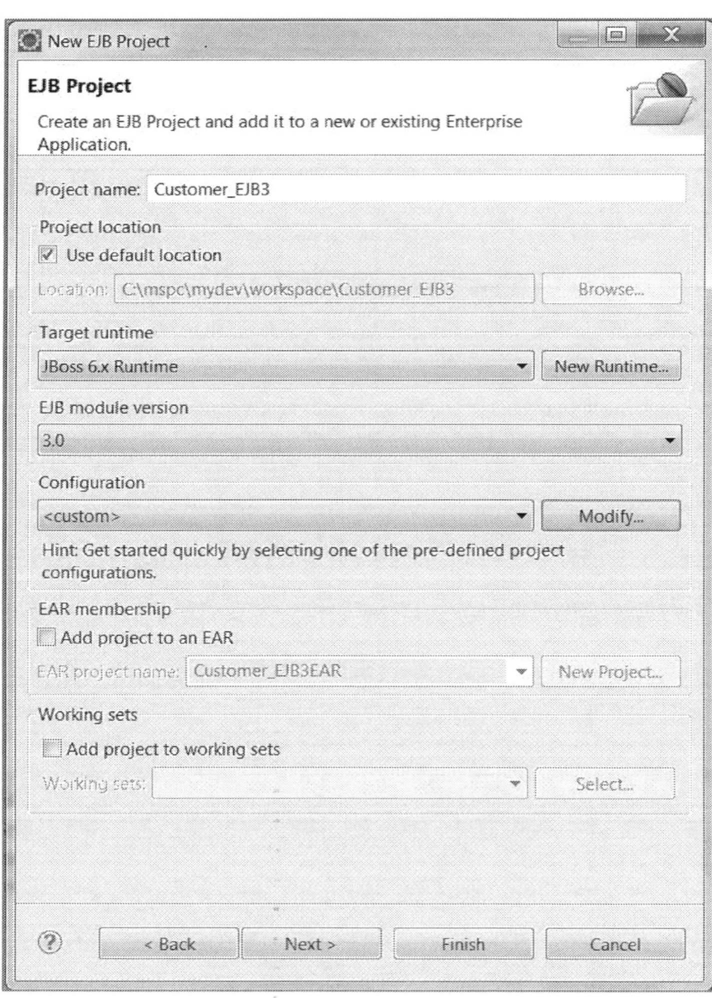

Figure 10.2 Project settings for the EJB 3 sample project

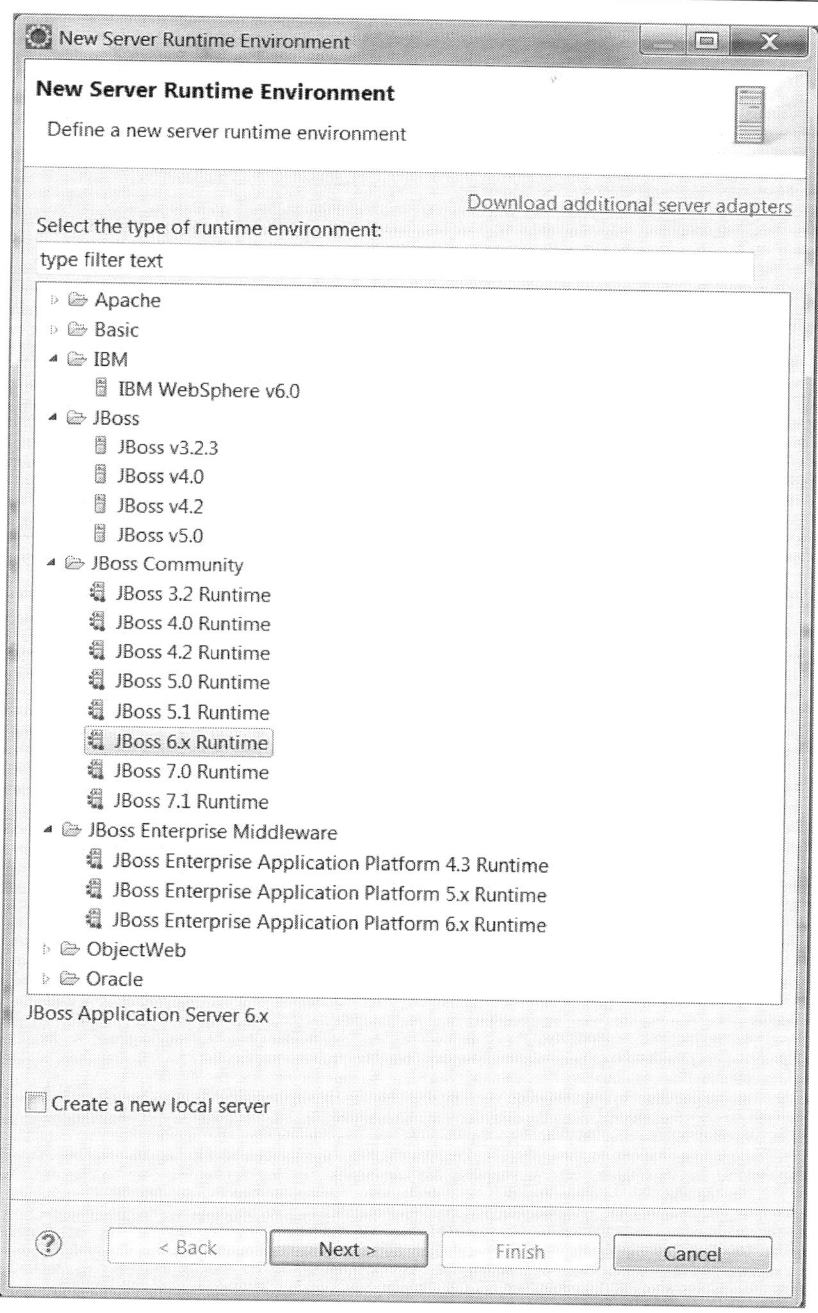

Figure 10.3 All Jboss Runtimes available as plug-ins on Juno Eclipse IDE

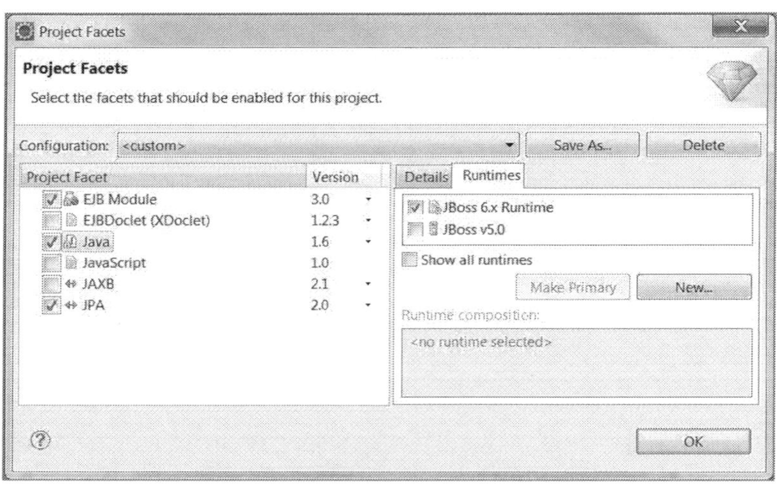

Figure 10.4 Configurable project facets for the EJB 3 sample project

After making sure all project settings have been entered as required as shown in Figure 10.2, click *Next* and then *Next* again. In the new dialog, select "*Generic 2.0*" for *Platform*, and "*Library Provided by Target Runtime*" for *JPA implementation*. We also need to create a MySQL Connection, since we have an EJB 3 database to connect to as described in §10.1.1. You can do this by clicking the "*Add connection ...*" link and referencing Figure 10.5.

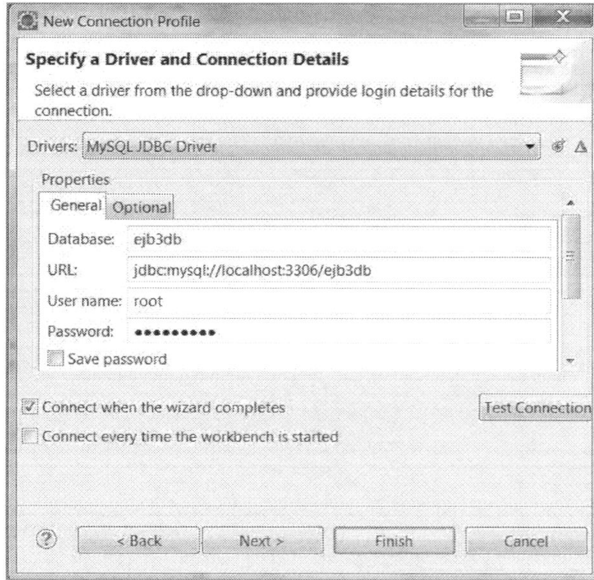

Figure 10.5 Creating a MySQL connection profile

Now the dialog should look similar to Figure 10.6. Click *Next* and then *Finish* to complete this task. When you are prompted for opening the project in Java EE perspective as shown in Figure 10.7, click *Yes*. Your newly-created *Customer_EJB3* project should look similar to Figure 10.8. The next step is to create JPA entities.

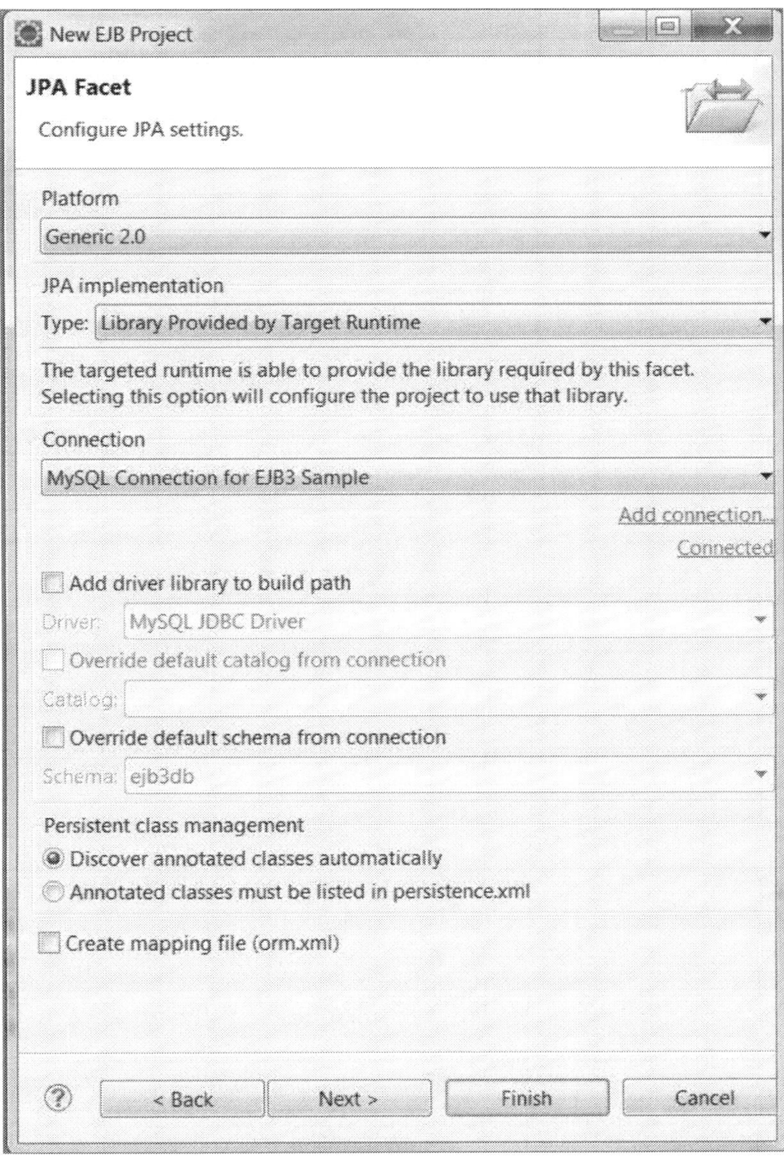

Figure 10.6 JPA Facet dialog

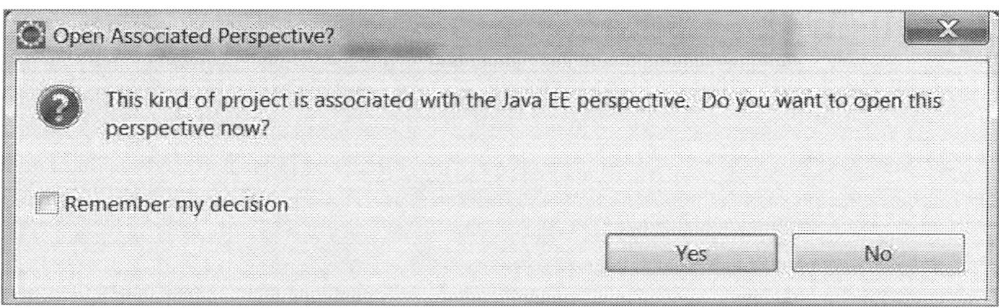

Figure 10.7 Open the Java EE perspective

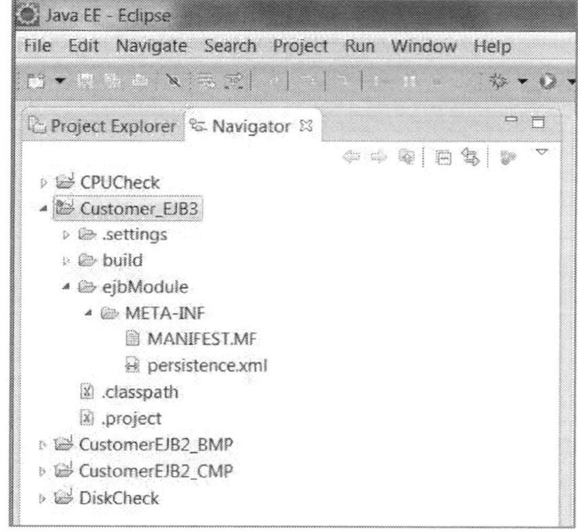

Figure 10.8 Newly-created Customer_EJB3 project

Task #2: Creating JPA entities

In this step, we create JPA entities directly from the two tables of BANKINGTX and CUSTOMER we created previously. Although you can create those JPA entities manually or copy/paste/modify existing ones (if any) with your project, it's more convenient to create them using an IDE like Eclipse with such built-in functionality. You may also want to know that behind the scenes a plug-in called *Dali* takes care of all the details of translating the settings entered on the GUI into actual Java code for the JPA entities created. You can check Eclipse *help* or online for more information about Dali. You may also want to go through a quick tutorial about JPA if you have never been exposed to it. We'll provide brief explanations about why we choose certain options over others, but we won't go too deeply into it, as our main focus here is to create an EJB 3 sample so that we can demonstrate how Spring-EJB integration works.

To create JPA entities for our EJB 3 sample, with your *Customer_EJB3* project selected, click *File → New → Other → JPA → JPA Entities from Tables*, as is shown in Figure 10.9. We select this option out of four possibilities under the JPA category (the other three are *JPA Entity*, *JPA ORM Mapping File*, and *JPA Project*), because we already have a database created *a prior* to work with. This is the preferred approach that you create your database schema first and then your JPA entities as your domain objects out of your database tables.

Click *Next* and you should see the *Select Tables* dialog similar to Figure 10.10. Make sure that you select the proper *Connection*, *Schema*, and *Tables* (in our case, the two tables of BANKINGTX and CUSTOMER we created previously). Also make sure that the "*Update class list in persistence.xml file*" check box is checked, as we need to have all JPA entity classes included in the `persistence.xml` file, which is the required configuration file for all JPA entities.

Now click *Next* and you should see the *Table Associations* dialog similar to Figure 10.11. Make sure that you click the second association and uncheck the "*Generate this association*" check box in its editing panel. This is because we don't have a many-to-many association between customers and banking transactions. What we have here is a one-to-many association between a customer and multiple transactions, as one banking transaction cannot be assigned to more than one customer. If you have a situation that a many-to-many association makes sense, then you need to deal with both.

Now click the first association, and click *Next*, which should bring up a dialog similar to Figure 10.12. Make sure you have selected the following options:

- **Key Generator**: Select "*auto*" so that database table keys will be generated automatically.
- **Entity Access**: Select "*Field*", which means that the instance variables (fields) of the persistence classes will be mapped to the corresponding table columns in the database. "*Property*" *entity access* means that getters of the persistence classes will be used to determine the property names that will be mapped to the table columns in the database. Note that JPA favors "Field" access, while Hibernate favors "Property" access.
- **Associations Fetch**: This is about how persisted entity data should be loaded from the database. *Eager fetching* (or *eager loading*) means "*loading even if data is not needed right away*," while *lazy loading* means "*do not load until data is needed*." The "*Default*" is to load property values, including references, eagerly while loading collections lazily. This is a delicate performance issue and should be dealt with carefully according to your application context and requirements.
- **Collection Properties Type**: This is about whether the *Set* or *List* type should be used for collections. Using *List* is just fine for most situations.
- **Source Folder and Package**: Eclipse chooses "*<project-name>/ejbModule*" for *Source Folder* by default and we use "*com.perfmath.ejb3.jpa*" for the package name here.

After clicking *Next*, a dialog similar to Figure 10.13 shows up, allowing each individual entity to be customized. We don't have a lot to customize here except that we can optionally change the "*t*" letter from lower case to upper case in the class name of "*Bankingtx*" to make it look like "*BankingTx*." Click "Finish" to complete the two JPA domain object entity classes for this EJB 3 sample. Listings 10.3 and 10.4 show the JPA classes of *Customer.java* and *BankingTx.java*. Some brief discussions are provided following Figure 10.13 and prior to Listing 10.3.

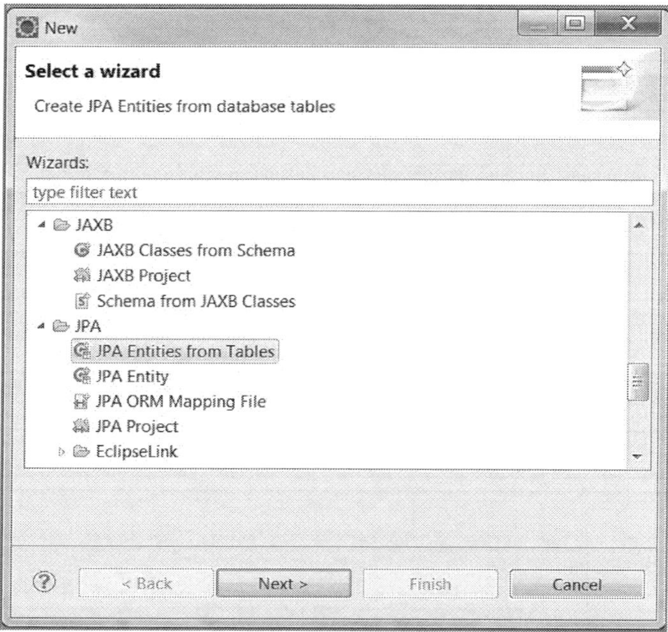

Figure 10.9 Creating JPA entities on Eclipse (Juno)

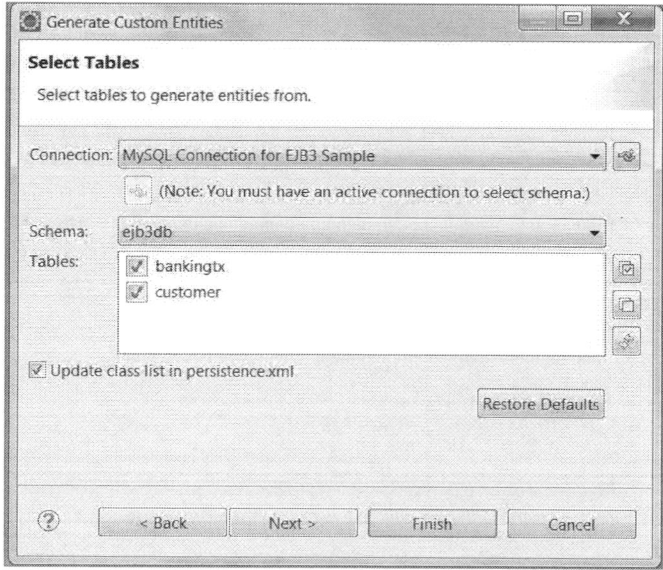

Figure 10.10 Select Tables step in creating JPA entities

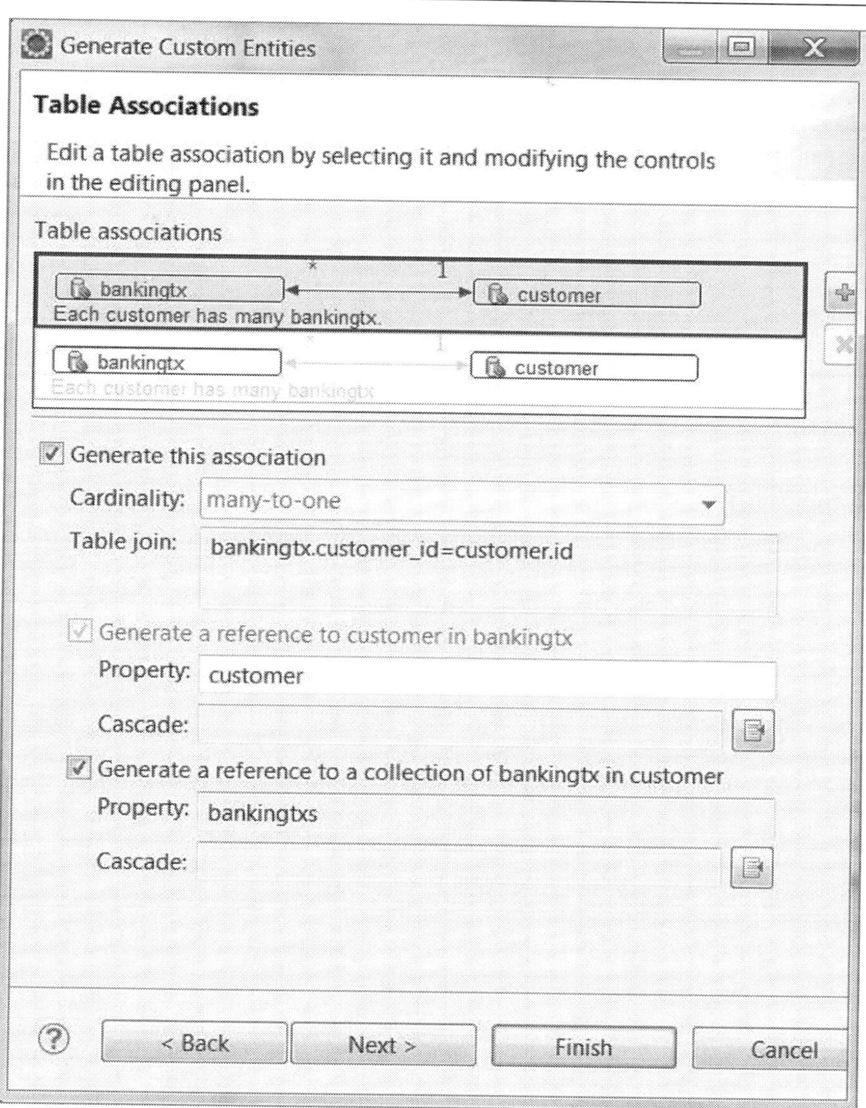

Figure 10.11 Table associations step in creating JPA entities

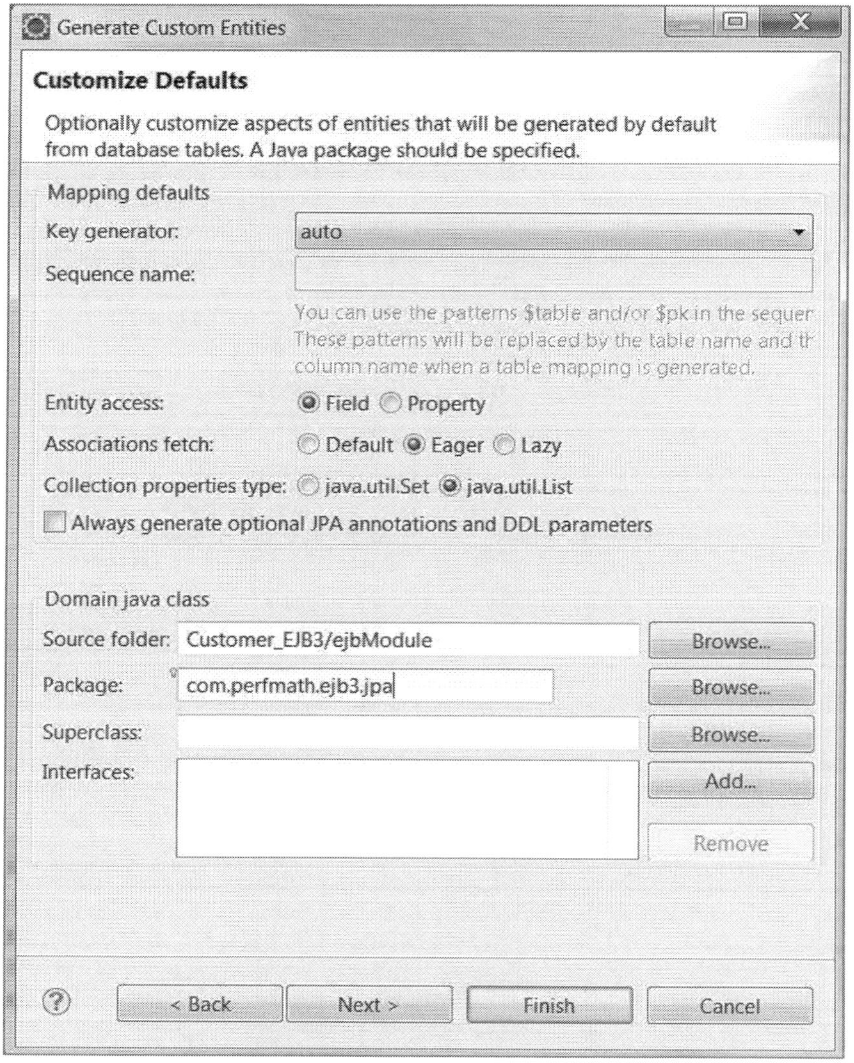

Generate Custom Entities

Customize Defaults

Optionally customize aspects of entities that will be generated by default from database tables. A Java package should be specified.

Mapping defaults

Key generator: auto

Sequence name:

You can use the patterns $table and/or $pk in the sequer
These patterns will be replaced by the table name and th
column name when a table mapping is generated.

Entity access: Field Property

Associations fetch: Default Eager Lazy

Collection properties type: java.util.Set java.util.List

Always generate optional JPA annotations and DDL parameters

Domain java class

Source folder: Customer_EJB3/ejbModule Browse...

Package: com.perfmath.ejb3.jpa Browse...

Superclass: Browse...

Interfaces: Add... Remove

< Back Next > Finish Cancel

Figure 10.12 Generate Custom Entities dialog

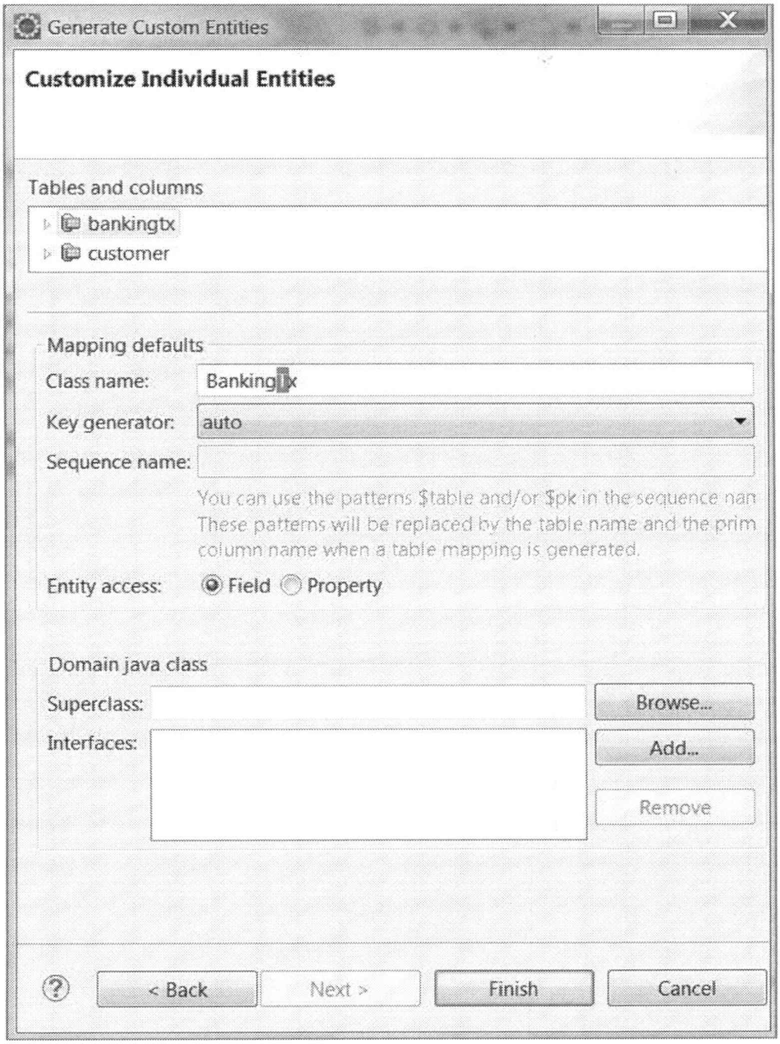

Figure 10.13 Customizing individual entities

By examining Listings 10.3 and 10.4, we notice that these entity classes are indeed much simpler than the EJB 2 entity beans such as the Customer entity bean discussed in my article "*A Retrospective View on EJB 2*." Secondly, notice how succinct these annotations are – there are only four of them here: *@Entity* annotation for declaring that this class is a JPA entity class, *@Id* for declaring that this field is an ID field, *@GeneratedValue* for specifying how ID values should be generated, and *@OneToMany* or *@ManyToOne* for declaring the association type. Of course, our sample here is a very simple one, and you might encounter more complicated situations for your project, in which case, you should consult EJB and JPA dedicated texts.

In addition to the entity classes of Customer.java and BankingTx.java, a JPA specific XML file of persistence.xml has also been created, as shown in Listing 10.5. This is a simple file that specifies the persistence-unit name of "Customer_EJB3" and the entity classes created. This file is generic and we'll have to overwrite it later when we deploy and test it on Jboss.

Note: The type for the *locked* field of the *Customer* entity class was *byte* when created initially by the JPA utility on the Eclipse IDE. We had to manually change it to *boolean* to be consistent with the simple type convention observed by Java programmers. This is an example of why IDE-auto-generated artifacts may require applying customizations afterwards. An IDE is convenient, but it cannot replace a developer's deep understanding of how things work at the source code level that only comes from experience.

Next, we demonstrate how to create an EJB 3 stateless session bean as a session façade for accessing the entities created above.

Listing 10.3 JPA domain object entity class Customer.java

```
package com.perfmath.ejb3.jpa;

import java.io.Serializable;
import javax.persistence.*;
import java.util.List;


/**
 * The persistent class for the customer database table.
 *
 */
@Entity
public class Customer implements Serializable {
    private static final long serialVersionUID = 1L;

    @Id
    @GeneratedValue(strategy=GenerationType.AUTO)
    private int id;

    private String email;

    private boolean locked;
```

```
private String name;

private String password;

//bi-directional many-to-one association to BankingTx
@OneToMany(mappedBy="customer", fetch=FetchType.EAGER)
private List<BankingTx> bankingTxs;

public Customer() {
}

public int getId() {
    return this.id;
}

public void setId(int id) {
    this.id = id;
}

public String getEmail() {
    return this.email;
}

public void setEmail(String email) {
    this.email = email;
}

public boolean getLocked() {
    return this.locked;
}

public void setLocked(boolean locked) {
    this.locked = locked;
}

public String getName() {
    return this.name;
}

public void setName(String name) {
    this.name = name;
}
```

```
    public String getPassword() {
        return this.password;
    }

    public void setPassword(String password) {
        this.password = password;
    }

    public List<BankingTx> getBankingTxs() {
        return this.bankingTxs;
    }

    public void setBankingTxs(List<BankingTx> bankingTxs) {
        this.bankingTxs = bankingTxs;
    }

}
```

Listing 10.4 JPA domain object entity class BankingTx.java

```
package com.perfmath.ejb3.jpa;

import java.io.Serializable;
import javax.persistence.*;
import java.math.BigDecimal;


/**
 * The persistent class for the bankingtx database table.
 *
 */
@Entity
public class BankingTx implements Serializable {
    private static final long serialVersionUID = 1L;

    @Id
    @GeneratedValue(strategy=GenerationType.AUTO)
    private String id;

    private BigDecimal amount;

    private String description;
```

```
private String type;

//bi-directional many-to-one association to Customer
@ManyToOne
private Customer customer;

public BankingTx() {
}

public String getId() {
    return this.id;
}

public void setId(String id) {
    this.id = id;
}

public BigDecimal getAmount() {
    return this.amount;
}

public void setAmount(BigDecimal amount) {
    this.amount = amount;
}

public String getDescription() {
    return this.description;
}

public void setDescription(String description) {
    this.description = description;
}

public String getType() {
    return this.type;
}

public void setType(String type) {
    this.type = type;
}

public Customer getCustomer() {
    return this.customer;
```

```
    }

    public void setCustomer(Customer customer) {
        this.customer = customer;
    }

}
```

Listing 10.5 The persistence.xml file for the EJB 3 sample

```
<?xml version="1.0" encoding="UTF-8"?>
<persistence version="2.0" xmlns=http://java.sun.com/xml/ns/persistence
xmlns:xsi="http://www.w3.org/2001/XMLSchema-instance"
xsi:schemaLocation="http://java.sun.com/xml/ns/persistence
http://java.sun.com/xml/ns/persistence/persistence_2_0.xsd">
    <persistence-unit name="Customer_EJB3">
        <class>com.perfmath.ejb3.jpa.BankingTx</class>
        <class>com.perfmath.ejb3.jpa.Customer</class>
    </persistence-unit>
</persistence>
```

10.1.3 Creating an EJB 3 Stateless Session Bean

To create an EJB 3 stateless session bean as a façade for accessing the *Customer* and *BankingTx* entities, right-click on the *Customer_EJB3* project, and then select *File → New → Other → EJB → EJB 3 Session Bean* (you can refer back to Figure 10.1 to locate the EJB 3 Session Bean option in the New EJB Project Wizard). After clicking *Next*, you should see a dialog similar to Figure 10.14 with the following default and manually entered options:

- **Source folder**: This was set to `Customer_EJB/ejbModule` by default.
- **Session Bean Type**: This was set to `Stateless` by default, which was also what we needed.
- **Bean Package**: Manually entered "`com.perfmath.ejb3.ejb`" for this session bean.
- **Bean Name**: Manually entered "`CustomerManager`" for this session bean.
- **Bean Class Name**: Automatically generated by the IDE with "`Bean`" appended to the fully qualified session bean name of "`com.perfmath.ejb3.ejb.CustomerManager`."
- **Remote Interface Package and Remote Interface Name**: All populated automatically as shown in Figure 10.14.

In is very interesting to see that this process does not do much. It creates two bare-minimum Java files only: The `CustomerManager.java` file and `CustomerManagerBean.java` file as shown in Listings 10.6 and 10.7, respectively (we will have to overwrite these two classes heavily later, but the purpose for showing them here as they are is to give you an opportunity to see what have been created by the IDE in the first place). Note that the former is a remote interface, while the latter is the bean implementation class. The annotations are also minimal: only one for each (`@Remote` for the remote interface, and `@Stateless` for the bean implementation class). This is significantly simpler than the EJB 2 session bean created with the EJB 2 sample discussed in my article "*A Retrospective View on EJB 2*" – All the "*octopus*" `ejbXXX ()` methods required by EJB 2 are gone now with EJB 3! This is a significant improvement, but EJB 3 components are still more complex than POJOs.

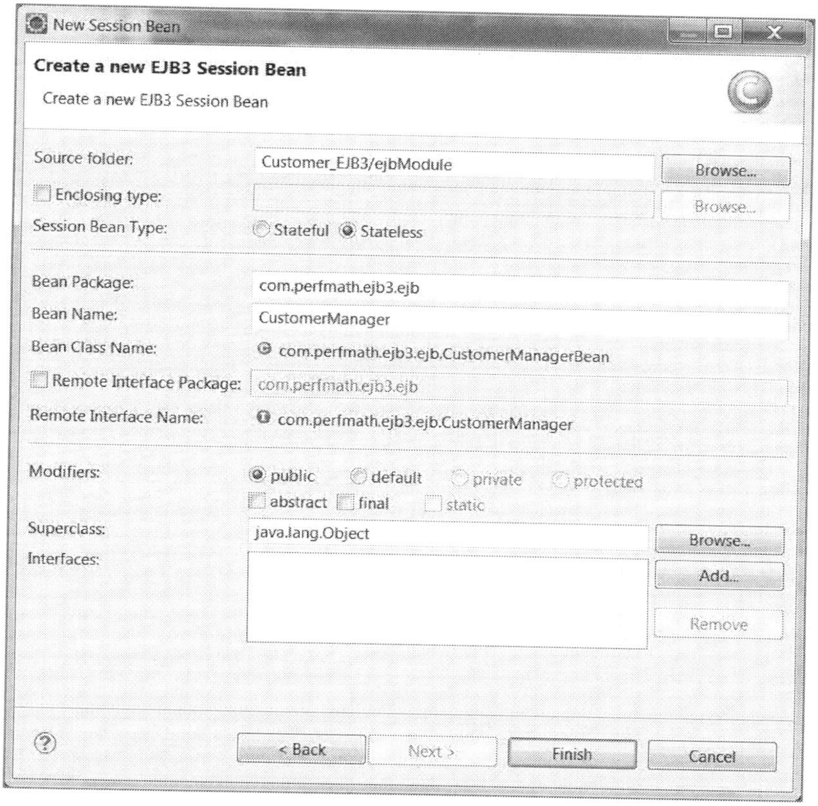

Figure 10.14 Creating a new EJB3 session bean

Listing 10.6 Eclipse-created CustomerManager.java

```
package com.perfmath.ejb3.ejb;

import javax.ejb.Remote;

@Remote
public interface CustomerManager {

}
```

Listing 10.7 Eclipse-created CustomerManagerBean.java

```
package com.perfmath.ejb3.ejb;

import javax.ejb.Stateless;
import com.perfmath.ejb3.ejb.CustomerManager;

public @Stateless class CustomerManagerBean implements CustomerManager {

}
```

In order to make it as realistic as possible, we need to make some adjustments here. The first adjustment we would make is to make the `CustomerManager` interface as shown in Listing 10.6 a more generic business interface by removing the following two statements:

```
import javax.ejb.Remote;
@Remote
```

We then manually add all business methods as shown in Listing 10.8. We can make a local interface (Listing 10.9 (a)) and a remote interface (Listing 10.9 (b)) by extending the generic interface shown in Listing 10.8 (we can also make a Web Services interface out of it, but it is not needed here). This way, the bean implementation class can implement both the local and remote interfaces as shown is Listing 10.10 so that it can be accessed either locally or remotely.

Note: The above practice of creating a common top non-EJB business interface is called the *Business Methods Interface pattern.* It provides the developer with the flexibility of swapping EJB out for POJOs when such needs arise later.

If you are not familiar with EJB 3 annotations, note the following annotations used in the bean implementation class:

- **@RemoteBinding**: Specifies jndi binding for remote access across JVMs.
- **@LocalBinding**: Specifies jndi binding for local access within the same JVM.
- **@PersistenceContext**: Specifies the persistence context for the persistence unit of "`CustomerEJB3`" (note that a persistence unit is a group of entities packaged together in an application module). This makes it possible to inject the `EntityManager` named `em` into the `CustomerManager` bean.

In addition, note the use of the `persist` and `createQuery` methods of the entity manager for the various business methods implemented. If you are interested in such details, consult dedicated EJB 3 texts.

Note: Before proceeding further, copy/overwrite the `CustomerManager.java`, `CustomerManagerLocal.java`, `CustomerManagerRemote.java`, and `CustomerManager.java` files contained in the *spring-integration.zip* download file into the `com.perfmath.ejb3.ejb` folder of your project.

Next, we demonstrate how to modify the `persistence.xml` file to use the Jboss Hibernate JPA implementation in the next section.

Listing 10.8 Generic interface CustomerManager.java

```
package com.perfmath.ejb3.ejb;

import java.math.BigDecimal;
import java.util.List;

import com.perfmath.ejb3.jpa.Customer;
import com.perfmath.ejb3.jpa.BankingTx;

public interface CustomerManager {

    public void createCustomer(String name, String password, String email, boolean locked);
    public List<Customer> findAllCustomers();
    public Customer findCustomerByName(String name);
    public Customer findCustomerById(int id);

    public void saveTxs(int customerId, BigDecimal amount,
            String description, String type);
    public List<BankingTx> findAllTxs(int customerId);
}
```

Listing 10.9 (a) Local interface CustomerManagerLocal.java

```
package com.perfmath.ejb3.ejb;

import javax.ejb.Local;

@Local
public interface CustomerManagerLocal extends  CustomerManager  {

}
```

Listing 10.9 (b) Remote interface CustomerManagerRemote.java

```
package com.perfmath.ejb3.ejb;

import javax.ejb.Remote;

@Remote
```

```
public interface CustomerManagerRemote extends  CustomerManager  {

}
```

Listing 10.10 Bean implementation class CustomerManagerBean.java

```
package com.perfmath.ejb3.ejb;

import java.math.BigDecimal;
import java.util.List;

import javax.ejb.Stateless;
import javax.persistence.*;

import org.jboss.ejb3.annotation.LocalBinding;
import org.jboss.ejb3.annotation.RemoteBinding;

import com.perfmath.ejb3.jpa.*;

@Stateless

@RemoteBinding(jndiBinding="CustomerEJB3.0/remote")
@LocalBinding(jndiBinding="CustomerEJB3.0/local")

public  class CustomerManagerBean implements CustomerManagerLocal,
                          CustomerManagerRemote {
    @PersistenceContext(unitName="CustomerEJB3")
    private EntityManager em;

    public void createCustomer(String name, String password, String email, boolean locked) {
        Customer customer = new Customer();
        customer.setName(name);
        customer.setPassword(password);
        customer.setEmail(email);
        customer.setLocked(locked);
        em.persist(customer);
    }
    public void saveTxs(int customerId, BigDecimal amount,
            String description, String type) {
        Customer customer = findCustomerById(customerId);

        BankingTx bankingTx = new BankingTx();
        bankingTx.setCustomer(customer);
```

```
        bankingTx.setAmount(amount);
        bankingTx.setDescription(description);
        bankingTx.setType(type);
        em.persist(bankingTx);
    }

    public List<BankingTx> findAllTxs(int customerId)
    {
        Query query = em.createQuery("FROM Customer where id=:id");
        query.setParameter("id", customerId);
        Customer customer = (Customer)query.getSingleResult();

        List <BankingTx>bankingTxs = customer.getBankingTxs();

        return bankingTxs;
    }
    public Customer findCustomerByName(String customerName)
    {
        Query query = em.createQuery("FROM Customer where name=:name");
        query.setParameter("name", customerName);
        Customer customer = (Customer)query.getSingleResult();

        return customer;
    }

    public Customer findCustomerById(int id)
    {
        Query query = em.createQuery("FROM Customer where id=:id");
        query.setParameter("id", id);
        Customer customer = (Customer)query.getSingleResult();

        return customer;
    }
    public List<Customer> findAllCustomers() {
        Query query = em.createQuery("FROM Customer");
        List<Customer> customerList = query.getResultList();

        return customerList;
    }
}
```

10.1.4 Modifying persistence.xml to Use the Hibernate JPA Implementation

The `persistence.xml` file shown in Listing 10.5 is generic and lacks required additional information to be usable for us to deploy and run this EJB 3 sample on a vendor-specific EJB 3 container. We pick *Jboss-6.1.0.Final* to run this EJB 3 sample as was used for running those EJB 2 examples discussed in my article "*A Retrospective View on EJB 2.*" Therefore, we need to modify the `persistence.xml` file shown in Listing 10.5 by replacing it with the `persistence.xml` file from the *spring-intergration.zip* file downloadable from this book's website. See Listing 10.11 for this modified `persistence.xml` file. By comparing the two `persistence.xml` files, notice that we have added the following information:

- **transaction-type**: "`JTA`" as specified.
- **provider**: "`org.hibernate.ejb.HibernatePersistence`" as specified.
- **jta-data-source**: "`java:/DefaultDS`" as specified in the `mysql-ds.xml` file of the Jboss-6.1.0.Final's *default* server configuration as explained in my article "*A Retrospective View on EJB 2.*"
- **hibernate**.dialect: `="org.hibernate.dialect.MySQLDialect"` as specified.

Next, we create a Jboss specific test client driver for testing this EJB 3 sample in the next section.

Listing 10.11 Jboss specific persistence.xml file

```
<?xml version="1.0" encoding="UTF-8"?>
<persistence version="2.0" xmlns=http://java.sun.com/xml/ns/persistence
xmlns:xsi="http://www.w3.org/2001/XMLSchema-instance"
xsi:schemaLocation="http://java.sun.com/xml/ns/persistence
http://java.sun.com/xml/ns/persistence/persistence_2_0.xsd">
    <persistence-unit name="CustomerEJB3" transaction-type="JTA">
    <provider>org.hibernate.ejb.HibernatePersistence</provider>
    <jta-data-source>java:/DefaultDS</jta-data-source>
    <class>com.perfmath.ejb3.jpa.BankingTx</class>
    <class>com.perfmath.ejb3.jpa.Customer</class>
    <properties>
        <property name="hibernate.dialect" value="org.hibernate.dialect.MySQLDialect"/>
    </properties>
    </persistence-unit>
</persistence>
```

10.1.5 Creating a JBoss Specific EJB 3 Test Client

In order to test this EJB 3 sample standalone, we need a test client driver. Listing 10.12 shows such a driver. Since this test client program is similar to the EJB 2 test drivers discussed in my article "*A Retrospective View on EJB 2,*" we would not explain further about how it works. Instead, in the next section, we explain how to deploy this EJB 3 sample and run it in the same Jboss environment as defined by the same Jboss-6.1.0.Final release we used with the EJB 2 samples discussed in my article "*A Retrospective View on EJB 2.*"

Listing 10.12 A Jboss specific EJB 3 test client driver

```
package com.perfmath.ejb3.client;

import java.math.BigDecimal;
import java.util.*;
import javax.naming.*;
import com.perfmath.ejb3.ejb.*;
import com.perfmath.ejb3.jpa.*;
import com.perfmath.ejb3.util.RandomID;

public class TestCustomerEJB3 {

    public static void main(String[] args) throws Exception {

        InitialContext ctx = null;
        try {
            ctx = getInitialContext();
        } catch (Exception ex) {
            System.out.println("Error in establishing initial context: "
                    + ex.getMessage());
        }

CustomerManager customerManager =
(CustomerManager)ctx.lookup("CustomerManagerEJB3/remote");

        String customerName = "customer" + (new RandomID()).getId();
        System.out.println ("creating " + customerName);
        customerManager.createCustomer(customerName, "password",
            "customer0@abc.com", false);

        System.out.println ("finding " + customerName);
        Customer customer = customerManager.findCustomerByName(customerName);

        String customerId = customer.getId ();
        System.out.println ("saving txs for customer with customer ID: " + customerId);
        customerManager.saveTxs(customerId, new BigDecimal(1000.0*Math.random()),
            "EJB 3 test", "test");

        System.out.println ("find all txs for " + customerName);
        List<BankingTx> txs = customerManager.findAllTxs(customerId);

        System.out.println("Listing txs for "+customer.getName());
        Iterator <BankingTx> iter = txs.iterator();
        while (iter.hasNext()) {
```

```
            BankingTx tx = iter.next();
            System.out.println("----------------");
            System.out.println("tx id: " + tx.getId());
            System.out.println("description: " +tx.getDescription());
            System.out.println("Type: " +tx.getType());
            System.out.println("amount: " +tx.getAmount());
        }
    }
    protected static InitialContext getInitialContext() throws NamingException {
        Hashtable<String, String> env = new Hashtable<String, String>();
        env.put("java.naming.factory.initial",
                "org.jboss.security.jndi.JndiLoginInitialContextFactory");
        env.put("java.naming.provider.url", "localhost:1099");
        env.put(Context.SECURITY_PRINCIPAL, "admin");
        env.put(Context.SECURITY_CREDENTIALS, "admin");
        return new InitialContext(env);
    }
}
```

10.1.6 Running the EJB 3 Sample on Jboss

To run this EJB 3 sample on JBoss, perform the following tasks to prepare your environment first:

- Make sure the same Jboss-6.1.0.Final environment you used with the EJB 2 samples as discussed in my article "*A Retrospective View on EJB 2*" is still available on your machine. If not, install and configure it per instructions given in that article.
- Copy the `setJboss.bat` and `build.xml` files from the downloaded Customer_EJB3 project folder mentioned previously into your project. Make sure the JBOSS_HOME and JBOSS_SERVER_CONFIG environment variables are set properly on your system.
- Create a *dist* folder in your project (if it does not exist) to hold the distribution jar file. Your Customer_EJB3 project should now look similar to Figure 10.15.

Note: Before proceeding further, make sure you have deleted the EJB 2 sample jar files left in the *$JBOSS_INSTALL\server\default\deploy* folder if any. In addition, replace "`ejb`" with "`ejb3db`" in the `<connection-url>` element in the `mysql-ds.xml` file located in the same folder of *$JBOSS_INSTALL\server\default\deploy.*

Then, perform the following tasks to run this EJB 3 sample:

- Start up a command prompt and make sure all environment variables, including JAVA_HOME, JBOSS_HOME and JBOSS_SERVER_CONFIG, are set properly on your system (you can use the `setJboss.bat` script included in the EJB 3 sample project download to set your Jboss environment variables, with my JBOSS_HOME replaced with yours in this script).

- Change to your *$JBOSS_INSTALL\bin* directory and issue the following command to start up your Jboss server:

  cmd>run.bat –b 0.0.0.0

- Open up a command prompt, change to your Customer_EJB3 project directory, execute the "`setJboss.bat`" script, and issue the following command to deploy this EJB 3 sample into your Jboss environment (of course, you should also have configured ANT per instructions given in my article "*A Retrospective View on EJB 2*" posted on my website):

  cmd>ant deploy

- Open up another command prompt, change to your *Customer_EJB3* project directory, execute the "`setJboss.bat`" script, and issue the following command to run the test client for this EJB 3 sample:

  cmd>ant run-testCustomerEJB3

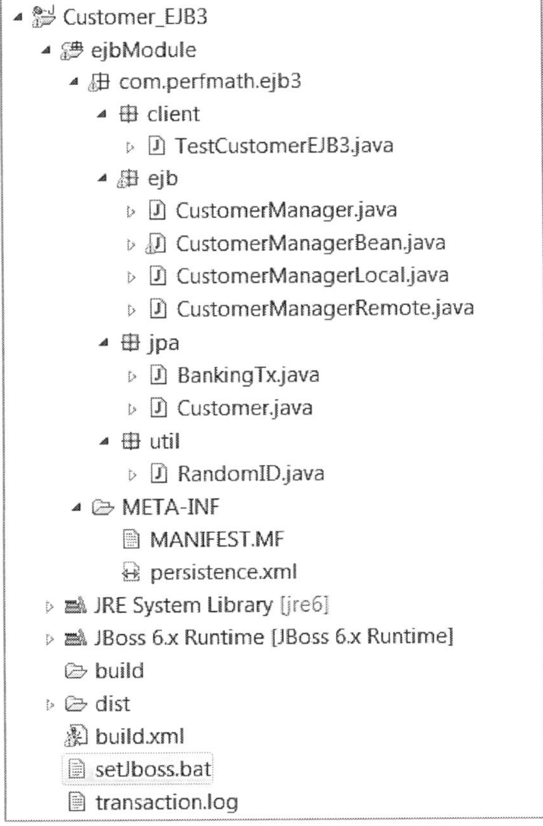

Figure 10.15 Final EJB 3 sample project structure

If everything goes well, you should see an example console output similar to the following:

```
run-testCustomerEJB3:
    [java] creating customer501521085
    [java] finding customer501521085
    [java] saving txs for for customer with customer ID: 2
    [java] find all txs for customer501521085
    [java] Listing txs for customer501521085
    [java] ----------------
    [java] tx id: 1
    [java] description: EJB 3 test
    [java] Type: test
    [java] amount: 807.15
```

This wraps up our endeavor of creating an EJB 3 sample and we move to demonstrating how to integrate Spring with EJB 3 in the next section.

10.2 ACCESSING EJB 3 COMPONENTS FROM SPRING

Thanks to the concepts of *dependency injection* and *IoC container*, accessing EJB components from Spring has been made really simple. The mechanism is as simple as the following three-step procedure:

1. In your Spring bean as the caller of your EJB component, perform the following three tasks:
    - Create an EJB business interface instance variable in your Spring bean to set up a reference for your Spring bean to use the EJB component you intend to use.
    - Create a corresponding setter method so that the EJB reference can be injected into your Spring bean as if it were a regular dependency.
    - Create a wrapper method that calls the business method(s) of the EJB component.
2. In your Spring bean configuration file, configure the EJB component as a Spring bean using Spring-specific rules. In the same bean configuration file, set the property of the EJB business interface variable as a "*ref*" property for your consuming Spring bean.
3. In your Spring application, create an *ApplicationContext* object for your Spring bean and use it by calling its wrapper method(s) with the EJB component working behind the scences.

In the remainder of this section, we do exactly what we described above to demonstrate how Spring-EJB integration works. The application context might differ from yours, but the procedure should be equally applicable. Let's start with creating a Spring-integration package in the existing SOBA project next.

10.2.1 Creating a Spring-EJB integration package

For convenience, we use the existing Ant-based SOBA project to demonstrate how Spring-EJB integration works. You can simply follow the steps given below and in the next few sections to complete this exercise.

Assuming that you have a working, Ant-based SOBA project, perform the following tasks:

- Add a package of "*com.perfmath.spring.soba.integration.ejb*" in your existing Ant-based SOBA project.
- Copy the *jbossall-client.jar* file from your $JBOSS_INSTALL/client folder and the *CustomerEJB3.0.jar* file from your *Customer_EJB3* project's *dist* folder to a folder of your choice. Add these two jar files to the *classpath* for your Ant-based SOBA project. This step helps make sure that our Spring bean will have access to the EJB business interface to be integrated with and all client utilities needed for performing EJB context lookups.

Note: This EJB 3 sample is Jboss specific and the above jars must be added as described above in order to verify that this sample works in your environment. If you choose a different EJB container vendor, such as GlassFish or WebLogic, you'll have to figure out how to make proper adjustments. Note that although the EJB is a common spec, the performance and scalability that the underlying EJB container exhibits may vary from vendor to vendor, or even from release to release with the same vendor. Before committing to a specific EJB container vendor, do your homework to help make sure that you don't end up with putting up your enterprise application on a vendor's EJB container that is so resource demanding that even fastest hardware can hardly meet the moderate performance and scalability requirements of your customers.

In the next section, we create the Spring bean in the integration package as created above.

10.2.2 Creating the Spring Bean that Consumes the EJB Component

We now need to decide how we are going to demonstrate Spring-EJB integration. First, by examining the Customer_EJB3 project we created earlier in this chapter, we know that we have a business interface defined in the `CustomerManager.java` class as shown in Listing 10.8. This interface defines six business methods, which are implemented by the corresponding bean implementation class named `CustomerManagerBean.java` as shown in Listing 10.10. Let's say that we'd like to access some of the methods defined in this interface in a Spring bean. For illustrative purposes, we do not need more than one method; therefore, let's just pick the `createCustomer` (...) method. Then, according to the three-step procedure given earlier in this section, we can define a Spring bean interface and its corresponding implementation class as shown in Listings 10.13 (a) and (b). Note the following in the Spring EJB-integration bean implementation class of `CustomerServiceImpl.java`:

1 The EJB business interface instance variable `customerManager`
2 The setter method of `setCustomerManager` (...) for this instance variable
3 The Spring bean wrapper method of `createCustomer` (...) that calls the `createCustomer` business method of the `CustomerManager` stateless session bean

In the next section, we describe how to create the Spring-EJB integration bean configuration file to define the EJB component bean and Spring bean so that both can be loaded up during starting up the Spring application.

Listing 10.13 (a) Spring EJB-integration bean interface CustomerService.java

```
package com.perfmath.spring.soba.integration.ejb;

public interface CustomerService {
    public void createCustomer(String name, String password, String email, boolean locked);
}
```

Listing 10.13 (b) Spring EJB-integration bean implementation class CustomerServiceImpl.java

```
package com.perfmath.spring.soba.integration.ejb;

import com.perfmath.ejb3.ejb.*;

public class CustomerServiceImpl implements CustomerService {
    private CustomerManager customerManager;

    public void setCustomerManager(CustomerManager customerManager) {
        this.customerManager = customerManager;
    }

    public void createCustomer(String name, String password, String email,
            boolean locked) {
        customerManager.createCustomer(name, password, email, locked);
    }

}
```

10.2.3 Creating Spring-EJB Integration Bean Configuration Files

Next, we need to create a Spring bean configuration file to define a *customerManager* bean out of the EJB component as the dependency of the *customerService* Spring bean, which also has to be defined in the same bean configuration file. In fact, there are three options for defining the EJB business interface bean, resulting in three different bean configuration files as shown in Listings 10.14 (a), (b) and (c), respectively. Each of these options are explained as follows:

- **Spring's JndiObjectFactoryBean**: Spring offers this factory bean to declare a JNDI object reference in its IoC container as shown in Listing 10.14 (a). This approach is simpler than the other two we will introduce next that it does not need to specify the EJB business interface. Note the `jndiEnvironment` property and the `jndiName` property, which are similar to the `getInitialContext` ( ) method and the context lookup statement as we saw in the EJB 3 sample test client shown in Listing 10.12, respectively.
- **Spring's SimpleRemoteStatelessSessionProxyFactoryBean**: Spring offers this factory bean to create a local proxy for a remote stateless session bean as shown in Listing 10.14 (b) (the equivalent factory bean for accessing a local stateless session bean would be `LocalStatelessSessionProxyFactoryBean`). With this option, it's necessary to specify a business

interface property, which takes the fully qualified EJB 3 interface name for its value. The other parts remain the same as with the previous `JndiObjectFactoryBean` option.

- **Spring's <jee:remote-slsb> element**: Spring offers this *jee* schema as an alternative to defining EJB business interface bean using either the `JndiObjectFactoryBean` or the `StatelessSessionProxyFactoryBean`. As is shown in Listing 10.14 (c), this option also requires defining an EJB business interface property as is the case with the `StatelessSessionProxyFactoryBean` option.

As is seen, all these three options only differ in *format*. I would recommend using the `JndiObjectFactoryBean`, since it does not require defining an EJB business interface and it mimics how an EJB component is accessed by a regular EJB client to some extent.

Next, we describe how to create a Spring-EJB integration test driver to test this Spring-EJB integration sample.

Listing 10.14 (a) Defining an EJB business bean using Spring's JndiObjectFactoryBean (beans-customer_0.xml)

```
<?xml version="1.0" encoding="UTF-8"?>
<beans xmlns="http://www.springframework.org/schema/beans"
    xmlns:xsi="http://www.w3.org/2001/XMLSchema-instance"
    xsi:schemaLocation="http://www.springframework.org/schema/beans
       http://www.springframework.org/schema/beans/spring-beans.xsd">
         <bean id="customerManager"
             class="org.springframework.jndi.JndiObjectFactoryBean">
        <property name="jndiEnvironment">
        <props>
        <prop key="java.naming.factory.initial">org.jboss.security.jndi.
            JndiLoginInitialContextFactory</prop>
        <prop key="java.naming.provider.url">localhost:1099</prop>
        <prop key="java.naming.security.principal">admin</prop>
        <prop key="java.naming.security.credentials">admin</prop>
        </props>
        </property>
        <property name="jndiName" value="CustomerManagerEJB3/remote" />
    </bean>
    <bean id="customerService"
            class="com.perfmath.spring.soba.integration.ejb.CustomerServiceImpl">
        <property name="customerManager" ref="customerManager" />
    </bean>
    </beans>
```

Listing 10.14 (b) Defining an EJB business bean using Spring's SimpleRemoteStatelessSessionProxyFactoryBean (beans-customer_1.xml)

```
<?xml version="1.0" encoding="UTF-8"?>
<beans xmlns="http://www.springframework.org/schema/beans"
    xmlns:xsi="http://www.w3.org/2001/XMLSchema-instance"
    xsi:schemaLocation="http://www.springframework.org/schema/beans
      http://www.springframework.org/schema/beans/spring-beans.xsd">
    <bean id="customerManager"
        class="org.springframework.ejb.access.
            SimpleRemoteStatelessSessionProxyFactoryBean">
        <property name="jndiEnvironment">
        <props>
        <prop key="java.naming.factory.initial">org.jboss.security.jndi.
            JndiLoginInitialContextFactory</prop>
        <prop key="java.naming.provider.url">localhost:1099</prop>
        <prop key="java.naming.security.principal">admin</prop>
        <prop key="java.naming.security.credentials">admin</prop>
        </props>
        </property>
        <property name="jndiName" value="CustomerManagerEJB3/remote" />
        <property name="businessInterface"
            value="com.perfmath.ejb3.ejb.CustomerManager" />
    </bean>
    <bean id="customerService"
        class="com.perfmath.spring.soba.integration.ejb.CustomerServiceImpl">
        <property name="customerManager" ref="customerManager" />
    </bean>
    </beans>
```

Listing 10.14 (c) Defining an EJB business bean using Spring's <jee:remote-slsb> element (beans-customer_2.xml)

```
<?xml version="1.0" encoding="UTF-8"?>
<beans xmlns="http://www.springframework.org/schema/beans"
    xmlns:xsi="http://www.w3.org/2001/XMLSchema-instance"
    xmlns:jee="http://www.springframework.org/schema/jee"
    xsi:schemaLocation="http://www.springframework.org/schema/beans
      http://www.springframework.org/schema/beans/spring-beans.xsd
      http://www.springframework.org/schema/jee
      http://www.springframework.org/schema/jee/spring-jee.xsd">
      <jee:remote-slsb id="customerManager"
          jndi-name="CustomerManagerEJB3/remote"
          business-interface="com.perfmath.ejb3.ejb.CustomerManager">
          <jee:environment>
              java.naming.factory.initial=org.jboss.security.jndi.
```

```
                JndiLoginInitialContextFactory
              java.naming.provider.url=localhost:1099
              java.naming.security.principal=admin
              java.naming.security.credentials=admin
           </jee:environment>
        </jee:remote-slsb>

    <bean id="customerService"
        class="com.perfmath.spring.soba.integration.ejb.CustomerServiceImpl">
        <property name="customerManager" ref="customerManager" />
    </bean>
</beans>
```

10.2.4 Creating a Spring-EJB Integration Test Driver

In this section, we demonstrate how to create a Spring-EJB integration test driver to test the *CustomerService* bean as shown in Listing 10.13. Such a test driver is shown in Listing 10.15. This program works as follows:

- First, it creates an *ApplicationContext* using one of the bean configuration files as discussed in the previous section (since we are using the `FileSystemXmlApplicationContext` instead of the `ClassPathXmlApplicationContext`, we must place the bean configuration file in the project's top directory).
- It then uses the usual `context.getBean` (…) method to retrieve the `customerService` bean instance.
- Finally, it calls the `createCustomer` (…) method to create a customer by invoking the same `createCustomer` (…) method of the underlying EJB 3 component.

As is seen, it's really not complicated to access an EJB component within a Spring bean, thanks to the simplicity of the Spring framework in general. Next, we describe how to run this test driver, given all we have presented so far.

Listing 10.15 A Spring-EJB integration test driver (CustomerServiceMain.java)

```
package com.perfmath.spring.soba.integration.ejb;
import org.springframework.context.ApplicationContext;
import org.springframework.context.support.ClassPathXmlApplicationContext;

import com.perfmath.spring.soba.util.RandomID;
public class CustomerServiceMain {
    public static void main (String[] args) {
        ApplicationContext context = new
                ClasspathXmlApplicationContext ("beans-customer_0.xml");
```

```
        CustomerService customerService =
                context.getBean("customerService", CustomerService.class);
        String customerName = "customer" + (new RandomID(9)).getId();
        System.out.println ("creating " + customerName);
        customerService.createCustomer(customerName, "password", "customer0@abc.com",
    false);
    }
}
```

10.2.5 Running the Spring-EJB Test Driver

To run the Spring-EJB integration test driver as shown in Listing 10.15 in the previous section, first, start up your Jboss and make sure that the EJB 3 sample itself works standalone per instructions given in §10.1. Then, simply right-click on the `CustomerServiceMain.java` class in the Ant-based SOBA project and select *Run As → 2 Java Application* (if you want, you can test other bean configuration files by substituting the *beans-customer_0.xml* file in the test driver with *beans-customer_1.xml* or *beans-customer_2.xml*). If everything works in your environment, you should see a console output similar to Figure 10.16. You can also check the customer created from your MySQL database.

```
Problems  Javadoc  Declaration  Console
<terminated> CustomerServiceMain [Java Application] C:\Program Files\Java\jre6\bin\javaw.exe (Jan 8, 2013 9:48:51 PM)
log4j:WARN No appenders could be found for logger (org.springframework.core.env.StandardEnvironment).
log4j:WARN Please initialize the log4j system properly.
creating customer739399525
```

Figure 10.16 Console output from running the Spring-EJB integration sample

10.3 ACCESSING EJB 2.X COMPONENTS

According to the Spring Reference Documentation, accessing EJB 2 session beans and EJB 3 session beans is largely transparent. This is because the Spring-EJB integration framework handles a home interface if found (EJB 2 style), or perform straight component invocations if no home interface is found (EJB 3 style). This transparency applies no matter how an EJB lookup is performed with one of the three options discussed previously.

At this point, we could have proved the above transparency statement by providing an example using one of the EJB 2 samples (BMP-based or CMP-based) presented in my article "*A Retrospective View on EJB 2.*" However, most of the readers may not be interested in going further along this line, so we leave it as an exercise for those who may want to pursue it on their own.

10.4 SPRING'S EJB IMPLEMENTATION SUPPORT CLASSES

To be complete, we have to mention that Spring provides convenience classes to help you implement EJB3. Their thinking is that we can put our business logic behind EJBs in POJOs while leave EJBs responsible for transaction demarcation and (optionally) remoting.

To implement a Stateless or Stateful session bean, or a Message Driven bean, we need only derive our implementation class from one of the following Spring classes:

- *AbstractStatelessSessionBean* for SLSBs
- *AbstractStatefulSessionBean* for SFSBs
- *AbstractMessageDrivenBean* for MDBs
- *AbstractJmsMessageDrivenBean* for JMDBs

However, this looks more like a cross-breeding approach between Spring and EJB, and you might be better off by choosing either Spring or EJB for your new project without getting into that kind of awkward situation of programming in both Spring and EJB. The Spring Reference Documentation explains further how it can be done programmatically, and you should consult it for more information if you indeed have such a need.

10.5 SUMMARY

In this chapter, we focused on demonstrating how Spring-EJB integration works. We first created a MySQL database with two tables of CUSTOMER and BANKINGTX, setting the stage for creating JPA entities for domain objects for our EJB 3 sample. We then demonstrated how to create JPA entities with Eclipse/Dali facilities, based on the two tables described above. This part shows a generally applicable approach to creating JPA entities based on a well-defined database schema.

Following creating the JPA entities, we demonstrated how to create an EJB 3 stateless session bean based on a non-EJB-specific business interface named *CustomerManager*. We created both a local and a remote EJB 3 interface as well as an EJB 3 stateless session bean implementation class. We went a few extra miles to demonstrate how to configure and run this EJB 3 sample on Jboss to help ensure that the sample actually works.

The second part of this chapter focused on presenting the specific steps for carrying out a Spring-EJB integration project. A three-step procedure was given with a full proof of concept using the EJB 3 sample created in the first part of this chapter. Overall, the Spring-EJB integration framework works by introducing a Spring bean based on the business interface of the underlying EJB 3 component, and then adding it as a property to the Spring integration bean that wraps the methods of the EJB 3 component with its own methods. We introduced the three options that Spring can look up an EJB component, which are:

- Using *JndiObjectFactoryBean*
- Using *[Local|SimpleRemote]StatelessSessionProxyFactoryBean*
- Using *<jee:remote-slsb>* or *<jee:local-slsb>*

Corresponding to the above three options, three specific bean configuration XML files were provided, showing exactly how each option works. We also created a Spring-EJB integration test driver, which was run on Jboss to demonstrate that the entire Spring-EJB integration suite presented in this chapter works.

This wraps up our coverage on the Spring-EJB integration framework.

10.6 RECOMMENDED READING

If you are interested in learning more about EJB 3, there are many similar texts available. You can also search the Internet for online free tutorials, especially from one of your preferred EJB container vendors.

For more information about Spring-EJB integration, refer to the Spring Reference Documentation: *Chapter 22 Enterprise JavaBeans (EJB) integration.*

10.7 EXERCISES

10.1 What are the differences among those three JPA associations fetch options as shown in Figure 10.12? Use specific examples to explain the pros and cons of each option.

10.2 Prove the Spring-EJB integration transparency statement as discussed in §10.3 by replacing the EJB 3 sample with one of the EJB 2 samples discussed in my article "*A Retrospective View on EJB 2*" available for downloading from this book's website.

11 Spring Web Flow Framework

You might wonder why there is a need for the Spring Web Flow Framework, given the fact that the Spring MVC Framework can be used to build Spring-based web applications. In this chapter, we will not only explain why there is such a need but also how to some parts of a Spring-based web application with the Spring Web Flow Framework. I'd like to point out that most online tutorials and Spring books present the Spring MVC Framework and the Spring Web Flow Framework standalone without illustrating how one can build a Spring-based web application using both frameworks, which is convenient but less practical, as a real Spring-based web application most likely need to use both frameworks. As you will see, this book distinguishes itself from others by using an integrated approach to demonstrating the Spring Web Flow Framework with the same SOBA sample already built with the Spring MVC Framework. With this unique approach, you will see the issues that occur only when both frameworks are used together and learn how to resolve them.

11.1 WHY THE SPRING WEB FLOW FRAMEWORK?

Assuming that you have learnt what the Spring MVC Framework is about, you already know how to implement a given use case - you have to have a page flow blueprint in your mind first before you start. Then, you code page flows through multiple views in JSP scripts (or other view technologies) together with various Java components configured as Spring beans, according to the flow blueprint in your mind. It's okay to take such a simple approach to building a simple Spring-based web application, but it could quickly become unmanageable with a large scale web application. For example, if a developer has to re-visit how a user case is coded, he will have to trace the page flows by examining all relevant JSPs and Java components, and if another developer needs to trace the implementation of the same use case, he will have to repeat the same manual process. This apparently is a waste of valuable resources and is also error-prone. Therefore, a medium to large-scale web application should be built with a web flow framework one way or the other.

The other disadvantage with the Spring MVC Framework is that it does not manage *state* across requests in order to complete a use case that can be considered as a transaction. For example, with the SOBA sample, a use case of signing up a new customer is that you first create a customer, then an account, and then a login identity for the user. Suppose the program execution fails mid-way, then a customer might be left with no account and/or no login ID. With the Spring Web Flow Framework, however, one can easily lump those three subsequent steps into a transactional flow so that it will succeed either *none* or *all*. In other words, following a standard to manage the states of a web application is one of the major driven-factors for having a formalized web flow framework such as the Spring Web Flow Framework.

Another disadvantage of not using a web flow framework such as the Spring Web Flow Framework is that there would be too much boilerplate code to write, which would result in poor *re-usability*. This is against one of the general software engineering principles and should be avoided as much as possible. Besides, with a well-designed web flow framework, one can have sub-flows under a given parent flow, which offers finer-granularity for building complex web applications. All in all, using the Spring Web Flow Framework should be mandate rather than optional for building complex Spring-based web applications.

In the next few sections of this chapter, we illustrate how to develop a Spring-based web application using the Spring WEB Flow Framework in conjunction with the Spring MVC Framework. Specifically, we will use the SOBA sample to demonstrate the following Spring Web Flow features:

- Integrating Spring Web Flow Framework with Spring MVC Framework
- Setting up Spring Web Flows
- Defining Spring Web Flows
- Using Expression Language (EL)
- Rendering Views
- Executing Actions
- Flow Managed Persistence
- Securing Flows

Since we already have a functioning SOBA sample, let's start with how to plug the Spring Web Flow Framework into the Spring MVC framework in SOBA's context. This may make practical sense, as you may want to use both frameworks to build your Spring-based web application based on your specific needs for each framework.

11.2 INTEGRATING SPRING WEB FLOW FRAMEWORK WITH SPRING MVC FRAMEWORK

There are two issues to deal with when integrating the Spring Web Flow Framework with the Spring MVC Framework: one is how to configure servlet mappings and the other is how to configure handler mappings and handler adapters. The complexities arise only when you attempt to integrate both frameworks, as is discussed next.

11.2.1 Configuring Servlet Mappings

Spring web flows are similar to web requests that they must be processed by the Spring dispatcher servlet defined by the `org.springframework.web.servlet.DispatcherServlet` class. If you have read other Spring web flow texts or articles, you might notice that they may suggest mapping a url pattern like "/`flow`/*" to the above servlet. You may also recall that we defined two servlet mappings with SOBA, that is, mapping both a specific url pattern of "*.htm" and the root url pattern of "/" to the above servlet. The question is if we need to separate Spring web flow requests to a separate url pattern like "/flow/*" with the SOBA project. It turns out that it's unnecessary to do so, as the root url pattern of "/" applies to the "/flow/*" url pattern automatically. However, it's beneficial from the maintenance point of view that Spring web flow specific configurations should be specified in their own configuration files such as `flow-service.xml` and `flow-servlet.xml`. See Listing 11.1 for a complete listing of the `web.xml` file that is applicable to both the Spring regular web requests and Spring web flow requests. We will cover web flow specific configurations later.

Listing 11.1 web.xml file

```
<?xml version="1.0" encoding="UTF-8"?>
<web-app version="2.4" xmlns="http://java.sun.com/xml/ns/j2ee"
   xmlns:xsi="http://www.w3.org/2001/XMLSchema-instance"
   xsi:schemaLocation="http://java.sun.com/xml/ns/j2ee
    http://java.sun.com/xml/ns/j2ee/web-app_2_4.xsd">
   <!-- Log4j configuration loading -->
   <listener>      <listener-class>org.springframework.web.util.Log4jConfigListener</listener-class>
   </listener>
   <context-param>
       <param-name>log4jConfigLocation</param-name>
       <param-value>/WEB-INF/classes/log4j.xml</param-value>
   </context-param>
   <!-- Bootstrapping context loading -->
   <listener>
       <listener-class>org.springframework.web.context.ContextLoaderListener</listener-class>
   </listener>
   <context-param>
       <param-name>contextConfigLocation</param-name>
       <param-value>
          /WEB-INF/soba-servlet.xml
      /WEB-INF/soba-services.xml
      /WEB-INF/soba-security.xml
      <!--  webflow  -->
      /WEB-INF/flow-service.xml
      /WEB-INF/flow-servlet.xml
      </param-value>
   </context-param>
   <context-param>
       <param-name>webAppRootKey</param-name> <param-value>soba.root</param-value>
   </context-param>

   <!-- session management listener -->
```

```
    <listener>
        <listener-class>org.springframework.security.web.session.HttpSessionEventPublisher
    </listener-class>
    </listener>
    <session-config>
        <!-- session times out if no activities for 30 minutes -->
        <session-timeout>30</session-timeout>
    </session-config>
    <!-- Security entry point -->
    <filter>
        <filter-name>springSecurityFilterChain</filter-name>
        <filter-class>org.springframework.web.filter.DelegatingFilterProxy</filter-class>
    </filter>

    <filter-mapping>
        <filter-name>springSecurityFilterChain</filter-name> <url-pattern>/*</url-pattern>
    </filter-mapping>

    <!-- defining the DispatcherServlet -->
    <servlet>
        <servlet-name>soba</servlet-name>
        <servlet-class>org.springframework.web.servlet.DispatcherServlet</servlet-class>
        <load-on-startup>1</load-on-startup>
    </servlet>

    <servlet-mapping> <servlet-name>soba</servlet-name> <url-pattern>/</url-pattern>
    </servlet-mapping>
    <servlet-mapping> <servlet-name>soba</servlet-name> <url-pattern>*.htm</url-pattern>
    </servlet-mapping>

<!-- defining the DefaultServlet -->
<servlet>
     <servlet-name>DefaultServlet</servlet-name>
     <servlet-class>org.apache.catalina.servlets.DefaultServlet</servlet-class>
   </servlet>
    <servlet-mapping>
        <servlet-name>DefaultServlet</servlet-name>
        <url-pattern>*.jpg</url-pattern>
    </servlet-mapping>
    <servlet-mapping>
        <servlet-name>DefaultServlet</servlet-name>
        <url-pattern>*.html</url-pattern>
    </servlet-mapping>
```

```
    <error-page> <error-code>404</error-code> <location>/WEB-INF/jsp/notfound.jsp</location>
    </error-page>
    <welcome-file-list>
        <welcome-file> login.jsp
    </welcome-file-list>
    <!-- Spring jsp tag lib -->
    <jsp-config>
        <taglib>
            <taglib-uri>/spring</taglib-uri>
            <taglib-location>/WEB-INF/tld/spring-form.tld</taglib-location>
        </taglib>
    </jsp-config>
</web-app>
```

11.2.2 Configuring HandlerMappings and HandlerAdapters

In order to have Spring web flow requests handled properly, an flow handler mapping of `org.springframework.webflow.mvc.servlet.FlowHandlerMapping` must be defined. One might think that just adding this handler mapping in the servlet configuration XML file would work fine. However, the way the Spring MVC Framework works is that it uses the default handler mappings of `org.springframework.web.servlet.mvc.annotation.DefaultAnnotationHandlerMapping` and `org.springframework.web.servlet.handler.BeanNameUrlHandlerMapping` to handle the annotated controllers and un-annotated or configured controllers, respectively. These default handler mappings would be created by default without having to be specified in the servlet configuration XML file if no other handler mappings were specified explicitly. Since the flow handler would not be created by default if it were not specified in the servlet configuration file explicitly, we have to declare it explicitly if we want to integrate the Spring Web Flow Framework with the Spring MVC Framework. Therefore, in order to work around this handler mapping issue caused by the requirement that both the regular Spring web requests and the Spring web flow requests must be handled in the same context, we have to declare the `DefaultAnnotationHandlerMapping` and `BeanNameUrlHandlerMapping` explicitly in the servlet configuration file. Otherwise, the Spring execution engine would attempt to handle regular Spring web requests as Spring web flow requests, which would result in failures and exceptions.

However, it is not the end of the story yet, as defining a handler mapping is just one side of an equation that there must be a corresponding handler adapter defined, which would carry out the actual executions for the web request or web flow request in question. For example, for the two default handler mappings for handling regular Spring web requests, the required handler adapters are `org.springframework.web.servlet.mvc.annotation.AnnotationMethodHandlerAdapter`, `org.springframework.web.servlet.mvc.method.annotation.RequestMappingHandlerAdapter`, and `org.springframework.web.servlet.mvc.SimpleControllerHandlerAdapter`. For a Spring web flow handler mapping defined with `org.springframework.webflow.mvc.servlet.FlowHandlerMapping`, the corresponding handler adapter is defined with `org.springframework.webflow.mvc.servlet.FlowHandlerAdapter`. Listing 11.2 and Listing 11.3 show how these handler mappings and handler adapters work together for regular Spring web requests and Spring web flow requests, respectively.

In Listings 11.2 and 11.3, you might notice the property of "`order`" specified for each handler mapping. This property specifies the precedence of the associated handler mapping, with lower number representing higher precedence. You might also notice the property of "`flowRegistry`" associated with the `flowHandlerMapping` and the property of "`flowExecutor`" associated with the `flowHnadlerAdapter` in Listing 11.3. We discuss these Spring Web Flow Framework infrastructural beans next.

Listing 11.2 A partial listing of the soba-servlet.xml file showing how handler mappings and handler adapters work together to handle regular Spring web requests

```
<beans xmlns="http://www.springframework.org/schema/beans"
    xmlns:xsi="http://www.w3.org/2001/XMLSchema-instance"
    xmlns:context="http://www.springframework.org/schema/context"
    xmlns:mvc="http://www.springframework.org/schema/mvc"
    xsi:schemaLocation="http://www.springframework.org/schema/beans
  http://www.springframework.org/schema/beans/spring-beans.xsd
  http://www.springframework.org/schema/context
  http://www.springframework.org/schema/context/spring-context.xsd
  http://www.springframework.org/schema/mvc
  http://www.springframework.org/schema/mvc/spring-mvc.xsd">

    <!-- the application context definition for the soba DispatcherServlet -->
    <context:component-scan base-package="com.perfmath.spring.soba.web" />
    <context:component-scan base-package="com.perfmath.spring.soba.model" />
    <context:component-scan base-package="com.perfmath.spring.soba.service" />
    <context:component-scan base-package="com.perfmath.spring.soba.restfulweb" />
    <context:annotation-config />

  <bean name="defaultHandler"
class="org.springframework.web.servlet.mvc.annotation.DefaultAnnotationHandlerMapping">
  <property name="order" value="0" />
  </bean>
    <bean name="beanNameUrlHandler"
class="org.springframework.web.servlet.handler.BeanNameUrlHandlerMapping">
  <property name="order" value="0" />
  </bean>
  <bean name="annotationMethodHandlerAdapter"
class="org.springframework.web.servlet.mvc.annotation.AnnotationMethodHandlerAdapter" />
  <bean
class="org.springframework.web.servlet.mvc.method.annotation.RequestMappingHandlerAdapter" />
```

```
    <bean name="simpleControllerHandlerAdapter"
class="org.springframework.web.servlet.mvc.SimpleControllerHandlerAdapter" />
......
</beans>
```

Listing 11.3 A partial listing of the soba-webflow.xml file showing how the flow handler mapping and the flow handler adapter work together to handle Spring web flow requests

```
<beans xmlns="http://www.springframework.org/schema/beans"
   xmlns:xsi="http://www.w3.org/2001/XMLSchema-instance"
   xmlns:webflow="http://www.springframework.org/schema/webflow-config"
   xsi:schemaLocation="http://www.springframework.org/schema/beans
      http://www.springframework.org/schema/beans/spring-beans.xsd
      http://www.springframework.org/schema/webflow-config
      http://www.springframework.org/schema/webflow-config/spring-webflow-config-2.4.xsd">

   <bean class="org.springframework.webflow.mvc.servlet.FlowHandlerMapping" >
   <property name="flowRegistry" ref="flowRegistry" />
   <property name ="order" value="1" />
   </bean>

   <bean name="flowHandlerAdapter"
class="org.springframework.webflow.mvc.servlet.FlowHandlerAdapter">
    <property name="flowExecutor" ref="flowExecutor" />
    </bean>
......
</beans>
```

11.3 SPRING WEB FLOW MECHANICS

At first glance, the Spring Web Flow Framework seems to be tedious and overwhelming. This is true but it's not unworkable. Once you understand the Spring web flow mechanics and follow a well-defined procedure, programming Spring web flows is no harder than programming other Spring components as we have gone through the SOBA project with various controllers, service beans, DAOs etc. This section focuses on helping you understand the Spring web flow mechanics, which constitutes the common base for programming all kinds of Spring web flows.

One part of the Spring web flow mechanics is defining the `flowHandlerMapping` and the corresponding `flowHandlerAdapter`, which you already learnt in the preceding section as shown in Listing 11.3. The next part of the Spring web flow mechanics is to define the dependencies for the `flowHandlerMapping` and the corresponding `flowHandlerAdapter`, such as the `flowRegistery` bean and the `flowExecutor` bean, as well as their dependency beans of such dependency beans. It's easier to explain all of this with the full listing of the `soba-webflow.xml` file as shown in Listing 11.4, which captures not only the `flowHandlerMapping` and the corresponding `flowHandlerAdapter` but also all remaining Spring web flow mechanics as we described above. Note that in Listing 11.4, we have shaded the first part, since it has been displayed in the previous section in order to explain the concrete `flowHandlerMapping` and the corresponding `flowHandlerAdapter` beans needed for configuring the Spring Web Flow Framework to work with the Spring MVC Framework. We explain the remaining part of the `soba-webflow.xml` file as illustrated in Listing 11.4 next.

Listing 11.4 soba-webflow.xml

```
<beans xmlns="http://www.springframework.org/schema/beans"
  xmlns:xsi="http://www.w3.org/2001/XMLSchema-instance"
  xmlns:webflow="http://www.springframework.org/schema/webflow-config"
  xsi:schemaLocation="http://www.springframework.org/schema/beans
    http://www.springframework.org/schema/beans/spring-beans.xsd
    http://www.springframework.org/schema/webflow-config
    http://www.springframework.org/schema/webflow-config/spring-webflow-config-2.4.xsd">

  <bean class="org.springframework.webflow.mvc.servlet.FlowHandlerMapping" >
  <property name="flowRegistry" ref="flowRegistry" />
  <property name ="order" value="1" />
  </bean>

  <bean name="flowHandlerAdapter"
class="org.springframework.webflow.mvc.servlet.FlowHandlerAdapter">
   <property name="flowExecutor" ref="flowExecutor" />
   </bean>

  <webflow:flow-registry id="flowRegistry">
    <webflow:flow-location
      path="/WEB-INF/flows/onlineService/onlineService.xml" />
    <webflow:flow-location
      path="/WEB-INF/flows/customerSearch/customerSearch.xml" />
    <webflow:flow-location
      path="/WEB-INF/flows/customerDetails/customerDetails.xml" />
    <webflow:flow-location
      path="/WEB-INF/flows/transferMoney/transferMoney.xml" />
  </webflow:flow-registry>

  <webflow:flow-executor id="flowExecutor">
    <webflow:flow-execution-listeners>
      <webflow:listener ref="securityFlowExecutionListener" />
      <webflow:listener ref="jpaFlowExecutionListener" />
    </webflow:flow-execution-listeners>
  </webflow:flow-executor>
```

```
  <bean id="securityFlowExecutionListener"
    class="org.springframework.webflow.security.SecurityFlowExecutionListener" />

  <bean id="jpaFlowExecutionListener"
    class="org.springframework.webflow.persistence.JpaFlowExecutionListener">
    <constructor-arg ref="entityManagerFactory" />
    <constructor-arg ref="jpaTransactionManager" />
  </bean>

  <bean id="customerCriteriaAction"
    class="org.springframework.webflow.action.FormAction">
    <property name="formObjectClass"
      value="com.perfmath.spring.soba.webflow.domain.CustomerCriteria" />
    <property name="propertyEditorRegistrar">
      <bean
        class="com.perfmath.spring.soba.webflow.web.PropertyEditors" />
    </property>
  </bean>

  <bean id="transferMoneyAction"
    class="org.springframework.webflow.action.FormAction">
    <property name="formObjectClass"
      value="com.perfmath.spring.soba.model.domain.TransferRecord" />
    <property name="propertyEditorRegistrar">
      <bean class="com.perfmath.spring.soba.webflow.web.PropertyEditors" />
    </property>
    <property name="validator"> <bean
      class="com.perfmath.spring.soba.webflow.services.TransferRecordValidator" />
    </property>
  </bean>
</beans>
```

Note that for illustrative purposes, this `soba-webflow.xml` file is imported in the `flow-servlet.xml` file, as is shown in Listing 11.5. You may also recall that the `flow-servlet.xml` file is specified in the `web.xml` file as shown in Listing 11.1, together with the `flow-service.xml` file that we will discuss later.

Listing 11.5 flow-servlet.xml

```
<beans xmlns="http://www.springframework.org/schema/beans"
  xmlns:xsi="http://www.w3.org/2001/XMLSchema-instance"
  xsi:schemaLocation="http://www.springframework.org/schema/beans
    http://www.springframework.org/schema/beans/spring-beans.xsd">
```

```
  <import resource="soba-webflow.xml" />
</beans>
```

11.3.1 Spring Flow Registry

As its name suggests, a Spring flow registry registers the Spring web flows. This is a centralized repository that helps the Spring `flowHandlerMapping` to map a web flow request to a well-defined web flow. As is shown in Figure 11.1, all Spring web flow examples associated with the SOBA project are located under the path of `src/main/webapp/WEB-INF/flows`. We have four web flow examples here, with each web flow consisting of an XML file and one or more jsp files. For example, the `onlineService` web flow consists of the `onlineService.xml` file and three jsp files of `onlineService.jsp`, `description.jsp`, and `moreInfo.jsp`. We will explain how a Spring web flow is defined and programmed later. For the time being, we only need to keep in mind that each Spring web flow has its own sub folder for its flow definition and view technology specific script files. This is how a Spring `flowHandlerMapping` can find a web flow, validate it, and then delegate it to the next stage to the corresponding `flowHandlerAdapter` for execution, which is discussed next.

11.3.2 Spring Flow Executor

A Spring web flow executor is configured with several flow execution listeners, based on the context of a web flow that is invoked. For example, in Listing 11.4 shown in the previous section, we see the `flowExecutor` defined with two flow execution listeners as follows:

```
......
<webflow:flow-executor id="flowExecutor">
      <webflow:flow-execution-listeners>
         <webflow:listener ref="securityFlowExecutionListener" />
         <webflow:listener ref="jpaFlowExecutionListener" />
      </webflow:flow-execution-listeners>
   </webflow:flow-executor>

   <bean id="securityFlowExecutionListener"
      class="org.springframework.webflow.security.SecurityFlowExecutionListener" />

   <bean id="jpaFlowExecutionListener"
      class="org.springframework.webflow.persistence.JpaFlowExecutionListener">
      <constructor-arg ref="entityManagerFactory" />
      <constructor-arg ref="jpaTransactionManager" />
   </bean>
......
```

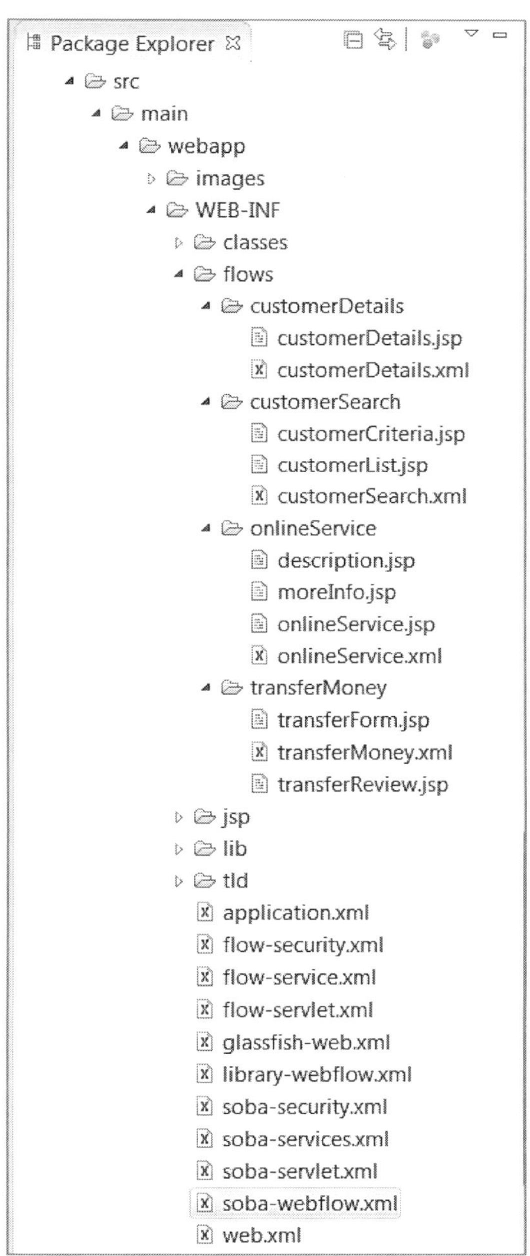

Figure 11.1 The SOBA web flow structure

In the above example, we see the following listeners:

- `org.springframework.webflow.security.SecurityFlowExecutionListener`: This listener is for securing web flows.
- `org.springframework.webflow.persistence.JpaFlowExecutionListener`: This listener is for supporting JPA-based persistence. If you choose to use Hibernate persistence instead of JPA persistence, then you would have to replace it with the Hibernate listener of `org.springframework.webflow.persistence.HibernateFlowExecutionListener`.

We will see how the above listeners are used with the examples to be presented later.

11.4 SPRING WEB FLOW PROGRAMMING

In the previous sections, we covered the following topics regarding the Spring Web Flow Framework:

- What a Spring web flow structure would look like
- How to integrate the Spring Web Flow Framework with the Spring MVC Framework
- The mechanics of defining a Spring web flow registry and a web flow executor

From this section on, we focus on how to program Spring web flows. We will three examples to assist illustrating how to program Spring web flows:

1 **onlineService**: This example helps illustrate how to define Spring web flows and how to create page views with Spring web flow IDs.
2 **searchCustomer**: This example demonstrates how to model web flows with various state types.
3 **transferMoney**: This example shows how to persist objects in Spring web flows.

Let's start with how to define a Spring web flow next.

11.4.1 Defining a Spring web flow

A Spring web flow can be defined with an XML-based flow definition language. In Listing 11.4 `soba-webflow.xml` file, four web flows are defined, each of which is specified with an XML file. The `onlineService` web flow is defined with the `onlineService.xml` file, as is shown in Listing 11.6. As is seen, each XML element defines a `view-state` with an `id` assigned. Let's summarize this web flow definition as follows:

- **The *`onlineService`* view state**: This *view state* is assigned an `id` of "`onlineService`" and defines how to transit from one view state to another. It consists of two *transitions*, each of which is specified with an "`on-to`" pair. The first transition specifies that the current view state should transit to the "`description`" view state upon the occurrence of the event "`next`", while the second transition specifies that the current view should transit to the "`moreInfo`" view state upon the occurrence of the event "`skip`".
- **The *description* view state**: This view state is assigned an `id` of "`description`" and illustrates how a view should be rendered and how to transit to another view state. The rendering part is defined with an `<on-render>` element, which is specified in an expression language (EL) in the format of `<evaluate expression="..." result="..."/>`. This is a mechanism to trigger an action for a view state before the view is rendered. The Spring Web Flow Framework supports Unified EL and ONGL, both of which are popular expression languages. You might wonder what the properties of

"expression" and "result" mean in that <on-render> <evaluate ...> </on-render> element. The *expression* part specifies the method to invoke, while the *result* part specifies where to store the result. To answer these questions, note that we have an OnlineService interface named OnlineService.java and the corresponding implementation class named OnlineServiceImpl.java that can be found in the package of com.perfmath.spring.soba.webflow.services (See Listings 11.7 and 11.8 for this interface and its implementation class). Note in Listing 11.9 flow-service.xml file that an onlineService bean is defined, which enables its getServices () method to be invoked when that expression of expression="onlineService.getServices()" is invoked on rendering (you can ignore the other parts in the flow-service.xml file as we will discuss them later). The *result* property defines the variable that will hold the result returned from the method call invoked through the expression definition. The scope of "requestScope" means that the variable named "services" will get allocated when the flow is called and destroyed when the flow returns. You can refer to the *Special EL variables* section of Chapter 4 *Expression Languages* (*EL*) of the *Spring Web Flow Reference Documentation* for other types of scopes such as *flowScope*, *viewScope* and *flasScope*, etc.

- **The *moreInfo* view state**: This view state is assigned an id of "moreInfo" and is the end view state for this web flow. This end view state has neither transitions nor <on-render> element specified. This is because it has no other actions to take other than displaying the static text we put in the moreInfo.jsp file as shown in Listing 11.10.

Each flow can be represented with a flow diagram to illustrate the flow from state to state. Figure 11.2 shows the flow diagram for the *onlineService* flow as defined in Listing 11.6.

Listing 11.6 onlineService.xml

```
<?xml version="1.0" encoding="UTF-8" ?>
<flow xmlns="http://www.springframework.org/schema/webflow"
  xmlns:xsi="http://www.w3.org/2001/XMLSchema-instance"
  xsi:schemaLocation="http://www.springframework.org/schema/webflow
    http://www.springframework.org/schema/webflow/spring-webflow-2.4.xsd">

  <view-state id="onlineService">
    <transition on="next" to="description" />
    <transition on="skip" to="moreInfo" />
  </view-state>

  <view-state id="description">
    <on-render>
      <evaluate expression="onlineService.getServices()"
        result="requestScope.services" />
    </on-render>
    <transition on="next" to="moreInfo" />
  </view-state>
```

```
    <view-state id="moreInfo"/>
</flow>
```

Listing 11.7 OnlineService.java

```
package com.perfmath.spring.soba.webflow.services;

import java.util.List;

public interface OnlineService {

    public List<String> getServices();
}
```

Listing 11.8 OnlineServiceImpl.java

```
package com.perfmath.spring.soba.webflow.services;

import java.util.ArrayList;
import java.util.List;

public class OnlineServiceImpl implements OnlineService {

    public List<String> getServices() {
        List<String> services = new ArrayList<String>();
        services.add("Online Banking");
        services.add("Mobile and Text Banking");
        services.add("Bill Payment Service");
        services.add("Online Statements");
        services.add("Online and Mobile Deposit");
        services.add("Electronic Funds Transfers");
        services.add("Check Images");
        services.add("Email and Text Alerts");
        services.add("Budget Tools");
        services.add("Interactive Demos");
        services.add("Frequently Asked Questions");
        return services;
    }
}
```

Listing 11.9 flow-service.xml

```
<beans xmlns="http://www.springframework.org/schema/beans"
```

```
    xmlns:xsi="http://www.w3.org/2001/XMLSchema-instance"
    xsi:schemaLocation="http://www.springframework.org/schema/beans
     http://www.springframework.org/schema/beans/spring-beans.xsd">

    <bean name="onlineService"
        class="com.perfmath.spring.soba.webflow.services.OnlineServiceImpl" />

    <bean id="customerService"
        class="com.perfmath.spring.soba.webflow.services.CustomerServiceImpl">
        <property name="customerDao" ref="customerDao" />
    </bean>

    <bean id="flow-dataSource" class="org.apache.commons.dbcp.BasicDataSource"
        destroy-method="close">
        <property name="driverClassName" value="${jdbc.driverClassName}" />
        <property name="url" value="${jdbc.url}" />
        <property name="username" value="${jdbc.username}" />
        <property name="password" value="${jdbc.password}" />
        <property name="initialSize" value="5" />
        <property name="maxActive" value="20" />
    </bean>

    <bean id="entityManagerFactory"
        class="org.springframework.orm.jpa.LocalContainerEntityManagerFactoryBean">
        <property name="dataSource" ref="flow-dataSource" />
        <property name="jpaVendorAdapter">
            <bean class="org.springframework.orm.jpa.vendor.HibernateJpaVendorAdapter">
                <property name="databasePlatform" value="org.hibernate.dialect.MySQLDialect" />
                <property name="showSql" value="true" />
                <property name="generateDdl" value="true" />
            </bean>
        </property>
    </bean>

    <bean id="jpaTransactionManager" class="org.springframework.orm.jpa.JpaTransactionManager">
        <property name="entityManagerFactory" ref="entityManagerFactory" />
    </bean>

</beans>
```

Listing 11.10 moreInfo.jsp

```
<html>
```

```
<head> <title>More Info</title> </head>
<body>
<h1>More Info</h1>
<h3>Bill Payment Service </h3>
Stop writing checks, making extra trips to the mailbox and standing in line at the post office. Instead, let SOBA Online make paying your bills easy with our online Bill Payment service.
<br>
<h3>With our Bill Payment service you can </h3>
For example:
<ul>
   <LI>Pay your bills when it's convenient for you &#8208 after payday, before the due date or whenever you'd like.</LI>
   <LI>Pay almost anyone, anytime, anywhere in the United States, from your mortgage lender to your newspaper carrier. </LI>
   <LI>Schedule single one-time payments up to one year in advance. </LI>
   <LI>Set up automatic recurring payments for your regular bills, such as your car or mortgage payment.</LI>
   <LI>Receive electronic bills (e-bills) so that you can view online versions of your paper bills.</LI>
   <LI>Receive notifications and email reminders when your payments are due.</LI>
   <LI>Track payments online with our Bill History screen, which shows you who you paid, the date and amount of each payment within the last two years.</LI>
</ul>
</body>
</html>
```

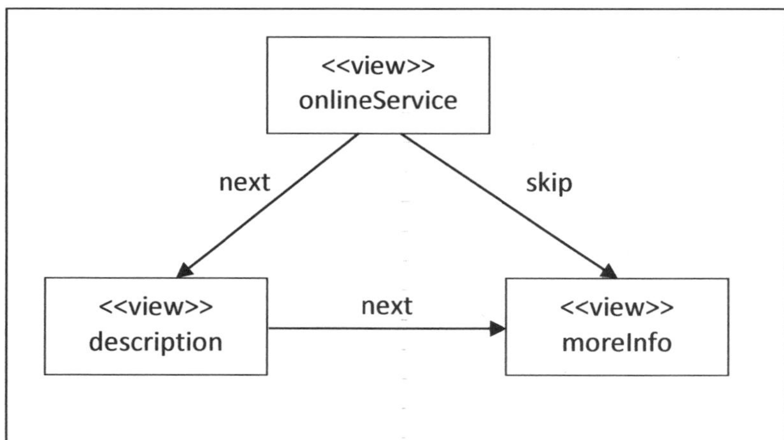

Figure 11.2 The flow diagram for the *onlineService* flow

11.4.2 Programming Page Views

After a web flow is defined, the next step is to create page views. Recall that we defined three view states in Listing 11.6 `onlineService.xml` with three different `id`'s of `onlineService`, `description`, and `moreInfo`. The convention is that the views should be located in the same folder as the flow definition file and their name should be the same as their corresponding view state id so that they can be loaded by default.

In terms of creating page views in web flow's context, it's not very different from creating regular page views in jsp except that you need to use the event id's specified in the flow definition file to guide the flow from one view state to another. The general format is:

```
<a href="${flowExecutionUrl}&_eventId=<event_id>">Event Alias</id>
```

where you should replace the part of "*<event_id>*" and "*Event Alias*" as illustrated above according to your specific needs. For example, you can easily identify the event id's in Listing 11.11 for the `onlineService.jsp` view and Listing 11.12 for the `description.jsp` view against the values of the "`on`" properties of the transitions defined in their respective view states.

Listing 11.11 onlineService.jsp

```
<html>
<head>
<title>Welcome</title>
</head>
<body>
<h2>Welcome to SOBA Online Service!</h2>
SOBA makes paying your bills easy with our online Bill Payment service. <p>
You can receive and pay bills, schedule recurring payments, and track <p>
payment history. You can even use our Popmoney® Personal Payment service <p>
to send money to friends, family, or acquaintences. These services are <p>
available to all SOBA members with a valid SOBA checking account <p>

To learn about our online bill payment service or for more information, please click the links below. <p>
<a href="${flowExecutionUrl}&_eventId=next">SOBA Online Service</a> <br> <br>
<a href="${flowExecutionUrl}&_eventId=skip">More Info</a>
</body>
</html>
```

Listing 11.12 description.jsp

```
<%@ taglib prefix="c" uri="http://java.sun.com/jsp/jstl/core" %>
<%@ taglib prefix="fmt" uri="http://java.sun.com/jsp/jstl/fmt" %>

<html>
<head>
<title>Description</title>
```

```
</head>

<body>
<h2>SOBA Online Services</h2>
<c:forEach items="${services}" var="service">
         <c:out value="${service}"/><br />
</c:forEach>
<br /><br />
<a href="${flowExecutionUrl}&_eventId=next">More Info </a>
</body>
</html>
```

If you are interested in running this `onlineService` web flow, you can build and deploy the project, start soba up, and enter the URL of https://localhost:8443/soba/onlineService. Then, ignore the certificate warning and you should see the first view of `onlineService` as shown in Figure 11.3. If you click the link of *SOBA Online Service*, it should take you to the *description* view as shown in Figure 11.4. Finally, if you click the link of *More Info*, it should take you to the *moreInfo* view as shown in Figure 11.5.

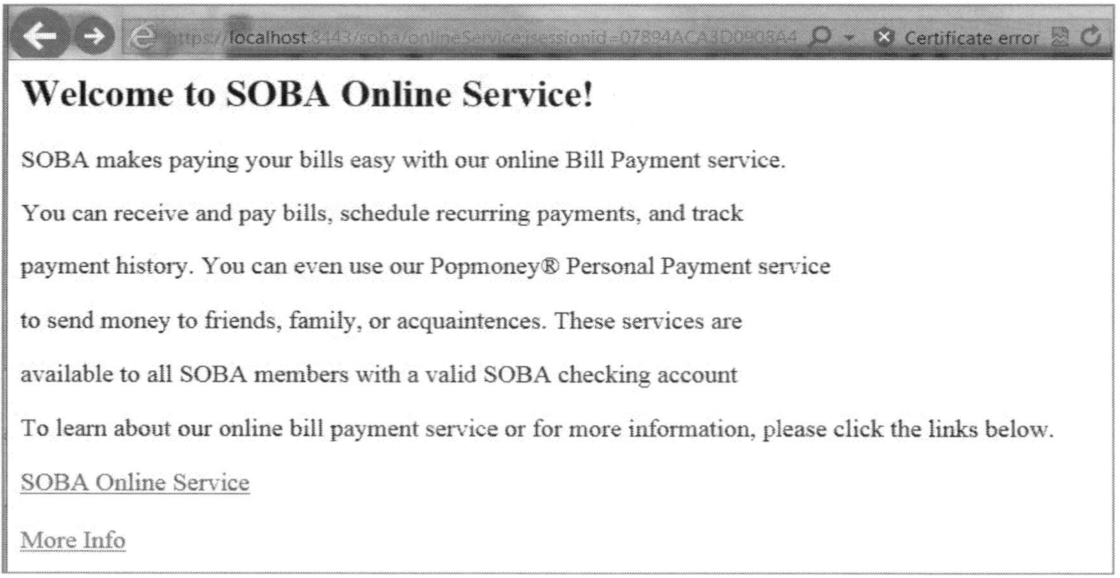

Figure 11.3 The *onlineService* view

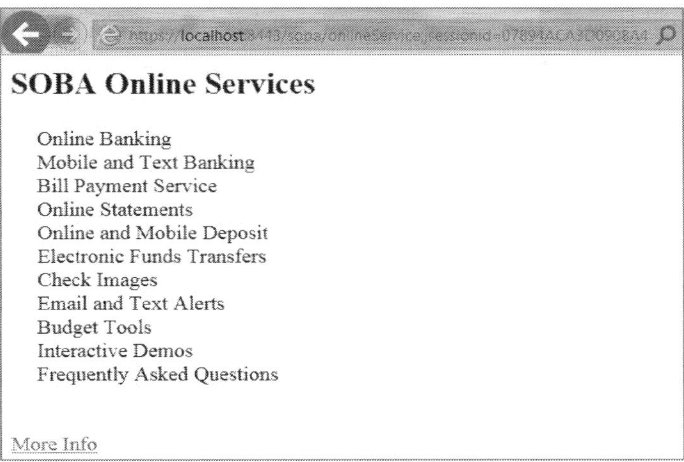

Figure 11.4 The *description* view

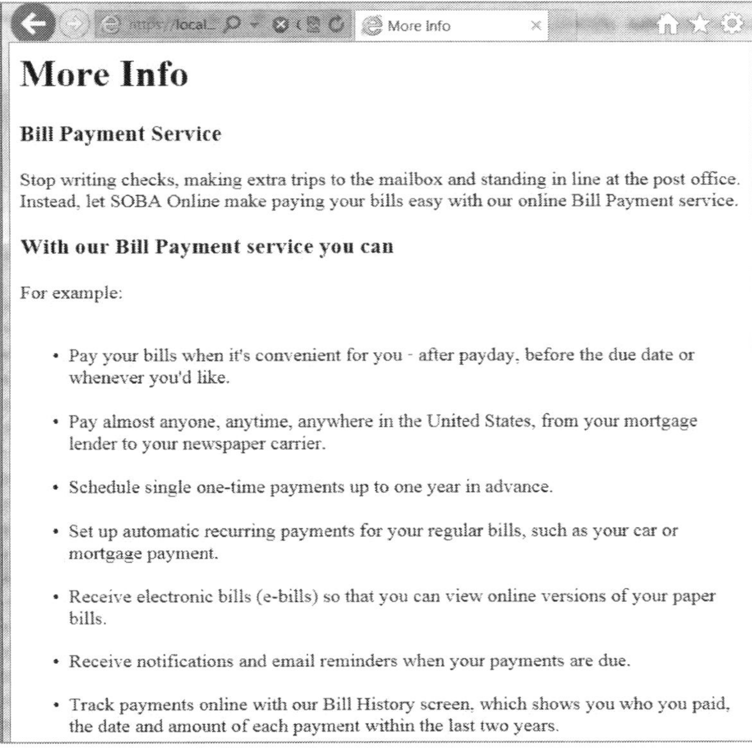

Figure 11.5 The *moreInfo* view

11.5 MODELING WEB FLOWS WITH VARIOUS STATE TYPES

The Spring Web Flow Framework is a very helpful feature for modeling UI activities that are typical with every web application. In the previous section, we presented a simple Spring web flow example of *onlineService* that can help customers understand what kind of online banking services are provided and how they can get started. Of course, my intention was to help give you a quick glimpse of how Spring Web Flow works. In this section, we discuss how to handle more complex flows with various state types and even sub flows. Let's start with what state types the Spring Web Flow Framework supports.

11.5.1 Built-in Spring Web Flow State Types

One can view a flow execution engine as a state machine that it moves the flow from state to state with well-defined states. Each state is uniquely identified with a unique id and has zero or more event IDs that control how state transitioning should proceed. In the previous example of the `onlineService` flow, we illustrated one of the most common state types, view-state. In this section, we introduce more Spring web flow state types.

Spring Web Flow supports the following five built-in state types:

- **View**: This state type renders a view to a user either by displaying some kind of information like the `onlineService` flow we presented in the previous section or displaying a form for the user to enter and submit. Upon the initial invocation, the flow will pause until the user takes some action, for example, clicking on a hyperlink or submitting a form, to advance the flow to the next state. We already saw this type of state with the previous `onlineService` flow example that the flow starts with a general summary about the online services, and then specific services provided, and finally a more detailed description about how to get started with the online services provided.
- **Action**: This state type allows certain actions to be executed for the current flow, such as interacting with the backend database, etc.
- **Decision**: This state type allows a Boolean expression to be executed to decide the next state that the flow should transit to.
- **Subflow**: This state type initiates a subflow under the current flow for a sub-task to be executed, after which it returns to the parent flow.
- **End**: This state type designates the end state of a flow, after which all flow variables will get invalidated.

Next, let's use a simple `customerSearch` web flow example to demonstrate the use of the above state types supported by the Spring Web Flow Framework.

11.5.2 customerSearch web flow

Search is a universal type of UI activities that every web application would have to support in various contexts. In this section, we present a Spring web flow example that allows SOBA customers to be searched based on certain criteria. This type of activity happens in reality whenever you need to call your bank or any service providers that you are associated with. In such situations, typically, you need to provide some information, for example, your customer id, last name, and so on, so that your service provider can look up your account based on the information you provide. With our customerSearch flow example, we use the *zipcode* and *last name* fields as the search criteria.

The search criteria mentioned above would be implemented as a form to collect the entries to be entered. Upon submission of the zipcode and/or last name entries, the SOBA database will be searched and matched customers will be returned. Listing 11.13 shows how this search criteria is implemented. Note that this class is a POJO and placed in a special package of com.perfmath.spring.soba.webflow.domain. Also note that this CustomerCriteria class must be made *serializable* by implementing the Serializable interface.

Listing 11.13 CustomerCriteria.java

```
package com.perfmath.spring.soba.webflow.domain;
import java.io.Serializable;
public class CustomerCriteria implements Serializable {

   private String zipcode;
   private String lastName;
//getters and setters are omitted
}
```

The next step is to create a customerService bean to fulfill the function of searching customers with a given search criteria. We use the same Customer domain object defined in the package of com.perfmath.spring.soba.model.domain, which is shown in Listing 11.14. The CustomerService.java interface is shown in Listing 11.15, while its implementation class CustomerServiceImpl.java is shown in Listing 11.16. As is seen in the interface, it defines two methods: one for searching all customers with a given criteria, and the other for finding a customer with a given customer ID. Both methods use the same CustomerDao bean to perform their operations (this bean is contained in the com.perfmath.spring.soba.model.dao package and we would not list here to save space). This service bean is defined in the flow-service.xml file as shown in Listing 11.9 as follows:

```
<bean id="customerService"
        class="com.perfmath.spring.soba.webflow.services.CustomerServiceImpl">
        <property name="customerDao" ref="customerDao" />
    </bean>
```

It is just a regular service bean with a dependency on a customerDao object.

Listing 11.14 Customer.java

```
package com.perfmath.spring.soba.model.domain;

import java.io.Serializable;
import java.sql.Timestamp;
```

```
public class Customer implements Serializable {

    private String customerId;
    private String firstName;
    private String lastName;
    private String phone;
    private String address;
    private String city;
    private String state;
    private String zipcode;
    private String email;
    private int status;
    private Timestamp createDate;

    //getters and setters omitted
}
```

Listing 11.15 CustomerService.java

```
package com.perfmath.spring.soba.webflow.services;

import java.util.List;
import com.perfmath.spring.soba.model.domain.Customer;
import com.perfmath.spring.soba.webflow.domain.CustomerCriteria;

public interface CustomerService {

  public List<Customer> search(CustomerCriteria criteria);
  public Customer findByCustomerId(String customerId);
}
```

Listing 11.16 CustomerServiceImpl.java

```
package com.perfmath.spring.soba.webflow.services;

import java.util.ArrayList;
import java.util.Iterator;
import java.util.List;

import com.perfmath.spring.soba.model.domain.Customer;
import com.perfmath.spring.soba.webflow.domain.CustomerCriteria;
import com.perfmath.spring.soba.model.dao.CustomerDao;
```

```
public class CustomerServiceImpl implements CustomerService {
    private CustomerDao customerDao;

  public void setCustomerDao(CustomerDao customerDao) {
        this.customerDao = customerDao;
   }

   public List<Customer> search(CustomerCriteria criteria) {
    String zipcode = criteria.getZipcode().trim();
    String lastName = criteria.getLastName().trim();

    List<Customer> customers = customerDao.getCustomerList ();

    List<Customer> results = new ArrayList<Customer>();
    Iterator it = customers.iterator();

    while (it.hasNext()) {
        Customer customer = (Customer) it.next();
       boolean zipcodeMatches = zipcode.length() > 0
            && customer.getZipcode().equals(zipcode);
       boolean lastNameMatches = customer.getLastName().equals(lastName);
       if (zipcodeMatches || lastNameMatches) {
          results.add(customer);
       }
    }
    return results;
  }

  public Customer findByCustomerId(String customerId) {
   Customer customer = customerDao.findByCustomerID(customerId);
    return customer;
  }
}
```

The views of the `customerSearch` flow consist of two jsp files: `customerCriteria.jsp` and `customerList.jsp`. These two files are shown in Listings 11.17 and 11.18, respectively. Note the line of `<input type="submit" name="_eventId_search" value="Search" />` shown in Listing 11.17, which shows that the event ID to be associated with the clicking *Submit* button event is `_eventId_search` for this `customerCriteria` view.

For the `customerList` view, two Spring flow specific hyperlinks are defined as follows:

```
<a href="${flowExecutionUrl}&_eventId=select&customerId=${customer.customerId}">
      ${customer.customerId} </a>
<a href="${flowExecutionUrl}&_eventId=newSearch">New Search</a>
```

The first hyperlink would initiate displaying the information on a specific customer with a given customer ID, whereas the second hyperlink would initial a new search. These definitions are not very different from what we discussed with the previous `onlineService` example, so we would not explain further.

Listing 11.17 customerCriteria.jsp

```
<%@ taglib prefix="form" uri="http://www.springframework.org/tags/form" %>

<html>
<head>
<title>Customer Criteria</title>
</head>

<body>
<form:form commandName="customerCriteria">
<table>
 <tr>
  <td>Zipcode</td>
  <td><form:input path="zipcode" /></td>
 </tr>
 <tr>
  <td>Last Name</td>
  <td><form:input path="lastName" /></td>
 </tr>
 <tr>
  <td colspan="2">
   <input type="submit" name="_eventId_search" value="Search" />
  </td>
 </tr>
</table>
</form:form>
</body>
</html>
```

Listing 11.18 customerList.jsp

```
<%@ taglib prefix="c" uri="http://java.sun.com/jsp/jstl/core" %>
<%@ taglib prefix="fmt" uri="http://java.sun.com/jsp/jstl/fmt" %>

<html>
<head>
<title>Customer List</title>
```

```
</head>
<body>
<table border="1">
 <tr>
   <th>customerId</th>
  <th>email</th>
  <th>Last Name </th>
  <th>First Name</th>
  <th>createDate</th>
  <th>zipcode</th>
 </tr>
 <c:forEach items="${customers}" var="customer">
 <tr>
  <td>
   <a href="${flowExecutionUrl}&_eventId=select&customerId=${customer.customerId}">
    ${customer.customerId} </a>
  </td>
  <td>${customer.email}</td>
  <td>${customer.lastName}</td>
  <td>${customer.firstName}</td>
  <td><fmt:formatDate value="${customer.createDate}" pattern="yyyy-MM-dd" /></td>
  <td>${customer.zipcode}</td>
 </tr>
 </c:forEach>
</table>
<a href="${flowExecutionUrl}&_eventId=newSearch">New Search</a>
</body>
</html>
```

Finally, Listing 11.19 shows how this `customerSearch` flow is defined (consult Listing 11.4 `soba-webflow.xml` file to see how this flow is registered in the `flowRegistry`). Next, we examine how those various Spring web flow state types are used with this `customerSearch` flow example, following the end of Listing 11.19.

Listing 11.19 customerSearch.xml

```
<?xml version="1.0" encoding="UTF-8" ?>
<flow xmlns="http://www.springframework.org/schema/webflow"
  xmlns:xsi="http://www.w3.org/2001/XMLSchema-instance"
  xsi:schemaLocation="http://www.springframework.org/schema/webflow
    http://www.springframework.org/schema/webflow/spring-webflow-2.4.xsd">
<!--
  <secured attributes=" ROLE_REP" />
-->
```

```
  <view-state id="customerCriteria">
    <on-render>
      <evaluate expression="customerCriteriaAction.setupForm" />
    </on-render>
    <transition on="search" to="searchCustomer">
      <evaluate expression="customerCriteriaAction.bindAndValidate" />
    </transition>
  </view-state>

  <action-state id="searchCustomer">
    <evaluate expression="customerService.search(customerCriteria)"
      result="flowScope.customers" />
    <transition on="success" to="checkResultSize" />
  </action-state>

  <decision-state id="checkResultSize">
    <if test="customers.size() == 1" then="extractResult"
      else="customerList" />
  </decision-state>

  <action-state id="extractResult">
    <set name="flowScope.customer" value="customers.get(0)" />
    <transition on="success" to="customerDetails" />
  </action-state>

  <view-state id="customerList">
    <transition on="select" to="customerDetails">
      <evaluate
        expression="customerService.findByCustomerId(requestParameters.customerId)"
        result="flowScope.customer" />
    </transition>
    <transition on="newSearch" to="newSearch" />
  </view-state>

  <subflow-state id="customerDetails" subflow="customerDetails">
    <input name="customer" value="flowScope.customer" />
    <transition on="newSearch" to="newSearch" />
  </subflow-state>

  <end-state id="newSearch" />
</flow>
```

#1 The view state of customerCriteria for the customerSearch flow

As is shown in the preceding listing, the customerSearch flow has two view states defined: the customerCriteria view state and the customerList view state. The first view state prepares a form so that a user can enter entries. This form is defined by the customerCriteria.jsp file as shown in Listing 11.17. The Spring Web Flow Framework provides a FormAction class for handling Spring web flow action forms. The corresponding bean is already defined in Listing 11.4 soba-webflow.xml as follows:

```
<bean id="customerCriteriaAction"
  class="org.springframework.webflow.action.FormAction">
  <property name="formObjectClass"
    value="com.perfmath.spring.soba.webflow.domain.CustomerCriteria" />
  <property name="propertyEditorRegistrar">
    <bean
      class="com.perfmath.spring.soba.webflow.web.PropertyEditors" />
  </property>
</bean>
```

This form action bean specifies that the customerCriteria form should be processed against the CustomerCritera class defined in the com.perfmath.spring.soba.webflow.domain package. Besides, in order to convert form field values into proper data types, we have to register custom property editors to this form action. For example, for this customerCriteriaAction bean, we specified a propertyEditorRegistrar bean of com.perfmath.spring.soba.webflow.web.PropertyEditors as shown above. Listing 11.20 shows how this propetyEditor bean is implemented exactly. Note that we really don't have a Date type entry to convert in the customerCriteria.jsp file, so this is for illustrative purposes only.

Listing 11.20 PropertyEditors.java

```
package com.perfmath.spring.soba.webflow.web;

import java.text.SimpleDateFormat;
import java.util.Date;

import org.springframework.beans.PropertyEditorRegistrar;
import org.springframework.beans.PropertyEditorRegistry;
import org.springframework.beans.propertyeditors.CustomDateEditor;

public class PropertyEditors implements PropertyEditorRegistrar {

  public void registerCustomEditors(PropertyEditorRegistry registry) {
    SimpleDateFormat dateFormat = new SimpleDateFormat("yyyy-MM-dd");
    dateFormat.setLenient(false);
    registry.registerCustomEditor(Date.class, new CustomDateEditor(
        dateFormat, true));
  }
}
```

Next, we saw the customerCriteria view state defined in Listing 11.19 customerSearch.xml as follows:

```
<view-state id="customerCriteria">
  <on-render>
    <evaluate expression="customerCriteriaAction.setupForm" />
  </on-render>
  <transition on="search" to="searchCustomer">
    <evaluate expression="customerCriteriaAction.bindAndValidate" />
  </transition>
</view-state>
```

This view state definition specifies that the setupForm () method of the form action customerCriteriaAction should be called first before rendering the view. Then, it defines a transition to the searchCustomer state, which is discussed next.

#2 The action state of searchCustomer for the customerSearch flow

Following the customerCriteria view state, an action state named searchCustomer is defined as follows:

```
<action-state id="searchCustomer">
    <evaluate expression="customerService.search(customerCriteria)"
      result="flowScope.customers" />
    <transition on="success" to="checkResultSize" />
  </action-state>
```

This action state performs a customer search with the given customerCriteria and stores the result in a variable named customers in flow scope. If the search is successful, meaning that no exceptions or errors occur, the flow transits to the checkResultSize state as is discussed next.

#3 The decision state of checkResultSize for the customerSearch flow

The decision state of checkResultSize is defined as follows as is shown in Listing 3.19:

```
<decision-state id="checkResultSize">
  <if test="customers.size() == 1" then="extractResult"
    else="customerList" />
</decision-state>
```

This decision state defines that if the returned result set has only one customer, then transit to the extractResult state; otherwise, transit to the customerList state. These two states are discussed next.

#4 The action state of extractResult for the customerSearch flow

This action state defines that if the result set as discussed previously has only one customer, then extract and assign the customer to the customer variable in flow scope; otherwise, transit to the customerList state, as is discussed next.

```
<action-state id="extractResult">
```

```
    <set name="flowScope.customer" value="customers.get(0)" />
    <transition on="success" to="customerDetails" />
  </action-state>
```

#5 The view-state of customerList for the customerSearch flow

The `customerList` view state simply displays all customers that match the `searchCriteria`. It also specifies that if a specific customer is selected with its `customerId` clicked, than it should transit to the `customerDetails` state, and before rendering the view, invoke the `findByCustomerId` method of the `customerService` bean and assign the result to the `customer` variable in flow scope. Note that this view state has another transition to the `newSearch` state on the event of `newSearch`. We will discuss this state after discussing the `customerDetails` state next.

```
<view-state id="customerList">
     <transition on="select" to="customerDetails">
        <evaluate
           expression="customerService.findByCustomerId(requestParameters.customerId)"
           result="flowScope.customer" />
     </transition>
     <transition on="newSearch" to="newSearch" />
  </view-state>
```

#6 The subflow state of customerDetails for the customerSearch flow

The `customerDetails` subflow state displays the detailed information about a customer using the `customer` variable passed down from its parent flow of `customerList` as discussed above. It also has another transition to a state named "`newSearch`" as is discussed next.

```
<subflow-state id="customerDetails" subflow="customerDetails">
     <input name="customer" value="flowScope.customer" />
     <transition on="newSearch" to="newSearch" />
  </subflow-state>
```

#7 The end state of newSearch for the customerSearch flow

The end state of `newSearch` is the simplest of all that it does not have any transitions defined at all, as is shown below:

```
  <end-state id="newSearch" />
```

At this point, you can build, deploy, and run the SOBA sample and check out the `customerSearch` flow with the URL of https://localhost:8443/soba/customerSearch.

11.6 PERSISTING OBJECTS IN WEB FLOWS: THE TRANSFERMONEY WEB FLOW EXAMPLE

So far, we have presented two Spring web flows in SOBA's context: one is the onlineService flow that is mostly view centric and the other is the customerSearch flow that involves using all Spring web flow state types. However, these examples do not involve persisting objects into the backend database in the flows. In this section, we present a web flow named transferMoney to help demonstrate how to persist objects in web flows.

Let's start with the object to be persisted next.

11.6.1 The Persistable Object TransferRecord

The object we choose to persist is described as shown in Listing 11.21 TransferRecord.java. This is a JPA-annotated object as denoted by the annotation of @Entity preceding the class definition. As is seen, this class actually maps to the TRANSFER table in the SOBA database. We named it TransferRecord rather than Transfer, as we intend to insert each money transfer request as a transfer record in the TRANSFER table so that the persisted transfer records could be processed in batches rather than in real time mode. Spring has a Batch Framework for programming batch jobs, but it is not covered in this text.

Since we have covered how to create JPA annotated entity classes in Chapter 10, we would not explain further here about how this TransferRecord class is annotated. We would dive directly into how to program this transferMoney flow next.

Listing 11.21 TransferRecord.java

```
package com.perfmath.spring.soba.model.domain;

import java.io.Serializable;
import java.util.Date;

import javax.persistence.Basic;
import javax.persistence.Column;
import javax.persistence.Entity;
import javax.persistence.Id;
import javax.persistence.Table;
import javax.persistence.Temporal;
import javax.persistence.TemporalType;

@Entity
@Table(name = "TRANSFER")
public class TransferRecord implements Serializable {
   private Long id=null;
   private Date transferDate;
   private String fromAccountId;
   private String toAccountId;
   private int fromTxId;
```

```
private int toTxId;
private double amount;
private String initiator;
private String description;
public TransferRecord () {
}
@Id
 @Column(name = "TRANSFER_ID", unique = true, nullable = false, precision = 10, scale = 0)
 public Long getId() {
     return id;
 }
 public void setId(Long id) {
     this.id = id;
 }
 @Temporal(TemporalType.TIMESTAMP)
 @Column(name = "TRANSFER_DATE")
 public Date getTransferDate() {
     return transferDate;
 }
 public void setTransferDate(Date transferDate) {
     this.transferDate = transferDate;
 }
 @Column(name = "FROM_ACCOUNT_ID", nullable = false, length = 10)
 public String getFromAccountId() {
     return fromAccountId;
 }
 public void setFromAccountId(String fromAccountId) {
     this.fromAccountId = fromAccountId;
 }
 @Column(name = "TO_ACCOUNT_ID", nullable = false, length = 10)
 public String getToAccountId() {
     return toAccountId;
 }
 public void setToAccountId(String toAccountId) {
     this.toAccountId = toAccountId;
 }
 @Column(name = "FROM_TX_ID", nullable = false, length = 10)
 public int getFromTxId() {
     return fromTxId;
 }
 public void setFromTxId(int fromTxId) {
     this.fromTxId = fromTxId;
 }
```

```
    @Column(name = "TO_TX_ID", nullable = false, length = 10)
    public int getToTxId() {
        return toTxId;
    }
    public void setToTxId(int toTxId) {
        this.toTxId = toTxId;
    }
    @Column(name = "AMOUNT", nullable = false)
    public double getAmount() {
        return amount;
    }
    public void setAmount(double amount) {
        this.amount = amount;
    }
    @Column(name = "INITIATOR", nullable = false, length = 10)
    public String getInitiator() {
        return initiator;
    }
    public void setInitiator(String initiator) {
        this.initiator = initiator;
    }
    @Column(name = "DESCRIPTION", nullable = false, length = 500)
    public String getDescription() {
        return description;
    }
    public void setDescription(String description) {
        this.description = description;
    }
}
```

11.6.2 The JPA Configuration File persistence.xml

In order to enable JPA persistence, we need to create a `persistence.xml` file first to define a persistence unit. For this example, the `persistence.xml file` is placed in the META-INF directory of the class root at *WEB-INF/classes* and has the contents as shown in Listing 11.22. Note that it has a simple definition of a persistence unit named "`soba`".

Next, we discuss how to set up the `entityManagerFactory` bean and the `jpaTransactionManager` bean to enable JPA persistence in Spring's context.

Listing 11.22 persistence.xml

```
<persistence xmlns="http://java.sun.com/xml/ns/persistence"
  xmlns:xsi="http://www.w3.org/2001/XMLSchema-instance"
```

```
    xsi:schemaLocation="http://java.sun.com/xml/ns/persistence
      http://java.sun.com/xml/ns/persistence/persistence_2_0.xsd"
    version="2.0">

    <persistence-unit name="soba" />
</persistence>
```

11.6.3 Setting up the entityManagerFactory Bean and the jpaTransactionManager Bean

In fact, we already shown the `entityManagerFactory` bean and the `jpaTransactionManager` bean in Listing 11.9 `flow-service.xml`, but we did not explain them there. For convenience, that part is duplicated here as follows:

```
<bean id="flow-dataSource" class="org.apache.commons.dbcp.BasicDataSource"
        destroy-method="close">
        <property name="driverClassName" value="${jdbc.driverClassName}" />
        <property name="url" value="${jdbc.url}" />
        <property name="username" value="${jdbc.username}" />
        <property name="password" value="${jdbc.password}" />
        <property name="initialSize" value="5" />
        <property name="maxActive" value="20" />
  </bean>

  <bean id="entityManagerFactory"
      class="org.springframework.orm.jpa.LocalContainerEntityManagerFactoryBean">
      <property name="dataSource" ref="flow-dataSource" />
      <property name="jpaVendorAdapter">
          <bean class="org.springframework.orm.jpa.vendor.HibernateJpaVendorAdapter">
              <property name="databasePlatform" value="org.hibernate.dialect.MySQLDialect" />
              <property name="showSql" value="true" />
              <property name="generateDdl" value="true" />
          </bean>
      </property>
  </bean>

  <bean id="jpaTransactionManager" class="org.springframework.orm.jpa.JpaTransactionManager">
      <property name="entityManagerFactory" ref="entityManagerFactory" />
  </bean>
```

As is seen, we first defined a `flow-DataSource` to be used for the flow persistence example discussed here. Then, this `flow-Datasource` is specified as the `dataSource` for the `entityManagerFactory` bean, together with a `jpaVendorAdapter` of `org.springframework.orm.jpa.vendor.`

HibernateJpaVendorAdapter. This entityManagerFactory bean is specified as the entityManagerFactory for the jpaTransactionManager bean.

The next step is to register the transferMoney flow in the soba-webflow.xml file.

11.6.4 Registering the transferMoney Flow

Refer to Listing 11.4 soba-webflow.xml and notice that the transferMoney flow has already been defined as follows:

```
<webflow:flow-location path="/WEB-INF/flows/transferMoney/transferMoney.xml" />
```

Since this flow requires to display a transfer form to a user, similar to the customerSearch flow example presented earlier, we need to define a transferMoneyAction as is shown in Listing 11.4 flow-service.xml as follows:

```
<bean id="transferMoneyAction"
      class="org.springframework.webflow.action.FormAction">
      <property name="formObjectClass"
         value="com.perfmath.spring.soba.model.domain.TransferRecord" />
      <property name="propertyEditorRegistrar">
        <bean class="com.perfmath.spring.soba.webflow.web.PropertyEditors" />
      </property>
      <property name="validator"> <bean
         class="com.perfmath.spring.soba.webflow.services.TransferRecordValidator" />
      </property>
   </bean>
</beans>
```

Unlike the customerCriteria form action, we added a validator to the transferMoney form action, which is defined in the TransferRecordValidator.java class as shown in Listing 11.23. Note that in addition to validating the description field, this also is where we can set various IDs that must be unique and are not required to enter by the user.

Next, we illustrate how to define the transferMoney flow.

Listing 11.23 TransferRecordValidator.java

```
package com.perfmath.spring.soba.webflow.services;

import java.sql.Timestamp;
import org.springframework.validation.Errors;
import org.springframework.validation.Validator;
import org.apache.commons.lang.StringUtils;
import com.perfmath.spring.soba.model.domain.TransferRecord;
import com.perfmath.spring.soba.util.RandomID;
```

```
public class TransferRecordValidator implements Validator {
    public boolean supports(Class clazz) {
        return TransferRecord.class.equals(clazz);
    }

    public void validate(Object object, Errors errors) {
        TransferRecord transferRecord = (TransferRecord) object;

      transferRecord.setId(new Long((new RandomID(10)).getId()));
      transferRecord.setFromTxId(Integer.parseInt(new RandomID(10).getId()));
      transferRecord.setToTxId(Integer.parseInt(new RandomID(10).getId()));
      transferRecord.setInitiator("self");
        transferRecord.setTransferDate(new Timestamp(System.currentTimeMillis()));
        if (StringUtils.isBlank(transferRecord.getDescription())) {
            errors.rejectValue("description", null,
                    "Description name must not be empty");
        }
    }
}
```

11.6.5 Defining the transferMoney Flow

The `transferMoney` flow is defined in the `transferMoney.xml` file in the `/WEB-INF/flows/transferMoney` folder as is shown in Listing 11.24 below:

Listing 11.24 transferMoney.xml

```
<?xml version="1.0" encoding="UTF-8" ?>
<flow xmlns="http://www.springframework.org/schema/webflow"
  xmlns:xsi="http://www.w3.org/2001/XMLSchema-instance"
  xsi:schemaLocation="http://www.springframework.org/schema/webflow
    http://www.springframework.org/schema/webflow/spring-webflow-2.4.xsd">

  <persistence-context />

  <view-state id="transferForm">
    <on-render>
      <evaluate expression="transferMoneyAction.setupForm" />
    </on-render>
    <transition on="proceed" to="transferReview">
      <evaluate expression="transferMoneyAction.bindAndValidate" />
    </transition>
    <transition on="cancel" to="cancel" />
```

```
  </view-state>

  <view-state id="transferReview">
    <on-render>
      <evaluate expression="transferMoneyAction.setupForm" />
    </on-render>
    <transition on="confirm" to="confirm">
      <evaluate expression="persistenceContext.persist(transferRecord)" />
    </transition>
    <transition on="revise" to="transferForm" />
    <transition on="cancel" to="cancel" />
  </view-state>

  <end-state id="confirm" commit="true" />

  <end-state id="cancel" />
</flow>
```

Note that we have to define a `<persistence-context />` to enable the Spring Web Flow Framework to manage the persistence context for the flow. Then, we see two view states: one is the `transferForm` view state for collecting input from the user, and the other is the `transferReview` view state so that the user can review the transfer to be submitted to decide whether to confirm or cancel. The `transferForm` view state is not very different from the `customerCriteria` form view state discussed previously except that this `transferForm` view state does not contain a transition that would invoke querying the backend database. The `transferReview` view state is unique that it invokes a call to `persistenceContext.persist (transferRecord)` upon the occurrence of a `confirm` event. This view state also contains other two transitions to allow revising or canceling a transfer. Finally, note that there are two end states defined for this `transferMoney` flow: one is the `confirm` end state and the other is the `cancel` end state. The `confirm` end state has a commit attribute that is set to "`true`" to initiate committing a transfer transaction.

Finally, we need to program the transfer form view and transfer review view in jsp files as discussed next.

11.6.6 Programming the Transfer Form and Transfer Review View in JSP Files

The transfer form view is defined in the `transferForm.jsp` file as shown in Listing 11.25. This is a regular Spring web flow view programmed with two event IDs of "`_eventId_proceed`" and "`_eventId_cancel`" for the `confirm` and `cancel` events, respectively.

Listing 11.25 transferForm.jsp

```
<%@ taglib prefix="form" uri="http://www.springframework.org/tags/form"%>

<html>
```

```
<head>
<title>Transfer Form</title>
 <style>
   .error { color: red; }
  </style>
</head>

<body>
    <form:form commandName="transferRecord">
        <table>
            <tr>
                <td>From Account ID</td>
                <td><form:input path="fromAccountId" /></td>
            </tr>
            <tr>
                <td>To Account ID</td>
                <td><form:input path="toAccountId" /></td>
            </tr>

            <tr>
                <td>Amount</td>
                <td><form:input path="amount" /></td>
            </tr>
            <tr>
                <td>Description</td>
                <td><form:input path="description" /></td>
                <td><form:errors path="description" cssClass="error"/></td>
            </tr>
            <tr>
                <td colspan="2">
                    <input type="submit" name="_eventId_proceed" value="Proceed" />
                    <input type="submit" name="_eventId_cancel" value="Cancel" /></td>
            </tr>
        </table>
    </form:form>
</body>
</html>
```

The `transferReview` view is shown in Listing 11.26 `transferReview.jsp` below. Once again, note the event IDs of `_eventId_confirm`, `_eventId_revise`, and `_eventId_cencel`, corresponding to the actions defined.

Listing 11.26 transferReview.jsp

```
<%@ taglib prefix="fmt" uri="http://java.sun.com/jsp/jstl/fmt"%>

<html>
<head>
<title>Transfer Review</title>
</head>

<body>
    <form method="POST">
        <table>
            <tr>
                <td>Transfer ID</td>
                <td>${transferRecord.id}</td>
            </tr>
            <tr>
                <td>Transfer Date</td>
                <td><fmt:formatDate value="${transferRecord.transferDate}"
                        pattern="yyyy-MM-dd" /></td>
            </tr>
            <tr>
                <td>From Account ID</td>
                <td>${transferRecord.fromAccountId}</td>
            </tr>
            <tr>
                <td>To Account ID</td>
                <td>${transferRecord.toAccountId}</td>
            </tr>
            <tr>
                <td>From Tx ID</td>
                <td>${transferRecord.fromTxId}</td>
            </tr>
            <tr>
                <td>To Tx ID</td>
                <td>${transferRecord.toTxId}</td>
            </tr>
            <tr>
                <td>Initiator</td>
                <td>${transferRecord.initiator}</td>
            </tr>
            <tr>
                <td>Amount</td>
                <td>${transferRecord.amount}</td>
            </tr>
```

```
        <tr>
            <td>Description</td>
            <td>${transferRecord.description}</td>
        </tr>
        <tr>
            <td colspan="2">
                <input type="submit" name="_eventId_confirm" ="Confirm" />
                <input type="submit" name="_eventId_revise" ="Revise" />
                <input type="submit" name="_eventId_cancel" value="Cancel" />
    </td>
        </tr>
      </table>
    </form>
</body>
</html>
```

At this point, you can build, deploy and run this example by starting with entering the URL of https://localhost:8443/soba/transferMoney.

11.7 SECURING SPRING WEB FLOWS

Securing Spring web flows is as easy to add a `<secured attributes="ROLE_X, ROLE_Y"/>` in the flow definition file for a flow (the ROLEs specified here must exist in your database). You can add a `match="all"` attribute to demand that all ROLEs must be satisfied. As a concrete example, you can add `<secured attributes="ROLE_REP"/>` to the `customerSearch.xml` file so that only a user who login as a rep can search customers. You can try this out with the *sobarep/sobarep* built-in user if you want.

11.8 SUMMARY

In this chapter, we introduced the Spring Web Flow Framework with three flow examples of `onlineService`, `customerSearch`, and `transferMoney`. We started with the simplest flow example of `onlineService` to illustrate how a Spring web flow works in general. We then used the `customerSearch` flow to demonstrate various types of states that can be used to construct a more complex flow. Finally, we used the `transferMoney` flow example to demonstrate how to persist objects in a flow.

We presented all these flow examples in the same SOBA context as we demonstrated in the previous chapters using the Spring MVC framework. The part of how to integrate the two frameworks of Spring MVC and Spring Web Flow by setting proper handler mappings and handler adapters should be particularly helpful if you came from a background of having already explored some Spring web flow examples based on the Spring Web Flow Framework alone.

This should give you a sufficient jump start with programming Spring web flows. You can consult the *Spring Web Flow Reference Documentation* for version 2.4 if you are interested in exploring some additional features that are not covered.

11.9 RECOMMENDED READING

Spring Web Flow Framework Reference Documentation (2.4 is the newest as of this writing):

Chapter 1 Introduction

Chapter 2 What's New

Chapter 3 Defining Flows

Chapter 4 Expression Language (EL)

Chapter 5 Rendering Views

Chapter 6 Executing Actions

Chapter 7 Flow Managed Persistence

Chapter 8 Securing Flows

Chapter 9 Flow Inheritance

Chapter 10 System Setup

Chapter 11 Spring MVC Integration

Chapter 12 Spring JavaScript Quick Refernce

Chapter 13 JSF Integration

Chapter 14 Portlet Integration

Chapter 15 Testing Views

Chapter 17 Upgrading from 1.0

11.10 EXERCISES

11.1 Under what circumstances will you use various flow states (view, action, decision, etc.)?

11.2 Draw the flow diagram for the `customerSearch` flow and `transferMoney` flow to verify that you have truly understood how these two examples work.

11.3 Try out the securing Spring web flow feature as discussed in §11.7 and verify that it works.

Appendix A Spring Resources

In addition to this book and other texts published about Spring that you can search easily online, you can refer to the following resources to learn more about Spring Frameworks.

A.1 Spring Guides and Tutorials

Spring 3 once had video and written tutorials located under http://www.springsource.org/tutorials. Spring 4 offers *guides* and *tutorials* at http://spring.io/guides.The guides were designed to be completed in 15-30 minutes, providing quick, hands-on instructions for building the "Hello World" of any development task with Spring. It's stated that in most cases, the only prerequisites are a JDK and a text editor. Spring may update those guides over time, but here is a list of guides it has to offer as of this writing (this is a long and interesting list, and it's worthwhile to take a glance at it):

- Building a RESTful Web Service: illustrating how to create a RESTful web service with Spring.
- Consuming a RESTful Web Service, illustrating how to retrieve web page data with Spring's RestTemplate.
- Consuming a RESTful Web Service with Spring for Android, illustrating how to retrieve web page data using Spring for Android's RestTemplate.
- Scheduling Tasks, illustrating how to schedule tasks with Spring.
- Detecting a Device, illustrating how to use Spring to detect the type of device that is accessing your web site.
- Building Java Projects with Gradle, illustrating how to build a Java project with Gradle.
- Building Java Projects with Maven, illustrating how to build a Java project with Maven.
- Accessing Relational Data using JDBC with Spring, illustrating how to access relational data with Spring.
- Uploading Files, illustrating how to build a Spring application that accepts multi-part file uploads.
- Authenticating a User with LDAP, illustrating how to secure an application with LDAP.
- Registering an Application with Facebook, illustrating how to register an application to integrate with Facebook.
- Building Android Projects with Maven, illustrating how to build an Android project with Maven.
- Messaging with Redis, illustrating how to use Redis as a message broker.
- Registering an Application with Twitter, illustrating how to register apps with Twitter.

- Messaging with RabbitMQ, illustrating how to create a simple publish-and-subscribe application with Spring and RabbitMQ.
- Accessing Twitter Data, illustrating how to access user data from Twitter.
- Accessing Facebook Data, illustrating how to access Facebook information from an application.
- Accessing Data with Neo4j, illustrating how to persist objects and relationships in Neo4j's NoSQL data store.
- Validating Form Input, illustrating how to perform form validation with Spring.
- Building Android Projects with Gradle, illustrating how to build an Android project with Gradle.
- Building a RESTful Web Service with Spring Boot Actuator, illustrating how to create a RESTful Web service with Spring Boot Actuator,
- Messaging with JMS, illustrating how to publish and subscribe to messages using a JMS broker.
- Consuming XML from a RESTful Web Service with Spring for Android, illustrating how to use Spring for Android's RestTemplate to consume XML from a RESTful Web service.
- Creating a Batch Service, illustrating how to create a basic batch-driven solution.
- Securing a Web Application, illustrating how to protect your web application with Spring Security.
- Building a Hypermedia-Driven RESTful Web Service, illustrating how to create a hypermedia-driven RESTful Web service with Spring.
- Accessing Data with GemFire, illustrating how to build an application using Gemfire's data fabric.
- Integrating Data, illustrating how to build an application that uses Spring Integration to fetch data, process it, and write it to a file.
- Installing the Android Development Environment, illustrating how to set up the Android development environment.
- Caching Data with GemFire, illustrating how to cache data in GemFire.
- Managing Transactions, illustrating how to wrap key parts of code with transactions.
- Accessing Data with JPA, illustrating how to work with JPA data persistence using Spring Data JPA.
- Accessing Data with MongoDB, illustrating how to persist data in MongoDB.
- Serving Web Content with Spring MVC, illustrating how to create a web page with Spring MVC.
- Converting a Spring Boot JAR Application to a WAR, illustrating how to convert your Spring Boot JAR-based application to a WAR file.
- Creating Asynchronous Methods, illustrating how to create asynchronous service methods.
- Handling Form Submission, illustrating how to create and submit a web form with Spring.
- Creating an Asynchronous, Event-Driven Application with Reactor, illustrating how to build an asynchronous, message-driven system.
- Building an Application with Spring Boot, illustrating how to build an application with minimal configuration.
- Using WebSocket to build an interactive web application, illustrating how to the send and receive messages between a browser and the server over a WebSocket
- Working a Getting Started guide with STS, illustrating how to import a Getting Started guide with Spring Tool Suite (STS).
- Handling Web Site Preference, illustrating how to use Spring to allow users to prefer a mobile or tablet view of your web site.
- Serving Mobile Web Content with Spring MVC, illustrating how to create a web page with Spring MVC and Spring Mobile

- Creating a stream of live twitter data using Spring XD, illustrating how to stream live data from twitter into a local file
- Consuming a RESTful Web Service with AngularJS, illustrating how to retrieve web page data with AngularJS.
- Consuming a RESTful Web Service with rest.js, illustrating how to retrieve web page data with rest.js.
- Consuming a RESTful Web Service with Backbone.js, illustrating how to retrieve web page data with Backbone.js.
- Consuming a RESTful Web Service with jQuery, illustrating how to retrieve web page data with jQuery.
- Consuming a RESTful Web Service with Sencha Touch, illustrating how to retrieve web page data with Sencha Touch.
- Consuming a RESTful Web Service from iOS, illustrating how to retrieve web page data from iOS.
- Enabling Cross Origin Requests for a RESTful Web Service, illustrating how to create a RESTful web service with Spring that support Cross-Origin Resource Sharing (CORS).
- Using WebSocket and msgs.js to build an interactive web application, illustrating how to the send and receive messages between a browser and the server over a WebSocket using msgs.js

Spring 4 tutorials were designed to be completed in 2-3 hours. In contrast with the guides listed above, the tutorials provide deeper, in-context explorations of enterprise application development topics. As of this writing, Spring 4 tutorials include:

- Designing and Implementing RESTful Web Services with Spring, illustrating how to design and implement RESTful web services with Spring
- Data Access with Spring, illustrating to use multiple data stores to persist and retrieve data with Spring
- Designing and Implementing a Web Application with Spring, illustrating how to design and implement a web app with Spring

If you have gone through this book already, you should find that many of the guides and tutorials are so familiar and so easy to understand now. Next, let us have a tour on Spring documentations.

A.2 SPRING DOCUMENTATIONS

With Spring 3, all documentations, including frameworks, security, etc., are located at http://www.springsource.org/documentation. For Spring4, docs are located at http://spring.io/docs . Figure A.1 shows all Spring projects as of this writing. By clicking on a project, you will have an option to view the Reference documentation or API documentation. For example, if you are interested in the Spring 4 Framework reference and/or API documentation, click on the Spring Framework project link and make your selection accordingly.

Spring Projects

Spring AMQP	Spring for Android
Spring Batch	Spring Data JPA
Spring Data Commons	Spring Data JDBC Extensions
Spring Data MongoDB	Spring Data Neo4J
Spring Data Redis	Spring Data REST
Spring Data Solr	Spring Flex
Spring Framework	Spring Data GemFire
Spring for Apache Hadoop	Spring HATEOAS
Spring Integration	Spring LDAP
Spring Mobile	Spring Roo
Spring Security	Spring Security OAuth
Spring Shell	Spring Social
Spring Social Facebook	Spring Social Twitter
Spring Web Flow	Spring Web Services
Spring Data JDBC Extensions	

Figure A.1 All Spring 4 projects as of this writing

A.3 SPRING COMMUNITY DOWNLOADS

With Spring 3, the community downloads page is at http://www.springsource.org/download/community. From there you could download the jars you're interested in. Spring 4 no longer provides such community downloads. Instead, you have to use Maven to configure your project dependencies. The website http://spring.io/projects has some instructions about how to configure Spring dependencies with Maven or Gradle. For this reason, I have removed the Ant-based approach to building SOBA from this version of the book. Whether you like it or not, you should get used to use Maven to build your Spring or other projects, as that's the moving trend anyway.

Appendix B Creating the SOBA Database

Before you start, you need to choose a relational database platform to host the SOBA database. I have tested the SOBA sample on MySQL, PostgreSQL, SQL Server 2012 SP1 and Oracle 11g R2, and any one of those should work. However, unless you have a specific interest in SQL Server or Oracle, I would recommend either MySQL or PostgreSQL, as these two leading open-source database platforms are of enterprise-class in performance and scalability and run both on Windows and on Linux. Whatever you choose, this appendix helps you create the SOBA database you need in no time.

Let us start with MySQL next.

B.1 Setting up the SOBA Database on MySQL

If you are new to MySQL, here is a brief and quick guide to helping you get familiar with it in a matter of hours, assuming that you have some minimum knowledge and experience in at least another commonly used database system. To make it relevant and easy, we will go in two sections. In the first section, I'll help you set up a MySQL environment and learn how to perform some of the routine tasks such as starting/stopping/restarting MySQL, and how to interact with MySQL, etc. In the second section, I'll show you how to set up the SOBA database in order to work with the sample application introduced in this book.

Let us start with how to set up a MySQL environment on Windows next (if you choose to work .

B.1.1 Setting up a MySQL Environment on Windows

Setting up a MySQL environment starts with downloading a proper version of MySQL. In our case, we use the community version of MySQL 5.5.22 available from http://dev.mysql.com/downloads/ (note that Oracle acquired MySQL in January 2010 and made it commercial with enhanced features). Click on the link of *MySQL Community Server* and select the proper version (in my case with a Windows 7 desktop, I selected Windows (x86, 64-bit) MSI Installer or the file *mysql-5.5.22-win64.msi*).

Next, download MySQL Workbench 5.2.38 (Windows (x86, 32-bit), MSI Installer, file *mysql-workbench-gpl-5.2.38-win32.msi*) as well as the JDBC driver or connector *mysql-connector-java-5.1.19.zip* for JDBC connections.

To start installing MySQL, double-click the downloaded msi installer and keep clicking until you are asked to choose a setup type. The remaining steps are as follows:

- Select *Typical* and then click *Install*. Note that you may need to check if there are Windows User Account Control pop-ups waiting for you to click *Yes* or *No*.
- Click *Next* on the MySQL Enterprise screen.
- Click *Next* on the MySQL Enterprise Monitor Service screen and then click *Finish*.
- Now you should be greeted with the *MySQL Server Instance Configuration Wizard*. Click *Next*.
- Select *Standard Configuration* since we are interested in a general-purpose configuration. Click *Next*.
- Keep all default settings of *Install As Windows Service*, *Service Name MySQL*, and *Launch the MySQL Server* automatically. Also, check the box for *Include Bin Directory in Windows PATH*. Click *Next*.
- Enter the root password and put it down as you will need it later when configuring SOBA to connect to MySQL. In my case, I used *MySql5522* for the root password. Click *Next*.
- Click *Execute*. Then click *Finish* to close the Wizard.
- Now you should see MySQL running from your Windows Services snap-in.

Next, let's install the MySQL Workbench. After starting up the installer for MySQL Workbench, keep clicking until you are greeted with the *Setup Type* screen. Select *Complete* and click *Next*. Then click *Yes* on the *User Account Control* pop-up and finish the installation. Then you should be greeted with the MySQL Workbench GUI as shown in Figure B.1.1. Close it now and I'll walk you through it later.

Now you should unzip the connector zip file to any folder of your choice, since we need to copy this driver jar file *mysql-connector-java-5.1.19-bin.jar* to the proper folders of your Eclipse and Tomcat installations as discussed in Chapter 2. Alternatively, you can find this jar file in the folder named *extras* from your SOBA download from this book's website.

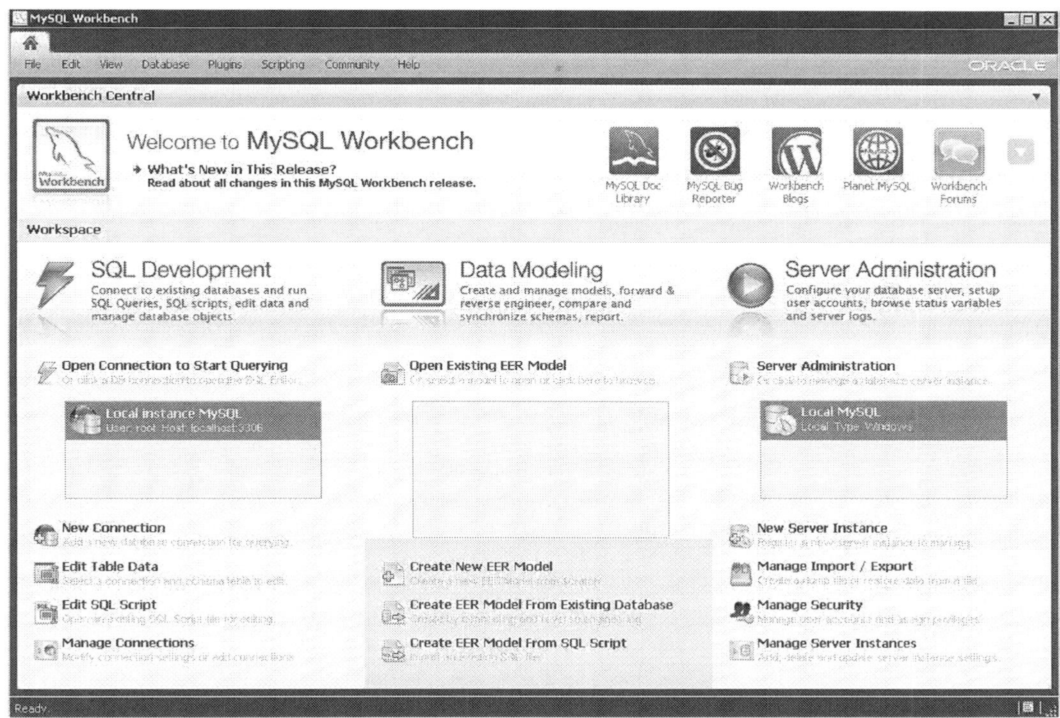

Figure B.1.1 MySQL Workbench console after initial installation

B.1.2 CREATING SOBA DATABASE ON MYSQL

Now start up the MySQL 5.5 *Command Line Client* from Windows *Start* … or open a DOS command line prompt and cd to `C:\Program Files\MySQL\MySQL Server 5.5\bin` if the MySQL *bin* folder is not on your Windows PATH. At this point, you can create the SOBA MySQL database by executing the `create_soba_mysql.sql` script as shown below (make sure *mysql* is on your bin path and replace the path with your own to the SQL script contained in the *soba_db_scripts/mysql* folder of your SOBA download):

```
cmd>mysql -h 127.0.0.1 -u root -p < create_soba_mysql.sql
```

Now when prompted, enter the root password for MySQL you entered when installing MySQL at the step described in the previous section.

Alternatively, you can execute the command `mysql -h 127.0.0.1 -u root -p`, enter your root password, and you should be greeted with the `mysql>` prompt. Then, execute each statement as shown in Listing B.1.1 to create an empty SOBA MySQL database.

At this point, you should see that the `soba` database has been created, along with four other pre-existing databases of `information_schema`, `mysql`, `performance_schema`, and `test`.

Listing B.1.1 create_soba_mysql.sql

```
create database soba;
grant usage on *.* to sobaadmin@localhost identified by 'sobaadmin';
grant all privileges on soba.* to sobaadmin@localhost;
show databases;
```

If you need to delete this database and user, simply execute the commands:

```
Mysql> drop database soba;
Mysql> drop user sobaadmin;
```

Now start up the MySQL Workbench from Windows *All Programs* …. You should now see three components from left to right: *SQL Development*, *Data Modeling*, and *Server Administration*, as shown in Figure B.1.1 illustrated previously. Double-click on the *Local MySQL* icon in the *Server Administration* section, enter your root password, and you should see the Server MySQL Admin Console, allowing you to view *Server Status*, manage security, perform startup/shutdown and export/import tasks, and change options for performance tuning purposes, and so on. This is your one-stop shop for performing all kinds of administrative tasks with MySQL.

Next, go back to the *Home* screen and in the *SQL Development* section, click the *New Connection* link and create a new connection named *sobaadmin* as shown in Figure B.1.2 (note the default TCP port of 3306 and you will need this to configure access to MySql when you configure SOBA later on Eclipse). You should click the *Test Connection button* and make sure that testing connection is successful as shown in Figure B.1.3. Now double click the newly created connection, enter the password for the *sobaadmin* user, and you should see an area that allows you to enter and execute SQLs. On the left side, you should see the *soba* schema created for the SOBA database (at this point, it is empty).

Next, follow the procedure below to create the soba database objects on your MySQL. First, open up a DOS command prompt and cd to the folder that contains all SOBA db scripts for MySQL downloadable from the download link provided with this book. Then make sure the access path to *mysql.exe* is added to your path environment variable or precede it with the access path "`C:\Program Files\MySQL\MySQL Server 5.5\bin`," which is where *mysql.exe* is located in my case.

Then execute the `create_all.sql` script as shown below to create all SOBA schema objects in MySQL. See Listing B.1.2 for the contents of this SQL script to be executed.

```
cmd>mysql soba -h 127.0.0.1 -u sobaadmin -p < create_all.sql
```

There also is a script named `drop_all.sql` included in the download that you can use to drop all objects from executing the script `create_all.sql` as described in the preceding step. Refer to that script for the actual drop statements if you are interested in them.

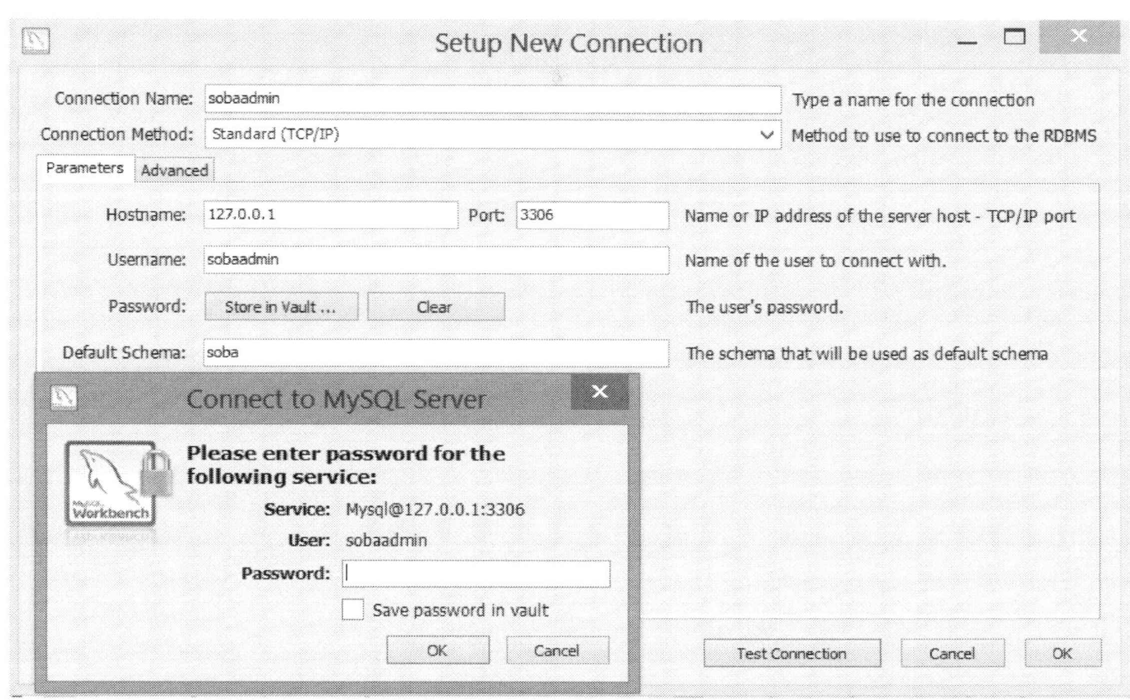

Figure B.1.2 MySQL: setting up a new connection

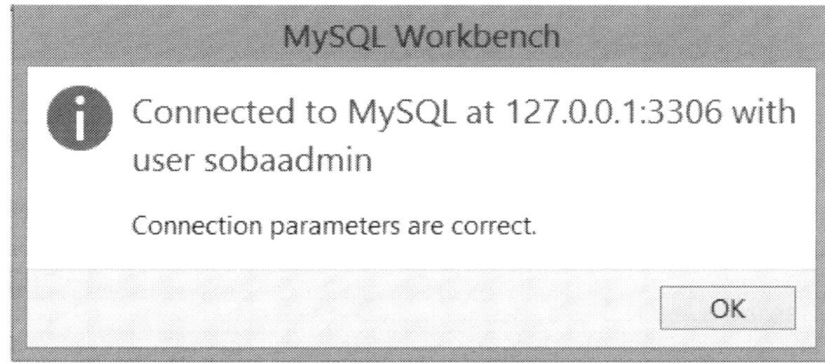

Figure B.1.3 Testing connection successful

Listing B.1.2 create_all.sql

```
source create_customer.sql
source create_account.sql
source create_banking_tx.sql
```

```
source create_loginuser.sql
source create_transfer.sql
source create_bill_payment.sql
source create_statement.sql
source create_activity_view.sql
source create_acl.sql
source create_users_view.sql
source create_authorities.sql
source create_func_compute_balance.sql
source create_func_random_string.sql
source create_index_tx_account_id_trans_date_ix.sql
source create_trigger_user_auth.sql
source create_trigger_account_balance_update.sql
source create_test_users.sql
```

B.1.3 EXPORTING AND IMPORTING SOBA DATABASE

At some point, you might want to back up or restore your SOBA database from a dump. Execute the following command to create a dump:

```
cmd> mysqldump --user=sobaadmin --password=sobaadmin --databases soba
>yourDump.sql
```

To restore from a dump, execute the following command:

```
cmd> mysql --verbose --user=sobaadmin --password=sobaadmin soba
<yourDump.sql
```

Now return to Chapter 2 and continue to configure the SOBA sample application with MySQL.

This appendix is brief, but it should give you all you need to get around with MySQL for SOBA.

B.2 SETTING UP THE SOBA DATABASE ON POSTGRESQL

Setting up the SOBA database on PostgreSQL is easy. This section describes how to set up the SOBA database on PostgreSQL on Windows and on Linux.

B.2.1 POSTGRESQL ON WINDOWS

I first downloaded the latest version of PostgreSQL on Windows named *postgresql-9.3.2-1-windows-x64.exe*, which has the admin GUI named pgAdmin III bundled as well. To install it, double click the image file and keep clicking until the Stack Builder 3.1 screen pops up. As we don't need to install any additional tools, close it to finish the installation process.

Then, execute the following the following command to create the SOBA database schema named '*soba*' with username/password = sobaadmin/sobaadmin:

```
cmd>psql -h localhost -U postgres -f create_soba_psql.sql
```

Then, create the SOBA database objects with the following command by entering "*sobaadmin*" for the password prompted:

```
cmd>psql -h localhost -U sobaadmin -d soba -f create_all.sql
```

Finally, start up the pgAdmin III GUI. Select *File*, and then *Add Server* to register the server to the Admin GUI. As is shown in Figure B.2.1, the *Service* entry should be left blank. Enter all other entries as indicated and then click OK. Now, verify against Figure B.2.2 for the SOBA database objects created (2 functions, 4 sequences, 12 tables, 2 triggers, and 2 views).

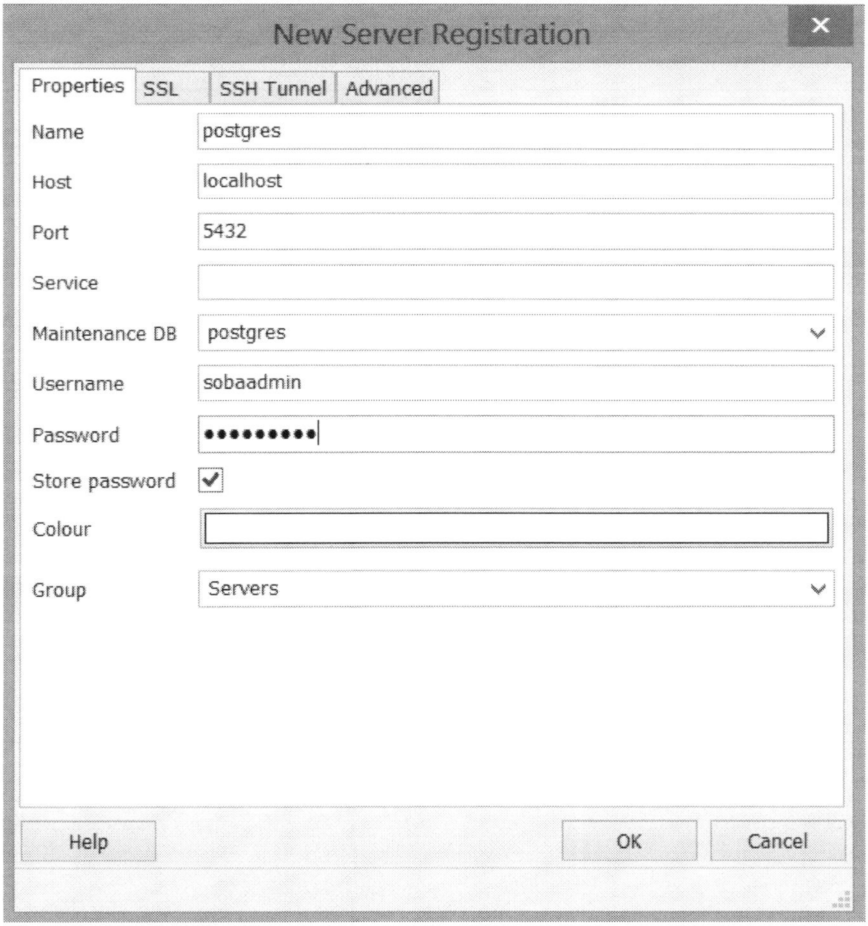

Figure B.2.1 PostgreSQL new server registration on pgAdmin Console

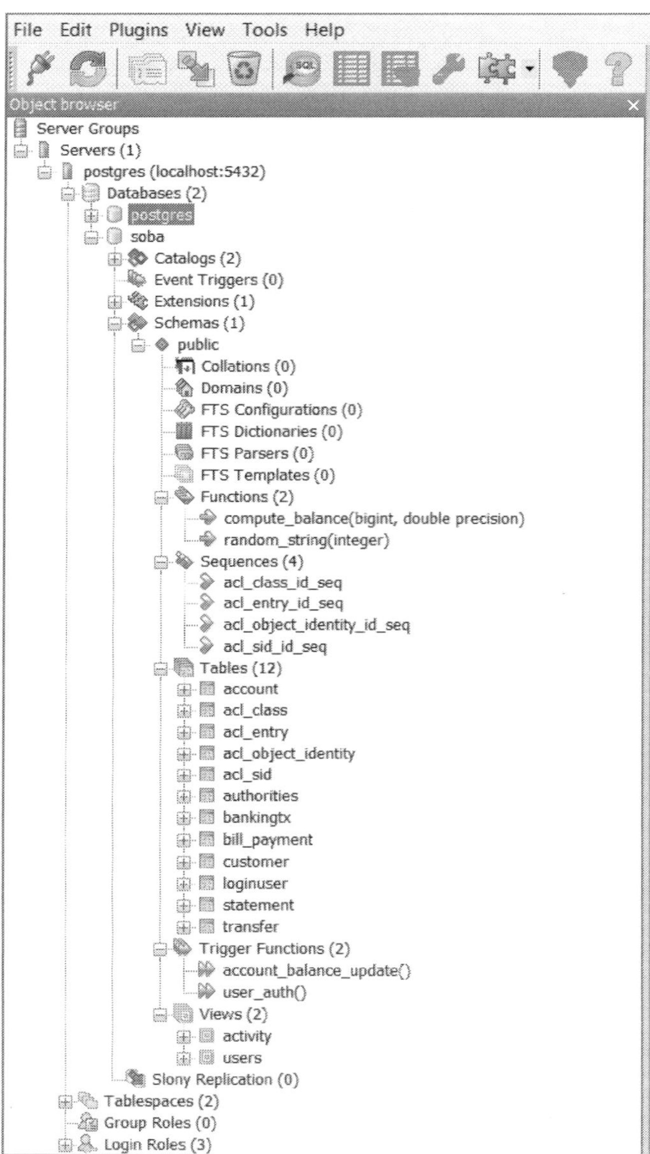

Figure B.2.2 SOBA database objects created on PostgreSQL

B.2.2 POSTGRESQL ON LINUX

The utility for installing PostgreSQL on Linux differs from vendor to vendor. Here is a summary on what utility to use on a given Linux OS such as Red Hat, SuSE, and Ubuntu:

- Red Hat: yum
- SuSE: zypper
- Ubuntu: apt-get

Next, I use SuSE to demonstrate how to set up SOBA database on Linux. The procedure is described as follows:

1 Installing PostgreSQL: sudo zypper install postgresql-server
2 Starting/stopping PostgreSQL: sudo /etc/init.d/postgresql [start|stop]
3 Installing pgadmin3: sudo zypper install pgadmin3
4 Changing password for user postgres:
$sudo su –
$passwd postgres (then enter postgres for the password)
5 Creating soba db (replace <ip> your server's ip):
$sudo psql –h <ip> –U postgres –f create_soba_psql.sql
6 Creating SOBA database objects with <ip> replaced with your server ip:
$sudo psql –h <ip> –d soba –U sobaadmin –f create_all.sql

If you want to connect pgAdmin GUI from Windows to your PostgreSQL on Linux, you need to make some changes to two files. First, add the following lines in /var/lib/pgsql/data/pg_hba.conf:

- host all all 192.168.0.18/32 trust
- host all all 192.168.0.0/24 md5

The "trust" line is for enabling connecting to the postgres db server with the specified IP remotely through pgadmin3 on Windows, while the "md5" line is for setting authentication for connecting from pgadmin3 on Windows that sits on the same subnet of 192.168.x.x.

Then, add the following line in /var/lib/pgsql/data/postgresql.conf

listen_addresses = '*'

To reload, execute: etc/init.d/postgresql reload

Now you can add your PostgreSQL server on Linux to your pgAdmin III GUI on Windows by entering proper entries as shown in Figure B.2.1 (enter the Linux server IP in the host box). If you get a connection error, most likely, you need to stop Firewall service on your Linux server.

B.3 SETTING UP THE SOBA DATABASE ON SQL SERVER 2012

If you are new to Microsoft SQL Server, here is a brief guide to help you get familiar with it quickly, assuming that you have some minimum knowledge and experience in at least another commonly used database system. To make it relevant and easy, we will go in two sections. In the first section, I'll help you set up a SQL Server 2012 environment and learn how to perform some of the routine tasks such as starting/stopping/restarting SQL Server 2012, and how to interact with it, etc. In the second section, I'll show you how to set up the SOBA database in order to work with the sample application introduced in this book.

B.3.1 SETTING UP A SQL SERVER 2012 ENVIRONMENT

First, download the SQL Server 2012 Express software named ENY\x64\SQLEXPWT-x64_ENU.exe, and then double-click it to kick off the installation. Keep clicking until you get to choosing SQL Server Feature Installation option. The remaining steps are as follows:

- Select *SQL Server Feature Installation* and then click *Next*. Select all default features. Click *Next* until you get to *Instance Configuration*. Select all default settings and keep clicking Next until:
- At the *Database Engine Configuration* screen, select *Mixed Mode* for the *sa* user.
- Continue and finish the installation.

Now you should see SQL Server 2012 (SQLEXPRESS) running from your Windows Services snap-in.

Next, startup SQL Server Configuration Manager from *Start -> All Programs -> Microsoft SQL Server 2012 -> Configuration Tools -> SQL Server Configuration Manager*. Click *SQL Server Network Configuration -> Protocols*. On the right-hand-side, select *TCP/IP* (make sure it's enabled). Right-click on it and select *Properties* and then *IP Addresses* tab. Scroll down to the bottom and under `IPAll`, you should see *TCP Dynamic Ports*. Put down the port # ('`58600`' in my case) and you'll need this when you configure the sample application to connect to your SQL Server.

Now you can start up the *Microsoft SQL Server Management Studio* and connect to your instance. This is your one-stop shop to interact with your SQL Server both for administrative tasks and SQL query executions.

B.3.2 CREATING SOBA DATABASE ON SQL SERVER 2012

Follow the procedure below to create the SOBA database on your SQL Server 2012 instance. First, open up a DOS command prompt and cd to the folder that contains all db scripts for SQL Server 2012 downloadable from the download link provided with this book. Then make sure the access path to *sqlcmd.exe* is added to your path environment variable or precede it with the access path "`C:\Program Files\Microsoft SQL Server\110\Tools\Binn`," which is where *sqlcmd.exe* is located. Then execute the following command to create the SOBA database. See Listing B.3.1 provided below for the contents of this SQL script to be executed.

```
cmd>sqlcmd -S LOCALHOST\SQLEXPRESS -U sa -P <your password> -i
create_sobadb_ss2k12.sql
```

Listing B.3.1 create_sobadb_ss2k12.sql

```
CREATE DATABASE soba;
GO
CREATE LOGIN sobaadmin
   WITH PASSWORD = 'sobaadmin',
   DEFAULT_DATABASE = soba;
USE soba;
GO
CREATE USER sobaadmin FOR LOGIN sobaadmin;
GO
EXEC sp_addrolemember 'db_owner', 'sobaadmin';
```

GO

Then execute the `create_all.bat` script to create all SOBA database objects. Before doing so, make sure you have replaced all `<server>\<instance>` entries in this script to match your settings. See Listing B.3.2 for the contents of `create_all.bat`.

Listing B.3.2 create_all.bat

```
sqlcmd -S localhost\SQLEXPRESS -U sobaadmin -P sobaadmin -i create_customer.sql
sqlcmd -S localhost\SQLEXPRESS -U sobaadmin -P sobaadmin -i create_account.sql
sqlcmd -S localhost\SQLEXPRESS -U sobaadmin -P sobaadmin -i create_banking_tx.sql
sqlcmd -S localhost\SQLEXPRESS -U sobaadmin -P sobaadmin -i create_loginuser.sql
sqlcmd -S localhost\SQLEXPRESS -U sobaadmin -P sobaadmin -i create_transfer.sql
sqlcmd -S localhost\SQLEXPRESS -U sobaadmin -P sobaadmin -i create_bill_payment.sql
sqlcmd -S localhost\SQLEXPRESS -U sobaadmin -P sobaadmin -i create_statement.sql
sqlcmd -S localhost\SQLEXPRESS -U sobaadmin -P sobaadmin -i create_activity_view.sql
sqlcmd -S localhost\SQLEXPRESS -U sobaadmin -P sobaadmin -i create_acl_ss.sql
sqlcmd -S localhost\SQLEXPRESS -U sobaadmin -P sobaadmin -i create_Users_view.sql
sqlcmd -S localhost\SQLEXPRESS -U sobaadmin -P sobaadmin -i create_authorities.sql
sqlcmd -S localhost\SQLEXPRESS -U sobaadmin -P sobaadmin -i
  create_func_compute_balance.sql
sqlcmd -S localhost\SQLEXPRESS -U sobaadmin -P sobaadmin -i create_trigger_user_auth.sql
sqlcmd -S localhost\SQLEXPRESS -U sobaadmin -P sobaadmin -i
   create_index_tx_account_id_trans_date_ix.sql
```

There is also a script named `drop_all.sql` that you can use to undo the effects from executing the `create_all.bat` script executed in the preceding step.

Now return to Chapter 2 of this book on how to configure the sample application with SQL Server 2012.

B.4 SETTING UP THE SOBA DATABASE ON ORACLE 11G R2

For Oracle 11g R2, the installation and configuration procedure is omitted here. If you are familiar with Oracle, follow the procedure below to create the SOBA database on your Oracle 11g R2 instance.

First, open up a DOS command prompt and cd to the folder that contains all db scripts for Oracle 11g R2 from the download link provided with this book. Then make sure the access path to *sqlplus.exe* is added to your path environment variable or precede it with the proper access path. See Listings B.4.1 and B.4.2 provided below for the contents of each SQL script to be executed (note that you need to replace the path to the data files with your own).

```
cmd>sqlplus sys/<password>@<connect_string> as sysdba
```

Then at the sqlplus command prompt, run:

```
@create_soba_tablespaces.sql
@create _soba_schema_user.sql
```

Listing B.4.1 create_soba_tablespaces.sql

```
CREATE TABLESPACE OnlineBanking DATAFILE 'D:\oradata\ora11gr2a\olbnk01.dbf' SIZE 50M EXTENT
MANAGEMENT LOCAL SEGMENT SPACE MANAGEMENT AUTO;

CREATE TEMPORARY TABLESPACE OBTemp TEMPFILE 'D:\oradata\ora11gr2a\obtemp01.dbf' SIZE 20M
REUSE EXTENT MANAGEMENT LOCAL UNIFORM SIZE 2M;
```

Listing B.4.2 create_soba_schema_user.sql

```
CREATE USER sobaadmin identified by sobaadmin DEFAULT TABLESPACE OnlineBanking TEMPORARY
TABLESPACE OBTemp;
GRANT CONNECT, RESOURCE to sobaadmin;
GRANT SELECT ANY DICTIONARY to sobaadmin;
GRANT CREATE VIEW TO sobaadmin;
GRANT CREATE SYNONYM TO sobaadmin;
```

Then login with `sobaadmin/sobaadmin` and run `create_all.sql` script shown in Listing B.4.3.

Listing B.4.3 create_all.sql

```
@@create_customer.sql
@@create_account.sql
@@create_banking_tx.sql
@@create_loginuser.sql
@@create_transfer.sql
@@create_bill_payment.sql
@@create_statement.sql
@@create_activity_view.sql
@@create_acl.sql
@@create_synonym_users.sql
@@create_authorities.sql
@@create_trigger_account_balance_update.sql
@@create_trigger_user_auth.sql
@@create_func_compute_balance.sql
@@create_func_random_string.sql
@@create_seq.sql
@@create_index_tx_account_id_trans_date_ix.sql
```

Now return to Chapter 2 of this book on how to configure the sample application with Oracle 11g R2.

Appendix C A Simpler Sample Built with Spring, Hibernate, MySQL and Maven 3

In this Appendix, I show you how to build a generic enterprise Web application with Spring, Hibernate, MySQL and Maven 3. Compared with SOBA, this is a lighter-weight, Spring MVC based, mini sample, simulating a *Notes Manager* application that would allow a user to add, view and delete notes. We care much less about its functionality for obvious reasons. By creating such an application yourself, you would learn:

- How to create an enterprise Web application with Maven from scratch to help bootstrap your project.
- A bare-minimum skeleton of a Spring MVC based enterprise application that you can expand and solidify to suit your own particular needs.

I assume that you have gone through all previous parts of this text, or at least cursorily, so that you don't need a detailed explanation about every step we go. Let's get started with building this sample with Maven 3 next.

C.1 Creating the Sample Database

Execute the following two SQL scripts on MySQL to create the `mydb` database and the `mynote` table for this sample.

```
Cmd>mysql –h 127.0.0.1 –u root –p < create_mydb.sql
Cmd>mysql mydb –h 127.0.0.1 –u mydbadmin –p <createMyNote.sql
```

See Listings C.1 and C.2 for the contents of these two scripts. The first script creates a `mydb` database with a user named `mydbadmin` whose password is also `mydbadmin`. The sample application will use these credentials to access the `mydb` database. The second script creates a table against the `mydb` database, which has seven attributes of id, username, password, category, subject, content, and created. The last field has the type of TIMESTAMP, which records the time when a note is created. We'll see how this type is annotated in Hibernate later.

Listing C.1 create_mydb.sql

```
create database mydb;
grant usage on *.* to mydbadmin@localhost identified by 'mydbadmin';
grant all privileges on mydb.* to mydbadmin@localhost;
show databases;
```

Listing C.2 createMyNote.sql

```
CREATE TABLE MYNOTE (
id          INT PRIMARY KEY AUTO_INCREMENT,
username    VARCHAR(12),
password    VARCHAR (8),
category    VARCHAR(20),
subject     VARCHAR(30),
content     VARCHAR(500),
created     TIMESTAMP DEFAULT NOW() );
```

C.2 CREATING THE SAMPLE WITH MAVEN

First, cd to your Eclipse workspace folder. Then, execute the following command to create the sample application (the entire command should be in one line).

```
cmd>mvn archetype:generate -DgroupId=com.perfmath.spring.mn
-DartifactId=MyNotes -DarchetypeArtifactId=maven-archetype-webapp
```

Creating this empty project may actually take some time. When asked to enter a number, enter a number like '6' (we will need to customize it a lot later anyway). For groupId, artifactId, package, enter com.perfmath.spring.mn, MyNotes, <empty>, respectively. Now you should have a project named MyNotes created with a structure similar to Figure C.1.

The next step is to convert this webapp into an Eclipse structure. First, cd to the MyNotes folder that has a pom.xml file in it. Then, issue the command "mvn eclipse:eclipse" and wait for a while until it is done. You should now see an output message of "BUILD SUCCESFUL".

Now on your Eclipse IDE, select *File->Import->Existing Maven Projects -> Next*. Select MyNotes as your root directory and complete importing. You should see a project structure similar to Figure C.2. Not surprisingly, it doesn't have much yet, but it's sufficient for bootstrapping your project. Now download the sample MyNotes project from this book's support website at http://www.perfmath.com/download.htm and unzip it to somewhere on your system. Create the dummy artifacts as described in the next few sections to pretend that you were creating your own. Then, replace those dummies with their downloaded counterparts (or you could simply import the entire downloaded project if you do not want to go through the hassle of repeating so many redundant tasks, since you already know how a real one of your own would be created).

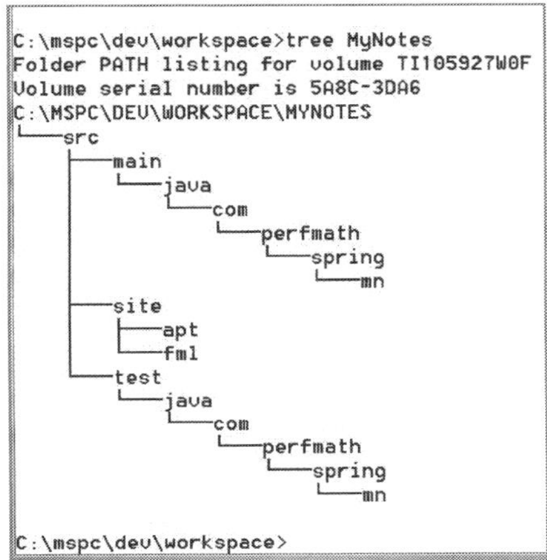

Figure C.1 An initial project structure created with Maven 3

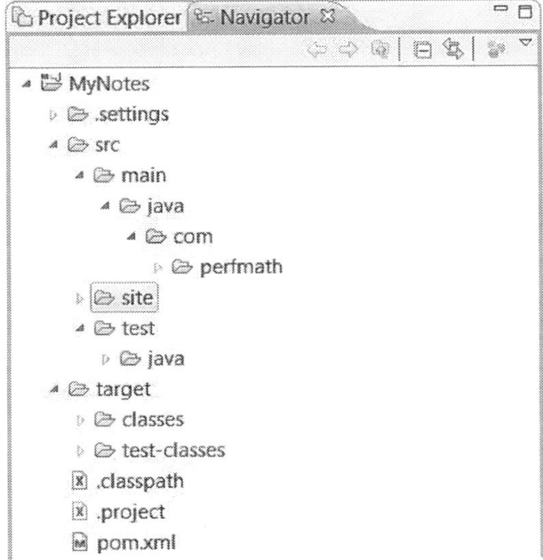

Figure C.2 Initial MyNotes structure on Eclipse

C.2.1 Creating Java Classes

This section creates all Java classes required for this sample in the directory of `src/main/java`.

- Create `Note.java` in the package of `com.perfmath.spring.mn.model.domain`. This is the `command` class in Spring that corresponds to the table `MYNOTE` in MySQL. See Listing C.3 for the contents of this class.
- Create the `NoteDAO.java` and `NoteDAOImpl.java` classes in the package of `com.perfmath.spring.mn.model.dao`. These are the DAO interface and its implementation class for this sample. See Listings C.4 (a) and (b) for the contents of this interface and its implementation class.
- Create the `NoteService.java` interface and `NoteServiceImpl.java` class in the package of `com.perfmath.spring.mn.service`. These are the service interface and implementation class for this sample. See Listings C.5 (a) and (b) for the contents of this interface and its implementation class.
- Create the `NoteController.java` class in the package of `com.perfmath.spring.mn.web`. This is the frontend controller that handles all incoming requests for managing all notes related operations like *create*, *delete*, etc. See Listing C.6 for the contents of this class.
- Create the `LoginController.java` class in the package of `com.perfmath.spring.mn.web`. We need this controller to emulate a user login process so that notes are accessed based on preset user login credentials. See Listing C.7 for the contents of this class. However, keep in mind that this is for demo purposes only. The main sample SOBA shows how authentication with a real application should be implemented.

C.2.2 Creating Java Resources

This section creates all resources required for this sample in the directory of `src/main/resources`, which should be added manually on your Eclipse IDE.

- Create the `hibernate.cfg.xml` file for specifying Hibernate configurations later. See Listing C.8 for the contents of this file.
- Create the `messages_en.properties` file for specifying the labels in the `note.jsp` file to be created later. See Listing C.9 for the contents of this file.

C. 2.3 Creating WebApp Resources

This section creates all webapp resources required for this sample in the directory of `src/main/webapp`, which should be added manually on your Eclipse IDE.

- Create the `login.jsp` file, which is the entry point for this sample. See Listing C.10 for the contents of this file. We discuss more about the logic associated with this jsp file later.
- Create the `WEB-INF` folder and the following files in it:
  - The `web.xml` file: See Listing C.11 for the contents of this file.
  - The `mn-servlet.xml` file: See Listing C.12 for the contents of this file.
  - The `jdbc.properties` file: See Listing C.13 for the contents of this file. You need to modify this file to point to your own MySQL.
  - The `jsp` folder and the `note.jsp` file in it: See Listing C.14 for the contents of this file.

Listing C.15 shows the contents of the `pom.xml` file. These are all we need for this sample application. Whether you imported all files or manually replaced all dummies as created above with their counterparts downloaded, their contents should be the same or similar to those shown in Listings C.3 through C.15. The next section summarizes some of the implementation highlights of this sample.

Listing C.3 Note.java

```
package com.perfmath.spring.mn.model.domain;
import java.util.Date;
import javax.persistence.Column;
import javax.persistence.Entity;
import javax.persistence.GeneratedValue;
import javax.persistence.Id;
import javax.persistence.Table;
import javax.persistence.Temporal;
import javax.persistence.TemporalType;

@Entity
@Table(name="MYNOTE")
public class Note {

    @Id
    @Column(name="ID")
    @GeneratedValue
    private Integer id;

    @Column(name="USERNAME")
    private String username;
    @Column(name="PASSWORD")
    private String password;
    @Column(name="CATEGORY")
    private String category;
    @Column(name="SUBJECT")
    private String subject;
    @Column(name="CONTENT")
    private String content;
    @Temporal(TemporalType.TIMESTAMP)
    @Column(name="CREATED")
    private Date created;

    // getters and setters omitted
}
```

Listing C.4 (a) NoteDAO.java

```
package com.perfmath.spring.mn.model.dao;
import java.util.List;
import com.perfmath.spring.mn.model.domain.Note;
public interface NoteDAO {
    public void addNote(Note note);
    public List<Note> listNote();
    public void removeNote(Integer id);
public List<Note> checkLogin(String username,  String password);
    public List<Note> listNoteByUser(String username);
}
```

Listing C.4 (b) NoteDAOImpl.java

```
package com.perfmath.spring.mn.model.dao;

import java.util.List;

import org.hibernate.SessionFactory;
import org.springframework.beans.factory.annotation.Autowired;
import org.springframework.stereotype.Repository;
import org.slf4j.Logger;
import org.slf4j.LoggerFactory;

import com.perfmath.spring.mn.model.domain.Note;

@Repository
public class NoteDAOImpl implements NoteDAO {

    @Autowired
    private SessionFactory sessionFactory;
    private static final Logger log = LoggerFactory.getLogger(NoteDAOImpl.class);
    public List<Note> listNote() {
         long startTime = System.nanoTime();
        List<Note> notes =  sessionFactory.getCurrentSession().createQuery
            ("from Note") .list();
        log.info("listNote() " + (System.nanoTime() - startTime)/1000
            + " microseconds");
        return notes;
        }
    public void addNote(Note note) {
         long startTime = System.nanoTime();
            sessionFactory.getCurrentSession().save(note);
            log.info("saveNote() " + (System.nanoTime() - startTime)/1000
```

```
                + " microseconds");
        }
    public List<Note> checkLogin(String username, String password) {
        long startTime = System.nanoTime();
        List<Note> notes = sessionFactory.getCurrentSession().createQuery
            ("from Note " + " where username = '" + username + "' and password = '"
            + password + "'").list();
            log.info("saveNote() " + (System.nanoTime() - startTime)/1000 + "
                microseconds");
            return notes;
        }
    public List<Note> listNoteByUser(String username) {
        long startTime = System.nanoTime();
        List<Note> notes = sessionFactory.getCurrentSession().createQuery
            ("from Note " + " where username = '" + username + "'").list();
            log.info("saveNote() " + (System.nanoTime() - startTime)/1000
                + " microseconds");
            return notes;
        }
    public void removeNote(Integer id) {
        Note note = (Note) sessionFactory.getCurrentSession().load(
                Note.class, id);
        if (null != note) {
            sessionFactory.getCurrentSession().delete(note);
        }
    }
}
```

Listing C.5 (a) NoteService.java

```
package com.perfmath.spring.mn.service;
import java.util.List;
import com.perfmath.spring.mn.model.domain.Note;
public interface NoteService {
    public void addNote(Note note);
    public List<Note> checkLogin(String username, String password);
    public List<Note> listNoteByUser(String username);
    public List<Note> listNote();
    public void removeNote(Integer id);
}
```

Listing C.5 (b) NoteServiceImpl.java

```
package com.perfmath.spring.mn.service;
import java.util.List;
import org.springframework.beans.factory.annotation.Autowired;
import org.springframework.stereotype.Service;
import org.springframework.transaction.annotation.Transactional;
import com.perfmath.spring.mn.model.dao.NoteDAO;
import com.perfmath.spring.mn.model.domain.Note;
@Service
public class NoteServiceImpl implements NoteService {
    @Autowired
    private NoteDAO noteDAO;

    @Transactional
    public void addNote(Note note) {
        noteDAO.addNote(note);
    }
    @Transactional
    public List<Note> listNote() {
        return noteDAO.listNote();
    }
    @Transactional
    public List<Note> checkLogin(String username, String password) {
        return noteDAO.checkLogin(username, password);
    }
    @Transactional
    public List<Note> listNoteByUser(String username) {
        return noteDAO.listNoteByUser(username);
    }
    @Transactional
    public void removeNote(Integer id) {
        noteDAO.removeNote(id);
    }
}
```

Listing C.6 NoteController.java

```
package com.perfmath.spring.mn.web;

import org.springframework.beans.factory.annotation.Autowired;
import org.springframework.stereotype.Controller;
import org.springframework.validation.BindingResult;
import org.springframework.web.bind.annotation.ModelAttribute;
import org.springframework.web.bind.annotation.PathVariable;
```

```
import org.springframework.web.bind.annotation.RequestMapping;
import org.springframework.web.bind.annotation.RequestMethod;
import org.springframework.web.servlet.ModelAndView;

import com.perfmath.spring.mn.model.domain.Note;
import com.perfmath.spring.mn.service.CreateNoteValidator;
import com.perfmath.spring.mn.service.NoteService;

@Controller
public class NoteController {

    @Autowired
    private NoteService noteService;

    @RequestMapping(value = "/createNote/username/{username}",
        method = RequestMethod.POST)
    public ModelAndView createNote(@PathVariable("username")
    String username, @ModelAttribute("note")
    Note note, BindingResult result) {
        System.out.println ("execute createNote");
        note.setUsername(username);
        ModelAndView mav = new ModelAndView ();
        new CreateNoteValidator().validate (note, result);
        if (!result.hasErrors ()) {
        noteService.addNote(note);
        mav.setViewName ("note"); // to note.jsp
        mav.addObject("username", username);
        mav.addObject("noteList", noteService.listNoteByUser(username));
        }
    return mav;
    }
    @RequestMapping(value = "/delete/username/{username}/noteId/{noteId}")
    public ModelAndView deleteNote(@PathVariable("username")
    String username, @PathVariable("noteId")
    Integer noteId) {
        noteService.removeNote(noteId);
        ModelAndView mav = new ModelAndView ();
        mav.setViewName ("note");
        mav.addObject("username", username);
        mav.addObject("note", new Note ());
        mav.addObject("noteList", noteService.listNoteByUser(username));
    return mav;
    }
```

```
}
```

Listing C.7 LoginController.java

```
package com.perfmath.spring.mn.web;

import java.util.List;

import javax.servlet.http.HttpServletRequest;
import javax.servlet.http.HttpServletResponse;
import org.slf4j.Logger;

import org.springframework.beans.factory.annotation.Autowired;
import org.springframework.stereotype.Controller;

import org.springframework.web.bind.annotation.RequestMapping;
import org.springframework.web.servlet.ModelAndView;
import org.springframework.web.servlet.mvc.AbstractController;

import com.perfmath.spring.mn.model.domain.Note;
import com.perfmath.spring.mn.service.NoteService;

@Controller
public class LoginController extends AbstractController {
    @Autowired
    private NoteService noteService;
    private Logger logger = org.slf4j.LoggerFactory.getLogger(this.getClass());

    @RequestMapping("/loginController")
    protected ModelAndView handleRequestInternal(HttpServletRequest request,
            HttpServletResponse response) throws Exception {
        logger.info("Testing logging from SLF4J ... it works");

        String viewString = "redirect:/"; // redirect to login.jsp
        String username = request.getParameter("username");
        String password = request.getParameter("password");
        List<Note> noteList = noteService.checkLogin(username, password);
        ModelAndView mav = new ModelAndView();
        if (noteList.size() > 0) {
            logger.info("returned " + noteList.size() + " notes for "
                    + username);
            viewString = "note"; // to note.jsp
            mav.addObject("username", username);
```

```
            mav.addObject("noteList", noteService.listNoteByUser(username));
            mav.addObject("note", new Note());
        } else {
            logger.info("User " + username + " login error. Create a user
                account or retry.");
        }
        mav.setViewName(viewString);
        return mav;
    }
}
```

Listing C.8 hibernate.cfg.xml

```
<?xml version='1.0' encoding='utf-8'?>
<!DOCTYPE hibernate-configuration PUBLIC
  "-//Hibernate/Hibernate Configuration DTD//EN"
  "http://hibernate.sourceforge.net/hibernate-configuration-3.0.dtd">
<hibernate-configuration>
  <session-factory>
    <mapping class="com.perfmath.spring.mn.model.domain.Note" />
  </session-factory>
</hibernate-configuration>
```

Listing C.9 messages_en.properties

```
label.subject=Subject
label.created=Created
label.content=Content
label.url=URL
label.addnote=Add Note
label.menu=Menu
label.title=Notes Manager
label.footer=&copy; Perfmath
```

Listing C.10 login.jsp

```
<%@ taglib prefix="c" uri="http://java.sun.com/jsp/jstl/core" %>
<html>
<head>
<title>Login</title>
</head>
<script language="javascript">
function focusOnUsername () {
```

```
    document.loginForm.username.focus();
}
</script>
<body onLoad="focusOnUsername ()"> <center>

<hr>  <br> Please Login ... <br>

<form name="loginForm" method="GET" action="<c:url value="/loginController" />">

<table align="center" width="300" border="7" CELLPADDING="7" CELLSPACING="10"
        BGCOLOR="#C6EFF7">
<th colspan="2" bgcolor="#00184A"><FONT COLOR="#FFFFFF">Please Login ...
        </FONT></th>
 <tr>
  <td >Username: </td>
  <td><input type="text" name="username" /></td>
 </tr>
 <tr>
  <td align="center">Password: </td>
  <td><input type="password" name="password" /></td>
 </tr>
 <tr>
  <td colspan="2" align="center">
   <input type="submit" value="Login" />
   <input type="reset" value="Reset" />
  </td>
 </tr>
</table>
</form>

</center>
<br> <br> <br> <hr>
<table align="center">
</table>
</body>
</html>
```

Listing C.11 web.xml

```
<?xml version="1.0" encoding="UTF-8"?>
<web-app xmlns:xsi="http://www.w3.org/2001/XMLSchema-instance"
xmlns="http://java.sun.com/xml/ns/javaee" xmlns:web="http://java.sun.com/xml/ns/javaee/web-
```

```
app_2_5.xsd" xsi:schemaLocation="http://java.sun.com/xml/ns/javaee
http://java.sun.com/xml/ns/javaee/web-app_2_5.xsd" id="WebApp_ID" version="2.5">
   <display-name>My Notes</display-name>
   <context-param>
          <param-name>webAppRootKey</param-name>
          <param-value>mn.root</param-value>
   </context-param>
   <welcome-file-list>
    <welcome-file>login.jsp</welcome-file>
   </welcome-file-list>
   <servlet>
    <servlet-name>mn</servlet-name>
    <servlet-class>
              org.springframework.web.servlet.DispatcherServlet
          </servlet-class>
    <load-on-startup>1</load-on-startup>
   </servlet>
   <servlet-mapping>
    <servlet-name>mn</servlet-name>
    <url-pattern>/</url-pattern>
   </servlet-mapping>
</web-app>
```

Listing C.12 mn-servlet.xml

```
<?xml  version="1.0" encoding="UTF-8"?>
<beans xmlns="http://www.springframework.org/schema/beans"
      xmlns:xsi="http://www.w3.org/2001/XMLSchema-instance"
      xmlns:aop="http://www.springframework.org/schema/aop"
      xmlns:context="http://www.springframework.org/schema/context"
      xmlns:jee="http://www.springframework.org/schema/jee"
      xmlns:lang="http://www.springframework.org/schema/lang"
      xmlns:p="http://www.springframework.org/schema/p"
      xmlns:tx="http://www.springframework.org/schema/tx"
      xmlns:util="http://www.springframework.org/schema/util"
      xsi:schemaLocation="http://www.springframework.org/schema/beans
http://www.springframework.org/schema/beans/spring-beans.xsd
http://www.springframework.org/schema/aop http://www.springframework.org/schema/aop/spring-
aop.xsd
http://www.springframework.org/schema/context
http://www.springframework.org/schema/context/spring-context.xsd
http://www.springframework.org/schema/jee http://www.springframework.org/schema/jee/spring-
jee.xsd
```

```
http://www.springframework.org/schema/lang http://www.springframework.org/schema/lang/spring-lang.xsd
http://www.springframework.org/schema/tx http://www.springframework.org/schema/tx/spring-tx.xsd
http://www.springframework.org/schema/util http://www.springframework.org/schema/util/spring-util.xsd">
    <context:annotation-config />
    <context:component-scan base-package="com.perfmath.spring.mn" />
    <bean id="jspViewResolver"
        class="org.springframework.web.servlet.view.InternalResourceViewResolver">
        <property name="viewClass"
            value="org.springframework.web.servlet.view.JstlView" />
        <property name="prefix" value="/WEB-INF/jsp/" />
        <property name="suffix" value=".jsp" />
    </bean>
    <bean id="messageSource" class=
        "org.springframework.context.support.ReloadableResourceBundleMessageSource">
        <property name="basename" value="classpath:messages" />
        <property name="defaultEncoding" value="UTF-8" />
    </bean>
    <bean id="propertyConfigurer"
    class="org.springframework.beans.factory.config.PropertyPlaceholderConfigurer"
        p:location="/WEB-INF/jdbc.properties" />
    <bean id="dataSource"
        class="org.apache.commons.dbcp.BasicDataSource" destroy-method="close"
        p:driverClassName="${jdbc.driverClassName}"
        p:url="${jdbc.databaseurl}" p:username="${jdbc.username}"
        p:password="${jdbc.password}" />
    <bean id="sessionFactory"
        class="org.springframework.orm.hibernate3.LocalSessionFactoryBean">
        <property name="dataSource" ref="dataSource" />
        <property name="configLocation">
            <value>classpath:hibernate.cfg.xml</value>
        </property>
        <property name="configurationClass">
            <value>org.hibernate.cfg.AnnotationConfiguration</value>
        </property>
        <property name="hibernateProperties">
            <props>
                <prop key="hibernate.dialect">${jdbc.dialect}</prop>
                <prop key="hibernate.show_sql">true</prop>
            </props>
        </property>
```

```
    </bean>
    <tx:annotation-driven />
    <bean id="transactionManager"
        class="org.springframework.orm.hibernate4.HibernateTransactionManager">
        <property name="sessionFactory" ref="sessionFactory" />
    </bean>
</beans>
```

Listing C.13 jdbc.properties

```
jdbc.driverClassName= com.mysql.jdbc.Driver
jdbc.dialect=org.hibernate.dialect.MySQLDialect
jdbc.databaseurl=jdbc:mysql://localhost:3306/mydb
jdbc.username=mydbadmin
jdbc.password=mydbadmin
```

Listing C.14 note.jsp

```
<%@taglib uri="http://www.springframework.org/tags" prefix="spring"%>
<%@taglib uri="http://www.springframework.org/tags/form" prefix="form"%>
<%@taglib uri="http://java.sun.com/jsp/jstl/core" prefix="c"%>
<%@taglib uri="http://java.sun.com/jsp/jstl/functions" prefix="fn"%>
<html>
<head>
    <title>My Notes </title>
</head>
<body>
<h3>My notes (username: ${username}) </h3>
<form:form method="POST" action="/mn/createNote/username/${username}"
commandName="note">

    <table>
        <tr>
<td><form:label path="category"><spring:message code="label.category"/></form:label></td>
        <td><form:input path="category" /></td>
    </tr>
    <tr>
        <td><form:label path="subject" ><spring:message
        code="label.subject"/></form:label></td>
        <td><form:input type="text" size="30" path="subject" /></td>
    </tr>
    <tr>
        <td><form:label path="content"><spring:message
```

```
            code="label.content"/></form:label></td>
            <td><form:input type="text" size="120" path="content" /></td>
        </tr>
        <tr>
            <td colspan="2">
                <input type="submit" value="<spring:message code="label.addnote"/>"/>
            </td>
        </tr>
</table>
</form:form>
<c:if  test="${!empty noteList}">
<table class="data">
<c:forEach var="column" items="Category, Subject, Content, Created, Action">
<th align="left" bgcolor="#00184A"><FONT COLOR="#FFFFFF">${column}
    </FONT></th>
</c:forEach>
<c:forEach items="${noteList}" var="note">
    <tr>
    <td>${note.category} </td>
    <td>${note.subject} </td>
    <td>${note.content} </td>
    <td>${fn:substring(note.created, 0, 10)}</td>
    <td><a href="/mn/delete/username/${username}/noteId/${note.id}">delete</a>
</td>
    </tr>
</c:forEach>
</table>
</c:if>
</body>
</html>
```

Listing C.15 pom.xml for the MyNotes sample

```
<?xml version="1.0" encoding="UTF-8"?>
<project>
    <modelVersion>4.0.0</modelVersion>
    <groupId>com.perfmath.spring</groupId>
    <artifactId>mn</artifactId>
    <packaging>war</packaging>
    <version>0.1</version>
    <description></description>
    <build>
        <plugins>
```

```
            <plugin>
                <artifactId>maven-compiler-plugin</artifactId>
                <configuration>
                    <source>1.5</source>
                    <target>1.5</target>
                </configuration>
            </plugin>
            <plugin>
                <artifactId>maven-war-plugin</artifactId>
                <version>2.1.1</version>
            </plugin>
        </plugins>
    </build>
    <dependencies>
        <dependency>
            <groupId>javax.servlet</groupId>
            <artifactId>servlet-api</artifactId>
            <version>2.5</version>
        </dependency>
        <dependency>
            <groupId>org.springframework</groupId>
            <artifactId>spring-beans</artifactId>
            <version>${org.springframework.version}</version>
        </dependency>
        <dependency>
            <groupId>org.springframework</groupId>
            <artifactId>spring-jdbc</artifactId>
            <version>${org.springframework.version}</version>
        </dependency>
        <dependency>
            <groupId>org.springframework</groupId>
            <artifactId>spring-web</artifactId>
            <version>${org.springframework.version}</version>
        </dependency>
        <dependency>
            <groupId>org.springframework</groupId>
            <artifactId>spring-webmvc</artifactId>
            <version>${org.springframework.version}</version>
        </dependency>
        <dependency>
            <groupId>org.springframework</groupId>
            <artifactId>spring-orm</artifactId>
            <version>${org.springframework.version}</version>
```

```
        </dependency>
        <dependency>
            <groupId>org.hibernate</groupId>
            <artifactId>hibernate-entitymanager</artifactId>
            <version>3.6.8.Final</version>
        </dependency>
        <dependency>
            <groupId>taglibs</groupId>
            <artifactId>standard</artifactId>
            <version>1.1.2</version>
        </dependency>
        <dependency>
            <groupId>javax.servlet</groupId>
            <artifactId>jstl</artifactId>
            <version>1.1.2</version>
        </dependency>
        <dependency>
            <groupId>mysql</groupId>
            <artifactId>mysql-connector-java</artifactId>
            <version>5.1.18</version>
        </dependency>
        <dependency>
            <groupId>commons-dbcp</groupId>
            <artifactId>commons-dbcp</artifactId>
            <version>20030825.184428</version>
        </dependency>
        <dependency>
            <groupId>commons-pool</groupId>
            <artifactId>commons-pool</artifactId>
            <version>20030825.183949</version>
        </dependency>
        <dependency>
            <groupId>org.slf4j</groupId>
            <artifactId>slf4j-log4j12</artifactId>
            <version>1.6.6</version>
        </dependency>
    </dependencies>
    <properties>
        <org.springframework.version>3.1.1.RELEASE</org.springframework.version>
        <project.build.sourceEncoding>UTF-8</project.build.sourceEncoding>
    </properties>
</project>
```

C.3 SAMPLE IMPLEMENTATION HIGHLIGHTS

This section highlights some noteworthy implementation details associated with this sample. Note that we would not go into lengthy explanations, since they have been covered in the main text of this book.

C.3.1 THE HIBERNATE PIECE

- Note in Listing C.3 how each attribute of the `Note` class is mapped to its counterpart column in the table named `MYNOTE`. Pay attention to how the MySQL `TIMESTAMP` type of column `created` is mapped. In this case, we have to use java `Date` type rather than the `java.sql.Timestamp` type with the @Temporal annotation. Most samples from other sources do not include this special MySQL `TIMESTAMP` type mapping.
- Because the domain object `Note` is annotated, there is no need to have a `Note.cfg.xml` mapping file any more. Besides, pay attention to how the `Note` object mapping is specified in Listing C.8 `hibernate.hbm.xml` file: It is defined in `<mapping class="..."/>` rather than `<mapping resource="..."/>`.
- This DAO object is annotated with two annotations: `@Repository` and `@Autowired`. The annotation `@Repository` hints that it's a DAO object, while the annotation `@Autowired` makes it unnecessary to specify the *sessionFactory* dependency in the bean configuration file.
- Note the `transactionManager` defined in Listing C.12 `mn-servlet.xml`. Since the `HibernateTransactionManager` is defined, there is no need to call `begin`, `commit`, and `rollback` methods in `NoteDAOImpl.java` any more. This is contrary to what was implemented in `HibernateBillPaymentDao.java` for SOBA as shown in Listing 5.9 (b), in which case, a JDBC transaction manager was defined in `soba-services.xml` as shown in Listing 5.1.

C.3.2 THE SERVICE LAYER

- Listings F.5 (a) and (b) represent the service layer for this sample. It uses annotated transactions as can be identified by the annotations of `@Transactional`. This is defined so with a line in Listing C.12: `<tx:annotation-driven />`.
- Also, note the other two annotations of `@Service` and `@Autowried` in Listing C.5 (b). The annotation `@Service` hints that it's a service layer object, while the annotation `@Autowired` makes it unnecessary to specify the `noteDAO` dependency in the bean configuration file. Also, note the `context:component-scan base-package` defined in the beginning of the `mn-servlet.xml` file.

You may have also noticed that we have a `CreateNoteValidtaor.java` class that validates a ***note*** object before it is created. This class is shown in Listing C.16. Note the annotation of `@Component` for this validation class.

Listing C.16 CreateNoteValidator.java

```
package com.perfmath.spring.mn.service;

import org.springframework.stereotype.Component;
import org.springframework.validation.ValidationUtils;
import org.springframework.validation.Validator;
```

```
import org.springframework.validation.Errors;

import org.apache.commons.logging.Log;
import org.apache.commons.logging.LogFactory;

import com.perfmath.spring.mn.model.domain.Note;

@Component
public class CreateNoteValidator implements Validator {

    /** Logger for this class and subclasses */
    protected final Log logger = LogFactory.getLog(getClass());

    public boolean supports(Class clazz) {
        return Note.class.isAssignableFrom(clazz);
    }

    public void validate(Object target, Errors errors) {
        Note note = (Note) target;
            ValidationUtils.rejectIfEmptyOrWhitespace(errors, "username",
                    "required.username", "username is required.");
    }
}
```

C.3.3 THE CONTROLLER LAYER

- Listings C.6 `NoteController.java` represents the frontend controller that handles all incoming requests for this sample after a user is authenticated through the login controller shown in Listing C.7. The annotations of `@Controller`, `@Autowired`, and `@RequestMapping` are not different from what we have seen in the main text for SOBA. See Table C.1 for a summary of annotations used for the objects at each layer.

Table C.1 Annotations Applied on the Objects at Each Layer

Layer	Annotations		
DAO	@Repository	@Autowired	
Service	@Service	@Autowired	@Transactional
Web	@Controller	@Autowired	@RequestMapping

Next, let's see how various parts are wired together to govern programming logic flows for this sample.

C.4 PROGRAMMATIC LOGIC FLOWS

The programming logic flows for this sample are defined as follows:

- A user accesses this application via https://localhost:8443/mn. This is defined by the `welcome-file` tag and `servlet-mapping` tag in the `web.xml` file as shown in Listing C.11. After a user enters *username* and *password* and clicks *Login*, control is turned to the `LoginController`. See *form action* defined in `login.jsp` (Listing C.10) and *@RequestMapping /loginController* defined in `LoginController.java` (Listing C.7). If a user fails to provide proper username and password, control is redirected back to the login page. Otherwise, the user's notes are retrieved and control is handed to the `note.jsp` file as specified by the statement of `viewString = "note"` in Listing C.7. Note that it's necessary to tuck a new *note* object in the returned `MapAndView` object, as there is a command object specified as *note* in `note.jsp`. This is a subtle issue that needs to be dealt with properly; otherwise, an exception would be thrown.
- In the `note.jsp` file, two actions are defined: *create a note* and *delete a note*. Such requests are handled by the `NoteController` as shown in Listing C.6.
- The `NoteController` calls the `NoteService` bean, which in turn calls the Hibernate-based `NoteDAOImpl` class to carry out the `addNote/deleteNote` operation eventually.
- After this call-chain ends, the `NoteController` redirects control to `note.jsp`.

You might want to take a look at the signature of the `createNote` and `deleteNode` methods of the `NoteController` class. In the `createNote` method, `@ModelAttribute("note") Note note, BindingResult result` are passed in, which is because this is the domain object that will be created. The `BindingResult result` argument is needed by the `CreateNoteValidator` class as shown there in the code. The `deleteNote` method does not have such requirements, as all it needs is a `noteId` to identify which *note* to delete.

As you see, the programmatic logic is indeed very simple, thanks to the Spring Framework for doing all the wiring and execution work behind the scene.

To run this sample, you need to install Tomcat by following the instructions described in Chapter 2. Then, create a user by executing the following MySQL command using the `create_mn_users.sql` script as shown in Listing C.17 (you can add more by replacing "`user0`" in the script):

```
cmd>mysql mydb –h 127.0.0.1 –u mydbadmin –p <create_mn_users.sql
```

Listing C.17 create_mn_users.sql

```
insert into mynote (username, password, category, subject, content, created) values
 ('user0', 'user0', 'sys created', 'sys created', 'sys created', current_timestamp);
```

Then, follow the below steps to build and run it:

- cd to the `MyNotes` project folder and execute the command of:

```
cmd> mvn clean -DskipTests package
```

- Copy the `mn-0.1` folder in the `target` folder and drop it to the `webapps` folder of your Tomcat install. Rename it to `mn` (**do not forget this step**).
- Start up your Tomcat server by executing `startup.bat` in the `bin` folder of your Tomcat install.
- Access it at https://localhost:8443/mn . You should see a login dialog form, which means that the `MyNotes` app is up and running, allowing you to login and manage your notes.

This wraps up this appendix showing how an enterprise Web application can be built with Spring, Hibernate, MySQL, and Maven.

Appendix D Deploying/Developing SOBA on Linux

Many organizations develop enterprise Java applications on Windows and then deploy them on Linux in production. Therefore, we first describe how to deploy SOBA on Linux in this appendix. However, if you are interested in actually developing SOBA on Linux, you should skip the first section and jump to section 2 for Ubuntu or 3 for OpenSuSE, based on which Linux variant you are interested in.

D.1 Deploying SOBA on a Linux Server

If your interest is in deploying and running SOBA on a Linux server, I strongly suggest that you build, deploy and test SOBA on Windows first and make sure that SOBA works on your Windows PC. Then, you can follow the procedure given below to deploy SOBA on Linux. This procedure includes the following tasks to be performed on a Linux system:

- Installing a JDK and Maven
- Installing Tomcat 7.0.29
- Installing MySQL 5.5.22
- Deploying SOBA

The Linux box I tested was a Red Hat Enterprise Linux Server release 6.0 (Santiago) system. If you have decided to deploy SOBA on Linux, I assume that you know how to get around on a Linux system and you know what necessary changes to make to suit your needs when you follow the procedure below. In addition, my directory on my Linux box for holding JDK, Tomcat and MySQL was */data1/dev*. I used *root* to perform all tasks.

You need to make sure you have enough disk space for the entire stack of MySQL, Tomcat, JDK and SOBA. If you do not have enough disk space, the install will fail midway. To check your disk space, use the following command:

```
$df
```

Then, if the disk space allocated to the user *root* is near 100% used, cd to the "/" directory and execute the next command to find out all files larger than 100 MB. This was actually what happened to my system, and I had to delete many files of **.sqlite* in *root*'s *cache* directory to make room for installing the entire SOBA stack.

```
$find / -type f -size +100000k -exec ls -lh {} \; | awk '{ print $NF ": " $5 }'
```

D.1.1 INSTALLING A JDK

The JDK I installed was jdk 1.6.0_33 from a downloaded file named *jdk-6u33-linux-x64.bin*. You can use any 1.6.0 build, for example, between u18 and the latest jdk1.6.0 update.

I first ftp-ed the above downloaded jdk file to the */data1/dev* directory on my Linux system. Then I executed the following commands:

```
$chmod +x jdk-6u33-linux-x64.bin
$./jdk-6u33-linux-x64.bin
$vi ~/.bash_profile
```

Added the JAVA_HOME environment variable to the PATH environment variable as follows:

```
JAVA_HOME=/data1/dev/jdk1.6.0_33
PATH=$PATH:$HOME/bin:${JAVA_HOME}/bin
```

Executed the following command at my bash command prompt:

```
$source ~/.bash_profile
```

Verified with the commands "*echo $JAVA_HOME*" and "*$JAVA_HOME/bin/java -version*" to make sure my JDK had been installed properly.

Installed Tomcat next.

D.1.2 INSTALLING TOMCAT

I first downloaded *apache-tomcat-7.0.29.tar.gz* from Apache's website, ftp-ed it to the */data1/dev* directory on my Linux box, and issued the command:

```
$tar xvfz apache-tomcat-7.0.29.tar.gz
```

to have Tomcat unfolded at */data1/dev/apache-tomcat-7.0.29*. Followed the procedure below to complete Tomcat install:

- Ran "*keytool –genkey –alias tomcat –keyalg RSA*" to create a keystore. This step described in §2.4.3 for installing Tomcat on Windows applies to Linux as well.
- Carried out those two steps for Tomcat 7 regarding *server.xml* and *tomcat-users.xml* given in §2.4.3 here on Linux – they all apply to Linux as well.

To start/stop Tomcat, cd to its *bin* directory and execute

```
$./startup.sh
```

or

```
$./shutdown.sh
```

accordingly.

You can check out if Tomcat works by trying out https://<yourLinuxHost>:8443/. If the page does not return successfully, fix the issue before moving forward.

The next step is to install MySQL.

D.1.3 INSTALLING MYSQL

First, I downloaded the MySQL server and client packages *MySQL-server-5.5.22-1.linux2.6.x86_64.rpm* and *MySQL-client-5.5.22-1.el6.x86_64.rpm* from http://downloads.mysql.com/archives.php?p=mysql-6.0&o=linux-, and ftp-ed them to my */data1/dev* directory on my Linux box. Download the proper packages of MySQL5.5.22 on to your Linux box and get ready for installing both MySQL server and MySQL client.

First, execute the command of

```
$ rpm –qa | grep –i mysql
```

to see if you already have MySQL installed. If you already have MySQL installed on your Linux box, you can use it or use the command of

```
$ yum remove <mysql-prefix>
```

to remove it all, where *<mysql-prefix>* is the part that does not include the numerical version number.

Now, execute the following command to install MySQL server:

```
$ rpm –i MySQL-server-5.5.22-1.linux2.6.x86_64.rpm
```

And similarly for the MySQL client

```
$ rpm –i MySQL-client-5.5.22-1.el6.x86_64.rpm
```

To start/stop MySQL, execute

```
$ /etc/init.d/mysql start
```

or

```
$ /etc/init.d/mysql stop
```

accordingly. After you start up your MySQL, execute the following command to change the password for the *root* user:

```
$ /usr/bin/mysqladmin –u root password 'MySql5522'
```

Note that I entered *'MySql5522'* for my install and you can certainly change it to anything you like. Also, note that *mysqladmin* tool comes only with the MySQL client install.

At this point, we need to set the variable *lower_case_table_names = 1* in the *my.cnf* file. The default values for this parameter are 0 on Linux, 1 on Windows, and 2 on Mac OS, where "0" means table names case sensitive, "1" means converting table names to lower case to make it case insensitive, and "2" means keeping the original case while making it case insensitive. Follow the steps below:

- Run the command "*find / -name *.cnf*" or "*locate *.cnf*" to find out where your MySQL configuration file *my.cnf* file resides. Mostly you probably don't see it in your /etc directory and you may see many of them in */usr/share/mysql/* directory. If this is the case, run the command "*cp /usr/share/mysql/my-large.cnf /etc/my.cnf*" to copy it to your */etc* directory. Note that you may choose a different file than *my-large.cnf* based on the capacity of your system.
- Edit your *my.cnf* file copied to the */etc* directory by adding a line of *lower_case_table_names* = 1 below the *thread_concurrency* line in the section as shown in Figure D.1 (if you add it in other places, it may not work).
- Start up your MySQL server.
- Verify that *lower_case_table_names* is set to 1 by running "*mysqladmin –u root –p variables*." This step is necessary, so make sure it's done properly.

```
# The MySQL server
[mysqld]
port            = 3306
socket          = /var/lib/mysql/mysql.sock
skip-external-locking
key_buffer_size = 256M
max_allowed_packet = 1M
table_open_cache = 256
sort_buffer_size = 1M
read_buffer_size = 1M
read_rnd_buffer_size = 4M
myisam_sort_buffer_size = 64M
thread_cache_size = 8
query_cache_size= 16M
# Try number of CPU's*2 for thread_concurrency
thread_concurrency = 8
lower_case_table_names = 1
```

Figure D.1 Adding *lower_case_table_names* parameter in *my.cnf* file

Then I ftp-ed the *soba_db_scripts* folder from the downloaded project zip file and unzipped it to my */data1/dev* directory on my Linux box.

To create the SOBA database, execute the following commands (you need to enter the *root* password for the first command and *sobaadmin's* password of "*sobaadmin*" for the second command):

```
$ mysql –h 127.0.0.1 –u root –p < create_soba_mysql.sql
$ mysql soba–h 127.0.0.1 –u sobaadmin –p <create_all.sql
```

Next, deploy SOBA on your Linux box.

D.1.4 DEPLOYING SOBA

I used my Maven 3 build of *soba4* and moved it to my */data1/dev* directory on my Linux box. Then I changed to the directory of */data1/dev/soba4* on my Linux box and issued the command

```
cp –a * /data1/dev/apache-tomcat-7.0.29/webapps/soba
```

to copy all files and directories over to Tomcat's *webapps* directory. In addition, copy *mysql-connector-java-5.1.10.jar* to Tomcat's *lib* directory. Then, start or restart Tomcat and try it out at https://<yourLinuxHost>:8443/soba. The above entire procedure works on my Linux system. Now you can test your SOBA deployment using the procedures given in Chapter 2 of this book.

D.2 DEVELOPING SOBA ON AN UBUNTU LINUX DESKTOP

First off, if you do not have a ready-to-use Ubuntu Linux desktop yet, it's really easy to convert one of your Windows PCs to a Linux desktop (either Ubuntu or OpenSuSE – I did both). For example, I converted one of my 64-bit Intel® Core i3 @ 2.40 GHz Windows 7 PCs into an Ubuntu 12.10 desktop within a matter of 2 – 3 hours. You first download the proper Ubuntu release as an .iso file, and then right-click on the downloaded file and burn it onto a DVD by selecting "Burn Disk Image" (note that you do not need to install any third-party software to burn an .iso file onto a CD/DVD on Windows 7).

In the following sections, I share the exact experience I had with setting up SOBA on my Ubuntu desktop.

D.2.1 INSTALLING A JDK AND MAVEN

The JDK I installed was jdk 1.6.0_35 named *jdk-6u35-linux-x64.bin*. You can use any 1.6.0 build, for example, between u18 and the latest jdk1.6.0 update.

Then I executed the following commands:

```
$chmod +x jdk-6u35-linux-x64.bin
$./ jdk-6u33-linux-x64.bin
$ move jdk1.6.0_35 from the Downloads directory to $HOME/myapp/
$vi ~/.bashrc
```

Next, I downloaded *Maven* and unzipped it to the *$HOME /myapp* directory.

Added the following lines in the *.bashrc* file:

```
export JAVA_HOME$HOME /myapp/jdk1.6.0_35
export PATH=$PATH:$JAVA_HOME/bin
```

Executed the following command at the bash command prompt:

```
$source ~/.bashrc
```

Verified with the command *"java -version"* and made sure that my JDK had been installed properly. Installed Tomcat next.

D.2.2 INSTALLING TOMCAT

Downloaded *apache-tomcat-7.0.29.tar.gz* and unzipped it to *$HOME/myapp*. Configured it according to the instructions given in Chapter 2. Installed MySQL next.

D.2.3 INSTALLING MYSQL

MySQL was installed by issuing the following command:

```
$sudo apt-get install mysql-server
```

The *root* password for MySQL Server was set to "MySql5522" to be consistent with my other MySQL installs on other platforms.

The MySQL workbench was installed using the Ubuntu Software Center feature. You can start/stop your MySQL server using the MySQL workbench or executing the following command:

```
$ sudo /etc/init.d/mysql start/stop
```

But before starting up your MySQL server, add the following line below the "*thread concurrency*" line in your */etc/mysql/my.cnf* file:

```
lower_case_table_names = 1
```

Then I located the *soba_db_scripts* folder from the SOBA project download zip file and copied it to my *$HOME /mydev/mysql* directory.

To create the SOBA database, execute the following scripts (you need to enter the *root* password for the first command and *sobaadmin's* password of "*sobaadmin*" for the second command):

```
$ mysql –h 127.0.0.1 –u root –p < create_soba_mysql.sql
$ mysql soba –h 127.0.0.1 –u sobaadmin –p <create_all.sql
```

D.2.4 INSTALLING ECLIPSE AND IMPORTING SOBA

Downloaded the latest 2012 Eclipse release of *eclipse-jee-juno-SR1-linux-gtk-x86_64.tar.gz* and unzipped it to my */home/henry/myapp* directory. To start up eclipse, I changed it to my $HOME/myapp/eclipse directory, executed the "*chmod +x eclipse*" command first and then the "*./eclipse*" command (we could not simply double-click on the eclipse file to start it up as on Windows). When the Workspace Launcher pops up, enter your eclipse workspace location (I entered *$HOME/mydev/workspace* in my case).

Now you can follow the same procedure as described in Chapter 2 to import SOBA into your eclipse workspace. Note that I modified the first two lines in the ant *build.properties* file as follows (you should make similar changes accordingly as well):

```
user.home=/home/henry
appserver.home=/home/henry/myapp/apache-tomcat-7.0.29
```

Then, follow the instructions given in Chapter 2 to configure, build, deploy and test SOBA.

D.3 DEVELOPING SOBA ON AN OPENSUSE LINUX DESKTOP

Between Ubuntu and OpenSuSE desktop, I would recommend Ubuntu over OpenSuSE if you have not made your choice yet, although both are very good. However, if OpenSuSE is your preference, here is a summary of my experience I had with setting up SOBA on my OpenSuSE 12.1 desktop.

D.3.1 INSTALLING A JDK AND ANT

The JDK I installed was jdk 1.6.0_35 named *jdk-6u35-linux-x64.bin*. You can use any 1.6.0 build, for example, between u18 and the latest jdk1.6.0 update.

Then I executed the following commands:

```
$chmod +x jdk-6u35-linux-x64.bin
$./ jdk-6u35-linux-x64.bin
$ move jdk1.6.0_35 from the Downloads directory to $HOME /myapp/
$vi ~/.bash_profile
```

Next, I downloaded *Maven* and unzipped it to the *$HOME /myapp* directory.

Added the following lines in the *.bash_profile* file:

```
export JAVA_HOME$HOME/myapp/jdk1.6.0_35
export PATH=$PATH:$JAVA_HOME/bin
```

Executed the following command at the bash command prompt:

```
$source ~/.bash_profile
```

Verified with the command *"java -version"* and made sure that my JDK had been installed properly. Installed Tomcat next.

D.3.2 INSTALLING TOMCAT

Downloaded *apache-tomcat-7.0.29.tar.gz* and unzipped it to *$HOME/myapp*. Configured it according to the instructions given in §2.4.3. Installed MySQL next.

D.3.3 INSTALLING MYSQL

MySQL was installed by downloading and installing each of the following components:

- MySQL-client-5.5.28-1.linux.2.6.x86_64.tar.rpm
- MySQL-server-5.5.28-1.linux.2.6.x86_64.tar.rpm
- MySQL-shared-compat-5.5.28-1.linux.2.6.x86_64.tar.rpm

The *root* password for MySQL Server was set to "MySql5522" to be consistent with my other MySQL installs on other platforms.

The MySQL workbench was installed using the *mysql-workbench.ymp* file. You can start/stop your MySQL server using the MySQL workbench or executing the following command:

```
$ sudo /etc/init.d/mysql start/stop
```

However, before starting up your MySQL server, add the following two lines below the "*thread concurrency*" line in your */etc/mysql/my.cnf* file (note the second parameter, which is not required on Ubuntu but must be present here):

```
lower_case_table_names = 1
log_bin_trust_function_creators = 1
```

Then I copied the *soba_db_scripts* folder from the downloaded SOBA project zip file and unzipped it to my *$HOME/mydev/mysql* directory.

To create the SOBA database, execute the following commands (you need to enter the *root* password for the first command and *sobaadmin's* password of "*sobaadmin*" for the second command):

```
$ mysql –h 127.0.0.1 –u root –p < create_soba_mysql.sql
$ mysql soba –h 127.0.0.1 –u sobaadmin –p <create_all.sql
```

D.3.4 INSTALLING ECLIPSE AND IMPORTING SOBA

Downloaded the latest 2012 Eclipse release of *eclipse-jee-juno-SR1-linux-gtk-x86_64.tar.gz* and unzipped it to my *$HOME/myapp* directory. To start up eclipse, I changed it to my $HOME/myapp/eclipse directory, executed the "*chmod +x eclipse*" command first and then the "*./eclipse*" command (we could not simply double-click on the eclipse file to start it up as on Windows). When the Workspace Launcher pops up, enter your eclipse workspace location (I entered *$HOME/mydev/workspace* in my case).

Now you can follow the same procedure as described in Chapter 2 to import SOBA into your eclipse workspace. Note that I modified the first two lines in the ant *build.properties* file as follows (you should make similar changes accordingly as well):

```
user.home=/home/henry
appserver.home=/home/henry/myapp/apache-tomcat-7.0.29
```

However, there was a specific bug with Eclipse on OpenSuSE, that is, whenever I tried to expand the imported soba4 project, Eclipse crashed immediately. The fix was to create a *startup_eclipse.sh* file with the following contents and use this script to start up Eclipse:

```
#!/bin/sh
export MALLOC_CHECK_=1
$HOME/myapp/eclipse/eclipse
```

Then, follow the instructions given in Chapter 2 to configure, build, deploy and test SOBA.

Appendix E SOBA on Mac OS X

In this appendix, we demonstrate how to set up a dev environment for developing SOBA on Mac OS X. The procedure applies to developing any Spring- and MySQL-based applications on Mac OS X. My Mac is a latest 13.3″ MacBookPro Retina with an Intel dual-core i5 @ 2.4 GHz, 8 GB, 256 GB SSD, running on Mac OS X Mavericks 10.9.2. You may need to choose different versions of software to be compatible with your own Mac OS X system.

First, I created a directory */Users/henry/mydev* to hold the entire SOBA stack. Then, the procedure including the following steps was followed:

- Installing a JDK
- Installing Tomcat 7.0.29
- Installing MySQL 5.5.22
- Installing Eclipse &Maven
- Importing and Building SOBA
- Deploying SOBA

Let's describe the above steps one at a time next.

E.1 Installing a JDK

Every Mac machine has a latest JDK pre-installed. However, for this version of OS X 10.9.2, it put the java executable in a folder named `Commands`, which made the Maven executable unable to find the java executable in the `bin` folder that it was supposed to look for. Because of that issue specific to that version of OS X, I had to install jdk1.7.0_51 and added the JAVA_HOME environment variable to the PATH environment variable as follows:

- $ vi ~/.bash_profile

```
export JAVA_HOME=/Library/Java/JavaVirtualMachines/jdk1.7.0_51.jdk/Contents/Home
export PATH=$PATH:${JAVA_HOME}/bin
```

- $ source ~/.bash_profile

You can verify with the commands "*echo $JAVA_HOME*" and "*$JAVA_HOME/bin/java –version*" to make sure your JDK has been installed properly. (If you happen to be on a different version of OS X, you might need to figure out how to set up your JAVA_HOME environment variable accordingly.)

Install Tomcat next.

E.2 INSTALLING TOMCAT

I first downloaded and un-archived Tomcat 7.0.29 to my *mydev* folder with a few quick and smooth clicks. Then I made all scripts executable by executing the following command:

- $ sudo +x /Users/henry/mydev/apache-tomcat-7.0.29/bin/*.sh

Then, I configured Tomcat as follows:

- Run "*keytool –genkey –alias tomcat –keyalg RSA*" to create a keystore. This step described in Chapter 2 for installing Tomcat on Windows applies to Mac as well.
- Carry out those two steps for Tomcat 7 regarding *server.xml* and *tomcat-users.xml* given in Chapter 2 here on Mac – they all apply to Mac as well.

To start/stop Tomcat, cd to its *bin* directory and execute

- $ ./startup.sh

or

- $ ./shutdown.sh

accordingly.

You can check if Tomcat works by trying out https://localhost:8443/. If Tomcat home page does not return successfully, fix the issue before moving forward.

The next step is to install MySQL.

E.3 INSTALLING MYSQL

First, I downloaded MySQL 5.5.22 (AMD64, installer format) named *mysql-5.5.22-osx10.6-x86_64.dmg* from http://downloads.mysql.com/archives.php?p=mysql-5.5&v=5.5.22. However, this build did not work on my Mac, saying "*… could not be recognized*" (bad luck). After a few random trials with older and newer versions, finally I found one that worked, which is version 5.6.5 as is shown in Figure E.1.

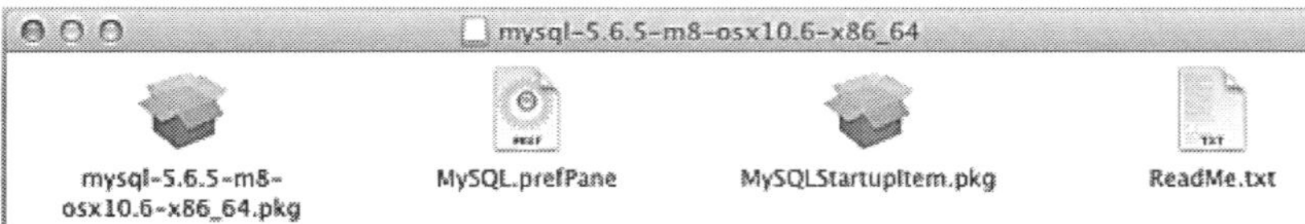

Figure E.1 Version of MySQL installable on Mac OS X 10.7.3

The remaining part was actually smooth. I took a few screenshots for your reference as shown in Figures E.2 – E.4, just in case you encounter problems.

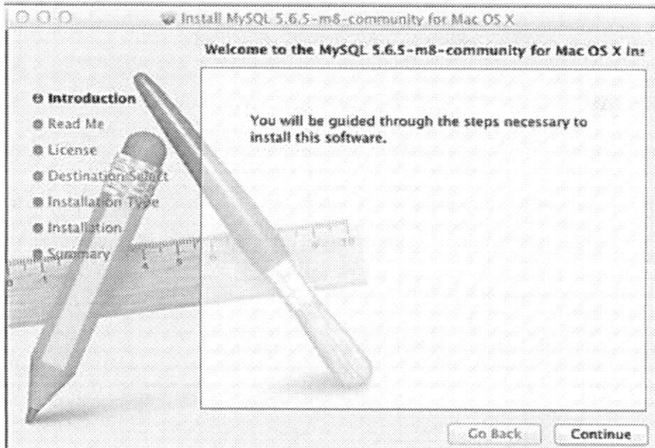

Figure E.2 MySQL 5.6.6 installation kicked off

Figure E.3 MySQL 5.5.6 installation requesting password to continue

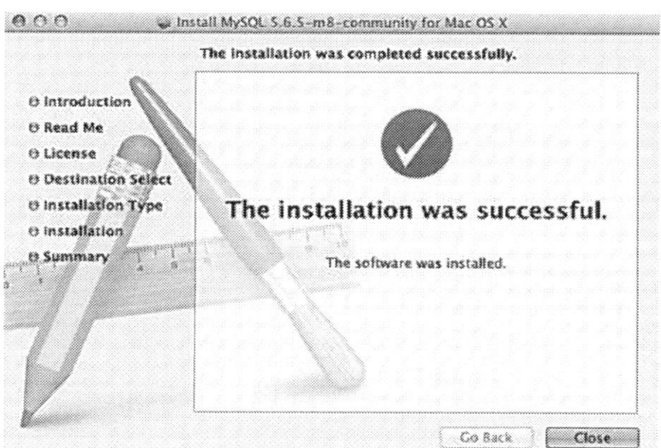

Figure E.4 MySQL 5.5.6 installed successfully on Mac

Note the third icon in Figure E.1 labeled *MySQL.StartupItem.pkg*. Double-click on it and install MySQL Startup Item utility. The Startup Item is installed into */Library/StartupItems/MySQLCOM*. The installation adds a variable MYSQLCOM=-YES- to the system configuration file */etc/hostconfig*. Change it to MYSQLCOM=-NO- if you want to disable the automatic startup of MySQL.

Now you can start/stop MySQL using MySQL StartupItem by executing the following commands:

- $ sudo /Library/StartupItems/MySQLCOM/MySQLCOM start

Or

- $ sudo /Library/StartupItems/MySQLCOM/MySQLCOM stop

You might be prompted for a password when you start up MySQL the first time.

You can also install the MySQL PreferencePane shown as the second icon in Figure E.1. Then, you can start/stop MySQL from the System Perferences tray, as is shown in Figure E.5.

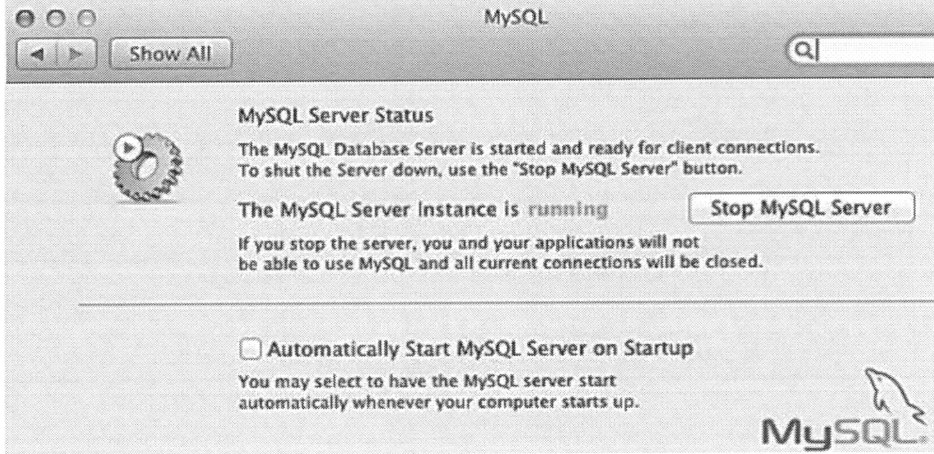

Figure E.5 MySQL PreferencePane

Next, you can install MySQL Workbench if you want. I downloaded mysql-workbench-gpl-5.2.40-osx-i686.dmg and installed it by simply dragging and dropping it in my Applications folder, but it's optional.

Now execute the following commands to create a *my.cnf* in the */etc* directory:

```
$ cp /usr/local/mysql-5.6.5-m8-osx10.6-x86_64/support-files/my-medium.cnf .
$ mv my-medium.cnf my.cnf
$ sudo cp my.cnf /etc
```

By default, MySQL sets up two users on Mac, root with no password and a blank user account, which allows you to access MySQL without any password. Execute the following commands to reset root's password and delete the blank user account:

```
$ /usr/local/mysql/bin/mysqladmin –u root password 'MySql565'
$ /usr/local/mysql/mysql –u root –p
mysql>use mysql;
mysql>delete from user where User=' ';
mysql>exit
$
```

Then I copied the *soba_db_scripts* folder from the project download zip file to my */Users/henry/mydev* directory on my Mac.

To create the SOBA database, I executed the following two scripts (Note: need to enter the *root* password for the first command and *sobaadmin's* password of "*sobaadmin*" for the second command):

- $ /usr/local/mysql/bin/mysql –h 127.0.0.1 –u root –p < create_soba_mysql.sql
- $ /usr/local/mysql/bin/mysql soba –h 127.0.0.1 –u sobaadmin –p <create_all.sql

Next, install Eclipse and Maven.

E.4 INSTALLING ECLIPSE AND MAVEN

I downloaded latest Mac OS version of Eclipse IDE for Java Developers (version: Luna M6 release) and expanded it to my `/Users/henry/myapp` folder, which is separate from my `/Users/henry/mydev/workspace` folder for all my eclipse projects (it's recommend that the `workspace` directory be created outside eclipse so that you would not lose your projects accidentally when you uninstall eclipse).

Then I downloaded Maven 3 from http://maven.apache.org/download.html by choosing the *apache-maven-3.0.4-bin.tar.gz* file. I expanded and moved it to my */Users/henry/myapp* directory. I executed the following commands to complete setting it up (Note: you can add the last two `export` commands to your `.bash_profile` file as you did with setting up your JAVA_HOME and PATH environment variables as described previously):

```
$ cd ~henry/myapp
$ ln –s apache-maven-3.0.4 maven
$ export M2_HOME=/Users/henry/myapp/maven
$ export PATH=${M2_HOME}/bin:${PATH}
```

Now, execute the command "*mvn –version*" to verify that Maven has been installed properly on your Mac. Follow the same procedure as shown in Section 2.5.3 to enable Maven on your eclipse environment.

The next step is to import and build SOBA on your Mac computer.

E.5 IMPORTING AND BUILDING SOBA

First, make sure you can start up your Eclipse IDE. If it complains about the required JDK missing, change to where your Eclipse was installed and start it up from the command line as follows:

```
$./eclipse –vm $JAVA_HOME/bin/java
```

To install SOBA on your Mac, follow the below procedure:

- First download the soba4 project file from my website at http://www.perfmath.com/download.htm.
- Unzip and copy the `soba4` folder to your eclipse `workspace` directory (make sure it is named `soba4`).
- Create a new Java Project named soba4 and choose the same soba4 folder as your new project folder.
- Right-click on your soba4 project and select *Fresh*.
- Right-click on your soba4 project and select *Validate*.

If you get any unexpected errors or issues, please send me an email and I can help you troubleshoot.

Next, deploy SOBA on your Mac computer.

E.6 DEPLOYING SOBA

I created a directory named *soba* in the */Users/henry/mydev/apache-tomcat-7.0.29/webapps* directory for deploying SOBA on Tomcat. I used my Maven 3 build of *soba4 a* and moved its contents to Tomcat's *soba* directory created above. In addition, I copied *mysql-connector-java-5.1.10.jar* to Tomcat's *lib* directory. Then, I changed to Tomcat's *bin* directory and started up Tomcat using the following command

- $ ./startup.sh

At last, I tried https://localhost:8443/soba and it worked like on Windows and Linux. This is the entire procedure I tested on my Mac. You may want to continue testing your SOBA deployment using the procedures given in Chapter 2 of the main text. After populating some data into your SOBA database, you might want to back up your database with the following command:

$/usr/local/mysql/bin/mysqldump --user=root --password=MySql565 --databases soba
>soba_dump_0.sql

To import your SOBA database, execute the following command:

$/usr/local/mysql/bin/mysql --verbose --user=root --password=MySql565 soba <soba_dump_0.sql

Appendix F Deploying SOBA and MyNotes Straight from Maven to Tomcat 7

Building and installing a real application are two separate processes in general that you first create a build and then run an installer to deploy your application in a given environment, either for internal testing or production. However, in a dev environment, it might be more convenient to run a quick test on an embedded server or standalone server with just one click or one command. In this appendix, a procedure is given on how you can deploy SOBA and MyNotes straight from Maven to Tomcat 7 so that you don't have to manually copy and rename either of them as was described in previous appendices.

To include deploying SOBA or MyNotes on Tomcat 7 into the Maven building process directly, follow the steps below:

Step 1: Add the following <plugin> element within the <plugins> section of the `pom.xml` file (replace *soba* with *mn* for the MyNotes sample):

```
<plugin>
    <groupId>org.codehaus.mojo</groupId>
    <artifactId>tomcat-maven-plugin</artifactId>
    <version>2.0-beta-1</version>
    <configuration>
    <url>http://localhost:8080/manager/html</url>
    <server>myTomcat</server>
    <path>/soba</path>
    </configuration>
</plugin>
```

Step 2: Locate the Maven `settings.xml` file (in *C:\Users\<yourLoginID>\.m2* on Windows) and add the following element (assuming that you have followed the instructions in the book to configure your tomcat with the following username and password):

```
<server>
  <id>myTomcat</id>
  <username>tomcat</username>
  <password>s3cret</password>
</server>
```

Step 3: Make sure your Tomcat server is running as you cannot perform deploy or redeploy operations if it is not running.

Step 4: cd to your project directory and execute the following commands to deploy or redeploy SOBA or MyNotes:

```
cmd> mvn -DskipTests tomcat:deploy
cmd> mvn -DskipTests tomcat:redeploy
```

Note that you might see errors on your Tomcat console after you redeploy multiple times. Whenever that happens, you need to manually stop your Tomcat server and start over.

Appendix G Deploying SOBA on GlassFish

Some readers are interested in deploying SOBA on GlassFish. Assuming that you have followed the instructions detailed in Chapter 2 and made sure that: 1) you have set up your MySQL and created the SOBA schema properly, and 2) you have built SOBA successfully in your environment, this appendix describes the steps for deploying SOBA on GlassFish 3.1.

Step 1: In SOBA's `web.xml` file, replace the "*default*" servlet with the "*DefaultServlet*" as shown below if it's not already replaced (the former only works on Tomcat):

```
<!--  this is necessary in order to make SOBA run on glassfish and jboss -->
<servlet>
     <servlet-name>DefaultServlet</servlet-name>
     <servlet-class>org.apache.catalina.servlets.DefaultServlet</servlet-class>
  </servlet>
    <servlet-mapping>
        <servlet-name>DefaultServlet</servlet-name>
        <url-pattern>*.jpg</url-pattern>
    </servlet-mapping>
<!--
    <servlet-mapping>
        <servlet-name>default</servlet-name>
        <url-pattern>*.jpg</url-pattern>
    </servlet-mapping>
    <servlet-mapping>
        <servlet-name>default</servlet-name>
        <url-pattern>*.gif</url-pattern>
    </servlet-mapping>
-->
```

Step 2: Open up a command prompt and execute the command *asadmin* from the `bin` directory of your GlassFish installation (you need to start up your domain by executing *asadmin> start-domain* first if your GlassFish server is not running):

```
asadmin> create-ssl --type http-listerner --certName sampleCert http-listener-2
```

Step 3: Verify the http listener created in the previous step by logging into your GlassFish admin console at http://localhost:4848/ and then navigating to *Configurations → server-config → Network Config → Network Listeners → http-listener-2*. Similar to Figure G.1, it should show the port 8181 for the HTTPS protocol (remember that later you need to use this port number of 8181 instead of 8443 to start up SOBA).

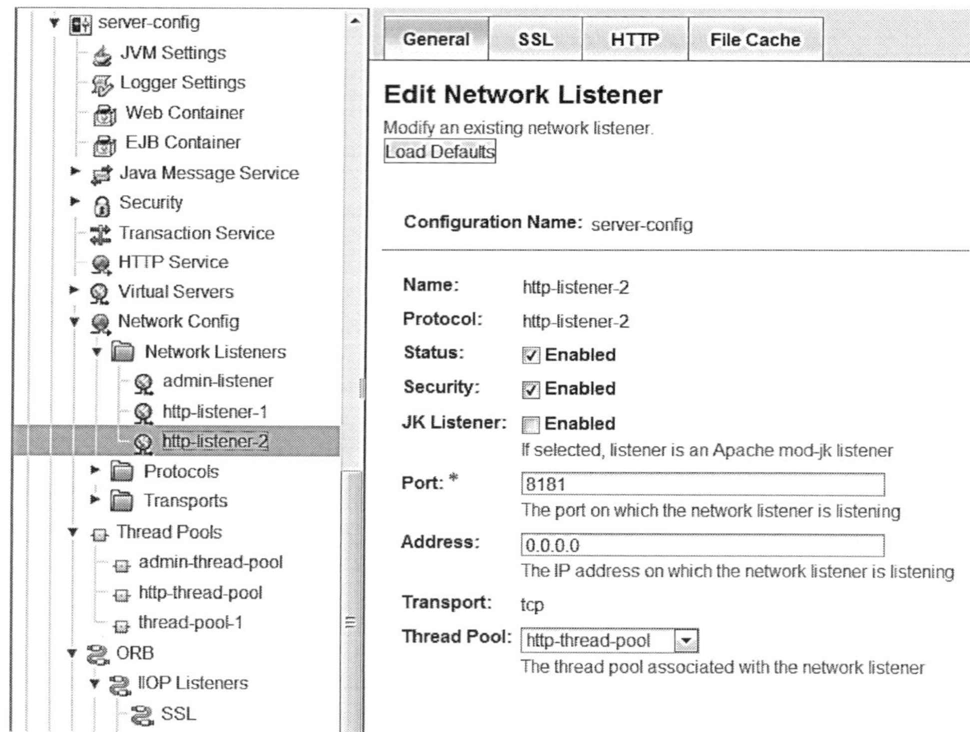

Figure G.1 GlassFish HTTPS/SSL configured to run at port 8181

Step 4: Copy the *soba* folder (you need to rename it to *soba* from its default name of *soba4 a* in your *target* directory built with Maven to the *domains/domain1/autodeploy* folder of your GlassFish installation (you can also use the *soba4.war* file but you need to rename it to *soba.war*).

Step 5: stop and restart your GlassFish server to be sure that SOBA is deployed successfully as follows:

```
asadmin> stop-domain
asadmin> start-domain
```

Now try https://localhost:8181/soba/login.jsp and you should see the normal SOBA login page (note that the context-root setting is ignored somehow by GlassFish, and https://localhost:8181/soba without adding `/login.jsp` would not work). That's all about how to deploy SOBA on GlassFish 3.1.

Appendix H Deploying SOBA on JBoss

Some readers are interested in deploying SOBA on JBoss. Assuming that you have followed the instructions detailed in Chapter 2 and made sure that: 1) you have set up your MySQL and created the SOBA schema properly, and 2) you have built SOBA successfully in your environment, this appendix describes the steps for deploying SOBA on Jboss 7.1.

Step 1: In SOBA's `web.xml` file, replace the "*default*" servlet with the "*DefaultServlet*" as shown below if it's not already replaced (the former only works on Tomcat):

```
<!--  this is necessary in order to make SOBA run on glassfish and jboss -->
<servlet>
     <servlet-name>DefaultServlet</servlet-name>
     <servlet-class>org.apache.catalina.servlets.DefaultServlet</servlet-class>
  </servlet>
   <servlet-mapping>
       <servlet-name>DefaultServlet</servlet-name>
       <url-pattern>*.jpg</url-pattern>
   </servlet-mapping>
<!--
   <servlet-mapping>
       <servlet-name>default</servlet-name>
       <url-pattern>*.jpg</url-pattern>
   </servlet-mapping>
   <servlet-mapping>
       <servlet-name>default</servlet-name>
       <url-pattern>*.gif</url-pattern>
   </servlet-mapping>
-->
```

Step 2: In your `standalone.xml` file located in the *standalone/configurations* directory of your Jboss 7.1 installation directory, add the https connector as shown as highlighted below:

```
   <subsystem xmlns="urn:jboss:domain:web:1.1"
default-virtual-server="default-host" native="false">
        <connector name="http" protocol="HTTP/1.1" scheme="http"
socket-binding="http"/>
        <connector name="https" protocol="HTTP/1.1" scheme="https"
socket-binding="https" secure="true">
           <ssl name="https" password="changeit"
certificate-key-file="../standalone/configuration/.keystore"/>
        </connector>
        <virtual-server name="default-host" enable-welcome-root="true">
           <alias name="localhost"/>
           <alias name="example.com"/>
        </virtual-server>
     </subsystem>
```

Step 3: Copy your .keystore file from your C:\Users\<login-name> directory to the *standalone/configurations* directory of your Jboss 7.1 installation. Refer to Chapter 2 if you missed the step of creating an SSL testing certificate. Tomcat and Jboss require this certificate be created *a priori*, whereas the GlassFish has a built-in certificate and therefore doesn't require this certificate be created.

Step 4: Copy the *soba.war* file (you need to rename it to *soba.war* from its default name of *soba4.war*) in your *target* directory built with Maven to the *standalone/deployments* folder of your Jboss installation.

Step 5: Start your Jboss server to get SOBA deployed successfully by executing the follow command (you may need to set your JBOSS_HOME environment variable first):

```
<jboss-install>/bin> set JBOSS_HOME=<yourPath>/ jboss-as-7.1.1.Final
<jboss-install>/bin> standalone.bat
```

Now try https://localhost:8443/soba/login.jsp and you should see the normal SOBA login page (note that the context-root setting is ignored somehow by Jboss, and https://localhost:8443/soba without adding `/login.jsp` would not work). That's all about how to deploy SOBA on JBoss 7.1

Appendix I Importing SOBA onto STS

Some readers are interested in building SOBA on the Spring Tool Suite (STS) IDE instead of a plain Eclipse IDE. This appendix describes the steps to make this happen.

I.1 Installing STS

STS can be installed either standalone or as plugins in Eclipse. I prefer a standalone install as the two IDEs (STS standalone and Eclipse with STS plugins) are identical, and I was afraid of messing up my existing Eclipse environment that hosts many of my projects.

To install STS standalone, download the proper version by starting from the link http://www.springsource.org/spring-tool-suite-download, which requires submitting a form with your personal information. I downloaded the *installer.exe* file for spring-tool-suite-3.0.0.RELEASE for my 64-bit Windows 7 PC. Clicking on this installer.exe would start the installation process as follows:

- Welcome: Click Next
- License: Click Accept and Next
- Target Path: I selected *c:\mspc\app\springsource* and you can choose your own
- Select Installation Packages (I selected all as shown by default in Figure I.1)
- JDK_PATH: I selected *C:\jdk1.6.0_31_64*
- … Finish

As is seen from Figure I.1, in addition to STS, the *vFabric tc Server*, *Spring Roo*, and *Maven 3* are installed as well. However, you may not see the `settings.xml` file in the *C:\Users\<login-name>\.m2* folder for Maven 3. Also, the tc Server may include a tomcat 6 and a tomcat 7 folder, but they are not the same as the standalone tomcat 6/7 installs. Here, I assume that you have installed tomcat and Maven 3 standalone, and we are only interested in the STS IDE.

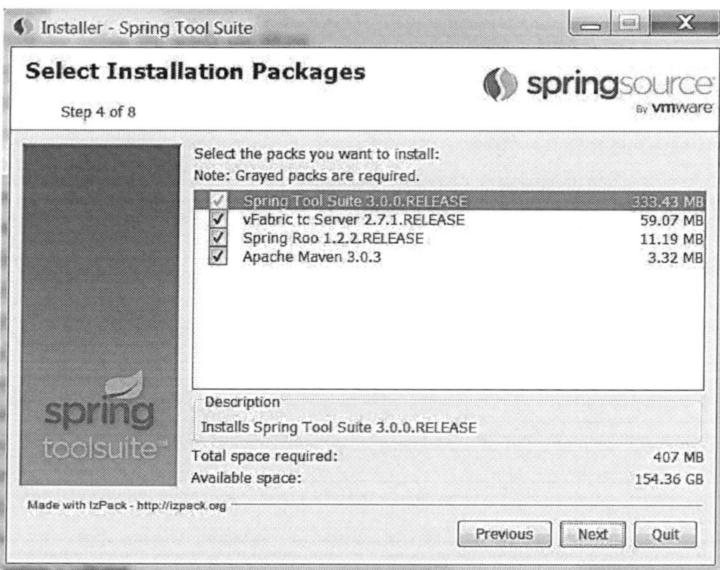

Figure I.1 STS packages

I.2 STS VERSUS ECLIPSE IDE

An STS IDE and an Eclipse IDE look similar to each other except that you would see a lot of Spring specific project templates and features as expected. The differences between an STS IDE and an Eclipse IDE are shown in Figures I.2 and I.3. For now, we ignore these differences, as the procedure to import SOBA into either IDE is the same.

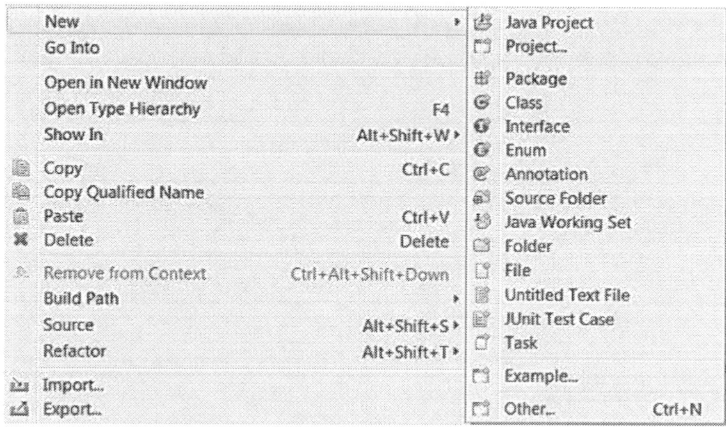

Figure I.2. A plain Eclipse IDE

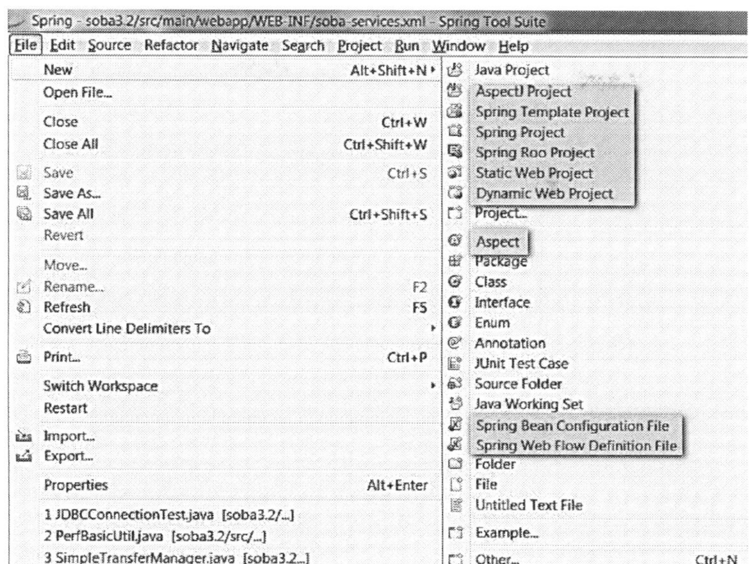

Figure I.3 An STS IDE

I.3 IMPORTING SOBA ONTO STS

There really is no difference between importing SOBA onto an STS IDE and an Eclipse IDE. So, please follow instructions given in Appendix E to complete importing SOBA into your STS IDE. Then, follow the steps in Appendix F to deploy SOBA straight from Maven to Tomcat 7.

Depending on the version of SOBA you downloaded, you might encounter a few errors after importing SOBA into your STS IDE. These errors appear in `soba-services.xml` if any, complaining "*no setter found for property ...*" associated with a few classes. Although these errors do not affect building SOBA successfully with Maven, you can fix them easily by applying the following changes if any:

- `SimpleAclTxManager.java` in the `service` package: change `setaclBankingTxDao` to `setAclBankingTxDao`
- `SimpleTransferManager.java` in the `service` package: change `setbankingTxDao` to `setBankingTxDao`
- `SimpleTxManager.java` in the `service` package: change `setbankingTxDao` to `setBankingTxDao`
- `PerfBasicUtil.java` in the `util` package
    - change `private static String profilingStatus;` to `private static String profilingStatus = "disabled";`
    - delete the corresponding `<property>` element in `soba-services.xml` file.
- Do a project "*clean*" and these errors should disappear.

From this point on, everything else is the same whether SOBA is hosted on STS or Eclipse.

Appendix J Deploying SOBA on WebLogic

This appendix helps readers deploy SOBA on WebLogic. First, follow the instructions detailed in Chapter 2 to: 1) set up your MySQL and create the SOBA schema properly, and 2) build SOBA successfully in your environment. Then, follow the below steps to deploy SOBA on WebLogic 12c R1.

Step 1: Install WebLogic 12c R1 with the features as shown in Figure J.1selected.

Step 2: In SOBA's `web.xml` file, make sure that the "*default*" servlet is set properly for the WebLogic 12c R1 using its *FileServlet* as shown below (if you don't make this change, SOBA would still work except that jpg files will not be rendered properly):

```
<!—DefaultServlet for WebLogic 12R1 -->
<servlet>
     <servlet-name>DefaultServlet</servlet-name>
     <servlet-class>weblogic.servlet.FileServlet</servlet-class>
  </servlet>
   <servlet-mapping>
       <servlet-name>DefaultServlet</servlet-name>
       <url-pattern>*.jpg</url-pattern>
<!--  necessary in order to run SOBA on glassfish and jboss (also works on tomcat)
<servlet>
     <servlet-name>DefaultServlet</servlet-name>
     <servlet-class>org.apache.catalina.servlets.DefaultServlet</servlet-class>
  </servlet>
   <servlet-mapping>
       <servlet-name>DefaultServlet</servlet-name>
       <url-pattern>*.jpg</url-pattern>
   </servlet-mapping>
-->
```

```
<!—this is the default servlet mapping on Tomcat
    <servlet-mapping>
        <servlet-name>default</servlet-name>
        <url-pattern>*.jpg</url-pattern>
    </servlet-mapping>
    <servlet-mapping>
        <servlet-name>default</servlet-name>
        <url-pattern>*.gif</url-pattern>
    </servlet-mapping>
-->
```

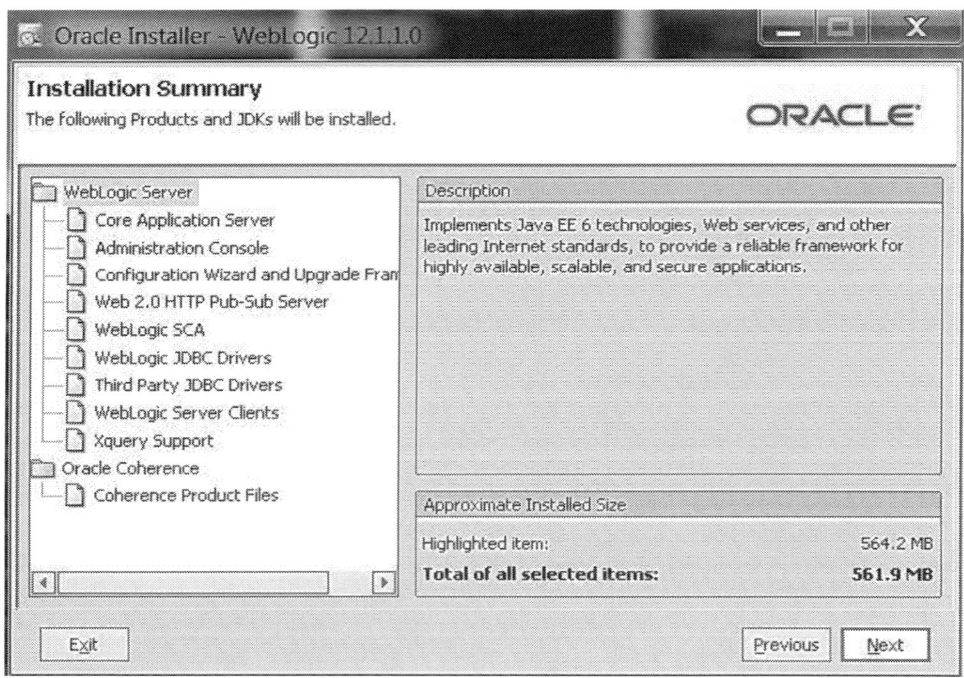

Figure J.1 Installed features with WebLogic 12c R1

Step 3: Configure SOBA to use HTTP rather than HTTPS on WebLogic. Edit the soba-security.xml file and remove the attribute "requires-channel="https" from the <intercept-url pattern="/**" requires-channel="https"/> XML element to make it look like

<intercept-url pattern="/**" />

Step 4: Locate the *soba4* directory from your *target* directory built with Maven. Copy it to the *<WebLogic_Install>\user_projects\domains\base_domain\autodeploy* directory and rename it to *soba* (note that *base_domain* is the domain you set up when installing WebLogic).

Step 5: Change to your *base_domain* directory and start your WebLogic server as follows:

base_domain> bin\startWebLogic.cmd

Step 6: Try http://localhost:7001/console and you should see the WebLogic server admin console as shown in Figure J.2 (note that you need to change the default port number of 7001 if you chose a different port number during your WebLogic installation process).

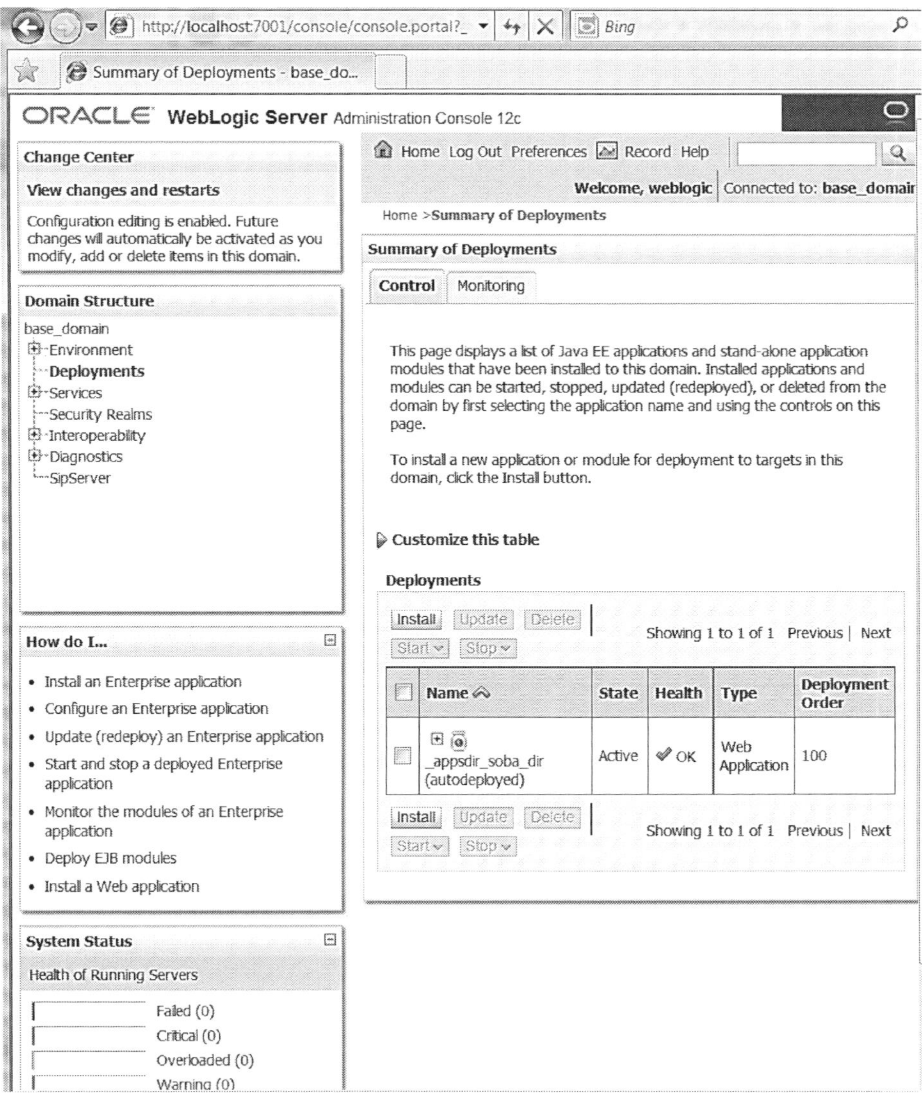

Figure J.2 WebLogic server admin console

Now log into the admin console with your credentials (like *weblogic/weblogic1211* in my case). After clicking on *deployments* under *domain structure*, you should see that SOBA has been deployed successfully with a green check-mark there. Otherwise, check the SOBA log file of *soba.log* located in *user_projects\domains\log\soba*. Or, if you need help, please send this file to me via email.

Step 7: If step 6 is successful, click one of the SOBA test points under the *Testing* tab as shown in Figure J.3. You should see the SOBA login page as shown in Figure J.4. That's all about how to deploy SOBA on WebLogic 12c R1.

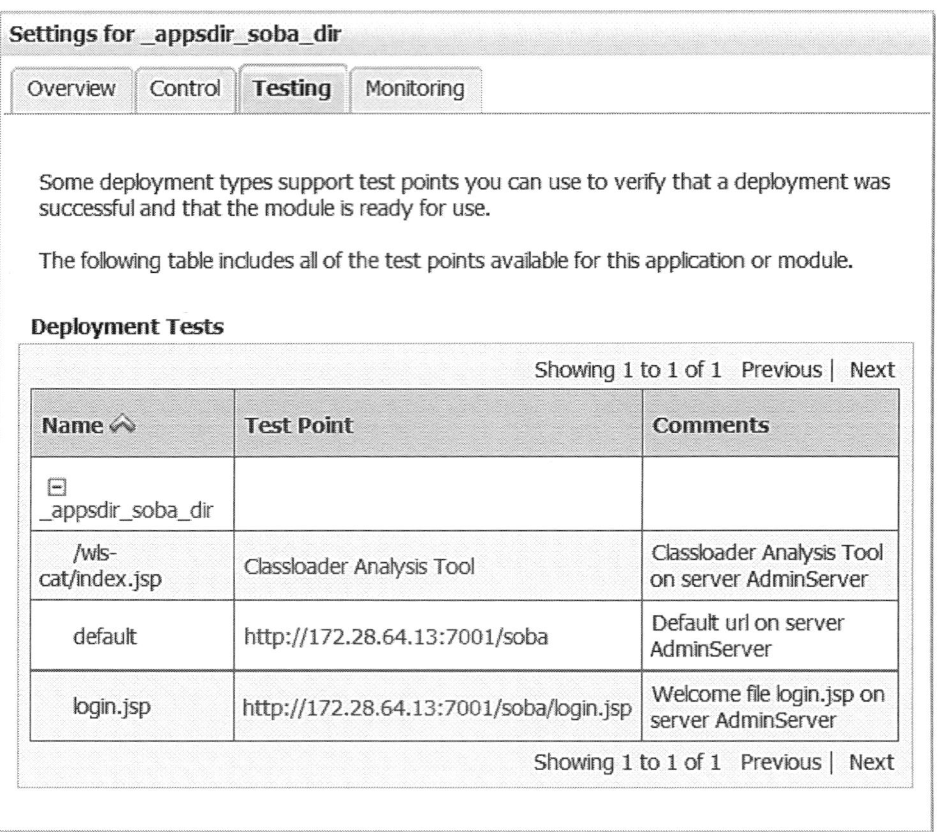

Figure J.3 Testing tab for SOBA on the WebLogic admin console

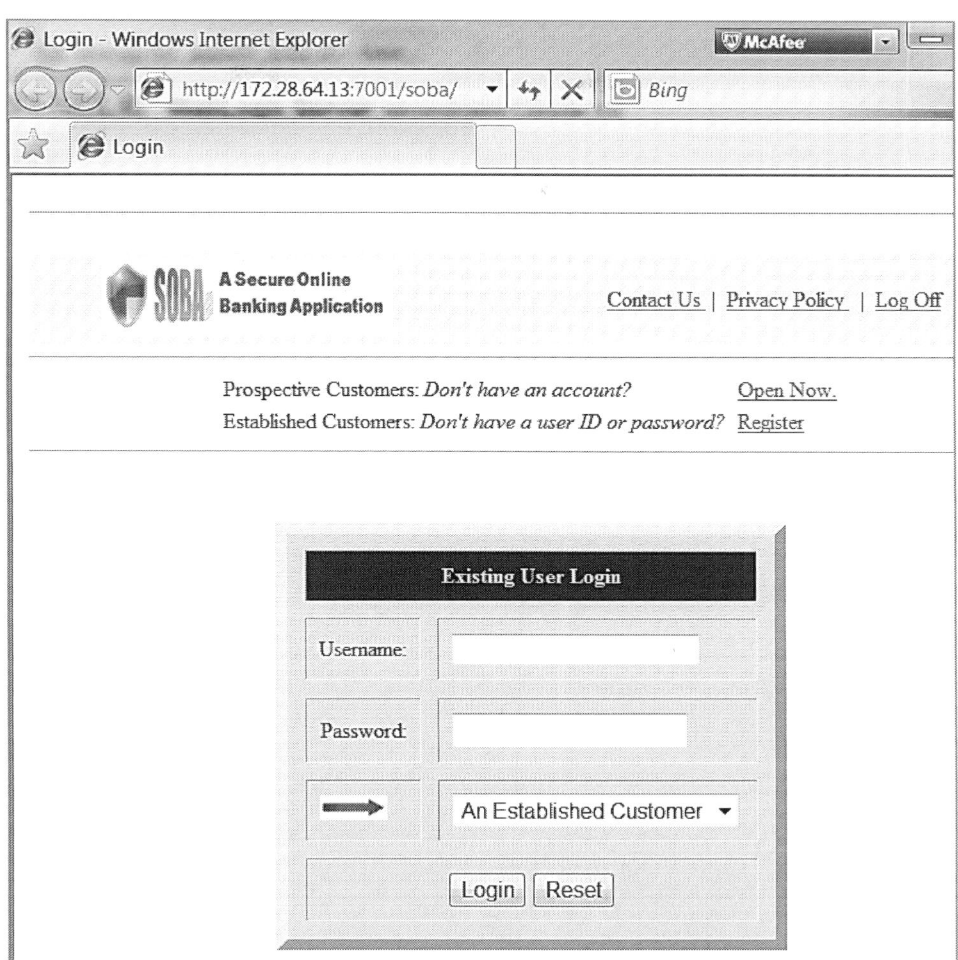

Figure J.4 The login page of SOBA on WebLogic 12c R1

Appendix K Publishing and Deploying SOBA From Eclipse to Tomcat

Some readers are interested in publishing and deploying SOBA from Eclipse to Tomcat using the Server feature available from Eclipse. In this appendix, we demonstrate how this can be done on the Mac OS X platform. The procedure applies to Windows as well except that one needs to enter the proper installation path for Tomcat on Windows. Besides, I'd like to emphasize that it's always a good practice to install and configure Tomcat separately as we have shown in Chapter 2. This appendix assumes that you have tested your Tomcat install and made sure that Tomcat and SOBA work in your environment. There are other ways to achieve the objective of publishing and deploying SOBA from Eclipse to Tomcat. You need to be very experienced with performing such tasks in general and know how to work around various issues that may occur with the alternative approach you take.

The approach to publishing and deploying SOBA from Eclipse to Tomcat introduced here consists of three steps:

1 Creating a new Server with Tomcat
2 Configuring the newly-created Tomcat Server
3 Editing the Run Configuration to set the heap size for Tomcat properly

Let's start with creating a new Server with Tomcat for SOBA on Eclipse.

K.1 Creating a New Server with Tomcat

To create a new Server with Tomcat, go through the following steps:

- Click File → New → Other → Server → Next.
- Under Apache, select Tomcat v7.0 Server, click Next and the Finish.

- Click Windows → Show View → Server → Servers. Make sure now you see the Tomcat Server you created under the Package Explorer / Servers tab.

K.2 CONFIGURING THE NEWLY-CREATED TOMCAT SERVER

To configure the newly-created Tomcat server, follow the below steps:

- Double-click the *Tomcat v7.0 Server at localhost.server* entry under the Servers tab to bring up its view, which should look similar to Figure K.1. Make sure for *Server Locations*, you have done the following:
  - Checked "*Use Tomcat installation …*" – the second radio button. In my environment, the first selection of "*Use workspace metadata …*" did not work.
  - Entered the proper path for your Tomcat server install.
- For Server Options, check "Modules auto reload by default"

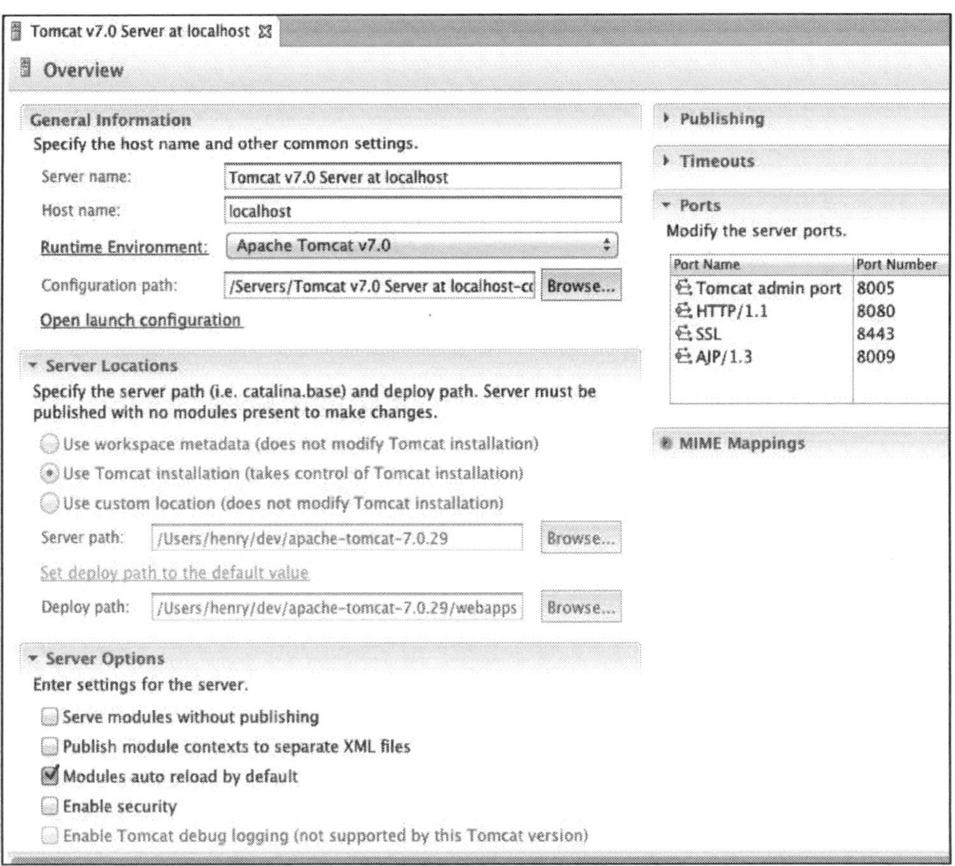

Figure K.1 Configuring Tomcat Server for publishing and deploying SOBA from Eclipse

K.3 SETTING PROPER HEAP SIZES FOR TOMCAT

It's very possible that you might encounter Out-Of-Memory errors when you start up Tomcat from your Eclipse IDE. To cure this issue, right-click on *Tomcat v7.0 Server at localhost.server*, then select Run As →Run Configurations…, which should bring up a dialog box similar to Figure K.2. Now click the Arguments tab, and add the JVM heap sizes for the Tomcat Server as highlighted in the *VM arguments* box (note that I tried to make similar changes in Tomcat's configuration files, which did not work, that is, the OOM errors did not disappear until it was done here).

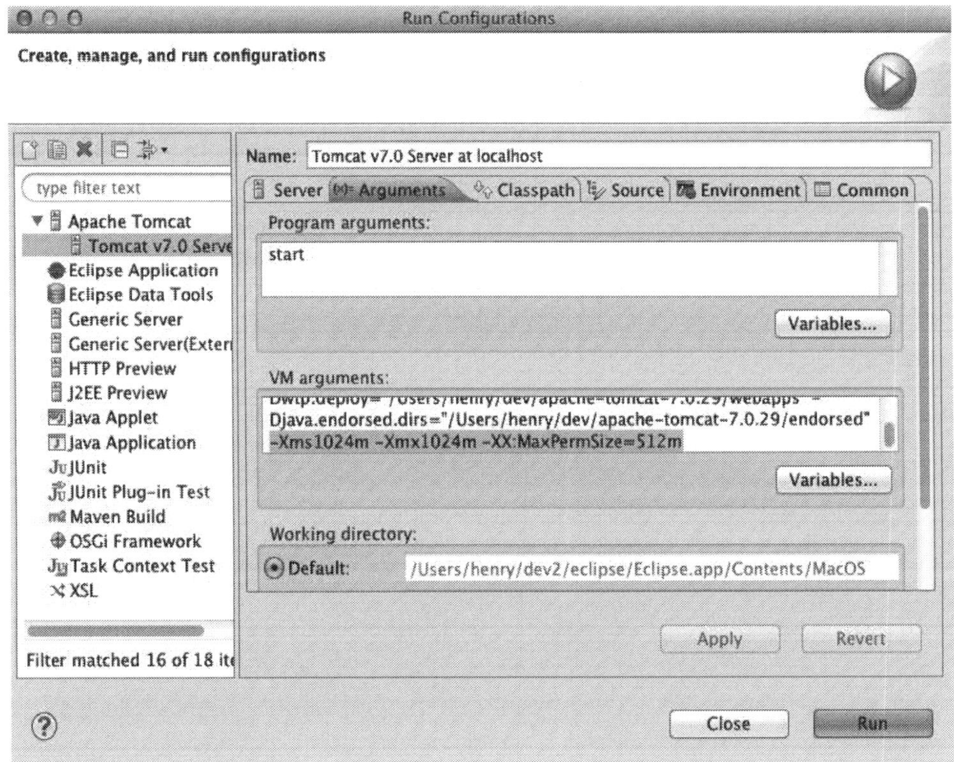

Figure K.2 Setting heap sizes for Tomcat server

K.4 PUBLISHING AND DEPLOYING SOBA FROM ECLIPSE TO TOMCAT

Now we need to perform a few additional steps before we can publish and deploy SOBA from Eclipse to Tomcat. First, rename the soba4 project to "soba" as this is the context path we need for deploying SOBA onto Tomcat. Secondly, copy all jars from *target/soba4/WEB-INF/lib* to *soba/src/main/webapp/WEB-INF/lib*.

At last, add the soba project as shown in Figure K.3 (a). You can then start Tomcat server and publish SOBA onto it as shown in Figure K.3 (b). You can view the Tomcat startup output lines under the Console tab.

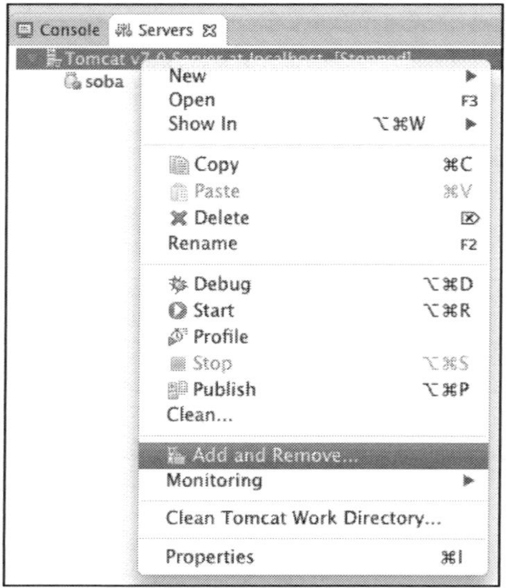

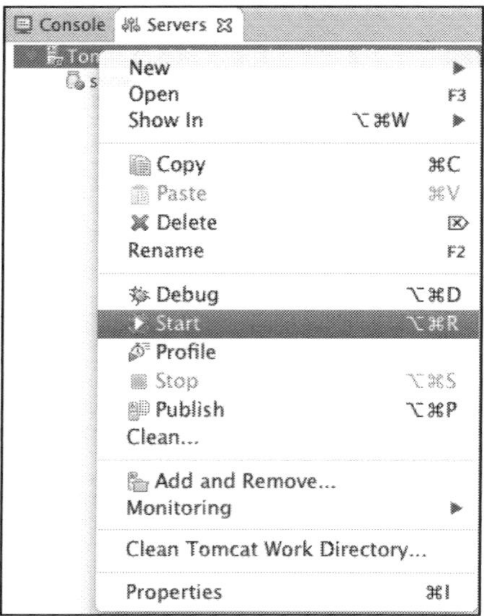

Figure K.3 (a): Add SOBA to the Tomcat Server; (b): Start Tomcat and publish SOBA

Index

Other texts by the same author:

- A quantitative text on *Java Performance and Scalability*
- A scientific, objective approach to learning Hadoop 2 MapReduce programming

34166945R00254

Made in the USA
Lexington, KY
25 July 2014